University 101
The Individual & Life
2018-2019

D1532900

Hampton University

Kendall Hunt
publishing company

Compiled by Dr. Eric Claville and Ms. Patra Johnson.

Part opener art contributed by Joseph F. Martin. Copyright © Kendall Hunt Publishing Company.

Cover photo and Hampton University seal courtesy of Hampton University.

Kendall Hunt
publishing company

www.kendallhunt.com
Send all inquiries to:
4050 Westmark Drive
Dubuque, IA 52004-1840

Copyright © 2014, 2015, 2016, 2017, and 2018 by Hampton University

PAK ISBN 978-1-5249-7610-1
Text alone ISBN 978-1-5249-7611-8

Kendall Hunt Publishing Company has the exclusive rights to reproduce this work,
to prepare derivative works from this work, to publicly distribute this work,
to publicly perform this work and to publicly display this work.

All rights reserved. No part of this publication may be reproduced,
stored in a retrieval system, or transmitted, in any form or by any
means, electronic, mechanical, photocopying, recording, or otherwise,
without the prior written permission of the copyright owner.

Published in the United States of America

Contents

Hampton University Alma Mater

O Hampton, a thought sent from Heaven above,
To be a great soul's inspiration;
We sing thee the earnest of broad human love,
The shrine of our heart's adoration.
Thy foundation firm and thy roof tree out spread,
And thy sacred altar-fires burning,
The sea circling 'round thee, soft skies overhead,
Dear Hampton, the goal of our yearning!

Refrain

O Hampton, we never can make thee a song
Except as our lives do the singing,
In service that will thy great spirit prolong,
And send it through centuries ringing!

Kind mother, we'll treasure the dear happy days
We've spent here in life's preparation,
Yet go with brave hearts upon our chosen ways,
Of service to God and our nation.
Still wearing thy colors, the blue and the white,

As pledge that our fond hearts will cherish
A love which for thee ever shines true and bright,
A loyalty that ne'er can perish!

Words by: Sarah Collins Fernandis, 1882
Music by: Chauncey Northern, 1924

Introduction

The college career is designed with past, present and future in mind. The past, with home and community as the student's familiar environment, which the student brings to campus; the present, in which the student learns skills, values, and expertise with which to successfully conquer the challenges of the 21st century; and the future, which will offer unknown challenges to his or her intellect and creativity. As our society transitions into an even more complex and technological community, Hampton University remains mindful of its success in offering a diverse and eclectic curriculum grounded in its core principles, that of academic rigor, a supportive learning environment, and commitment to basic ethical values. Hampton is proud of its history, and we remain in the forefront of teaching the leaders of tomorrow, those who will affect change and improve communities, within our nation and across the globe.

© Martial Red/Shutterstock.com

Welcome Students!

You are about to embark on a life changing journey. Each year, hundreds of new students join the Hampton University Family. We have high expectations of our students and create an enriching environment to support students in reaching their full potential.

This course is geared to help freshmen and transfer students become acclimated to university life, learn about student resources available, and foster community among peers. In turn, the University becomes more aware of and responsive to the needs of its new students. There is a deliberate emphasis on Hampton's values and traditions so that all new students will embrace Hampton's rich heritage and perpetuate its legacy. Using the Hampton model, you will be EMPOWERED to EXPLORE and use the tools in this book to help you EXCEL inside and outside the University.

Part 1
EMPOWER

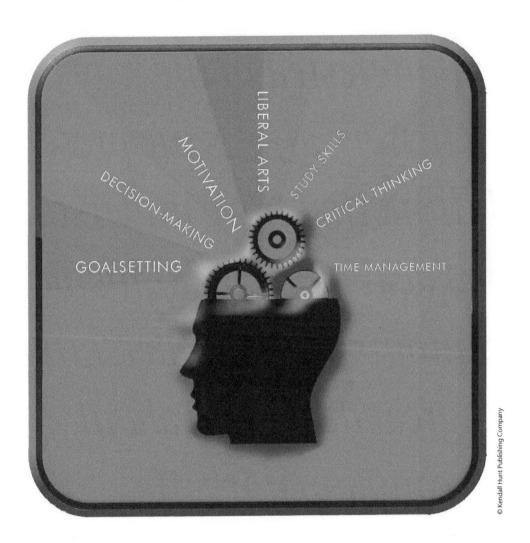

© Kendall Hunt Publishing Company

*"A good head and a good heart are always a formidable combination.
But when you add to that a literate tongue or pen,
then you have something very special."*

NELSON MANDELA

"I'm interested in the way in which history affects the present, and I think that if we understand a good deal more about history, we automatically understand a great deal more about contemporary life."

—Toni Morrison, *Time Interview*
January 21, 1998

CHAPTER 1
Hampton University History

"We should emphasize not Negro history, but the Negro in history. What we need is not a history of selected races or nations, but the history of the world void of national bias, race hate, and religious prejudice."

—Carter Woodson

Upon completion of this chapter, you will be able to:

- **Acquaint** yourself with Hampton University's history
- **Review** major milestones
- **Identify** individuals who made significant contributions to the growth and development of the University

Hampton University History

HBCUs Past and Present

College—Your Gateway to the Future

Going to college is a major milestone in your life. You are standing on the cusp of new experiences and new opportunities—indeed a whole new world. You are feeling happy, excited, and reinvigorated by the promise and opportunity ahead. At the same time, it is also likely that you may be feeling anxious and fearful of the unknown. Or, maybe even self-doubt. Such wide-ranging emotions are common among students during this period of transition. Nonetheless, you've worked hard, planned well, and maintained discipline. Within the four walls of the university, you will translate hopes and dreams into achievable action steps. College brings you one step closer to realizing your life's dreams.

Why College Matters

Enrolling in college is the most important decision you will make on your journey toward the realization of your hopes and dreams. It pays—literally—to go to college. Over the years, numerous studies have examined the relationship between higher education and income. These studies have found that earnings over the course of a lifetime are determined in large part by education. In other words, your level of education will dictate your earning potential.

Going to college greatly increases your lifetime earning potential. According to the U.S. Census Bureau, the median household income of a family comprised of high school graduates is $28,744. For a family comprised of individuals with at least four years of college, the median household income nearly doubles to $50,549. In short, going to college means you will increase your lifetime earning potential nearly 50%.

Disparity in earning potential among high school and college graduates. The margin further widens when one pursues education beyond the bachelor's level; for instance, a master's or doctoral degree.

Beyond immediate earning potential, college is important because your course of study will allow you to develop skills crucial to employment and success in the high-tech, global economy of the twenty-first century. For example, you will develop a skill set anchored on the application of critical thinking, writing, and analysis. These are crucial skills relevant for whatever profession you plan to pursue in future, be it in the Humanities, Social Sciences, Education, Medicine, Business, Law, the Ministry, or Public Life.

Your college experience will not be limited to professional development. You will also blossom socially. You will have a social life and participate in extracurricular activities. You will find many people with much in common with you. At the same time, you will also meet and interact with people from different cultural

From *A Customized Version of Thriving in College and Beyond* by Carolyn W. Mbajekwe. Copyright © 2012 by Kendall Hunt Publishing Company. Reprinted by permission.

backgrounds. You will have the opportunity to learn and experience a new culture or a new language. Such experiences will make you a well-rounded individual, a true citizen of the world.

Historically Black Colleges and Universities: Early History

Snapshot

The American Missionary Association (AMA) was a Protestant-based abolitionist group founded in 1846.

Recognizing a link between education and equality, the AMA established hundreds of schools for African Americans.

HBCUs founded by the AMA include: Fisk, Atlanta, Dillard, and Talladega.

Pursuing your undergraduate education at a historically black college or university is a proven route to success in life. America's historically black colleges and universities (HBCUs) have a long history of producing students who go on to achieve immense success and who make positive contributions to the world. From the ivory towers to executive boardrooms to legal chambers across America, HBCU graduates are highly visible.

Today, there are 103 HBCUs in America. As a group, these institutions reflect the diversity that defines higher education. Among their ranks are public and private institutions; single-sex and co-ed; as well as 4-year bachelor's degree and 2-year associate's degree schools. With regard to their institutional outlook, the HBCUs engage a variety of specializations, including research-intensive universities, small liberal arts colleges, as well as professional schools. HBCU student populations range from less than 500 to upwards of 10,000.

The history of America's HBCUs constitutes what is often called a "unique chapter" in higher education. Most HBCUs were founded in the aftermath of the Civil War (post-1865) for the specific purpose of educating African Americans. Legal mandates and social mores of the era prevented African Americans from attending post-secondary schools established for whites. With a few exceptions, most HBCUs were established in the southern United States.

Northern White Missionaries and the Rise of Black Colleges in the South

The private colleges were the first institutions to emerge. The private schools were established under the supervision of a number of groups and organizations, including northern white missionaries, black church groups, and black communities. Of these various constituencies, much has been written about the particular role northern white missionaries played in the development of black education in the South. The northern white missionaries were devout Christian men and women who believed in the innate humanity of African Americans and the efficacy of education to improve the conditions of blacks.

Of the northern white religious groups, organizations such as the American Missionary Association (AMA), the American Baptist Mission Society, and the Methodist Episcopal Church were leaders. The AMA established Atlanta University (1865); Fisk University in Nashville, Tennessee (1867); Talladega College in Talladega, Alabama (1867); Hampton University in Hampton, Virginia (1868); and Straight University, the forerunner of Dillard University, in New Orleans, Louisiana (1869).

Schools established by the American Baptist Home Mission Society include Virginia Union in Richmond, Virginia (1865); Shaw University in Raleigh, North Carolina (1865); Benedict College in Columbia, South Carolina (1870); Morehouse College in Atlanta, Georgia (1867); and Spelman College in Atlanta, Georgia (1881).

The northern Methodist Episcopal Church established Claflin College in Orangeburg, South Carolina (1869); Bennett College in Greensboro, North Carolina (1873); and Wiley College in Marshall, Texas (1873). The northern Presbyterians initiated Johnson C. Smith University in Charlotte, North Carolina (1867); Barber Scotia College in Concord, North Carolina (1867); and Knoxville College in Knoxville, Tennessee (1875). St. Katharine's Sisters of the Blessed Sacrament founded Xavier University in New Orleans, Louisiana, in 1915. Xavier is the only historically black Catholic university in the Western Hemisphere.

The Role of the Black Church in the Establishment of Black Colleges

In addition to northern whites, African Americans themselves also played a critically important role in efforts to initiate higher education for blacks in the South. The work of African Americans in the field was spearheaded by black religious organizations. Four groups in particular—the African Methodist Episcopal Church (AME), the African Methodist Episcopal Zion Church, the Colored Methodist Episcopal Church, and the Black Baptist Church—were at the forefront of this endeavor. The work of the black denominations in establishing schools for African Americans is truly noteworthy because the black church organizations were started by ex-slaves— by men and women who came out of bondage with nothing by way of material possessions. Nonetheless, despite not having access to comparable resources, black churches were able to sponsor a number of higher education institutions for members of their race.

The AME Church was at the helm of the black denominational drive to establish institutions of higher education. The AME started and maintained Edward Waters College in Jacksonville, Florida (1866); Allen University in Columbia, South Carolina (1870); Morris Brown College in Atlanta, Georgia (1881); and Shorter College in Little Rock, Arkansas (1886). The Colored Methodist Episcopal Church founded Lane College in Jackson, Tennessee (1882); Paine College in Augusta, Georgia (1882); Texas College in Tyler, Texas (1894); and Miles College in Birmingham, Alabama (1905). The Black Baptists took over the support of several black institutions that were founded by the northern white American Baptist Home Mission Society. In other cases, black Baptists started their own colleges. The institutions that operated under the auspices of the black Baptists include Selma University in Selma, Alabama (1878); Arkansas Baptist College in Little Rock, Arkansas (1901); and Morris College in Sumter, South Carolina (1908).

Booker T. Washington

Founder of Tuskegee Institute

Other private institutions resulted from the efforts of visionary individuals. Of this group, the legacy of Booker T. Washington looms large. In 1881, W.F. Foster and Arthur L. Brooks, two white men newly elected to the Alabama Senate, drafted and sponsored legislation authorizing $2,000 for the creation of a school for African Americans at Tuskegee. With the appropriation in hand, a committee of black Tuskegee citizens wrote to Samuel C. Armstrong, principal of Hampton Institute in Hampton, Virginia, with a question. Could he recommend a teacher? Armstrong sent his young protégé, Booker T. Washington. The curriculum Washington implemented at Tuskegee emphasized "industrial education," or training in skill trades. By 1900,

Courtesy of Library of Congress, Prints and Photographs Division, Washington, DC 20540 (2004672766)

Booker T. Washington (1856–1915)

Booker T. Washington established Tuskegee University in 1881.

Courtesy of Library of Congress, Prints and Photographs Division, Washington, DC 20540 (2003654395)

Dr. Martin L. King, Jr. (1929–1968)

On August 28, 1963, more than 200,000 demonstrators gathered at the Lincoln Memorial to take part in the March on Washington for Freedom and Jobs. Dr. Martin Luther King, Jr., stood before the marchers and delivered his now-famous "I Have a Dream" speech.

Courtesy of Library of Congress, Prints & Photographys Division, Carl Van Vechten Collection, (2004662602).

Dr. Mary McLeod Bethune (1875–1955)

Dr. Mary McLeod Bethune established Bethune-Cookman College in Daytona Beach, Florida, in 1904.

because of his conservative politics and influence with wealthy white philanthropists such as Andrew Carnegie and John D. Rockefeller, Washington was the most powerful black man in America. When Washington died in 1915, Tuskegee could claim an endowment value of $1.5 million, one of the largest for any black college in America. In addition to Washington, other black men left their mark on the education of African Americans. James E. Shepard, for instance, founded North Carolina Central University in Durham, North Carolina, in 1910.

Joseph C. Price

Founder of Livingstone College

Livingstone College in Salisbury, North Carolina, owes its existence to Joseph C. Price. Price was born in 1854 in Elizabeth City, North Carolina, the son of a slave and a free black woman. In 1875 Price entered Lincoln University, a Presbyterian-sponsored school for African Americans in Pennsylvania, where he received training for a career in the ministry. Price returned to North Carolina in 1881 and rapidly rose through the ranks of the African Methodist Episcopal Church. Shortly afterwards, he was tapped by AME Zion leaders to spearhead efforts at putting fledgling Zion Wesley Institute, a minister training school sponsored by the denomination, on a firm foundation. In September 1881, Price conducted a speaking tour in Great Britain to raise money for Zion Wesley. Price returned to the United States in 1882 having raised nearly ten thousand dollars. In September 1882, Price was named president of Zion Wesley, and continued his work of building and expanding the institution that would become Livingstone College.

Mary McLeod Bethune

Founder of Bethune-Cookman University

African American women established two institutions of higher education. Mary McLeod Bethune established Bethune-Cookman College in Daytona Beach, Florida, in 1904. Bethune was born in 1875 in Mayesville, South Carolina, to Samuel and Patsy McLeod, former slaves. Mary was the fifteenth of seventeen children; and the first to be born free. She entered the Presbyterian-sponsored Mayesville Mission School when she was eleven years old, and quickly came under the influence of the school's founder, Emma Jane Wilson. After Bethune completed the Mayesville course of study, Wilson recommended her for a scholarship to attend Scotia College, Wilson's alma mater.

Upon graduation from Scotia in 1894, Bethune was awarded a scholarship to the Moody Bible Institute in Chicago. Bethune returned South in 1896 and embarked on a number of teaching stints, including her alma mater, Mayesville Institute; Haines Institute in Augusta, Georgia; and Kindell Institute in Sumter, South Carolina. Bethune's tenure at Haines Institute was an especially formative experience because there she worked under the visionary school founder, Lucy Craft Laney. In 1904, Bethune opened the Daytona Literary and Industrial School for Training Negro Girls. In building the school that would become Bethune-Cookman University Mary McLeod Bethune drew heavily on the models and examples of both Emma Jane Wilson and Lucy Craft Laney.

Dr. Bethune's reach and influence would eventually transcend education. By the 1930s, Bethune was the most influential black person in America. She was a recognized leader of women (she founded the National Council of Negro Women in 1935), an adviser to U.S. presidents, and a tireless fighter for racial equality.

Elizabeth Evelyn Wright
Founder of Voorhees College

Finally, Voorhees College in Denmark, South Carolina, resulted from the efforts of its founder, Elizabeth Evelyn Wright. Wright was born in Talbotton, Georgia, in 1872. At the age of sixteen, she left her hometown and enrolled in Tuskegee Institute in Alabama, where she came under the influence of Booker T. Washington. Learning from Washington to "try to help my fellow men to help themselves," Wright committed herself to being the "same type of woman as Mr. Washington was of a man." Wright graduated from Tuskegee, relocated to Demark, South Carolina, and in 1897 established the Denmark Industrial School as a replica, or "off-shoot" of Tuskegee. Wright and Denmark Industrial benefitted immensely from the Tuskegee connection. This was evidenced in 1902 when Ralph Voorhees, a wealthy New Jersey industrialist, donated 380 acres of land to the school. The name of the school was changed to Voorhees Industrial in tribute to Voorhees.

The Second Morrill Act of 1890
Genesis of Public Historically Black Colleges

The advent of the public system of higher education for African Americans was a product of the Second Morrill Act of 1890. The Act provided land-grant colleges for blacks in states were land-grant institutions existed for whites. Nineteen colleges for blacks were established under the Land-Grant mandate. These include Southern Agricultural and Mechanical College in Louisiana; North Carolina Agricultural and Technical State College; Florida Agricultural and Mechanical College; Alabama Agricultural and Mechanical College; and the South Carolina Agricultural and Mechanical College.

Historically Black Professional Schools

The historically black college community is also home to several professional schools. There are currently four historically black medical schools: Howard University College of Medicine, Morehouse School of Medicine, Meharry Medical College, and the Charles R. Drew University of Medicine and Science. Xavier University of Louisiana and Florida A&M University are home to outstanding schools of pharmacy. There are four historically black colleges with law schools: Howard University, Texas Southern University, North Carolina Central University, and Southern University.

The United Negro College Fund

During their early years, black colleges received financial support from several sources. The General Education Board, founded in 1902 by oil magnate John D. Rockefeller, invested significantly in the development of education in the South, with a special focus on black education. Other extant philanthropies, such as the Rosenwald Fund and the Phelps-Stokes Fund, contributed to education for blacks. In 1944, Dr. Frederick D. Patterson, then president of Tuskegee Institute, established the United Negro College Fund (UNCF) to raise funds for private black colleges. The UNCF was higher education's first collective financial campaign. Today, with 39 member institutions and assets of $278 million, the United Negro College Fund has grown to become America's most successful higher education assistance organization.

A Mind is a Terrible Thing to Waste.
—The United Negro College Fund

Historically Black Colleges in the Age of Segregation

The early years of the black colleges coincided with the period historian Rayford W. Logan called the "nadir," or low point, of race relations in America. As black colleges were rising from the soil of the South, Reconstruction, a period characterized by systematic efforts to incorporate African Americans into the social and political fabric of America, was coming to an end. The collapse of Reconstruction was followed by Redemption, an era that witnessed the rise and entrenchment of widespread racial repression. African Americans were deprived of the right to vote, excluded from public facilities and institutions by mandate of Jim Crow segregation laws, and lived under the constant threat of racial violence.

The racial fallout of this time period presented numerous challenges to the growth and development of higher education institutions for blacks in the South. For instance, black elementary and secondary education in the South lingered in a state of major underdevelopment. Generations of African Americans were denied the prerequisite secondary education required for higher learning. This, in turn, hindered the growth and development of black colleges by robbing the schools of thousands of potential students. The racial politics of the era affected the development of black colleges in many other ways, ranging from assigning black schools the limited role of educating African Americans exclusively to starving black institutions of funding.

Throughout this time period, the primary mission of the black college was to uplift and improve the conditions of African Americans through education. Black leaders of the immediate post-Emancipation era believed strongly that education was the key to freedom and prosperity. As one historian writes, the faith African Americans placed in education was "mythical" in nature. Because of this strong belief in the empowering quality of knowledge, the acquisition of education became the central focus of the black political struggle for racial advancement. The mission of the black college, the majority of which started as teacher training schools, was to produce leaders, who in turn would go out and train future generations. The Supreme Court ruling in the 1954 Brown vs. Board of Education case, which overturned segregation in elementary and secondary education, paved the way for the eventual prohibition of legally enforced racial segregation in higher education.

Black Colleges and Social Change

Because of the progressive atmosphere created by black college presidents of the mid-twentieth century, much of the black political and social activism of the era centered on the black colleges. W.E.B. Du Bois wrote pioneering studies of race in America while on the faculty at Atlanta University. From his post at Dillard University, Horace Mann Bond produced seminal research on the stagnating effect of segregation on black education in the South. In the 1940s, the Howard University trio of E. Franklin Frazier, Abram Harris, and Ralph Bunche published groundbreaking studies on issues related to the black experience in the fields of sociology, economics, and politics. Much of the scholarship produced by black scholars teaching at black colleges influenced a generation of public policy.

The black colleges made direct contributions to the dismantling of racial segregation in America. Howard University produced Thurgood Marshall and the cohort of black lawyers who challenged the legal underpinning of racial segregation, culminating in the Supreme Court desegregation ruling in the 1954 Brown v. Board of Education case. The black college produced civil rights activists Martin Luther King, Jr., Andrew Young, Ralph Abernathy, Jesse Jackson, Stokely Carmichael, and John Lewis. In 1960, students from North Carolina A&T State University initiated the

Courtesy of Library of Congress, Prints and Photographs Division, Washington, DC 20540 (2003681451)

W.E.B. Du Bois (1868–1963)

W.E.B. Du Bois was the first African American to earn a Ph.D. from Harvard University. Du Bois served on the faculty of Atlanta University from 1897 to 1910. In 1909 he helped to establish the National Association for the Advancement of Colored People (NAACP).

sit-in protest against segregated public facilities. Students from Morehouse and Spelman Colleges organized the first formal protest against segregation in stores and shops in downtown Atlanta. Students from Tougaloo College, Jackson State University, Claflin College, South Carolina State College, and numerous other HBCUs made similar contributions. In 1935 Mary McLeod Bethune founded the National Council of Negro Women (NCNW) to advocate for equal rights for women of color. The contributions of this generation of black college leaders and students were instrumental in the eventual passage of the 1964 Civil Rights Act, which overturned segregation in public facilities, and the 1965 Voting Rights Act, which removed barriers to black voting.

Finally, the black colleges pioneered the idea of diversity in higher education. As earlier stated, the black colleges were interracial in origin, created by a coalition of African Americans and progressive northern whites. The black colleges were also the first institutions in America to enroll students from Africa. Kwame Nkrumah, who in 1957 was appointed the first African prime minister of Ghana, and Nnamdi Azikiwe, who in 1960 was appointed the first indigenous president of Nigeria, are both graduates of historically black Lincoln University. Throughout their long and illustrious history, the black colleges stood as models of the democratic ideal in higher education.

Courtesy of Library of Congress, Prints and Photographs Division, Carl Van Vechten Collection (2004662647).

Ralph Bunche (1904–1971)

Dr. Ralph Bunche chaired the Department of Political Science at Howard University from 1928 to 1950.

Black Colleges Today

Today the HBCUs remain at the forefront of change and progress in America. They produce 30 percent of undergraduate degrees earned by African Americans, and train the lion's share of African Americans who go on to pursue a Ph.D. Under the leadership of dynamic and visionary men and women, the schools are revitalizing their campus and academic infrastructure to meet the demands of higher education in the twenty-first century. Welcome to the culture of excellence!!

Public Schools Revisited, the Black Community and the Hampton Normal and Agricultural Institute

By the end of the Civil War, there were around twenty-five thousand black refugees living in settlements in or near Hampton, and many of them had been there for much of the war. Than many people, most of them new to the area, needed a great deal of help: "The majority of blacks spent their first years of freedom in wretched poverty, confined to inadequate housing in refugee camps, and barely able to subsist on irregular government wages or scanty government rations." Help did come from Northern missionaries:

> *The American Missionary Association was the first Northern benevolent organization to send aid to Southern contrabands . . . The Association was already fifteen years old by 1861 and from its inception, had been dedicated to "preaching the Gospel free from all complicity with slavery and caste." Though officially a nonsectarian evangelical society, the Association was closely allied with the Congregational and Presbyterian Churches; it was this form of evangelical Chrishanty that it sought to spread in the South. Its leadership had strong ties to the abolitionist movement and was deeply committed to the uplift of the black man, whether slave or free.*

The American "slave codes" laid down very specifically what could and could not be done by and to slaves: for example, slaves could not own property. One of the more specific prohibitions had to do with education. Virginia law, in the Revised Code of 1819, stated. "All meetings or assemblages of slaves, or free negroes or mulattoes mixing and associating with such slaves at any meeting house, &c., in the night: or at any school or schools for teaching them reading or writing, either in the day or night, under whatsoever pretext, shall be deemed and considered an unlawful assembly." The punishment for such an offense could be "at the discretion of any justice of the peace, not exceeding twenty lashes."

The law was applied unevenly throughout the state, and when the missionaries arrived in Hampton in September 1861, black residents were already being taught to read by Mary Peake. She was the daughter of a Frenchman and a mulatto woman, and her father had paid for her to be educated. She had established her school in Brown Cottage, next to the abandoned Chesapeake Female Seminary between Hampton and Fort Monroe. At that time, there were forty-nine pupils, with more expected. Mary and her husband. Thomas, were leaders in the free black community before the war and took their responsibilities seriously:

> Mary did not allow her education to go to waste. She taught reading to free blacks and slaves alike. Teaching slaves was, of course, against Virginia law, but like so much else in ante-bellum Hampton, it went unchallenged by white residents so long as it was done discretely and caused no problems. Mrs. Peake continued her school openly after the war began and was one of the first teachers of ex-slaves in the Civil War South.

The missionaries had often acted as liaisons between the contraband and the Union army, and this was especially true in regard to schools. By December 1861, the AMA (American Missionary Association) had helped start three more schools, in addition to the one taught by Mary Peake. All these early classes were taught by local African Americans. By the end of 1863, the schools were established institutions and were taught mainly by missionaries: "The goal was to provide each student with a 'good English education' and to make each a 'good Christian' . . . The missionaries interspersed education with Union politics; they meant to teach freedom as well as the 'three Rs." Adults as well as children benefitted from the missionaries' efforts: "A large number of 'Union Primers' [were distributed] among the blacks, and . . . working men took every moment of leisure to study their books, and teach each other to read."

The interest in education and the ability of black students to learn so readily surprised the AMA teachers: "To some degree, however, they were victims of their own abolitionist propaganda. In the effort to promote antislavery sentiment in the North, the abolitionists may have overdrawn number of white and colored schools was accidental . . . [the state tried to] avoid everything that would even present the appearance of unfairness." The main concern across the state was the need for funds to support this education that was being offered free to all children. The idea that "a specific tax of one mill in the dollar . . . on the assessed value of the property of the State should be levied to meet this demand [the cost of supporting the Public Free Schools of the State] was proposed by the legislature." Where this idea was put to a local vote, the people approved; school was a necessity.

Here are some statistics of the early years of Virginia's postwar public school system. Only about half of the counties had been able to open their schools at the beginning of the school year in 1870. It was encouraging to note that "a large proportion of these schools have heretofore existed as private schools, which, by the concurrence of those concerned, have now been adopted into the State system, and made free to all." By the end of the school year, "the number of schools had increased to more than 2,000, with about 130,000 pupils and more than 3,000 teachers." A few more statistics are of interest: teachers received about $30 a month as salary; the length of the school year was five months: and there was a "difficulty in procuring qualified teachers for the colored schools." The Normal School at Hampton would soon meet that need.

Elizabeth City County, which included the town of Hampton, had eleven schools open in 1871, eight white (one of which was the Hickman School) and three black. In addition, there were three white and three black private schools, with 50 white children and 83 black children enrolled. The county school population between five and twenty-one years of age) included 340 white males, 314 white females, 810 black males and 810 black females. Of that population. 372 white children and 277 black children were enrolled in school. The average attendance for white children was 230 while that of black children was 174. Nine children were furnished with schoolbooks at public expense. Illiteracy in the county of people aged ten and over included 2.308 who could not read and 3.055 who could not write. The free public schools had arrived just in time.

Six years later, there was marked improvement. One goal of the state superintendent was to "lengthen the school term from five months to nine of ten months." He recognized that this was a problem because some parents were "compelled to use the labor of their children during a large part of the year." Elizabeth City County in 1877 had an enrollment of 419 white children, or 33 percent of the white school population, and 875 black children, or 51 percent of the black school population. The average monthly attendance was 357 white students and 732 black students. Fifty children were supplied with textbooks at public expense. The good news was that more children were in school; the bad news was that many children were not. The Butler School on the Normal School property and the Lincoln School downtown had the largest enrollment of black children, and the Little England Chapel may have been used as a day school. Samuel Chapman Armstrong, in his report of the Hampton Normal School for the year 1877, declared, "The hard times and the scarcity of money in the South, contrary to expectation, have not caused a diminished attendance this year . . . the school may hope to graduate annually from fifty to sixty trained teachers." Those graduates would teach in the black schools across the South, but many of the local alumni would teach in Hampton. That was unqualified good news.

The Black Community

At the close of the Civil War, the black community in Hampton was still evolving. The changes actually began several years earlier: "With each passing day after the spring of 1862. Hampton's original contraband were becoming more and more of a minority in their own black community. By the first wartime census in 1864, they were already outnumbered by more than two to one." This was a problem because the newcomers had experienced much less freedom and had exercised little responsibility in their own lives:

> Many slaves, given a choice, would risk their lives to be free rather than stay on the plantations. More uncertain was their understanding of freedom. Having had far less opportunity to exercise certain degrees of freedom than native blacks of Hampton, would they use it wisely or abuse it and prove the long-standing claim of white Southerners that the black man without slavery was a savage?

How was the new postwar black community to survive with the original contrabands and the less experienced newcomers sharing space? In addition to eliminating crime from their neighborhoods, black residents had to find constructive occupations for the citizens of their communities. Idleness and the neighborhood saloon proved to be a temptation for some of the freedmen. "A missionary teacher appealed that a 'good temperance man' be sent to Hampton because it was "becoming a very wicked place". The black community could organize itself and avoid some of those problems. There were already successful black families living in the area. Could a successful black man help another black man from "reverting to savagery" and thus condemning all other black men with him? The answer was found when more black men became literate, acquired higher educations and developed salable skills. The training and discipline required to achieve these goals, along with active participation in the black church, prepared new leaders in the black community. The freedmen of both groups who availed themselves of these opportunities became the black elite of Hampton. They were able to set a standard for the community and see to its enforcement:

> The black professional group although small in number, was of vital importance to the black community of Hampton. Members of this group were the acknowledged leaders of the community. They played a large role in shaping the goals and directions of its inhabitants. Anyone who sought respectability within the community had to belong to a church, and it was the ministers who spelled out the norms of acceptable social and religious behavior. Teachers, accepting the Hampton Institute belief in "formative work" among their pupils, did far more than teach reading, writing, and arithmetic. They helped reinforce the norms taught on Sunday in church, and passed on to their students the belief in the importance of education that had typified blacks of Hampton since 1861. Black lawyers played a crucial role in helping blacks acquire property and in protecting them from being cheated out of it once they had it. Black professionals also played another vital, if less concrete, role in shaping the community. They symbolized to the young of the town the heights to which black people might aspire.

Earlier, however, the harsh conditions in the refugee camps during the Civil War and the absence of meaningful work for both men and women created a situation where the safest reaction was the passive resistance that had been useful on the plantations. Freedom meant having choices, and the ex-slaves during the war had few, if any, real options—there was little chance to practice being free. Those who were given the chance often succeeded:

> Those freedmen who had the opportunity to rent farms from the Bureau of Negro Affairs, which became possible in the last year and a half of the war, fared better than the others and did much to prove that blacks could support themselves if given the chance . . . In Elizabeth City County in 1865, 37 farms were rented to 138 tenants and their families. All the farms were reported in good condition and none of the tenants defaulted on their rent payments. Unfortunately, most of the freedmen on the Peninsula never had the opportunity to rent and farm land independently during the war. Those who did were primarily the original contraband from Hampton village.

When the war ended, black residents had to put their lives together, starting with the basic family unit. Many from the upcountry plantations had been separated from their families and did not know exactly who belonged to whom:

> The unorthodox familial patterns which the later refugees brought from slavery created more problems for blacks, and for missionaries, than simply

determining which wife belonged to which husband. Freedwomen willingly accepted the responsibilities for caring for their children and for keeping proper homes, but not all knew how to do so. On many plantations, one "black mammy" was charged with the care of all slave children The missionaries continually called for a school to teach the women the habits of "good housewivery [sic]." to teach the care and discipline of their children. Black freedwomen lacked many of the skills considered to be essential by the missionary ladies. They did not know how to sew, or to cook, or to keep a clean house. More importantly, they lacked knowledge of infant and child care.

The newly freed black men also faced very real problems. There were fewer jobs to be had, and more men were looking for work. "By 1865, 40,000 freedmen were concentrated on the Peninsula; 7,000 were in the village of Hampton alone . . . The unclear division of authority between military and civilian agencies fostered the breakdown of civil order. Lawlessness was rampant and clashes between the races were almost daily occurrences." Much of this lawlessness was probably caused by the criminal element from both races. Freedom cannot be enjoyed nor life lived to the fullest in such circumstances. Reasonable people needed to take charge:

The priority, second only to defense of freedom itself, became greater social responsibility and stability within their communities. Most freedmen appear to have been supporters, if not active participants, in the armed defense of black settlements and black rights. At the same time, they seemed equally near unanimity in opposing the criminal element among them, black or white. Much of the theft and violence within postwar black communities was perpetrated by blacks. Black church and political leaders joined forces with the Freedmen's Bureau and even the civil authorities to bring peace to their settlements.

These settlements were primarily in three areas of Hampton and Elizabeth City County, Property in some parts of town could be bought fairly cheaply and thus was available to the black population. The first was the area known as "Newtown" and was that part of the county bordered on the north by Electric Avenue and on the west by LaSalle Avenue and that extended on the east nearly over to Sunset Creek. "In 1869. Daniel Cock divided a thirty-five acre triangular section of his property into thirty-three lots with the intention of selling the parcels to black buyers. His plat, a drawing by a surveyor which shows individual parcels of land, was titled 'Cock's Newtown.' The first six lots were sold in March of that year for fifty dollars each.

The Little England Chapel was built on a small lot at the edge of Newtown as the neighborhood gathering place. It got its start around 1877 when a teacher from the Normal School noticed three children playing on the beach next to his cottage one Sunday morning. He invited them in, they sang hymns and a Sunday school tradition was begun. By the spring of 1878, 75 people were attending, and "by January 1879, the Sunday School had an enrollment of [110], ranging in age from four to seventy-five. A larger space was definitely needed. A neighborhood fund drive was conducted, and the Normal School president General Armstrong "promised to give one dollar for every four dollars that the neighborhood gave . . . Daniel Cock offered the use of a small site close to the black community to be used for building a church or a schoolhouse." Thus Newtown gained its own chapel.

Students at the Normal School were encouraged "to provide Christian service to the black neighborhoods near the school . . . An example was . . . students [going] across the river to the Newtown neighborhood to teach Sunday School." A more practical assistance was provided when sewing classes were offered in 1889–90:

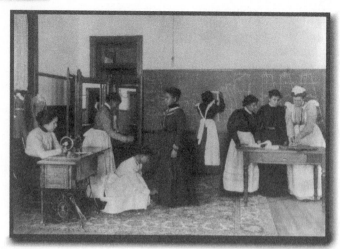

A class in dressmaking. Hampton Institute, circa 1899. The girls are receiving lessons in sewing and tailoring. They will use these skills to teach the women at Little England Chapel. They also make the male students' uniforms. The men are organized into a corps of cadets and wear a military-style uniform, thus eliminating the need for "proper" college clothes, which few had. From Engs. Educating the Disfranchised and Disadvantaged. *photograph courtesy of Library of Congress. LC-USZ62-38151.*

The Normal School ladies cut all the material before taking it to the Little England and Slabtown [Buckroe] sewing schools and often prebasted it as well. The women participating in the classes were required to pay half the price of the material they used. As an incentive, the merchants of the town of Hampton lowered the prices of their goods. The other part of the costs was donated by Northerners interested in supporting a worthy project.

The two sewing schools together used fifteen hundred yards of material in a single year, making two hundred sixty garments as well as numerous sheets, towels and other articles. So many women wanted to attend the sewing schools that the buildings could not accommodate all of them.

A second area of black property ownership was roughly north of Queen Street and west of King Street. The third black settlement was between Fort Monroe and the Soldiers' Home. Both of these properties were put on the market by the court to settle two bankruptcy cases in 1868. At that time.

the court-appointed administrators of the estates struck upon the idea of laying out streets and dividing the estates into city lots. The lots were extremely narrow, sometimes only thirty to fifty feet along the street front, and very deep, usually half a block. One group would be most interested in such property, the blacks, and the administrators clearly had them in mind. Prices were very low sometimes as little as eighty-five dollars: the administrators themselves carried the mortgages for many who could not pay the full amount upon purchase.

As these areas were settled, black residents had effectively established their own business and residential communities: "From the beginning of Queen Street at Hampton bridge westward to the end of the then settled area just west of Armistead Avenue, as many as half of all businesses were owned by blacks. A similar pattern existed along King Street northward to the edge of town." The largest store in downtown was a combination grocery and dry goods store owned by Thomas Harmon, a black merchant. Early on, the area was "a ramshackle business district of black-owned boarding-houses, barbershops, eating places, and saloons intermixed with a few imposing structures and homes such as St. John's Church, the Courthouse, and the residences of black sheriff Andrew Williams and black Commissioner of Revenue R.M. Smith. More substantial brick buildings would come later, as the financial affairs of both black and white townspeople improved with the development of the seafood industries and the return of wealthy tourists to the area. One thing that remained from that early time was the naming of the streets: Grant, Union, Lincoln and Liberty indicate choices of the black population. The school that the area children attended was the Lincoln School. The court plan of selling the second estate in small lots worked as well in the new settlement across Mill Creek from Fort Monroe, which came to be called Phoebus.

Black residents were now property owners, and jobs were available in construction, skilled crafts—such as blacksmiths and shoemakers—and the seafood industry. With the establishment of the black church, the community had taken responsibility for its own self-improvement: "One of their first cooperative acts was to institutionalize [religion] in separate churches under their own control. In 1863 they founded Zion Baptist Church at Hampton…and First Baptist Church of Hampton." These were not the missionary-led organizations of ex-slaves. The freedmen had discovered real choices: "Freedom meant the right to control one's own life, to pray in one's own way, and to suffer the consequences of one's own mistakes….black acceptance of [the missionary] values came only after most missionaries had departed and blacks could make the choice because of their own needs, rather than because of needs imposed upon them."

The Hampton Normal and Agricultural Institute

Like the Soldiers' Home, the Hampton Normal and Agricultural Institute would never have come into existence except as a result of the Civil War. The people who would be the founders of the school and those who would attend the classes came together during the conflict and stayed during the period of transition that followed. The American Missionary Association came to Hampton in 1861 to assist the newly freed slaves and remained throughout the war as teachers to the black population. When the war ended, the AMA continued its emphasis on education as a way to "uplift" the freedmen. To train black teachers, the AMA "in 1867 and 1868, founded eight teacher-training schools in Macon. Savannah and Atlanta, Georgia: Charleston. South Carolina; Louisville. Kentucky: Nashville. Tennessee; Talladega, Alabama; and Hampton, Virginia."

From the beginning, the school in Hampton was different from the others, due to the character of its first principal and the goals he established for the institute. Samuel Chapman Armstrong had served in the Union army and came to Hampton after the war as the local director of the Freedmen's Bureau. The bureau's main task was to aid the ex-slaves in their transition to freedom, and an essential part of that task was to develop local educational facilities. Armstrong was literally placed in the midst of the two things that would occupy him for the rest of his life: black youth and their education. His vision of a school to train the newly freed black youth was based on his army experience and missionary training:

First, his military experience, and his success in it, had persuaded him that blacks needed a more rigid, disciplined educational environment than other missionaries advocated. Second, his upbringing as his father's assistant in organizing schools for indigenous Hawaiians had wedded him to the idea of "industrial education" as a primary means of advancement for "backward peoples." Third, that same background had inspired in him a grandiose notion of "saving races." Thus he set out to design a system that would give the black masses at least a rudimentary education.

Before he could lead such a school, however, he had to be asked; the AMA was in charge. First, he pushed for the purchase of land in Hampton and finessed the AMA into buying the property: "The site agreed upon was 125 acres of a former plantation called Little Scotland, or, less elegantly. Wood's Farm." Despite being on hand and available. Armstrong had to wait until the first person offered the position of principal declined, whereupon he readily accepted the offer. The Hampton Normal and Agricultural Institute opened on April 6, 1868, with Samuel Chapman Armstrong in charge.

The April opening of the school was an auspicious occasion, but "in 1868, the new Hampton Institute was not much to look at. It consisted of some old army barracks, the remnants of Chesapeake Army Hospital, and the decrepit mansion house of the former Little Scotland plantation." All that would change as Armstrong set about acquiring financial support:

In March, 1872, the General Assembly of Virginia passed an Act, giving the institution one-third of the Agricultural College land grant of Virginia. Its share was one hundred thousand acres, which were sold in May 1872, for $95.000. Nine-tenths of this money was invested in State bonds, bearing six per cent interest; the other tenth has been expended in the purchase of additional land, increasing the size of the home farm to one hundred and ninety acres.

After acquiring the land grant and the much-needed funds, 'the Institute was virtually independent of the American Missionary Association." By 1885, the "entire property of the School is…valued at about $400,000. most of which has been paid for by private contributions." The large brick buildings of the 1880s campus were constructed in part from money received as gifts from those Northern benefactors.

The essential purpose of the Hampton Normal School was to train black teachers who would then go out into the hinterland of the South and teach black students. The curriculum of a "Normal" school was built around this idea: "During their three years— the "Junior," "Middle," and "Senior"— students completed the equivalent of a high school education…Seniors were required to engage in practice teaching at the 'Butler School' for black youngsters on Hampton's campus." There was one very important addition to the course of study in Hampton: it also incorporated a trade school requirement:

Southern black schools usually were in session less than six months a year. Hampton alumni needed to learn other skills simply to support themselves and their families during the remaining months. In short, manual labor education at Hampton was, originally, a means to important ends. It would provide graduates with moral character and additional skills needed so that they could pursue their primary task of teaching others.

Hampton was also unusual in that it was coeducational and emphasized a "home" atmosphere where moral values would be learned within the institute family:

Armstrong believed that immorality was a major weakness of the black race. Therefore, women would have to play an equal role in uplifting the black race.

Hampton Institute campus. 1899. On a calm winter day, the buildings of the Normal School stand out against the sky. From left to right: Principal's House, Memorial Chapel and Clock Tower. Academic Hall and the Huntington Industrial Works. The pier and boathouse are in the center. Courtesy of Library of Congress LC-USZ62-68934.

By teaching men and women together under the close supervision of their teachers, the school could inculcate the habits and values that had to be passed on to their pupils and communities.

The black students seem to have taken all this in stride; they were young, away from home for the first time and making new friends. They were probably enjoying themselves as college students always have. As they became more sophisticated, many realized that they could acquire an education and later decide on their own goals in life. "It is true that most of them became teachers, but very few were *only* teachers. They were also lawyers; they were ministers, newspaper editors, actors, musicians. Pullman porters, postal workers, and politicians…about 10 percent went on to advanced training in northern white schools."

Three different aspects of the early Hampton Normal School experience are given special attention here: the Trade School Course, the Indian School and Regulations for both male and female students. The Trade School was greatly needed to give the students a source of income: "Most of Hampton's early students were like the young Booker T. Washington, who simply arrived at Hampton's gates and sought acceptance." They could not pay for their education nor support themselves while in attendance: "Students' labor is generally faithful, but school boys' work is not equal to that of hired hands. It is, however, paid at the price of the latter, regardless of the demand for it, not only as needed stimulus but as necessary to their support. Courses were added to the curriculum to provide that work. The Trade School Course was developed in 1879:

Class in capillary physics at Hampton Institute. Female students have joined the men in what appears to be a physics lab. The men are wearing the uniform of the cadet corps. http://hdl.loc.gov/loc.pap/iph.3e08065. courtesy of Library of Congress. LC-USZ62-108065.

It was four years in length. During the first three of those years, boys spent forty-nine hours a week in "Shop Practice" and a total of sixteen hours in academic pursuits, along with eight hours in activities such as mechanical drawing mechanics, gymnastics/drill, and trade discussion. Additionally, they spent twelve hours a week in "Supervised Study." Only in the fourth year did students spend the bulk of their time pursuing the Normal Course curriculum.

By 1884, the school owned two large farms, a sawmill, a machine shop, a carpenter shop, a harness shop, a tin shop, a paint shop and a shoe shop, and a wheelwright and blacksmith were operating on campus. The uses for these are self-explanatory and would offer students a wide choice of trades. All of the equipment, buildings and instruction were expensive and also needed the infusion of Northern money. The girls were offered training suitable to their sex that would be useful in their future lives as teachers and housewives. In the Stone Memorial Building, "we come first to the Girls' Industrial Room and Sewing and Tailoring Department. Here all the mending and making of garments is done, and uniforms for the students are made… On the same floor we come to the Knitting Department. Here the manufacture of mittens is carried on. The products of this department are taken by a firm in Massachusetts." The girls who led the sewing classes at Little England Chapel would have received their own training here.

One of the trades is of special interest: the Printing Office and Book Bindery. This department was run as an actual business and printed several magazines as well as the Soldiers Home weekly newspaper, the *Soldiers' Home Bulletin*. A business such as this had to meet deadlines and work on a schedule. An official staff was employed to do most of the work, with from twelve to fifteen boys as assistants. The office was a good example of using your best resources, wherever they can be found; several veterans from the Soldiers Home were at work, "while the book-binder also wears the uniform of Uncle Sam."

The logical outlet for the items produced in the various trades and crafts was the village of Hampton, and that meant competition for the local businesses. The institute's local alumni came to the aid of their school when charges were brought to that effect: "It was the black delegates in the legislature and black merchants in Hampton village who led the defense in refuting charges in 1886 and 1887 that the Institute's various shops constituted an illegal restraint on local trade Things probably evened out over the long run, as the students were allowed to shop in town once a week.

That the Trade School was successful in the early years at Hampton can be seen in the career of one of its best-known graduates. Booker T. Washington, class of 1875, "began his education in a prototype of what evolved into the [Trade] School, and he later came back to oversee it." His work as president of Tuskegee Institute showed that he had absorbed both the lessons and goals of Hampton Institute and that he endeavored to replicate them in rural Alabama.

Since the students could not pay for their tuition, room and board. Principal Armstrong had to acquire funding elsewhere. As has been noted, money came to the institute from Northern benefactors. It is interesting to see how those connections were made, Armstrong had a "product" to sell: his school for black ex-slaves. To draw attention to the uniqueness of his program, he "borrowed an idea from Hampton's sister AMA school, Fisk University in Nashville. Armstrong created a choral group, 'The Hampton Singers," modeled after Fisk's successful "Jubilee Choir" As in many other things relating to the school. Armstrong devoted his full attention to the development of his choir: "Armstrong traveled about Virginia with his music director. Thomas Fenuer, searching for talented singers in the fields and in the tobacco factories of Richmond," Once the choir was assembled and trained, the group went on tour to the major Northeastern cities to raise money:

> *The tour was a grand success. The group received rave reviews in Troy, Rochester, and New York City. It did not fare quite as well in Boston, apparently because the concert followed a disastrous 1872 fire in that city, and philanthropists were giving their money to a cause closer to home. The tour continued on through Philadelphia and reached its climax as the "Singers" performed in the Capitol Rotunda and before President Ulysses S. Grant on the White House steps.*

Virginia Hall, the largest building on campus, was completed in 1874, "partly through the efforts of the "Hampton Singers," in a three year's [*sic*] singing campaign." Armstrong's choir had achieved success and fulfilled its purpose: the moneyed elite of the Northeast now knew and approved of this Southern black school.

In April 1878, the first Native Americans arrived at Hampton from the western plains by way of Florida:

> *In 1874, some 150 Kiowa, Comanche, and Arapaho Indians who had participated in an uprising in the Indian Territory of Oklahoma were incarcerated at Fort Marion, Florida. Their warden was Lt. Richard Henry Pratt, a United States Army officer who had commanded black troops during the Civil War. The exiled Indians had been imprisoned without regard to actual guilt in the uprising. Such injustice outraged Pratt. He barraged officials in Washington with letters begging for the release of those who were innocent and for some provision for "civilizing" the others. Finally, in 1877, the army and then Indian Commissioner E.A. Hayt agreed to the release of Pratt's charges and to their education in eastern schools if they desired it.*

Samuel Armstrong decided to add another of the "backward races" to his educational program, and Lieutenant Prau accepted the offer, since "eastern whites wanted no part of Praty's partially tamed 'savages. Hampton Normal School gained not only a new teaching challenge but also a financial boost. "The United States pays $167 a piece per annum toward the board and clothes of 120 Indians: allowing nothing for tuition, [which costs about $70 each per annum], or for buildings for their accommodation. For which, about $50,000 have been paid by the school. For this sum, amounting to about $35.000 annually, the School looks to the friends of both races." A new worthy project was offered to those wealthy friends, and they must have come through. The school would eventually build two separate dormitories for the Native American students, the Wigwam for the men and Winona Lodge for the women. Coeducation was deemed essential for the "uplift" of the Indian, as it was for the black students.

Armstrong and his staff tried to blend the two groups of students into one community, but the differences were too great. For one thing, most of the Native Americans knew very little English and had only a rudimentary education when they came to the school. A separate program had to be established. "The first three years of the Indian School program concerned 'oral training in English,' with rudiments of writing. Only in the fourth year did students actually begin to study texts. History, mathematics, geography, and art also were included in the curriculum. The Indian students…had particular difficulty with mathematical concepts."

Another problem appeared early in the experiment: the men of the two races did not like one another. The black men were not sure that the Native American men were sufficiently "tamed," and the Native Americans felt superior to the black men." These were differences that could not be solved in an academic setting, and eventually, two separate schools were formed. As part of their training, Native American students were also required to learn manual skills, and in 1887, they "studied in a 'technical shop', in which they received a modest amount of training in a variety of trades." The Native American women worked with the black women in housekeeping skills:

The Indian men were organized in separate companies of the school cadet corps and were inspected daily by student officers. As with black students, the process of teaching civilization continued into the evenings. Indian students attended their required study halls and participated in there own debate society, prayer meetings, temperance association, and social events at Winona Lodge. On special occasions, such as Founders' Day, they joined the black students in social affairs.

A problem occurred in the lives of the Native American students that was unrelated to attitude or aptitude; many became sick in the hot, humid climate of southeastern Virginia. They had grown up in the high western plains and "were described as suffering from 'weak lungs.' They frequently were plagued by scrofula, an early manifestation of tuberculosis, and many of them later contracted pneumonia and tuberculosis." The school staff tried its best to help the students entrusted to its care by creating a separate kitchen and dining room to cater to their special needs: "Even these precautions were not entirely sufficient; of the 427 Indian students who attended Hampton between 1878 and 1888, 31 died. Another 111 had to be returned to their reservations because of poor health."

The Indian School at Hampton Institute was designed as a five-year program. Unfortunately, the government scholarships were for three years of study, so most American Indian students returned to their reservations with only a smattering of proper education. There was not enough work for the men back home, and "the vast majority of Hampton's Indian male graduates became subsistence farmers. An overwhelming majority of the women became the wives of such men and the mothers of their children." A few students went on to graduate programs in medicine, teaching or law and returned to work with their own people.

In 1912, the government subsidy was removed and "so brought about the demise of Hampton's Indian School. Indians, though in much smaller numbers, continued to attend the institute for another decade, supported by private charities. The attempt to form the two races into one community could not be termed a success, but it is to be hoped that they gained something positive from the experience.

General Armstrong's idea of a rigid, disciplined educational experience for the students at the Normal School was worked out in detail. The goal was not only to educate but also to prepare the young black students to succeed in the white society around them. They would need self-discipline to survive:

Accordingly, Hampton's teachers instituted a rigid set of behavioral regulations and an almost draconian disciplinary system. Hampton students were regimented from "Rising Bell" at 5:15 A.M. until "Taps" or "Lights-out" at 9:30. Each half hour or hour of their day was programmed. After breakfast at 6 A.M., their rooms were inspected. They attended chapel twice daily. Male students were organized into a corps of cadets. Uniforms were required of all male students [a boon for many of them who otherwise could not have afforded decent clothing]. The men marched to classes, meals, and work details. Women were not so regimented, but were supervised as closely by their teachers and matrons in the dormitories. Students were allowed only one afternoon a week to go into nearby Hampton village for necessities, a day carefully chosen so that it did not coincide with "market day," when local rowdies might be around to corrupt them.

The students who could not accommodate themselves to such a program were disciplined by receiving demerits. "Excessive demerits could result in fines [an impractical device, since most students had no money]: exile to the almost primitive conditions on the school farm at Shellbanks, several miles from the campus; or incarceration in the campus guardhouse." The idea of a school "jail" sounds extreme today, but it must have been better than calling in the civil authorities from the town of Hampton. The main idea was to save as many young black people as possible, and the institute succeeded in that.

The village of Hampton in particular benefitted from its graduates, who came home to teach in the new black public schools. They also pursued professions in the "ministry and the law, both of which usually led to political involvement as well." Black men were elected to office in the town and county, and to the Virginia legislature. Some became merchants, and John Mallory Phillips founded his own seafood industry. Its graduates signaled the success of the Hampton Normal and Agricultural Institute.

Samuel C. Armstrong

Samuel Chapman Armstrong (January 30, 1839–May 11, 1893) was an American educator and a commissioned officer in the Union Army during the American Civil War. He is best remembered for his work after the war as the founder and first principal of the normal school which is now Hampton University.

The son of missionaries, Armstrong was born in Maui, Hawaii, the sixth of ten children. He attended Punahou School in Honolulu, Hawaii. In 1860 his father suddenly died, and Armstrong, at age 21, left Hawaii for the United States and attended Williams College in Massachusetts, graduating in 1862.

When Armstrong was assigned to command the USCT, training was conducted at Camp Stanton near Benedict, Maryland. While stationed at Stanton, he established a school to educate the black soldiers, most of whom had no education as slaves.[3]

At the end of the war, Armstrong joined the Freedmen's Bureau. With the help of the American Missionary Association, he established the Hampton Normal and Agricultural Institute—now known as Hampton University—in Hampton, Virginia in 1868. The Institute was meant to be a place where black students could receive postsecondary education to become teachers, as well as training in useful job skills while paying for their education through manual labor.

During Armstrong's career, and during Reconstruction, the prevailing concept of racial adjustment promoted by whites and African Americans equated technical and industrial training with the advancement of the black race. This idea was not a new solution and traced its history to before the American Civil War. But especially after the war, blacks and whites alike realized the paradox that freedom posed for the African American population in the racist south. Freedom meant liberation from the brutality and degradation of slavery, but as W. E. B. Du Bois described it, a black person "felt his poverty; without a cent, without a home, without land, tools, or savings, he had entered into competition with rich, landed, skilled neighbors. To be a poor man is hard, but to be a poor race in a land of dollars is the very bottom of hardships."[4] Although the end of slavery was the inevitable result of the Union victory, less obvious was the fate of millions of penniless blacks in the South. Former abolitionists and white philanthropists quickly focused their energies on stabilizing the black community, assisting the newly freed blacks to become independent, positive contributors to their community, helping them improve their race, and encouraging them to strive toward a standard put forth by American whites.

In the aftermath of Nat Turner's slave rebellion in 1831, the Virginia General Assembly passed new legislation making it unlawful to teach slaves, free blacks, or mulattoes to read or write. Similar laws were also enacted in other slave-holding states across the South.[5] The removal of these laws after the Civil War helped draw attention to the problem of illiteracy as one of the great challenges confronting these people as they sought to join the free enterprise system and support themselves.

One instrument through which this process of racial uplift could take place was schools such as the Hampton Normal and Industrial Institute. The Hampton Institute exemplified the paternalistic attitudes of whites who felt it was their duty to develop those they regarded as lesser races. General Samuel Armstrong molded the curriculum to reflect his background as both a wartime abolitionist and the child of white missionaries in Hawaii. Armstrong believed that several centuries of the institution of slavery in the United States had left its blacks in an inferior moral state and only whites could help them develop to the point of American civilization. "The solution lay in a Hampton-style education, an education that combined cultural uplift with moral and manual training, or as Armstrong was fond of saying, an education that encompassed 'the head, the heart, and the hands.' "[6] The general insisted that blacks should refrain from voting and politics because their long experience as slaves and, before that, pagans, had degraded the race beyond responsible participation in government. "Armstrong maintained that it was the duty of the superior white race to rule over the weaker dark-skinned races until they were appropriately civilized. This civilization process, in Armstrong's estimate, would require several generations of moral and religious development."[7] The primary means through which white civilization could be instilled in African Americans was by the moral power of labor and manual industry.[8]

At the heart of the early Hampton-style education during Armstrong's tenure was this emphasis on labor and industry. However, teaching blacks to work was a tool, not the primary goal, of the Institute. Rather than producing classes of individual craftsmen and laborers, Hampton was ultimately a normal school (teacher's school) for future black teachers. In theory, these black teachers would then apply the Hampton ideal of self-help and industry at schools throughout the U.S., especially the South. To this end, a prerequisite for admission to Hampton was the intent to become a teacher. In fact, "approximately 84 percent of the 723 graduates of Hampton's first twenty classes became teachers."[8] Armstrong strove to instill in these disciples the moral value of manual labor. This concept became the crucial component of Hampton's training of black educators.

Legacy

Perhaps the best student of Armstrong's Hampton-style education was Booker T. Washington. After coming to the school in 1872, Washington immediately began to adopt Armstrong's teaching and philosophy. Washington described Armstrong as "the most perfect specimen of man, physically, mentally and spiritually. . . ." Washington also quickly learned the aim of the Hampton Institute. After leaving Hampton, he recalled being admitted to the school, despite his ragged appearance, due to the ability he demonstrated while sweeping and dusting a room. From his first day at Hampton, Washington embraced Armstrong's idea of black education.[9] Washington went on to attend Wayland Seminary in Washington, D.C., and he returned to Hampton to teach on Armstrong's faculty. Upon Sam Armstrong's recommendation to Lewis Adams, Washington became the first principal of a new normal school in Alabama, which became Tuskegee University. Many religious organizations, former Union Army officers and soldiers, and wealthy philanthropists were inspired to create and fund educational efforts specifically for the betterment of African Americans in the South by the work of pioneering educators such as Samuel Armstrong and Dr. Washington.

As the ever-increasing numbers of new teachers went back to their communities, by the first third of the 20th century, over 5,000 local schools had been built for blacks in the South with private matching funds provided by individuals such as Henry H. Rogers, Andrew Carnegie, and most notably, Julius Rosenwald, each of whom had arisen from modest roots to become wealthy. Dr. Washington later wrote that, by requiring matching funds, the benefactors felt they were also addressing self-esteem. The recipients locally would have a stake in knowing that they were helping themselves through their own hard work and sacrifice. In many communities, the histories of the so-called Rosenwald schools reflect that to have proved true.

In time, the normal schools which had been originally established primarily to work with blacks at Hampton, Tuskegee, and elsewhere evolved from their primary focus on industrial training, practical skills, and basic literacy into institutions of higher education focused not only upon training teachers, but teaching academics of many types, many eventually becoming full-accredited universities.

Samuel Armstrong suffered a debilitating paralysis in 1892 while speaking in New York. He returned to Hampton in a private railroad car provided by his multimillionaire friend, Collis P. Huntington, builder of the Chesapeake and Ohio Railway and Newport News Shipbuilding and Drydock Company, with whom he had collaborated on black-education projects.

Sam Armstrong died at the Hampton Institute on May 11, 1893. He was interred in the school's cemetery.

Armstrong High School in Richmond, Virginia, was named after Samuel C. Armstrong in 1909.

REFERENCES

1. Official Records, Series 1, Volume XLII/3 [S# 89].
2. Bates, Samuel P. (1868–1871). History of the Pennsylvania Volunteers, 1861–1865. Harrisburg: State Printers.
3. Talbot, Edith Armstrong (1904). Samuel Chapman Armstrong: A Biographical Study. New York: Doubleday, Page & Company. p.109. ISBN 0837115124. http:/books.google.com/books? id=RMxBAAAAIAAJ&dq=%22benedict, &pg=PA 109&ci=225,905,388,36&source=bookclip.
4. Du Bois, W.E.B. (1990). The Souls of Black Folk. New York: First Vintage Books. p. 12. II.
5. Lewis, Rudolph. "Up From Slavery: A Documentary History of Negro Education." Rudolph Lewis. http://www.nathanielturner.com/educationhistorynegro6.htm. Retrieved on 2007-09-05.
6. Adams, David Wallace (1995). Education for Extinction: American Indians and the Boarding School Experience, 1875–1928. Lawrence: University Press of Kansas. pp. 45, 326. ISBN 0700608389.
7. Anderson, James D. (1988). The Education of Blacks in the South, 1860–1935. Chapel Hill: University of North Carolina Press. p. 328. ISBN 0807842214.
8. Anderson, James D. (1988). The Education of Blacks in the South, 1860–1935. Chapel Hill: University of North Carolina Press. pp. 33–47. ISBN 0807842214.
9. Washington, Booker T. The Story of My Life and Work, Vol. 1. Harlan: Smock, and Kraft. p. 21.

- Engs, Robert Francis. Educating the Disfranchised and Disinherited: Samuel Chapman Armstrong and Hampton Institute, 1839–1893. U. of Tennessee Press, 1999. 207 pp.
- Fear-Segal, Jacqueline. "Nineteenth-century Indian Education: Universalism Versus Evolutionism" Journal of American Studies 1999 33(2): 323–341. ISSN 0021-8758.

The History of Hampton University in Correlanon to African-American History from 1868–Present

African Americans during 1868–1880

Amazingly, African Americans made large strides on the political front during this time. The first African-American governor was seen during this time. P.B.S. Pinchback, the elected lieutenant governor of Louisiana, served as governor for forty-one days when H.C. Warmoth was removed from office. Francis L. Cardozo, an accomplished black who had been educated at the University of Glasgow and in London, was secretary of the state of South Carolina from 1868 to 1872. He was also the state treasurer from 1872 to 1876. As for the state of Mississippi, three blacks held very important prestigious positions in the government. In 1873, A. K. Davis was lieutenant governor, James Hill was the secretary of state, and T. W. Cardozo was the superintendent of education. In 1872, John R. Lynch was also the Speaker of the House in Mississippi (Franklin, Moss, 238).

South Carolina saw the election of the first African American to their state supreme court in 1870. He served until 1876 (Franklin, Moss, 240).

Two African Americans were elected to the Senate during this time. Hiram R. Revels was elected to the United States Senate to fill the seat previously held by Jefferson Davis, the ex-Confederate president. Blanche K. Bruce was elected to the Senate in 1874, becoming the only black to be elected to a full term until the election of 1966 where Edward Brooke, a Republican from Massachusetts, became the next black (Franklin, Moss, 242).

The Later Armstrong Years: 1881–1893

Many other buildings sprang up in the. "Later Armstrong Years." To make up for the fire that destroyed the first Academic Hall in 1879, the Academy Building was constructed and dedicated on the old foundations of Academic Hall on May 19, 1881. Stone Manor was completed on April 15, 1882. Marshall Hall was completed to house the library and the principal's and treasurer's offices in 1882. The historic Memorial Chapel was dedicated in 1886. The Whittier School, which was a primary school on the campus that served as a practicing teaching site for Hampton students, was dedicated on November 23, 1887. The Holly Tree Inn was completed in 1888.

A new school was started in 1891 when faculty member Alice Bacon began the Hampton Training School for Nurses on the campus.

The "Later Armstrong Years" were brought to a close on May 11, 1893 when General Samuel Chapman Armstrong, Hampton Normal and Agricultural Institute, died (Hampton University, University 101, The Individual and Life, 301–305).

African Americans during 1881–1893

During this next time, political unrest began to occur and more blacks were seen in the government less frequently. South Carolina was one of the states that made voting for blacks extremely difficult. The law of 1882 required that special ballots and boxes be placed at every polling place for each office of the ballot and that voters put their ballots in the correct boxes. No one was allowed to speak to a voter, and if he failed to find the correct box, his vote was thrown out (Franklin, Moss, 256). The Populist, or People's, Party was the political agency of the resurgent farmers. In 1892, the Populists sought to win back the black vote in most of the Southern states and in many instances resorted to desperate measures to secure the franchise for blacks in communities where by custom and practice they had been barred from voting for more than a decade. The blacks surprisingly stood by the populists, who advocated political, if not social, equality (Franklin, Moss, 257).

Hollis Burke Frissell

Hampton University Principal: 1893–1918

The second twenty-five years of Hampton Normal and Agricultural Institute began when Hollis Burke Frissell was appointed the school's second principal on May 24, 1893. It was during this time in November 1894 that Hampton was able to acquire Henry O. Tanner's painting, The Banjo Lesson, one of the first paintings received at Hampton.

Many new buildings also were built during Frissell's tenure at Hampton. Cleveland Hall, an addition to Virginia Hall, was completed in 1901. The Collis P. Huntington Memorial Library was dedicated in 1903. Clarke Hall was dedicated in 1913.

New departments within the school and new standards for the school were also established during this time. On November 6, 1896, the Armstrong-Slater Memorial Trade School was dedicated. The Business Department, the forerunner of the School of Business, was established in September 1898. In 1904, the academic course was lengthened from three years to four years of study and, in 1916, Hampton Institute was approved as a four-year secondary school by the Department of Public Instruction of the Commonwealth of Virginia.

Hampton also drew national attention to the school when on November 20, 1909, United States President William Howard Taft visited Hampton as a recently elected trustee for the school. The Hampton Basketball Team won the school's first intercollegiate championship in 1916 (Hampton University, et al. 128–129).

African Americans during 1893–1918

Frissell became president at a turning point in history. He was the only Hampton University president to be in office before and after the turn of the century.

The 1900s were a time of serious changes for African Americans. Rioting and other disturbances became very common. From July 24 to July 27, 1900, a very serious race riot broke out in New Orleans. Many black schools and homes were destroyed by the disturbance (Hornsby, 3). From September 22 to September 24, 1906, a major race riot in Atlanta, Georgia left twelve people dead. The rioting was attributed to an irresponsible press and attempts to disenfranchise blacks (Hornsby, 7). Yet another race riot occurred in Springfield, Illinois from August 14 to August 19, 1908. This led concerned whites to call for a conference which led to the founding of the NAACP (The National Association for the Advancement of Colored People) on February 12, 1909 (Hornsby, 9).

Booker T. Washington, one of Hampton's most famous alumni, dined with United States President Theodore Roosevelt at the White House on October 16, 1901. The dinner meeting was viewed by many whites, especially the oppressive Southerners, as a marked departure from racial etiquette and was bitterly criticized (Hornsby, 3).

W.E.B. DuBois began to become a big force in the advancement of African-American people. In 1903, W.E.B. DuBois' The Souls of Black Folk was published. The book crystallized black opposition to the policies of Booker T. Washington, W.E.B. DuBois and William Monroe Trotter spearheaded the Niagara Movement, which was a meeting of black intellectuals from across the nation (Hornsby, 5). DuBois also became the first editor of the NAACP's first publication, the Crisis (Hornsby, 9).

African-American intellectuals also began to take strides during this time. In 1907, Alain Locke won a Rhodes Scholarship. No other African American won this honor again for more than a half a century (Hornsby, 8). On February 9, 1906, the African-American community lost an important intellectual. Paul Laurence Dunbar, a black poet who made Negro dialect an accepted literary form, died in Dayton, Ohio.

Many noble people in the fight for the African-American cause died during this period. Harriet Tubman, "the Moses of her people," died in Auburn, New York on March 10, 1913 (Hornsby, 10). Booker T. Washington, the most noted African American between Frederick Douglass and Martin Luther King, Jr., died at Tuskegee Institute on November 14, 1915. Bishop Henry McNeal Turner, a black Pan-Africanist leader and A.M.E. churchman, died on November 14, 1915 as well (Hornsby, 11).

Two Supreme Court cases also helped the cause of African Americans in their struggle for equality. On June 21, 1915, the United States Supreme Court (Guinn v. The United States) outlawed the "Grandfather Clauses" used by Southern states to deny blacks the right to vote (Hornsby, 10). On November 5, 1917, the Supreme Court, in Buchanan v. Warley, ruled a Louisville, Kentucky law unconstitutional which forbade blacks and whites from living on the same block (Hornsby, 13).

James E. Gregg

Hampton University Principal: 1918–1930

Hampton Institute inducted James E. Gregg as its third principal on November 1, 1918. With Gregg's induction came many new changes for the institute.

Even more buildings were built and dedicated as additions to Hampton's rapidly growing campus. In 1918, Robert C. Ogden Auditorium was completed. Coleman duPont Hall was completed in 1928 to house Natural Sciences, Biology, Mathematics, Chemistry, and Physics. Armstrong Field was dedicated on October 6, 1928.

More departments were added to the curriculum of the institute. In 1919, R. Nathaniel Dett established the Musical Arts Society. The first Bachelor's Degree was awarded for Agricultural Education in 1922.

Gregg's tenure also brought about something that had not happened while the previous two principals were in office. On October 6, 1928, the first issue of The Hampton Script was officially published (Hampton University, et al., 129).

African Americans during 1918–1930

President Gregg's tenure basically happened during the 1920s, which was a prosperous period for the United States as a whole. But even though the American economy was in good shape, this did not necessarily mean that the plight of African Americans got better.

More race riots prevailed. From July 13–October 1, 1918, major race riots occurred across the nation in what James Weldon Johnson called the "Red Summer."

More than 25 riots left more than 100 people dead and more than 1,000 people wounded. Federal troops had to be called in to suppress the uprisings in some areas. By December 1918, eighty-three lynchings had been recorded for the year (Hornsby, 17). It was only towards the end of 1929 that the number of lynchings began to decrease. By late 1929, only ten lynchings were recorded (Hornsby, 25).

Many black accomplishments took place during President Gregg's tenure. Robert Nathaniel Dett, an instructor at Hampton Institute from 1913–1931, was awarded the Bowdoin Prize by Harvard University for an essay entitled "The Emancipation of Negro Music" in August 1920. He was a composer, arranger, and a conductor (Hornsby, 19). George Washington Carver of Tuskegee Institute received the Springers Medal, the NAACP's highest honor, for distinguished research in agricultural chemistry on September 2, 1923 (Hornsby, 21). Garrett A. Morgan, a black inventor, developed the automatic traffic light in late 1923 (Hornsby, 22). Roland Haves was named a soloist with the Boston Symphony and Orchestra on July 1, 1924 (Hornsby, 22). On January 10, 1925, Adelbert H. Roberts was elected to the Illinois state legislature, becoming the first black to serve in a state assembly in twenty-five years (Hornsby, 22). James Weldon Johnson was honored on June 30, 1926 by the NAACP for his careers as a executive secretary for the NAACP, a member of the United States Consul, and editor and poet (Hornsby, 23). Oscar de Priest was elected congressman from Illinois on November 6, 1928 (Hornsby, 24).

One important Supreme Court case made an impact during this time. On March 7, 1927, the United States Supreme Court, in the case of Nixon v. Herndon, outlawed a Texas law that excluded blacks from the Democratic parties in that state (Hornsby, 23).

The major black contribution to the country in this time period was the Harlem Renaissance, which took place from 1922–1929. It was a time of great achievement in the areas of African-American art and literature. The writings and poetry of Langston Hughes, Countee Cullen, James Weldon Johnson, Claude McKay, and Zora Neale Hurston drew critical attention and popular acclaim from both blacks and whites. Claude McKay, the first important figure in this time period, was noted for his Harlem Shadows (1922), a collection of bitter, but eloquent poems on the condition of the Negro in postwar America (Hornsby, 21).

The most important occurrence in this part of history, however, was the New York stock market crash on October 29, 1929. This began the Great Depression (Hornsby, 24).

George P. Phenix

Hampton University Principal/President: 1930–1931

On January 30, 1930, George P. Phenix was elected the fourth and last principal of Hampton Institute by the Board of Trustees. Because of the short time span that Phenix was principal, he was not able to accomplish nearly as much as his predecessors. On July 1, 1930, Hampton Normal and Agricultural Institute became merely Hampton Institute. Phenix also changed the title of "principal" to that of "president," making him the first president of Hampton Institute.

As for academics, Hampton Institute's School of Nursing began offering diplomas after a three-year program (Hampton University, et al., 130).

African Americans during 1930–1931

During President Phenix's short tenure, a few substantial events occurred in African-American history.

Two people made headlines for their recognitions. On March 31, 1930, U.S. President Hoover appointed Judge John J. Parker of North Carolina, a known racist, to the Supreme Court. This made the NAACP launch a successful campaign against Parker's confirmation. On a happier note, on June 22, 1930, Mary McLeod Bethune, a Florida African-American educator, feminist leader, and civil rights spokesperson, was named one of America's fifty leading women by the historian Ida Tarbell (Hornsby, 25).

In court cases, nine black youths who were accused of raping two white women of a dubious reputation on a freight train went on trial for their lives in Scottsboro, Alabama. Many people, including African-American organizations, liberal whites, and the Communist Party vied to defend "the Scottsboro Boys." The boys were quickly convicted but, by 1950, all were free by either parole, appeal, or escape (Hornsby, 25).

In deaths, Daniel Hale Williams, a pioneer heart surgeon and founder of Provident Hospital, a predominantly black institution, died in Chicago, Illinois (Hornsby, 26).

Arthur Howe

Hampton University President: 1931–1940

Arthur Howe was inaugurated as the fifth president on January 1, 1931. During Howe's tenure, many new departments opened on campus. The first class in the School of Music graduated on June 3, 1931. The first Master's of Arts Degree was awarded on May 21, 1932. On April 21, 1932, Hampton Institute was accredited by the Southern Association of Colleges and Trade Schools as a "Class B" school, only to be elevated to "Class A" on January 24, 1933. The George P. Phenix School, which was the City of Hampton's Senior High School for African Americans until the 1960s, was completed on campus in 1932.

Two traditions were started during this time. After a vote headed by the Hampton Script, the students selected "Pirates" as the name of the school's mascot. In Fall 1940, the first Annual Fall Convocation was held (Hampton University, et al., 130).

African Americans during 1931–1940

President Howe resided over Hampton University during the Great Depression, a horrible time for both blacks and whites, but more so for blacks.

In 1932, Franklin D. Roosevelt was elected the President of the United States, promising a "New Deal" to all in the Depression-ridden nation (Hornsby, 261).

On March 15, 1933, the NAACP began its attack on segregation and discrimination in American schools and colleges. The NAACP sued the University of North Carolina on behalf of Thomas Hocutt. They later lost the case because a black educator responsible for certifying the academic record of the applicant refused to do so (Hornsby, 28).

African Americans made strides on the political front as Arthur L. Mitchell, a Democrat, defeated Republican Congressman Oscar de Priest, becoming the pioneer black member of his party in Congress on November 7, 1934.

As for religion, Elijah Muhammad succeeded W.D. Fard as the leader of the Black Muslim movement in the United States in November 1934 (Hornsby, 28).

On the sports front, Joe Louis defeated Primo Canera, a white man, at Yankee Stadium in New York on June 25, 1935 (Hornsby, 29). Jesse Owens made his own contributions to the legacy of African-American athletes when he won four gold medals at the Summer Olympics in Berlin (Hornsby, 30).

More promotions and appointments for African Americans also came in this period of time. John Hope, now president of Atlanta University, was honored in New

York City by the NAACP for his achievements as an educational and civil rights leader on July 3, 1936. President Franklin D. Roosevelt, continuing to organize his unofficial "Black Cabinet," appointed Mary McLeod Bethune director of the Division of Negro Affairs of the National Youth Administration on December 8, 1936. William H. Hastie, a black lawyer, was confirmed as the first African-American federal judge on March 26, 1937 (Hornsby, 30–31).

In Supreme Court cases, the case of Gibbs v. Board of Education of Montgomery county, Maryland was filed by the NAACP. The decision of this case set the precedent for equalizing the salaries of black and white schoolteachers (Hornsby, 30). In the case of Missouri ex rel Gaines, supported by the NAACP, the U.S. Supreme Court declared that states must provide equal, even if separate, educational facilities for blacks within their boundaries on December 12, 1938. The plaintiff, Lloyd Gaines, mysteriously disappeared following the Court's decision (Hornsby, 35).

In the entertainment business, Marion Anderson, world-renowned singer, was refused permission to sing in Constitution Hall in Washington D.C. by the Daughters of the American Revolution in March 1939. The Secretary of the Interior provided the Lincoln Memorial as the site for her concert. Anderson was later awarded the Spingarn Medal later in the year (Hornsby, 35).

Malcolm McLean

Hampton University President: 1940–1944

Malcolm McLean was inaugurated as the sixth president of Hampton Institute on November 25, 1940. While McLean was president, Hampton Institute saw a change and a few new additions to the campus. The U.S. Naval Training School, which was the first offered at a historically black college, was activated and ran until August 1945. The baccalaureate nursing program began under the Hampton Institute Division of Nurse Education, graduating its first class of three women in 1946. The Charles White mural "The Contribution of the Negro to Democracy in America" was unveiled and dedicated in Clarke Hall on June 25, 1943. Scrolls were presented to the thirty-nine charter members of the quarter Century Club at Convocation on October 29, 1943. The Division of Trades and Industries was closed in 1944 (Hampton University, et al., 130).

African Americans during 1940–1944

In the section of the arts, many new events occurred. Native Son, written by Richard Wright, was published and became a bestseller in February 1940. Hattie McDaniel received an Academy Award for Best Performance by an Actress in a Supporting Role for her performance as Mammy in Gone with the Wind, becoming the first African American to win an Oscar in March 1940 (Hornsby, 35).

African Americans continued receiving appointments to higher positions and various awards. Benjamin O. Davis, Sr. was appointed brigadier general in the United States Army, becoming the highest ranking black officer in the armed services on October 16, 1940 (Hornsby, 36). George Washington Carver was awarded an honorary Doctor of Science degree by the University of Rochester on June 18, 1941 (Hornsby, 38). William L. Dawson, for two decades the dean of black congressmen, was elected to the United States House of Representative from Chicago on November 3, 1942 (Hornsby, 40).

President Roosevelt played a large role in African-American history at this time. On June 25, 1941, the president issued an Executive Order forbidding racial and religious discrimination in defense industries and government training programs. The president established a Fair Employment Practices Committee to monitor discrimination against Negroes in defense industries (Hornsby, 38).

As for deaths, Marcus Garvey died in London on June 10, 1940 (Hornsby, 35). George Washington Carver died in Tuskegee, Alabama on January 5, 1943 (Hornsby, 40).

Ralph P. Bridgman

Hampton University President: 1944–1949

Ralph P. Bridgman was inaugurated as Hampton Institute's seventh president on February 12, 1944. Even though he was president of Hampton for five years, not much was accomplished. The only true milestone during his presidency was when graduate courses in Education and Guidance Techniques began in October 1944 (Hampton University, et al., 130).

African Americans during 1944–1949

The years 1944–1949 were years filled with many more advances for African Americans.

In the year 1944, the U.S. Supreme Court ruled in the Smith v. Allwright case that the white primary, which had excluded Negroes from voting in the South, was unconstitutional on April 3. Also during that year, black women were permitted to enter the Women's Naval Corp (WAVES) (Hornsby, 41).

On March 12, 1945, New York established the first state Fair Employment Practices Commission to guard against discrimination in the workplace. The United Nations Charter was approved in San Francisco in June. Several blacks, including W.E.B. DuBois, Ralph Bunche, and Mary McLeod Bethune, took part in the processes (Hornsby, 42).

Nineteen forty-six brought in former federal judge William H. Hastie as governor of the Virgin Islands, the first black to govern a U.S. state or territory since Reconstruction on May 1. June 5 was the day that the U.S. Supreme Court, in the case of Morgan v. Virginia, prohibited segregation in interstate bus travel. Jack Johnson, the first great African-American boxing hero, died on June 10 in Raleigh, North Carolina (Hornsby, 44).

In 1947, "Freedom riders" were sent into the South by the Congress of Racial Equality (CORE) to test the Supreme Court's June 3, 1946 ban against segregation in interstate bus travel on April 9. Jackie Robinson joined the Brooklyn Dodgers on April 10, becoming the first Negro baseball player in the major leagues (Hornsby, 44).

During 1948, the U.S. Supreme Court ruled in the court case Sipuel v. University of Oklahoma that a state must provide legal education for blacks at the same time it is offered to whites on January 12. On May 3, the Court decided in the case Shelley v. Kraemer that the courts could not enforce restrictive housing covenants. Professor Ralph J. Bunche, a noted black political scientist, was confirmed by the United Nations Security Council as temporary UN mediator in Palestine (Hornsby, 46–47).

Nineteen forty-nine brought William H. Hastie, a former District Court judge and governor of the Virgin Islands, an appointment to Judge of the Third U.S. Circuit Court of Appeals (Hornsby, 47).

Alonzo G. Moron

Hampton University President: 1949–1961

Hampton Institute's eighth and first African-American president Alonzo G. Moron was inaugurated on April 26, 1949. Four new additions and one subtraction came with his presidency. The Entrance Gate, which was designed by William Moses and was built by Trade School students, was completed in 1950. John Biggers' bronze sculpture of General Armstrong was unveiled on February 2, 1952. The auditorium of Clarke Hall was named in honor of John H. Wainwright, Hampton alumni of the class of 1888, and dedicated in 1956. Hampton Institute was admitted to the Southern Association of Colleges and Secondary Schools on December 2, 1957, and the School of Agriculture and Engineering closed in 1955 (Hampton University, et al., 130).

African Americans during 1949–1961

Hampton University President Moron became president during the beginning of a time filled with turmoil in history for African Americans.

In 1950, Charles R. Drew, the pioneering African-American hematologist who was often at times called the father of the "Blood Bank," died in Burlington, North Carolina on April 1. Gwend<ill/> Brooks was awarded the Pulitzer Prize for poetry, making her the first African American to have received the honor, on May 1. The U.S. Supreme Court decided in the case of McLaurin v. Oklahoma on June 5 that once a black student is admitted to a previously all-white school, no distinctions can be made on the basis of race. On September 22, Ralph Bunche was awarded the Nobel Peace Prize for mediating the Palestinian dispute (Hornsby, 48–49). Nineteen fifty-one brought the University of North Carolina's admitting black students to their institutions (Hornsby, 49).

But probably the most influential event that took place during this time was the Montgomery bus boycott of 1956. The blacks of Montgomery boycotted the city bus lines to avoid the alleged abuse of black passengers by white drivers, to obtain a more satisfactory seating regulation, and to secure the employment of black drivers on buses serving predominantly black sections. In the end, the bus boycott was successful with the whites giving in to the demands of the blacks (Franklin, Moss, 467).

Jerome H. Holland

Hampton University President: 1961–1970

Jerome H. Holland was inaugurated as the ninth president of Hampton Institute on April 29, 1961. During Holland's presidency, many new buildings were dedicated and moves were made to organize the University Archives. February 2, 1964 brought the dedication of the Samuel Chapman Armstrong Hall, which is the Communications and Music Building. Martin Luther King, Jr. Hall, the Social Sciences Building, was dedicated on September 26, 1968. William A. Freeman Hall, the Nursing Building, was dedicated on February 6, 1969. 1968 brought the completion of the Natural Sciences Building which was dedicated Thomas W. Turner Hall on January 29, 1978. Virginia Hall, the Academy Building, the Mansion House, and the Memorial Chapel were first included on the Virginia Landmark Register on September 16, 1969. Also, the first steps were taken to organize the University Archives which eventually resulted in the 1972 establishment of the

Hampton Institute Archives under the direction of Fritz J. Malval (Hampton University, et al., 131).

African Americans during 1961–1970

The 1960s brought with them many times of crisis and protests in support of the Civil Rights cause. The most important event of the 1960s was the March on Washington for the civil rights movement. On August 28, 1963, in one of the largest public gatherings that Washington, D.C. had ever seen, more than 200,000 people gathered at the foot of the Lincoln Memorial and heard the speeches from their leaders of the civil rights movement. A. Philip Randolph, Martin Luther King, Jr., Roy Wilkins, Walter Reuther, and other notables spoke to the eager crowds. This was the scene of Dr. King's famous "I Have A Dream" speech (Franklin, Moss, 505–506).

The 1960s also unwillingly became a decade of assassinations. On November 22, 1963, a major setback seemed to have occurred for the cause of the civil rights movement. This was the day that President John Fitzgerald Kennedy was shot in Dallas, Texas (Franklin, Moss, 507). But when Lyndon Baines Johnson was sworn in as the thirty-sixth president of the United States, he made it quick to be known that he was a strong supporter of Kennedy's civil rights programs (Franklin, Moss, 507). Malcolm X was murdered in 1965 in an auditorium and Dr. Martin Luther King, Jr. was assassinated on April 4, 1968 while in Memphis, Tennessee, where he was working on getting rights for garbage workers (Franklin, Moss, 518).

Roy D. Hudson

Hampton University President: 1970–1977

President Roy D, Hudson was inaugurated as Hampton Institute's tenth president on October 24, 1970. During Hudson's presidency, the Ceremonial Mace was presented to the College at the Commencement on May 28, 1972. On January 3, 1973, W.E.B. DuBois Hall was dedicated. On September 19, 1974, fifteen acres of the Hampton Institute campus were designated a national Historic District citing the historical importance of Virginia Hall, Academy Building, Mansion House, Memorial House, Memorial Chapel and the Emancipation Oak. And lastly, on April 24, 1976, the Dr. William Robinson Lecture Series was begun by the Department of Secondary Education (Hampton University, et al., 131–132).

African Americans during 1970–1977

African Americans made many strides in all areas during this time.

The *Flip Wilson Show* ran from 1970 until 1974, the first variety show hosted by an African American to be consistently rated among the top programs in television (Franklin, Moss, 488).

Representative Shirley Chisholm began campaigning for the office of United States president for the Democratic party, becoming the first African-American woman to do so in 1972 (Franklin, Moss, 527).

Arthur Ashe, an African-American tennis player, became the first African-American Wimbledon champion in 1975. To accomplish this feat, he defeated fellow American Jimmy Connors (Franklin, Moss, 488).

In the election of 1976, the power of the African-American vote was demonstrated in favor of Democratic nominee Jimmy Carter. More than 90 percent of all black voters supported Jimmy Carter. Except for the state of Virginia, Jimmy Carter swept the southern states. Carter made sure to thank the black voters by appointing Patricia Harris to the Cabinet as secretary of housing and urban development and Andrew Young as ambassador to the United Nations (Franklin, Moss, 528).

Carl M. Hill

Hampton University President: 1977–1979

On October 9, 1977, Carl M. Hill became the eleventh president of Hampton Institute. President Hill's short tenure was filled with building dedications. The dedication of the early Childhood Laboratory School, named in honor of Dr. Eva C. Mitchell, took place on January 29, 1978. The dedication of the Jerome H. Holland Physical Education Center occurred on March 11, 1978. Lastly, on May 20, 1978, Ethel C. Buckman Hall, the Business School, was dedicated (Hampton University, et al., 132).

African Americans during 1977–1979

On February 3, 1977, the "Roots" miniseries, based on Alex Haley's novel of the same title in which he traced his ancestry to Africa and slavery, ended eight nights of presentations on the ABC television network (Hornsby, 278).

On January 15, 1978, Walter Payton, an African-American running back for the Chicago Bears, was named the National Football League's Most Valuable Player for the 1977 season. Payton received 57 out of 87 votes cast by sportswriters and broadcasters, three from each league city (Hornsby, 289).

In 1979, Andrew J. Young, the African-American United States Ambassador to the United Nations, resigned, saying that he "could not promise to muzzle himself and stay out of controversies that might prove politically embarrassing to President [Jimmy] Carter." The President received the ambassador's resignation with much regret (Hornsby, 304).

Dr. William R. Harvey

Hampton University President: 1979–Present

Photo courtesy of Hampton University

Dr. William Harvey is president of Hampton University and 100% owner of the Pepsi Cola Bottling Company of Houghton, Michigan. A native of Brewton, Alabama, he is a graduate of Southern Normal High School and Talladega College. He earned his doctorate in College Administration from Harvard University in 1972. Before coming to Hampton forty years ago, he held administrative posts at Harvard, Fisk and Tuskegee universities.

As President of Hampton University since 1978, Dr. William R. Harvey has introduced innovations which have solidified Hampton's stellar position among the nation's colleges and universities. His innovative leadership is reflected in the growth and quality of the University's student population, academic programs, physical facilities, and financial base. His outstanding leadership skills are exemplified by the appointment of fourteen former Hampton University administrators to CEO positions at other institutions during his tenure.

Since Dr. Harvey became President, student enrollment has increased from approximately 2,700 to approximately 6,300. Seventy-six new academic programs have been introduced including PhD's in physics, pharmacy, nursing, atmospheric and planetary science, physical therapy, educational management, and business administration. During that time, he has built 26 new buildings.

Dr. Harvey promotes a learning environment that encourages faculty research rivalling that of major research universities across the nation. Hampton University has built the first proton therapy cancer treatment center in the commonwealth of Virginia—an unparalleled hub for cancer treatment, research, and technology. Weather satellites have been launched to study noctilucent clouds to determine why they form and how they may be related to global climate change. From Alzheimer's research and alternative fuels to nanodevices combining diagnostic and therapeutic functions for early diagnosis and treatment of arthritis, under the competent leadership of President Harvey, Hampton University is poised to become a leader in research and technology not only in the Hampton Roads area and Virginia, but nationwide. These new programs, together with existing ones, have placed and kept Hampton on the cutting edge of higher education.

An astute businessman, the budget has been balanced with a surplus every year of his presidency. Dr. Harvey initiated a university-owned commercial development consisting of a shopping center and 246 two-bedroom apartments. All after-tax profits from the Hampton Harbor Projects are primarily utilized for student scholarships. Additionally, the Project creates jobs, provides services, has increased the number of African-American entrepreneurs, and expanded the tax base in the City of Hampton.

As a fundraiser, he is considered one of the best in the country. When Dr. Harvey became president, Hampton's endowment was at $29 million. Today, that endowment stands in excess of $250 million.

His achievements have been recognized through inclusion in personalities of the South, Who's Who in the South and Southeast, Who's Who in Education, International Who's Who of Intellectuals, Two Thousand Notable Americans, Who's Who in Business and Finance, and Who's Who in America.

Works Cited

Franklin, John Hope & Alfred A. Moss, Jr. From Slavery to Freedom: A History of African-Americans, Seventh Edition. McGraw-Hill, Incorporated: New York, St. Louis, San Francisco, Auckland, Bogota, Caracas, Lisbon, London, et al., 1994.

Hornsby, Jr., Alton. Milestones in Twentieth-Century African-American History. Visible Ink Press: Detroit, Washington, D.C., 1993.

Salzman, Jack & Cornel West. Struggles in the Promised Land: Toward a History of Black-Jewish Relations in the United States. Oxford University Press: New York, Oxford, 1997.

Sullivan, Patricia. Days of Hope: Race and Democracy in the New Deal Era. The University of North Carolina Press: Chapel Hill and London, 1996.

Various Authors. Hampton University: University 101: The Individual and Life. Tapestry Press, Ltd., Acton, MA, 1998.

Among the Halls of Distinction

Through the years, Hampton has been blessed with many able, visionary leaders. Succeeding the founder, General Samuel Chapman Armstrong (1868–1893), exemplary direction has been provided by Drs. Hollis B. Frissell (1893–1917), James Gregg (1917–1929), George Phenix (1929–1930), Arthur Howe (1930–1940), Malcolm MacLean (1940–1943), Ralph Bridgman (1944–1948), Alonzo Moron (1948–1959), Jerome Holland (1959–1970), Roy D. Hudson (1970–1977), Carl M. Hill (1977–1978) and now William R. Harvey.

Hampton also has recruited many prominent businessmen, academicians, lawyers and diplomats to serve on its Board of Trustees, among them: U.S. Ambassador Ellsworth Bunker; John T. Dorrance, Jr., Chairman of Campbell Soup Company; William M. Ellinghaus, President of American Telephone and Telegraph Company; John C. Duncan, Chairman of St. Joe Minerals Corp.; the Honorable Linwood Holton, former Governor of Virginia; the Honorable Benjamin L. Hooks, Executive Director of the National Association for the Advancement of Colored People; the Honorable Samuel R. Pierce, Secretary of Housing and Urban Development; Henry Hockheimer, president of Ford Aerospace and Communications Corporation; Robert C. Upton, Retired Whirlpool Corporation Vice President, and the late Dr. Margaret Mead, famed anthropologist who served as a trustee for 34 years.

Additionally, 11 U.S. Presidents have been associated with the University. William Howard Taft served as Chairman of the Board while President and Chief Justice of the U.S. Supreme Court. Continuing this traditional relationship between the college and the White House, Presidents Ronald Reagan and George Bush have called on Dr. Harvey for advice and counsel. Our first African America President, Barack Obama, was Hampton University commencement speaker in May 2010. President Obama appointed President William Harvey as the Chair at the HBCU Initiative for the White House.

Financial support for Hampton has come from many sources. Historically, corporate leaders such as John D. Rockefeller, George Foster Peabody, Coleman DuPont, Arthur Curtiss James, Edward S. Harkness, Collis Porter Huntington, John Lee Pratt, Walter G. Ladd and William Jay Schieffelin have given generously to the college. Federal agencies such as the National Aeronautics and Space Administration and the National Science Foundation have funded faculty research projects. The university has five chairs for distinguished professorships supported by endowments.

Many significant events have fashioned the Hampton tradition as demonstrated by the number of educational firsts initiated by the university. These unique milestones include: the establishment of experiential education of learning to work by doing; pioneering formal Indian education in this country when the first group of Indians came to Hampton in 1878; and the training of black petty officers for the U.S. Navy during World War II. Hampton was one of the first schools to eliminate sex discrimination; the university has always accepted male and female students and teachers. What is now known as vocational education was the primary instruction at the school during the late 1890s. The Armstrong-Slater School offered classes in blacksmithing, welding, carpentry, furniture making, electricity, machinist skills, painting, plumbing, printing and tailoring, but the importance of academic education was always emphasized.

All of the academic areas have been accredited by the Southern Association of Colleges and Schools since 1932 with several disciplines including Architecture, Nursing, Chemistry, Music and Teacher Education enjoying specialized accreditation.

Some 28 schools, colleges and other institutions have been outgrowths of Hampton—among them St. Paul's College, Bowling Green Academy, Princess Anne Academy, Kittrell College and Tuskegee Institute. The founder and first principal of Tuskegee was also one of Hampton's most famous alumni—Booker T. Washington. Serving as a model of educational excellence and moral decency to institutions and individuals alike, Hampton Institute has continued its role as an institution which educates students for life and institutions for service.

Looking Back at Years of Excellence

President William Howard Taft

President William Howard Taft was elected trustee of Hampton Institute in 1909 and served as the President of the Board from 1914 until his death in 1930.

Armstrong-Slater

The Armstrong-Slater Memorial Trade School was the trade instruction center of the college. Erected in 1896, it contained classes in Horseshoeing, Blacksmithing, Welding, Automobile Mechanics, Carpentry, Furniture Making, Electricity, Machinist Skills, Painting, Plumbing, Printing and Tailoring. The building was planned by Ludlow and Peabody and built by the Hampton trade students.

Winona Lodge

In the Dakota language "Winona" means a female's eldest sister. Winona, a residence for Indian girls, was constructed in 1882. The building was located in the women's area of the campus and served as a center for many social activities for Indian students. In 1912 when the Indian enrollment began to dwindle. The dormitory housed both Indian and black girls. The old Winona Lodge was razed to make space available for a new girls dormitory, Davidson Hall.

Robert C. Ogden

Mr. Robert C. Ogden was a member of the Board of Trustees from 1874 and served as President of that body from 1894 until his death in 1914. Mr. Ogden devoted much time, thought, money, and influence to the building of Hampton. Ogden Hall, long known as a cultural center in Hampton Roads, stands in his memory on the campus.

Sarah Collins Fernandis

Sarah Collins Fernandis (Class of 1882) wrote the inspiring words of the Hampton Alma Mater. Mrs. Fernandis lived in Washington, D.C. where she directed a settlement project for the underprivileged in her own house.

Booker T. Washington

Hampton Institute's most illustrious alumnus, Booker T. Washington (Class of 1875), founded Tuskegee Institute and became a national leader. "No race that has anything to contribute to the markets of the world is long in any degree ostracized. It is important and right that all privileges of the law be ours, but it is vastly more important that we be prepared for the exercise of those privileges."

Stone Building

Stone Memorial Building was constructed in 1882 as a boys' dormitory. It was a gift from Mrs. Valerie Stone of Massachusetts in memory of her husband Samuel Stone. This Victorian style building was constructed, in part, by Hampton students. Stone has served a number of purposes in addition to its initial use as a boys' dormitory. It presently houses administrative offices and also serves as a dormitory.

Collis P. Huntington Library (Museum)

Erected in 1903, the library was the gift of Mrs. C. P. Huntington as a memorial to her husband who was a trustee of Hampton Institute. The library housed the University Archives as well as the G. F. Peabody collection of over 25,000 volumes on and by the African-American. It is one of the largest and most valuable collections on this subject in the country.

Susan La Flesche Picotte

Susan La Flesche Picotte (Class of 1886) graduated salutatorian of her class. Daughter of an Omaha chief, she was the first Indian woman to receive the degree of Doctor of Medicine.

R. Nathaniel Dett

R. Nathaniel Dett was a noted composer, conductor, pianist, poet and faculty member. In 1919, he organized the Musical Arts Society in which an annual series of concerts and recitals of music and dance made Ogden Hall an outstanding cultural center.

Administration Building Marshall-Palmer Hall

Marshall-Palmer Hall, known as the Administration Building, was built in 1882 in honor of General J. F. B. Marshall, first Treasurer of Hampton. When the building was enlarged in 1918, the addition was named Palmer Hall in honor of General William Jackson Palmer, as funds for the addition and renovation were appropriated from the Palmer Fund through Mr. George Foster Peabody.

Dr. Thomas Wyatt Turner

Dr. Thomas Wyatt Turner was the first Black to earn a doctorate degree in botany. Dr. Turner served on the Hampton Institute faculty from 1924–45. Turner Natural Science Building stands today in his memory.

Hampton Cadets

All male students were organized into Cadet Battalions from 1878 until the 1930s. They were required to wear uniforms as a part of their training at Hampton. In 1881, the Hampton Cadets marched in the inaugural procession of President Garfield who for six years had been a trustee of Hampton.

President James A. Garfield

President James A. Garfield was an incorporator of Hampton, and served on the Board of Trustees from 1870–1876. Garfield made his last known speech to a group of Hampton students near the campus at Bethesda Chapel (Veterans' Administration area), before his assassination.

Hampton's Centennial

On April 25th, 1968, Hampton Institute celebrated the college's Centennial. The design of the Centennial Medallion includes Emancipation Oak, symbolizing freedom; church tower symbolizing Hamptom's code of ethics and values; book of knowledge explains the purpose of education; plow represents agriculture and allied trades of our spacecraft represents science, engineering, humanities, and social sciences as our commitment of today; and stars represent the great heights to which our graduates have reached and the place of our design for living for tomorrow.

The Hampton University Seal

On June 9, 1875 a proposed official seal was submitted and accepted as the corporate seal of the Board of Trustees. On May 29, 1930, the Trustee minutes reflect the design of a new seal that shortened the name from Hampton Normal and Agricultural Institute to Hampton Institute. Finally, on July 27, 1984 the Board of Trustees adopted the name Hampton University and reorganized the University to include Hampton Institute, the Undergraduate College; the Graduate College; and the College of Continuing Education, Hence, the name on the seal was changed once more. The symbols on the seal are interpreted as plow and sheaths of grain; books of knowledge (or hymnals) surmounted by a globe of the world; Bible stand; old-fashioned printing press; and sunrise over Hampton Creek which symbolizes the rise of educational opportunities. The boat on the water symbolizes the principal medium of transportation to Hampton during its early history.

Proton Therapy Institute

Hampton University Proton Therapy Institute (HUPTI) is the largest free-standing proton therapy institute in the world. Proton therapy is one of the most precise forms of radiation treatment. Dr. William R. Harvey initiated the process for establishing the proton center. HUPTI began seeing patients in August of 2010.

Special Note: Richard Morris Hunt, known as the Dean of Architecture, was the architect for the Academy Building and Virginia Hall. Hunt's other works include the base of the Statue of Liberty, Biltmore Mansion and Yorktown Monument.

National Historic Landmarks

Mansion House 1828

The Mansion House was purchased as part of the Hampton Institute site from the Drummond Family who called their home "Little Scotland." In early years, the Mansion House served as a residence for teachers. The principal, General Armstrong, and his family lived in a section of the house as well. Today, Mansion House serves as the official residence for the first family and is used for entertaining official guests of the University.

Virginia-Cleveland Hall 1878

Virginia Hall, a girls' dormitory, was partly "sung up" by the Hampton Singers in 1874. It is the oldest of the women's dormitories, and houses on the first floor part of the cafeteria known as Macedonia and the Office of the Director of Food Services. This is a four and a half story and basement brick building which houses freshman girls.

Cleveland Hall, a girls' dormitory, was built in 1901, with funds contributed by former pupils of Charles Dexter Cleveland of Philadelphia. Cleveland

Hall was connected to the back of Virginia Hall when built, thus the name, Virginia-Cleveland Hall.

Wigwam Building 1878

Wigwam, which means a lodge or dwelling, was constructed in 1878. It was originally built to house Indian male students, the first of whom were admitted in that same year. The dormitory was built in part by Hampton students. The building once housed visiting athletic teams and the Commissioner for the Central Intercollegiate Athletic Association (CIAA). Today the building is used as an Educational Resource Center which was added in 1976 and houses the Career Planning and Placement Center.

Academy Building 1881

The Academic Hall was erected in 1870 and was destroyed by fire in 1879. A second Academy Building was completed in 1881. The bell outside of the building was used to call students to classes, meals and daily chapel. Selected students earned their money by being responsible for ringing the bell for various activities. The name Schurz Hall was given to this structure in 1915 in honor of the Honorable Carl Schurz, Secretary of the Interior, who was a loyal friend and supporter of Hampton.

Memorial Chapel 1886

Photo courtesy of Hampton University

Memorial Chapel was built in 1886. The church tower stands 150 feet high and has a four-faced illuminated clock with chimes. The pews are made of yellow pine and built by Hampton Trade School students. Its style of architecture is Italian Romanesque and J. C. Cady of New York served as the architect. Cost for construction of the Chapel was the gift of the Frederick D. Marquant Estate through Elbert B. Monroe, President of the Board of Trustees, and Mrs. Monroe. At the front entrance stands a coral stone from the foundation of the Kawaiaho Church in Honolulu built in 1842 by the Reverend Richard Armstrong, father of General Samuel Armstrong and given to Hampton Institute by Colonel William N. Armstrong in 1895. The baptismal font was made by students from Koa wood from the Reverend Armstrong's Church, The Chapel serves as a sanctuary for nondenominational religious services and will seat approximately 1,000 persons. At the right entrance is a plaque which commemorates all persons connected with Hampton Institute who died during World War I.

Emancipation Oak

Photo courtesy of Hampton University

Ninety-eight feet in diameter, Emancipation Oak is the site where President Lincoln's Emancipation Proclamation was read to the citizens of Hampton Roads. A live oak. Emancipation Oak's foliage remains green year round. It is listed as one of the Great Trees of the World. This is a national historic landmark.

History of the National Hampton Alumni Association, Inc.

As in the providence of God, our alma mater will have been in successful operations 10 years at the close of this session. As it is custom of the graduates of all well-established schools and colleges to assemble within the walls of their alma mater, we think it will be fitting to hold a reunion, I the decennial year, composed of all the graduates or as many as can make it convenient at this time, for the purpose of forming the Alumni Association of the Hampton Normal and Agricultural Institute.

Nearly one hundred forty years ago, the above quotation was included as a part of the original constitution of the Hampton Alumni Association. The writing of this document was one of the preliminary steps leading to the origin of the Association. Its preplanning and final organization were carefully guided by the following farsighted alumni: David Evans, 1875; George W. Davis, 1874; L. B. Phillips, 1874; R. B. Jackson, 1876; W. T. Greenhow, 1874; W. L. Coleman, 1877; G. W. Latimer, 1871; A. M. Hamilton, 1877: A. W. McAdoo, Secretary, 1876; N. B. Clark, Chairman, 1877.

Photo courtesy of Hampton University

The Hampton Alumni Association was partially organized in May, 1878. George W. Davis, 1874, was elected the first president and Alice S. Harris, 1877, became the organization's first secretary. In May, 1881, at the first triennial meeting, the Association was fully recognized and a constitution, including the opening quotation and provision for triennial meetings, was adopted. At this first 1881 meeting, the following officers were elected:

President
Booker t. Washington, 1875

Secretary
William H. Das, 1878

Corresponding Secretary
William M. Reid, 1876

The original constitution provided for triennial reunions. However, through the years, the reunion intervals have changed from triennial to the present annual reunion meeting. With the strong belief that the Association could better serve itself and its alma mater, the Association became incorporated on May 7, 7986 under the 1950 code of Virginia and the register office in the City of Hampton, VA is the Office of Alumni Affairs, Hampton University. The purposes are exclusively charitable and educational and are stated in the ratified Constitution and Bylaws of 1988.

During its one hundred and seventeen year history, The Hampton Alumni Association has pushed forward with momentum and direction designed to create in Hampton Alumni an abiding sense of personal commitment and individual responsibility for *the Life and Growth of Hampton Institute*, now *Hampton University*. The Association has operated in a spirit of family togetherness with other sectors of the University to insure its effective involvement in recruitment, fundraising, image enhancement and other activities of concern for the welfare of *Alma Mater*. The Association has continued to function with strong alumni

Photo courtesy of Hampton University

Photo courtesy of Hampton University

leadership and with an unbroken line of 23 presidents spanning the years 1878 to present. The past presidents of the Association and more history details are listed on pages xi-xiv of the 1994 Alumni Directory.

According to Robert Jones '93, in addition to the environmental influences, the class was also intrigued by onyx, a shiny black gemstone that is solid and brilliant.

Little did the Class of 1993 know that their class name was far from original. In fact, the Class of 1984 created the class name Onyx. "At our class meeting people gave suggestions for the motto and class colors," said Angela Nixon Boyd '84. "WE were Onyx, our colors were black and silver and our motto was 'Black United.'"

Not until mid-semester did the Class of 1993 realize that they were actually Onyx II.

The newest class name is Quintessence. "Leon Howard came up with the name," said Stacy Mason Howard '92. We looked in the dictionary and saw that Quintessence means perfection. We voted and ended up with McDonald's colors, red and yellow, and everyone teased us about it."

Since 1991, students have decided to stick with tradition and pass on their senior class name to the incoming freshman. Ogre Phi Ogre, Quintessence and Onyx are the three names that are used today, "When I started at HU, we were told that our class name was Onyx VI," said Erica Taylor Harrod '05. "There was never any discussion about changing our class name at all. Our motto is, 'We are Hamptonians by choice, Onyx by nature.'"

Dr. Sheila Mingo Jones of the first Ogre Phi Ogre is amazed at how class names have become an HU tradition. "You never know how what you do impacts the future," she said.

"Quintessence six?," exclaimed Howard. "I can't believe it has lasted this long. Everyone teased us and said Quintessence would not last!"

As HU alumni discussed their class names, there was a sense of pride, joy, and amazement. Many couldn't believe that after more than 30 years, Ogre Phi Ogre continues and more names have been created. In the fall HU welcomed the Class of 2017, Onyx X.

What's Your Class Name?

Graduating Class	Class Names	Graduating Class	Class Names
2014	Onyx IX	1994	Ogre Phi Ogre VIII
2013	Quintessence VIII	1993	Onyx II
2012	Ogre Phi Ore XIV	1992	Quintessence
2011	Onyx VIII	1991	Ogre Phi Ore VII
2010	Quintessence VII	1990	Dynasty
2009	Ogre Phi Ogre XIII	1989	Genesis II
2008	Onyx VII	1988	Ogre Phi Ogre VI
2007	Quintessence VI	1987	Essence

Graduating Class	Class Names	Graduating Class	Class Names
2006	Ogre Phi Ogre XII	1986	Genesis
2005	Onyx VI	1985	Ogre Phi Ogre V
2004	Quintessence V	1984	Onyx
2003	Ogre Phi Ogre XI	1983	Radiance
2002	Onyx V	1982	Ogre Phi Ogre IV
2001	Quintessence IV	1981	Eminence
2000	Ogre Phi Ogre X	1980	Ubiquity
1999	Onyx IV	1979	Ogre Phi Ogre III
1998	Quintessence III	1978	Creative Source
1997	Ogre Phi Ogre IX	1977	New Birth
1996	Onyx III	1976	Ogre Phi Ogre II
1995	Quintessence II	1973	Ogre Phi Ogre

What's in a Name?

Ayana P. Gibson '04—Quintessence V

When the Hampton University Class of 1973 hears the word Ogre, they're not referring to the big green ogre in the movie "Shrek." Instead, the word makes 1973 HU alumni reminisce about their freshman year at HU and how their rebelliousness led to a now treasured HU tradition of class names. They were the first Ogre Phi Ogre class. But how in the world did they come up with Ogre Phi Ogre? And how has it been able to last this long?

Photo courtesy of Hampton University

Over the past 42 years, HU has carried out a tradition that has been a mystery to most of us who have passed through the University's doors. Many have questioned, "Why are the class names Ogre Phi Ogre, Quintessence and Onyx, and how did this tradition begin?" There are many versions of how the tradition started, but we have unfolded the mystery.

It all began in the fall of 1969, when HU freshmen were considered to be at the bottom of the food chain and the upperclassmen ruled the campus. According to Dr. Pollie Murphy '73, the upperclassmen were able to participate in many organizations, more so than the freshmen. "At that time upperclassmen were able to pledge social organizations during the fall semester and Greek organizations during the spring semester," said Murphy. "We couldn't participate as freshmen."

"The school was much smaller so you knew just about everyone," said Hilary Jones '73. "Freshman men lived in James Hall and everyone knew everyone."

According to Jones, one night a group of the freshman guys were hanging out in James Hall and came up with the name Ogre Phi Ogre. "There was no grand plan," he said. "We were just a very close-knit class that did everything together. Everyone picked up on it and we were cool; we were just Ogres."

But who would ever think of Ogre Phi Ogre as a class name? "A couple of us guys were always sitting around James Hall arguing about something," said Sidney Ricks

'73. "This time we were arguing about what was strong enough to kill a wildebeest, and David Jones said, 'An Ogre.'"

According to Ricks, the heated debate led to the discussion of how the freshmen were treated poorly on campus. "We would go to off-campus parties with freshman women and they would be allowed in but the freshman guys would be excluded," said Ricks. "Someone decided that as freshmen, we would start our own organization, Ogre Phi Ogre."

They named their class Ogre Phi Ogre, but they needed to spread the word. "We pulled the fire alarm in James Hall so everyone had to assemble on Bemis field," he said. "Dean Campbell had to check every room before they were able to release us, so while he was doing that we were spreading the word that we were Ogres, and Bernard Thompson, also known as 'Lil' Dino,' was granted the official title, king of the Ogres."

In order to spread the word to the female freshmen, Ricks said they picked a topic and arranged a seminar in the lobby of Harkness Hall. "The real plan was to get the group together, put on some music, and get to know each other," he said. "Hey, it worked. The next thing I know the guys were chanting Ogre Phi Ogre and the ladies were chanting Ogre Phi Ogrettes, and the rest is history."

Just because the groovy Class of 1973 was graduating didn't mean that Ogre Phi Ogre had to die. They decided to continue their legacy and pass the name on to the freshman class, the Class of 1976. And over the next seven years there were three Ogre Phi Ogre classes carrying on the tradition.

By the fall of 1973, the incoming freshmen, Class of 1977, decided that their class should have a name too. Debra (Long) Chambers 77, was the freshman class president and remembers exactly how they chose their class name. "There was a musical group out at the time named New Birth, but more importantly we liked the symbolism of the name," she said. "We weren't Ogres, so we thought of something that would describe our class, special, different and something new that no one had seen before. Zoe Vaughn was a cheerleader at the time and suggested New Birth, and Louis Mosley, architecture major, designed a logo using our chosen colors, blue and white. Like the Ogres, we thought our class name would be passed from class to class, but that wasn't the case; the incoming freshmen of 1976 (Class of 1980), didn't want our name.

Photo courtesy of Hampton University

Creating new class names continued with the Class of 1978. By the time they came to HU, Ogre Phi Ogre and New Birth were already in place, so the Class of 1978 needed another great class name. "During freshman week we voted for Creative Source to be our class name and red and black for our colors," said 1978 graduate Joan Wickham.

"We didn't want to take the senior class name; I think it was New Birth," said 1980 graduate Herbert Allen. "This was an early indication of our independence and leadership."

"Ubiquity," Allen said with a chuckle as he reminisced of his days at HU. "Billy Taylor, also known as Billy T., suggested the name Ubiquity. It was two-fold because at the time Roy Ayers, a popular jazz musician, was in a group named Ubiquity and we liked the definition."

Ubiquity is the noun form of the word ubiquitous meaning present everywhere at the same time. "It was both something that was contemporary and had substance because we were a diverse group coming from a number of places and at the same time coming together," said Allen.

Ubiquity began and ended with the Class of 1980, but according to Allen, that was the plan. "We didn't want anyone to take our name, we were original," he said.

The Class of 1980 wasn't the only class with originality on their minds. According to Sylvia Woody Rose '81, during one of her first freshman class meetings, people submitted names for the class name vote. The Class of 1981 voted for the name Eminence. The 1981 yearbook says, "Something prominent or lofty; a condition or station of superiority is what the senior class is about. As the graduating class of 1981, Eminence has indeed shown prominence, both collectively and individually."

"We chose it and kept it because of the definition. We thought that it represented our class well," said Rose.

By 1983 the new tradition was set. Each incoming class was presented with the option of taking the name of the graduating senior class or creating their own class name. The latter was the most popular at this time, because every class wanted to be original. Somehow during the creation of new names Ogre Phi Ogre was able to survive.

Photo courtesy of Hampton University

"We were a large freshman class," said Royzell Dillard 83. "We were a rebellious group who wanted a new and innovative name. The freshman class created a committee, came up with names, and voted on them during a freshman class meeting."

The Class of 1983 voted for Radiance. According to Dillard, Class of 1983 seniors purposely did not enthusiastically "sell" their class name to the incoming freshmen because it was the trend to be unique and original.

The remaining classes had the same idea to be inventive and one of a kind. Some classes were honored that others wanted to take their name, but most were eager to stand out and be the one and only class with that name. The Class of 1986, Genesis, voted on their name to establish their own identity and start from the beginning, suggested Damita (Salters) Prince 86.

To create the class names, students turned to their major influences for help, including, music, television, and current events. The alumni of 1990 were freshmen during the run of a popular soap opera in 1986, Dynasty. The pastel colors, pink and blue were staple colors at that time and became the colors of the Class of 1990, Dynasty.

In the fall of 1989 the rap group Onyx was very popular for their hit single, "Slam." At this time, gangster rap was emerging. Black pride was back, and influenced the Class of 1993 to name themselves Onyx.

Hampton University Alumni
Darryl and Sandra Randolph Classes of 1960 and 1961

"Oh Hampton, a thought sent from Heaven above"

Darryl and Sandra Randolph met on the campus of Hampton Institute in the Fall of 1958. Even though their majors were different they shared a required Art Class in Bemis Hall, where they met. They enjoyed strolling on the campus, attending basketball and football games, as well as sitting on the beautiful waterfront. There were few buildings on campus during that time. The newest dorms were Harkness and Davidson Halls. The Student Union (Student Center) was known as "The Grill." Today that building serves as the University Computer Center (the building located next to Stone Manor) located on the "The Block."

Courtesy of Darryl and Sandra Randolph

"To be a great soul's inspiration"

Even then Hampton's Dress Code was in full effect. During that time Hampton female students were required to wear dresses while on campus and in town. Only on Saturday afternoons after class were pants allowed to be worn by female students. Attendance was mandatory for all freshmen at Sunday evening Vespers in Ogden Hall; you were marked absent if you were not in your assigned seat. All Freshman students were required to wear hats called "Beanies."

"Thy foundation's firm and thy rooftree outspread"

Darryl Randolph was born and raised in Richmond, VA, where he graduated from Armstrong High School prior to attending Hampton University. Sandra is a native of Washington, DC, and graduated from Spingarn Senior High. The Randolphs actually met during her sophomore and his junior year. In addition to having been married since graduation 49 years ago, the Randolphs have many lifelong friends whom they met during the time spent at Hampton University. Mr. Randolph had the pleasure of marching with his 50 year class of 1960 for The 140th Annual Commencement on May 09, 2010 at which the Honorable Barack Obama, President of the United States, was the Commencement Speaker and Honorary Degree Recipient. Mrs. Randolph is looking forward to marching with her 50 year class at the 141st Annual Commencement on May 08, 2011.

"In service that will thy great spirit prolong"

Even though Mr. Randolph was a five year Architectural Engineering major his first love was flying. He pursued this dream after graduation when he joined the U.S. Army where he spent his military career flying helicopters and flew for two tours of duty in Vietnam. After spending four years in Germany on assignment, the family settled in Newport News, Virginia. Mr. Randolph continued his education and received a second BS degree in information science management from Christopher Newport University in Newport News, VA. At the present time Mr. Randolph is giving back to his alma mater by volunteering weekly at the University Museum, where he does much of the computer work. He recently consulted with the Freshman Studies staff on the layout and design of this publication. Both Mr. and Mrs. Randolph are very active in the National Hampton University Alumni Association and the Hampton University Booster Club. Mrs. Randolph is currently employed at Hampton University in the Department of Freshman Studies. She believes that every student should take University 101 and become familiar with the history of Hampton University.

"And send it through centuries ringing"

The Randolphs have two children and three grandchildren. For the Randolphs, Hampton University was a stepping stone to a wonderful life and longtime friendships.

Hampton University's Notable Alumni

Business

- Fred Anderson, Senior Vice President, Wachovia Bank
- Carl Brooks, President, Executive Leadership Council
- Wesley Coleman, former Executive Vice President, Disney Corp.
- Frank Fountain, Senior Vice President, Daimler Chrysler
- Kay Cole James, President and Founder, Gloucester Institute
- Derek R. Lewis, Senior VP and General Manager, Pepsi North America Field Operations
- George R. Lewis, former President and CEO, Phillip Morris Capital Corporation
- Clarence Lockett, former Vice President and Controller, Johnson & Johnson
- Leslie Jones Patterson, Partner, Ernst & Young
- Charles Phillips, former President, Oracle Corporation

Education

- Booker T. Washington, Hampton's most illustrious alumnus, Founder, Tuskegee University
- Septima Poinsette Clark, Educator and Civil Rights Leader
- St. Clair Drake, Renowned Sociologist and Anthropologist
- Martha Louise Morrow Foxx, Educator for the blind
- John Garland, President, Central State University
- Freeman A. Hrabowski III, President, University of Maryland, Baltimore County
- Alberta Williams King, Educator, Mother of Dr. Martin Luther King, Jr.
- Kimberly Oliver, 2006 National Teacher of the Year
- Dianne Boardley Suber, First Female President of Saint Augustine's University
- Stephen J. Wright, Former President of Fisk University and the United Negro College Fund

Government & Military

- Major General (Retired) Wallace C. Arnold, U.S. Army and Former President of Cheney State University
- Danielle Crutchfield, Assistant to the President and Director of Scheduling, President Obama
- Al Eisenberg, Politician
- Lt. General Robert S. Ferrell, U.S. Army
- The Honorable Vanessa Gilmore, United States District Judge, Southern District of Texas
- Algie Thomas Howell Jr., Politician
- Spencer Overton, Lawyer and Interim President and CEO of the Joint Center for Political and Economic Studies

Photo courtesy of Hampton University

- The Honorable McKinley Price, Mayor of Newport News, Virginia
- The Honorable Charles Wesley Turnbull, former Governor of U.S. Virgin Islands
- The Honorable Robin R. Sanders, former U.S. Ambassador to DR Congo and Nigeria

Arts & Entertainment

- John T. Biggers, Artist and Educator
- Benjamin Brown, Actor
- Ruth Carter, Costume Designer
- RaaShaun Casey (DJ Envy), American DJ and Radio Personality
- Christopher Henderson, Grammy award-winning Producer, Jamie Foxx "Blame It'
- Samella Sanders Lewis, Artist; Educator; Founder of the International Review of African American Art
- Dorothy Maynor, Concert Singer
- Robi Reed, Emmy award-winning Casting Director
- M. Carl Holman, Poet; Playwright; and Author
- Wanda Sykes, Comedian; Actress; Voice Artist; and Emmy award-winning Writer, "The Chris Rock Show"

Journalism & Communications

- Robert S. Abbott, Founder/Publisher/Editor of the *Chicago Defender*
- Angela Burt-Murray, Former Editor-in-Chief of Essence Magazine
- Spencer Christian, Television Broadcaster and Former Weather Forecaster for ABC's Good Morning America

- John H. Sengstacke, Newspaper Publisher
- Emil Wilbekin, Entertainment Journalist
- Andrew Sturgeon "Doc" Young, Sports Journalist and Author

Sports

- Johnnie Barnes, NFL, Carolina, Detroit, and Dallas
- Ataveus Cash, NFL, Jets, Giants, and Redskins
- Jazwyn Cowan, NBA, Austin Toros
- Justin Durant, NFL, Jaguars, Lions, and Cowboys
- Devin Green, NBA, Lakers
- Kendall Langford, NFL, Rams and Dolphins
- Rick Mahorn, NBA Player and Coach, Washington and Detroit
- Jerome Mathis, NFL, Texans and Redskins
- Francena McCorory, Olympic Medalist (Gold)
- Greg Scott, NFL, Redskins and Bengals
- Zuriel Smith, NFL, Cowboys, Giants, and Patriots
- Cordell Taylor, NFL, Jaguars and Seahawks
- Terrence Warren, NFL, Seahawks and 49ers
- Kellie Wells, Olympic Medalist (Bronze)

Photo courtesy of Hampton University

Learning about the History of Your School

The following exercise is designed to help you learn the history of your college and to determine how that history relates to the overall development of America's HBCUs.

Name of Your College _____

Location _____

Year Established _____

Name of Founder _____

Affiliation (Public/Private) _____

Stated Reason for the Establishment of Your College _____

_____

_____

"Hampton University has come a long way."

Write your thoughts about this statement. _____

_____

_____

_____

_____

_____

_____

_____

_____

_____

_____

_____

_____

_____

_____

_____

_____

Briefly summarize the contributions of the following:

1. Samuel Chapman Armstrong _____

    _____

    _____

    _____

2. Booker T. Washington _____

    _____

    _____

    _____

3. Dr. R. Nathaniel Dett _____

    _____

    _____

    _____

4. Rosa Parks _____

    _____

    _____

    _____

Hampton Helped Me!

Tyra Jackson

Photo courtesy of Hampton University

Tyra Jackson received a Bachelor of Science in Business Management with a concentration in Marketing from Hampton University in 2009. Since graduation, she has worked for various government contracting companies, each time being stationed at the U.S. Department of State. Her career with the Department began with a summer internship in 2007 and has since spanned from combatting human trafficking to marketing a federal assistance management system used by the entire agency.

Ms. Jackson is very active in the NHAA, Inc.'s Northern Virginia Chapter, serving as Community Service Committee Chair since 2012. In this capacity, she has brought the chapter's service involvement to new heights after partnering with Fairfax County Public Schools, food banks, and other local non-profits, Tyra is the 2014 recipient of the chapter's highest honor, the Wallace C. Arnold Award, recognizing her involvement in public service.

CHAPTER 2
Academic Excellence at Hampton

"A mission statement is not something you write overnight . . . But fundamentally, your mission statement becomes your constitution, the solid expression of your vision and values. It becomes the criterion by which you measure everything else in your life."

—Stephen Covey

Upon completion of this chapter, you will be able to:

- **Review** the mission of Hampton University
- **Identify** the University's core values
- **Explore** the campus and student support services
- **Review** general academic policies and procedures

Academic Excellence at Hampton

Mission

Hampton University is a historically black comprehensive institution of higher education committed to the promotion of multiculturalism and dedicated to the promotion of learning through outstanding teaching, research, scholarship, and service. Its curricular emphases are scientific and professional, with a strong liberal arts under girding.

Core Values

Joining the Hampton Family is an honor and requires each individual to uphold the policies, regulations, and guidelines established for students, faculty, administration, professional and other employees, and the laws of the Commonwealth of Virginia. Each member is required to adhere to and conform to the instructions and guidance of the leadership of his/her respective area. Therefore, the following are expected of members of the Hampton Family:

1. To respect himself or herself
2. To respect the dignity, feelings, worth, and values of others
3. To respect the rights and property of others and to discourage vandalism and theft
4. To prohibit discrimination, while striving to learn from differences in people, ideas and opinions.
5. To practice personal, professional, and academic integrity and to discourage all forms of dishonesty, plagiarism, deceit, and disloyalty to the Code of Conduct.
6. To foster a personal, professional work ethic within the Hampton University Family
7. To foster an open, fair, and caring environment.

Now that you have reviewed the mission and core values of Hampton, take a look at the campus map and services available to you. Connect with the campus!

Academic Excellence at Hampton

General Academic Policies and Regulations

The graduation requirements of the University, which must be met for completion of a degree program, are those published in the Academic Catalog in force at the time of the student's admission to the University through one of the Colleges. Information concerning registration, grading, class attendance, grievances, academic probation and dismissal, and other matters of University-wide applicability can be found on the following pages. Program requirements specific to an undergraduate, graduate or professional program of study are provided in that program's description within the applicable school and college.

Registration for Classes

All students at the University must be properly admitted in order to register for classes. Certain students of the Graduate College and the College of Education and Continuing Studies at Hampton University may take courses in the Undergraduate College if special permission is granted and the student pays all applicable tuition and fees. Registration has no official standing until fully validated.

Photo courtesy of Hampton University

Program planning is the responsibility of the individual student. Each regular degree-seeking student, whether part-time or full-time, has a faculty advisor assigned to assist him or her in planning a program and sequence of courses. This Catalog lists the courses required in each program and shows typical sequences of the courses for meeting the requirements for the various degrees and major programs of study. Each academic department prepares materials to assist students in program planning and keeping requirements of the major field of study up to date and coordinated with current professional certification, licensing, and other requirements. Each student should review his or her own personal plan before each early registration period and be prepared for the preregistration conference with his or her academic advisor.

Early registration is conducted in mid-semester for the following semester. It is to each student's advantage to preregister for classes and make early financial arrangements. The student meets with his or her advisor as scheduled, and completes all preregistration forms for courses in the advisor's office or major department. Billing shortly follows, and all early registration for the next semester can be completed before the end of the current semester. The student who registers early and pays early has priority in most classes, avoids a portion of the registration fee, and can return for the semester with minimal check-in processing.

Changes in Registration

After an initial registration for a group of courses is fully validated, a student may make adjustments in courses or sections, if approved by the faculty advisor or major department chairperson, using HUNet (online registration.) The change, if allowable, and if done before the published deadline, will be recorded in the student's computer-based record. It is the student's responsibility to correct any "errors"/misinterpretations before leaving HUNet. A course change made personally by the student in this manner, or through his or her dean's problem terminal, is recorded in the system, and the student should print a copy of his/her schedule as a personal record of transactions completed. The University recognizes that any change made is binding upon the student. Should the student experience problems or need special help, each school has a help area for assistance.

The period in which courses may be added or dropped and grading status changed, ends approximately one week after the start of classes for each semester. The Official Academic Calendar contains the current dates. No schedule changes may be made after this period ends. All approved changes must be entered by the student using HUNet during the Add/Drop period. Any exception to the deadline will require a course request form signed by the advisor, chair, dean and provost and then the completed form is submitted to the Registrar for processing.

The period in which a student may withdraw from a course with a grade of WP (Withdrew Passing) or WF (Withdrew Failing) ends shortly after the mid-semester evaluation period. The Official Academic Calendar contains the current dates. No courses may be withdrawn after this period ends. The vehicle for this application to the Registrar is the completed course withdrawal form.

Photo courtesy of Hampton University

After the end of the course withdrawal period through the last day of classes (i.e., *before* the final examination period), a student can only withdraw completely from the University (i.e., from all courses). Each course will still receive a grade of WP (Withdrew Passing) or WF (Withdrew Failing). The vehicle for this application to the Registrar is the completed Petition for Separation Form.

Changing grade status (e.g., to and from S/U, Audit, regular grading) requires the student to complete a Course Request Form to eliminate the original registration and to "ADD" the new registration for the course(s). Changing S/U grade status is not permitted after the "ADD" period ends.

Auditing a course must be elected, approved, and fully processed before the end of the Audit period. The auditing student pays one-hour tuition for the course.

A graduating senior who lacks no more than six (6) semester hours of course work to complete the bachelor's degree, may request approval from the Graduate College to register for up to six (6) semester hours graduate credit from the 500 level courses while still enrolled in the Undergraduate College. The courses must not be required courses in the student's undergraduate program. The request must also be approved by the chairperson of the major department, and the Dean of the Graduate College. Grades made in these graduate courses must be "B" or better to be applied to a graduate degree program. Under no circumstances will an undergraduate student be allowed to register for graduate-only (600 and 700) level courses.

Grades and Grade Reports

A grade report is sent at the end of each semester to each student. Mid-term evaluations are sent to the student at mid-semester. The mid-term evaluations are not recorded on the student's permanent record. The student's local address of record is

The Grading System Effective Fall 1994

Letter Grade	Numerical Grade	Quality Points
A+	98 - 100	4.1
A	94 - 97	4.0
A−	90 - 93	3.7
B+	88 - 89	3.3
B	84 - 87	3.0
B−	80 - 83	2.7
C+	78 - 79	2.3
C	74 - 77	2.0
C−	70 - 73	1.7
D+	68 - 69	1.3
D	64 - 67	1.0
D−	60 - 63	0.7
F	Below 60	0.0

used for all reporting and other communication during the semester, and the student's permanent address of record is used at semester's end and other times.

AU   Audited work. Not computed in, and not applicable to, cumulative grade point average (GPA).

I   Incomplete work. Not computed in and not applicable to cumulative grade point average (GPA) but converts to "F" if work not completed within a year for undergraduate students and to a "Z" after one semester for graduate students. The student does not need to be enrolled to remove an "I" grade. A grade of "I" indicates that the student has maintained a passing average, but for reasons beyond his or her control, some specific item such as an examination, a report, a notebook, or an experiment has not been completed. The student holding a grade of "I" is responsible for taking the initiative in arranging with the instructor for changing the grade.

IP   Students separating from the University because of mobilization in the Armed Forces will receive grades of "IP"("In Progress") and will have up to three years from the date "IP" grades were issued to remove the "IP" grades. During that three-year period, the students will not be charged tuition for attending courses in which "IP" grades were awarded.

S   Satisfactory at the "C" or higher grade for undergraduate courses, or "B" or higher for graduate courses. Not computed in the cumulative GPA, grade point average.

U   Unsatisfactory below the "C" level (i.e., C−, D+, D, D−, F) for undergraduate courses or "B" level for graduate courses. Not computed in the cumulative GPA grade point average.

Photo courtesy of Hampton University

WP   Withdrew Passing - Not counted in cumulative average.
WF   Withdrew Failing - Not counted in cumulative average.
Z   Blank/No grade submitted.

Repetition of Courses

All courses taken and grades for them will appear on the student's record. A student may not elect the Satisfactory/Unsatisfactory basis for a repeated course. Repeated courses will be calculated in the cumulative grade point average. However, a course may be counted only once toward the degree, regardless of the number of times taken. All grades earned are used in the calculation of the Cumulative Grade Point Average for graduate and professional students. Effective Fall 2006, undergraduate students may repeat any course taken Fall 2006 and beyond in which a final grade of "C−" through "F" has been earned. All grades remain on the permanent record with an indication that the course has been repeated on both the original and the most recent grade. However, only the most recent grade will be calculated in the cumulative GPA. This policy is applicable only to courses taken at Hampton University.

For undergraduate students, English 101 and 102, Communication 103, and all required major courses must be passed with a grade of "C" (2.0) or better. A Grade of "C−" or below in these courses will require repeated enrollment until the required minimum grade has been attained for each such course. Each major degree program may impose a minimum grade requirement upon other courses as specified in the program description in this Catalog.

Auditing a Course

A student may audit a course, with the approval of his or her academic advisor, if class size permits. The auditing fee is the same as the normal registration fee for one credit hour. Auditing students are required to attend class regularly as specified by the instructor, but may not take the examinations. A student may choose to audit a course or change from credit to audit up through 30 days after the first day of classes.

Satisfactory/Unsatisfactory (S/U) Option

Any course, except those specified by the college or the student's major department, may be taken under the Satisfactory/Unsatisfactory (S/U) grading system. Satisfactory means that the undergraduate student has achieved at the "C" or higher academic level and the graduate student has achieved at the "B" or higher academic level. Unsatisfactory means that the undergraduate student has achieved below the "C" level (i.e., C−, D+, D, D−, F) or below "B" level for a graduate student. A student cannot take more than two courses on the S/U basis per semester and cannot take more than 18 semester hours of S/U credit to be applied to degree requirements. School Deans or departments may set lower limits for their undergraduate students. The master's or doctoral comprehensive course and the dissertation defense course are the only S/U credit courses that count toward degree requirements for graduate students. The credit hours for graduate courses taken on an S/U basis are not counted toward degree requirements. Students should also be aware that most employers and graduate schools do not favorably consider applicants who excessively use the nontraditional grading options. Departments may offer entry level, developmental courses on an S/U basis. The S/U basis may not be used for a repeated course or any lecture course in the major discipline.

Withdrew Passing/Withdrew Failing (WP/WF)

A student who withdraws from a course after the established deadline for dropping a course and before the deadline to withdraw from a course will receive a Withdrew Passing (WP), or Withdrew Failing (WF), grade that reflects the student's academic performance as of the effective date of withdrawal. Students who officially separate from the University will receive "WP" or "WF" grades for all courses for that semester or term. The WP/WF grades carry no quality points and do not contribute to the student's grade point average.

Calculation of Grade Point Average

The Grade Point Average (GPA) is computed by dividing the total number of grade points earned (also called quality points, QPTS) by the total number of academic GPA Hours (GPAHRS). All courses recorded on the student's undergraduate transcript with a final grade ranging from "A+" through "F" generate quality points that are included in the total number of quality points. The grade point average for graduate students is determined by grades in graduate courses only. The number of quality points from each course is the product of the credit hours attempted times the quality point value for the grade as listed in the table "The Grading System." The credit hours attempted for these courses are included in the total number of GPA Hours. Courses with no grades (e.g., transfer credit, credit by examination or advanced placement credit) and those with other grades (AU, I, IP, S, U, WF, WP and Z) are excluded from the grade point average. For example, the grades in the table below produce a grade point average of 2.208 obtained from 26.5 Total Quality Points divided by 12.0 Total GPA Hours.

Sample Grade Point Average Calculation

Course	Credit Hours (CrHr)	Final Letter Grade	Earned Hours (EHrs)	GPA Hours (GPAHrs)	Quality Points (QPts)	Grade Points Average
BIO 101	3.0	F	0.0	3.0	0.0	–
ENG 101	3.0	C+	3.0	3.0	6.9	–
HEA 200	2.0	B+	2.0	2.0	6.6	–
HIS 106	3.0	B	3.0	3.0	9.0	–
MAT 151	4.0	S	4.0	N/A	N/A	–
UNV 101	1.0	A	1.0	1.0	4.0	–
Totals	16.0	–	13.0	12.0	26.5	2.208

Examinations and Other Graded Work

Each course has periodic examinations and a final examination or evaluation. Final examination times are announced at least two weeks in advance of the first scheduled final examination. Students are required to take all of their final examinations at times scheduled. The University does not authorize re-examination, nor will changes in final examination times be permitted unless the student has an examination conflict or has four or more examinations scheduled in one calendar day.

Absence from examinations should be discussed with the instructor before the examination so that the instructor can determine if there is sufficient reason to excuse the student or reschedule the examination for the student.

Photo courtesy of Hampton University

Absence from the final examination or otherwise not completing course assignments within the scheduled time of the course is generally not excusable. Only debilitating illnesses or other emergencies are considered reasonable causes for being excused from final examinations and not completing course assignments as scheduled. If the final examination or other assignments are postponed with the consent of the instructor, an "I" is recorded on the student's record to show the course work is "Incomplete." If the work/examination is not completed within one calendar year, the "I" automatically becomes an "F."

Postponed examination and other assignments: A deferred examination is provided by the instructor for a student who has been excused by the instructor from taking an examination or completing other course work at the scheduled time. The student must arrange with his or her instructor to take the missed examination or complete the missing assignment as soon as possible. Except under very extraordinary conditions, the student is not permitted to postpone the taking of a deferred examination beyond the second occasion provided by the instructor.

Class Attendance Requirements

Faculty members should establish attendance requirements in each of their courses. Instructors are responsible for clearly informing the students in the course syllabus at the beginning of the semester of the attendance requirements and the consequences of poor attendance.

Additional Regulations

1. Absence from class does not relieve any student of the responsibility for completing all class assignments. Instructors are not obligated to provide make-up work for students who have missed classes unless the student is able to render a satisfactory explanation for his or her absence. The student shall be responsible for arranging make-up work with the instructor, who shall be the sole judge of the satisfactory completion of the work.
2. Students may not be allowed to make up or complete work, which is missed as a result of suspension or dismissal from the University. Suspension or dismissal before the end of the semester involves the loss of academic credit for the entire semester.

Tardiness Policy

Classes are scheduled to provide students with 10-15 minutes for transition to their next class, depending upon the day of the week. Specifically, classes schedules for Monday, Wednesday or Friday end 10 minutes before the hours (e.g., 9-10:50), giving students 10 minutes to transition to their next class; classes scheduled for Tuesday or Thursday end 15 minutes after or 15 minutes before the hour (e.g., 9-10:15 or 10:30-11:45), giving student 15 minutes to transition to their next class. Students will be given an additional five minutes to arrive for class without penalty, e.g. 9:05 or 10:35. Students who enter class after the five minute period will be governed by the tardiness policy stated on the course syllabus. Instructors are expeced to end their classes promptly at the announced time.

Class Absences

1. As a general rule, students will be responsible for resolving class absences directly with the instructor. It will be the instructor's responsibility to excuse or not excuse an absence as he or she so judges in accordance with the explanation rendered by the student.
2. Any student who is ill should notify his or her instructors that he or she will not be attending classes because of illness.
3. It is the responsibility of a student planning a prearranged absence for personal or school purposes to notify his or her instructors at least 24 hours prior to the absence. Absences for school purposes may be verified by the staff or faculty member directly involved with the activity.
4. A student having to be absent because of a death or serious illness or for an extended period of time should inform his or her residence hall director and the appropriate office of either the Dean of Men or Women. The respective Dean's office will, in turn, notify the student's instructors that it received notice of the absence and will issue a verification by letter, e-mail or Verification slip.
5. Instructor absence:
   a. An instructor who, for any cause, is unable to meet his or her class will make arrangements for a substitute to carry on the work or for the students themselves to carry on the class activities.
   b. If no such arrangements have been made, the students may assume, after the first ten minutes of the class period, that the class will not be held. Supplementary rules on attendance not inconsistent with these general rules may be adopted by the academic departments of the University. The Provost has the authority to dismiss or expel any student who fails to meet scholarship requirements or to abide by academic regulations.

Grievance Procedure for Hampton University Students

Step One   START AT THE SOURCE OF THE PROBLEM.
               A) Schedule a conference with the instructor of the course.
               B) Be prepared to discuss issues of concern clearly. Do not speculate.
               C) Proceed to the next level of authority if the problem or concern is not resolved.

Step Two   SCHEDULE A CONFERENCE WITH ACADEMIC ADVISOR.
               Repeat steps B and C as stated in Step One.

Step Three   SCHEDULE A CONFERENCE WITH THE ADMINISTRATIVE HEAD OF THE DEPARTMENT OR ACADEMIC UNIT.
               Repeat steps B and C as stated in Step One.

Step Four   SCHEDULE A CONFERENCE WITH DEAN OF THE SCHOOL.
               Repeat steps B and C as stated in Step One.

Step Five   SCHEDULE A MEETING WITH GRIEVANCE COUNCIL OF THE SCHOOL. Repeat steps B and C as stated in Step One.

               Step Six SCHEDULE A CONFERENCE WITH THE PROVOST OR DESIGNEE.

NOTE: If steps one through five have been omitted, the Provost will refer the case back to the step that was omitted.
               Hampton University has policies which have been established to resolve student problems and issues in a fair and impartial manner.

Our most important business is to help students learn while
maintaining high academic and ethical standards.
It is recommended that each learner "follows the counsel of those
wise faculty members who have dedicated their lives to meeting
the needs of students who are willing to take responsibility for
their own education."

Separation from the University

Leaving the University for any reason is separation from the University and is cate-
gorized as:

Official Withdrawal

As defined by the University, "withdrawal" means that the student ceases to attend
all classes and is no longer considered enrolled in the University. Leave of absence
is included within official withdrawal. Official withdrawal follows from the student informing the appropriate Dean of Men/Women of intent to withdraw and
completing the University Separation form. A student who withdraws before the
end of the course drop period will have his or her entire semester registration record removed from the permanent record. Withdrawing after the end of the drop
period – but before 4:00 p.m. on the last day of classes–causes "WP" or "WF" entries for each course of the student's current enrollment. Withdrawing after the last
day of classes results in grades as earned for the term being recorded in the permanent record.

Academic Dismissal

Dismissal for Academic Deficiencies results when a student does not meet the minimum academic standard. A minimum cumulative grade point average of 2.000 is the
standard for all undergraduate students, but there is a sliding scale standard rising to
2.000 at 63 semester hours attempted. The purpose of the rising sliding scale standard is to allow time for the insufficiently prepared student to make up deficiencies
in academic preparation for college work. Students who maintain a cumulative grade
point average at or just above 2.000 place themselves in jeopardy of being dismissed
without any other warning any time their semester average drops below 2.000.

Social Dismissal

Dismissal for not meeting generally accepted social standards and levels of decorum
may occur at any time a student violates his or her trust in these matters. The University reserves the right to separate any student from the University for nonpay-
ment of accrued charges, for ill health, or for disciplinary reasons.

Unofficial Withdrawal

Unofficial withdrawal results when a student who is matriculated for a degree and is
in good standing does not enroll in a consecutive semester (excludes summer school).
If an undergraduate student leaves during a term without notifying the Dean of Men
or Dean of Women and does not file a separation form, he or she is considered
unofficially withdrawn. A student who withdraws unofficially has not established an

official date of separation and consequently cannot be given a pro-rated refund for which he or she otherwise may be eligible. An unofficial withdrawal may also obligate the student to repay loans more quickly or in higher amounts than expected.

Readmission to the Undergraduate College after separation, for whatever reason (including all types outlined above) requires a current formal application for admission to Hampton University. Admission procedures are enumerated in this catalog's section on admission.

Photo courtesy of Hampton University

Taking Courses at Another Institution

Hampton University students may be permitted to earn credit for courses taken at another accredited institution of higher education. Concurrent registration at one of the institutions in the Tidewater Consortium of Higher Education affords the student with academic credit and quality points for courses passed and impacts the student's grade point average at Hampton University. Approved transfer credit from another accredited institution of higher education affords the student with academic credit only.

Concurrent Registration

The Tidewater Consortium of Higher Education affords students the opportunity to take enrichment courses, not taught at the home school, at another member institution. Certain restrictions and regulations of the Consortium, the host schools, and Hampton University apply. This opportunity is open to full-time undergraduate students with a cumulative grade point average of 2.000 or better and is designed to make available a wider variety of upper-division, elective courses. Graduate students require a minimum grade point average of 3.000, or better, and special permission from the Dean of the Graduate College.

Transfer Credit

A student may elect to take a course at any accredited institution of higher education. To protect the student and to ensure that the student is able to have the course and its credit, not quality points, transferred back to his or her program at Hampton University, the student must secure permission from his or her academic advisor, department chairperson, and school dean before the end of the Hampton semester prior to taking the course(s) at the other school. Standard forms and instructions may be obtained in each department. Transfer credit can only be posted to the student's record if the student is currently registered when the transaction is received in the Registrar's Office. The student is responsible for having an official transcript mailed to the Registrar's Office when the work has been completed. Credit hours will be awarded for approved courses carrying a letter grade of "C", or better for undergraduate courses and a "B", or better for graduate courses. No credit will be awarded undergraduate students for courses with grades of "C–", or less. The appropriately approved, posted transaction will appear on the student's record when the current term is completed.

The cumulative grade point average of each student will be calculated on work (courses) taken at Hampton University. All credits earned at other institutions, including those earned by students seeking re-entry to the University, as well as those with approved permission to take courses at another institution, will be treated/classified as transfer credits. They may be used to reduce the number of hours required for graduation. However, they will not be used in calculating the cumulative grade point average.

Good Academic Standing

Students whose cumulative averages are equal to or greater than the average for their tenure and who have met their financial obligations, and whose conduct is in keeping with the standards of membership in the university will be considered in good academic standing. Students in good academic standing are entitled to continue registration and class attendance and are eligible to apply for a degree upon completion of the necessary requirements. They are entitled to all the privileges of membership in the university, including residence, class attendance, examinations, participation in student activities (except as set forth below) and use of facilities under the regulations of the university. They are entitled to receive regular reports of their progress, to have transcripts and other official documents issued upon request, and to use the placement and other student services of the university. Any student on academic probation may be retained in accordance with the university's regulations. An undergraduate student placed on probationary status is allowed to retain status as a student with the following provisions:

1. The student may not register for more than thirteen hours per semester. Exceptions to this rule must be approved by the Provost.
2. The student may not participate in extracurricular activities, which are not class-related; and the student may not travel in the name of the university or at university expense. Exceptions to this rule must be approved by the Vice President for Student Affairs or the Provost.

Satisfactory Progress

Any undergraduate student enrolled as a regular degree student who maintains the cumulative average required by regulations and is enrolled in at least twelve (12) semester hours of course work each semester shall be considered to be maintaining satisfactory progress toward a degree. As an exception, a student's cumulative grade-point average may fall below 2.00, but not less than the minimum set forth below for the number of Grade Point Average hours attempted during which time he or she shall be placed on academic probation. The probationary student is subject to dismissal if the student fails to achieve the required minimum cumulative grade-point average in the following semester.

Any graduate student enrolled as a regular degree student who maintains at least a 3.00 cumulative GPA and is enrolled in at least nine (9) semester hours of course work each semester shall be considered to be maintaining satisfactory progress toward a degree.

Regulations for Probation and Academic Dismissal of Undergraduate Students

- A student who does not pass any courses at the end of any semester is subject to dismissal from the university.
- A student who has a cumulative grade point average below 1.0 after 9 GPA Hours will be subject to dismissal from the university.

- A student who has a cumulative grade point average below 1.5 after 18 GPA Hours is subject to dismissal from the university.
- A student who has a cumulative grade point average below 1.6 after 27 GPA Hours is subject to dismissal from the university.
- A student who has a cumulative grade point average below 1.7 after 36 GPA Hours is subject to dismissal from the university.
- A student who has a cumulative grade point average of less than 1.8 after 45 or more GPA Hours is subject to dismissal.
- A student who has a cumulative grade point average of less than 1.9 after 54 or more GPA Hours is subject to dismissal.
- A student who has a cumulative grade point average of less than 2.0 after 63 or more GPA Hours is subject to dismissal.
- If the major department chairperson, the school dean of the major area, and the Provost approve, a student with a cumulative grade point average between 1.95 and 1.999 after 63 or more GPA hours may be given special permission to enroll for one additional semester in order to achieve the required 2.0 cumulative grade point average. A student with a GPA between 1.95 and 1.999 who has been dismissed for the second time may be given special permission to enroll during the summer term as a provisional student and must earn a GPA of 3.0 in non-repeat academic courses. Concurrence must be obtained from department chair and school dean.
- Academically deficient students will generally only be dismissed at the end of the spring semester.
- A student with less than a 2.0 cumulative grade point average is placed on academic probation.
- A student on academic probation must take a reduced class load not to exceed 13 semester hours.
- A student who has been dismissed for academic deficiencies may apply for readmission upon obtaining and presenting evidence of increased academic maturity. Academic courses taken at another institution to be presented as evidence of increased academic maturity should not be those previously attempted at Hampton University. Further, these courses should involve the use of computational and verbal skills.
- University regulations governing dismissal and academic probation are summarized in the table below.

Academic Probation and Dismissal

Level of Enrollment (by credits earned)	Cumulative GPA for Dismissal	Cumulative GPA for Academic Probation for Those Students Not Dismissed
1 Semester	0.000	Below 2.0
9 to 17	Below 1.0	Below 2.0
18 to 26	Below 1.5	Below 2.0
27 to 35	Below 1.6	Below 2.0
36 to 44	Below 1.7	Below 2.0
45 to 53	Below 1.8	Below 2.0
54 to 62	Below 1.9	Below 2.0
63 or more	Below 2.0	Below 2.0

In cases where a student has been dismissed, the student may appeal suspected errors in grade point average computation to the Registrar, and circumstances of illness with a physician's certification to the Provost. A student has 10 days from the date of the letter announcing his or her dismissal to appeal his or her dismissal. A student dismissed for academic reasons will normally not be readmitted within six months of the dismissal nor be readmitted until he or she can demonstrate a high level of academic achievement and maturity.

Regulations for Probation and Academic Dismissal of Graduate Students

1. The minimum standard for graduate work leading to a master's degree is a 3.0 grade point average.
2. A student whose overall grade point average falls below 3.0 at the end of any term will be placed on academic probation and must raise this average to 3.0 by the time he or she completes nine (9) additional hours. A student who fails to comply with this requirement will be subject to dismissal from the degree program or from the Graduate College by the Graduate Council based on the recommendation of the department chair or the Dean of the Graduate College.
3. Grades below "C" carry no credit. However, such grades will be used in computing the overall grade point average. An earned grade below "C" in any course requires that the course be repeated.
4. An accumulation of no more than eight (8) hours of grades below "B" may be counted toward degree requirements.
5. The University reserves the right to terminate the registration of any student whose record falls below the standard acceptable to Hampton University. The department, with the concurrence of the Graduate Dean, can recommend to the Graduate Council that a student be withdrawn from the degree program for unsatisfactory performance.

Continuance as an Undergraduate Student – Minimum Standards for Continuance

Through an instructional program supplemented by faculty advising and counseling as necessary and as requested by the student, the University gives the student every encouragement to achieve academic excellence. The University expects the undergraduate student to make reasonable academic progress. The minimum acceptable standard is to achieve and maintain a cumulative grade point average of 2.000 ("C" level) or better across all courses taken for credit. However, to assist students who are

Semester Hours Attempted	Cumulative GPA
9 to 17	1.0
18 to 26	1.5
27 to 35	1.6
36 to 44	1.7
45 to 53	1.8
54 to 62	1.9
63 or more	2.0

insufficiently prepared academically to achieve at the level of 2.000 cumulative grade point average on first entering, the University allows continuance on probation at less than 2.000 cumulative grade point average according to the following scale. A student who does not pass any courses at the end of his or her first semester will normally be dismissed from the University, as will the student who does not meet the level of achievement listed below (and printed in the table above).

Academic Probation

Any undergraduate student who falls below a cumulative grade point average of 2.000 and is not dismissed for academic deficiency is placed on academic probation by the Provost of the University. A student on academic probation is limited to a 13 semester-hour load each semester while on probation and may not participate in extramural activities unless the activity is class related. A student may be dismissed for academic deficiency without ever having been on probation or without any other warning than a cumulative grade point average near or below 2.000.

Academic Dismissal

A regular student matriculating for a degree is dismissed for academic deficiency, with or without a period of probation or a period of warning, by the University Provost when the student's cumulative grade point average falls below the level required for the number of GPA Hours attempted, as shown above under minimum standards for continuance. Hampton University normally dismisses academically deficient students at the end of the spring semester; however, a student may be dismissed at the end of the previous fall and summer session for poor performance in its major program of study.

Appealing a Dismissal for Academic Deficiency

There is no appeal of a dismissal for academic deficiency if the student's cumulative grade point average is below the minimum standards for continuance unless the student suspects an error in calculation of his or her grade point average, or the student has had a recent medical or other emergency that has prevented satisfactory completion of a course or courses in the most recent semester of the Undergraduate College. An appeal based upon suspected miscalculation of one's GPA is addressed to the University Registrar.

Academic Warning

An academic warning notice is sent to an undergraduate student if his or her **semester** grade point average is below 2.000, but his or her cumulative grade point average is 2.000 or higher. **A student may be placed on probation or be dismissed without any other warning than a grade point average near or below 2.000.**

Credit by Examination

A student may request credit by examination for the purpose of validating knowledge of the material presented in a course. Prior to processing the request, the "Application for Credit by Examination" form must be approved by the chairperson of the student's department, the chairperson of the department offering the examination, and the appropriate deans. Approval by the Provost is required prior to fee payment. A copy of the completed examination must be filed with the appropriate dean. **Credit by examination shall not be attempted for a course previously taken or failed by the student.**

No student will be allowed over two examinations for credit per semester, up to a maximum of 30 credit hours per degree. No freshman student will be allowed to earn credit by examination for 300 or 400 level courses. Only the Provost may make an exception to these rules upon the recommendation of the school dean.

Letter grades **will not** be given for credit by examination. The number of credit hours earned will be indicated on the student's transcript.

Release of Information from Student Academic Records

1. Reports: The University periodically sends written reports of the student's academic progress to the student.
2. Access to student records is governed by the Federal and State of Virginia Freedom of Information Acts/Policy and the Policy of Hampton University.
3. Access to student records by officers and staff of the University is based on need to know in one's official capacity.
4. Access to his or her own permanent official academic record by the student is achieved by ordering a transcript of courses attempted and grades earned. Access to various temporary and other work files in operating offices in the University is by application to the individual office. All attempts will be made to quickly satisfy legal and reasonable record access requests of the student to his or her own record. However, an appointment up to four weeks from the date of the written request from the student may have to be used during periods of the University closing and unavailability of staff to provide data and to monitor their review.
5. All persons other than staff of the University and the individual student of legal age may access a student's record only with the student's written permission. The original signature of the student must be on the written request identifying the allowed access given to the University office of record for the student's information. No access is allowed to a student's information on file at the University except for standard directory information and access by those legal entities and agencies as allowed under the Privacy Acts of the Federal Government and the State of Virginia.
6. A student may request transcripts of his or her academic record as necessary. A fee is charged for each transcript.

Photo courtesy of Hampton University

Release of Information Policy

This is to inform students that Hampton University intends to comply fully with the Family Educational Rights and Privacy Act of 1974, as amended. This Act was designated to protect the privacy of education records, to establish the rights of students to inspect and review their education records and to provide guidelines for the corrections of inaccurate or misleading information and complaints with the Family Educational Rights and Privacy Act Office (FERPA) concerning alleged failures by the institution to comply with the Act. Local policy explains in detail the procedures to be used by the institution for compliance with the provisions of the Act. The policy can be read in the Office of the University Registrar. This office also maintains a directory of record, which lists all education records maintained on students by this institution.

Hampton University designates the following information as public or directory information. Such information may be disclosed by the institution at its discretion: name, address, telephone number, dates of attendance, previous institution(s) attended, major field of study, awards, honors (including Dean's List), degree(s) conferred (including dates), past and present participation in officially recognized sports and activities, physical factors (height, weight of athletes), date and place of birth.

Currently enrolled students may withhold disclosure of any category of information under the Family Educational Rights and Privacy Act of 1974, as amended. To withhold disclosure, written notification must be received in the Office of the Registrar, First Floor, Whipple Barn no later than 10 days after classes have started. Forms requesting the withholding of "Directory Information" are available in the Registrar's Office.

Hampton University assumes that failure on the part of any student to specifically request the withholding of categories of "Directory Information" indicates individual approval for disclosure.

Hampton Helped Me!

Brandon M. Northington

Photo courtesy of Hampton University

A Georgetown, Kentucky, native **Brandon M. Northington** is a proud Hampton University alumni Class of 2010, Quintessence 7. Brandon, presently, resides in Washington, District of Columbia, and is a licensed attorney in the state of Maryland.

Brandon went on to attend law school at Florida A&M University College of Law and ultimately earned a Juris Doctor degree in May of 2013. At the College of Law, he was a member of the Black Law Student Association, Phi Alpha Delta International Law Fraternity, and a member of the schools Toastmasters Chapter. Additionally, Brandon was a student attorney with the Office of the State Attorney Ninth Judicial Circuit, and he was the 2013 student commencement speaker.

In his free time, Brandon enjoys spending time with family and friends, movies, and a good game of spades.

Hampton Helped Me!

Mrs. Ebony Majeed

Photo courtesy of Hampton University

Mrs. Ebony Majeed was born and raised in Hampton, Virginia. She attended Hampton University's Laboratory School during her elementary years and later graduated from its Upward Bound program after high school. While studying at Hampton University, she was a member of Student Support Services and became a Ronald E. McNair Scholar. She completed her studies in 2007 and holds a Bachelor of Arts degree in Spanish.

CHAPTER 3

Liberal Arts and General Education

"The ability to recognize opportunities and move in new – and sometimes unexpected – directions will benefit you no matter your interest or aspirations. A liberal arts education is designed to equip students for just such flexibility and imagination."

—Drew Gilpin Faust

Upon completion of this chapter, you will be able to:

- **Appreciate** the meaning, purpose and benefits of liberal arts
- **List** major division and subject areas in the Liberal Arts curriculum
- **Explain** the value of a liberal arts education
- **Examine** transferable lifetime learning skills
- **Develop** a strategic plan for making the most out of general education

Liberal Arts and General Education

3

What It Means to Be a Well-Educated Person in the 21st Century

ACTIVATE YOUR THINKING | *Reflection* **3.1**

LEARNING GOAL

To appreciate the meaning, purpose, and benefits of the liberal arts and develop a strategic plan for making the most out of general education.

Before you launch into this chapter, do your best to answer the following question:

Which one of the following statements represents the most accurate meaning of the term *liberal arts*?

1. Learning to be less politically conservative

   _____

   _____

   _____

2. Learning to be more artistic

   _____

   _____

   _____

3. Learning ideas rather than practical skills

   _____

   _____

   _____

4. Learning to spend money more freely

   _____

   _____

   _____

5. Learning skills for freedom

   _____

   _____

   _____

From *Thriving in College and Beyond: Research-Based Strategies for Academic Success and Personal Development* by Cuseo et al. Copyright © 2013 by Kendall Hunt Publishing Company. Reprinted by permission.

Author's Experience I was once advising a first-year student (Laura) who intended to major in business. While helping her plan the courses she needed to complete her degree, I pointed out to her that she still needed to take a course in philosophy. Here's how our conversation went after I made this point.

Laura (in a somewhat irritated tone): Why do I have to take philosophy? I'm a business major.

Dr. Cuseo: Because philosophy is an important component of a liberal arts education.

Laura (in a very agitated tone): I'm not liberal and I don't want to be a liberal. I'm conservative and so are my parents; we all voted for Ronald Reagan in the last election!

Joe Cuseo

The Meaning and Purpose of a Liberal Arts Education

If you're uncertain about what the term *liberal arts* means, you're not alone. Most first-year students don't have the foggiest idea what a liberal arts education represents (Hersh, 1997; American Association of Colleges & Universities [AAC&U], 2007). If they were to guess, like Laura, many of them might mistakenly say that it's something impractical or related to liberal politics.

Laura probably would have picked option 1 as her answer to the multiple-choice question posed at the start of this chapter. She would have been wrong; the correct choice is option 5. Literally translated, the term *liberal arts* derives from the Latin words *liberales*, meaning "to liberate or free," and *artes*, meaning "skills." Thus, "skills for freedom" is the most accurate meaning of liberal arts.

The roots of the term *liberal arts* date back to the origin of modern civilization—to the ancient Greeks and Romans, who argued that political power in a democracy rests with the people because they choose (elect) their own leaders. In a democracy, people are liberated from uncritical dependence on a dictator or autocrat. In order to preserve their political freedom, citizens in a democracy must be well-educated critical thinkers so that they can make wise choices about whom they elect as their leaders and lawmakers (Bishop, 1986; Bok, 2006)

The political ideals of the ancient Greeks and Romans were shared by the founding fathers of the United States, who also emphasized the importance of an educated citizenry for preserving America's new democracy. As Thomas Jefferson, third president of the United States, wrote in 1801, "I know of no safe depository of the ultimate powers of a society but the people themselves; and if we think them not enlightened enough to exercise control with a wholesome discretion [responsible decision-making], the remedy is not to take power from them, but to inform their discretion by education" (Ford, 1903, p. 278).

Thus, the liberal arts are rooted in the belief that education is the essential ingredient for preserving democratic freedom. When citizens are educated in the liberal arts, they gain the breadth of knowledge and depth of thinking to vote wisely, preserve democracy, and avoid autocracy (dictatorship).

The importance of a knowledgeable, critically thinking citizenry for making wise political choices is still relevant today. Contemporary political campaigns are using more manipulative media advertisements. These ads rely on short sound bites, one-sided arguments, and powerful visual images that are intentionally designed to appeal to emotions and discourage critical thinking (Goleman, 1992; Boren, 2008).

"Knowledge will forever govern ignorance; and a people who mean to be their own governors must arm themselves with the power which knowledge gives."

—James Madison, fourth president of the United States, cosigner of the American Constitution, and first author of the Bill of Rights

Remember

The original purpose of higher education in America was not just to prepare students for a future profession, but to prepare them for citizenship in a democratic nation.

Over time, the term *liberal arts* has acquired the more general meaning of liberating or freeing people to be self-directed individuals who make personal choices and decisions that are determined by their own well-reasoned ideas and values, rather than blind conformity to the ideas and values of others (Gamson, 1984; Katz, 2008). Self-directed critical thinkers are empowered to resist manipulation by politicians and other societal influences, including:

- Authority figures (e.g., they question excessive use or abuse of authority by parents, teachers, or law enforcers);
- Peers (e.g., they resist peer pressure that's unreasonable or unethical); and
- Media (e.g., they detect and reject forms of advertisement designed to manipulate their self-image and dictate their material needs).

In short, a liberal arts education encourages you to be your own person and to ask, "Why?" It's the component of your college education that supplies you with the mental tools needed to be an independent thinker with an inquiring mind who questions authority and resists conformity.

"It is such good fortune for people in power that people do not think."

—Adolf Hitler, German dictator

"If a nation expects to be ignorant and free, it expects what never was and never will be."

—Thomas Jefferson, principal author of the United States Declaration of Independence and third president of the United States

Student Perspective

"I want knowledge so I don't get taken advantage of in life."

—First-year college student

Author's Experience

I must admit that I graduated from college without ever truly understanding the purpose and value of liberal education. After I became a college professor, two colleagues of mine approached me to help them create a first-year experience course. I agreed and proceeded to teach the course, which included a unit on the meaning and value of a liberal arts education. It was only after preparing to teach this unit that I began to realize that a college education is first and foremost a process of developing enduring (lifelong) learning skills and "habits of mind" that can empower all college graduates to succeed in any career they may pursue. If I hadn't taught a first-year experience course, I don't think I ever would have truly understood the process that was essential to the purpose of a college education and to my role as a college professor.

Joe Cuseo

The Liberal Arts Curriculum

The first liberal arts curriculum (collection of courses) was designed to equip students with (1) a broad base of knowledge that would ensure they would be well informed in various subjects and (2) a range of mental skills that would enable them to think deeply and critically. Based on this educational philosophy of the ancient Greeks and Romans, the first liberal arts curriculum was developed during the Middle Ages and consisted of the following subjects: logic, language, rhetoric (the art of argumentation and persuasion), music, mathematics, and astronomy (Ratcliff, 1997; AAC&U, 2002, 2007).

The original purpose of the liberal arts curriculum has withstood the test of time. Today's colleges and universities continue to offer a liberal arts curriculum designed to provide students with a broad base of knowledge in multiple subject areas and equip them with critical thinking skills. The liberal arts curriculum today is often referred to as *general education*—representing general knowledge and skills that are applicable to a wide variety of situations. General education is what all college students learn, no matter what their major or specialized field of study may be (AAC&U, 2002).

On some campuses, the liberal arts are also referred to as (1) the *core curriculum*, with "core" standing for what is central and essential for all students to know and do because it contributes to successful performance in any field, or (2) *breadth requirements*, meaning that they are broad in scope, spanning a wide range of subject areas.

Remember

Whatever term is used to describe the liberal arts on your campus, the bottom line is that they are the foundation of a college education upon which all academic specializations (majors) are built; they are what all college graduates should be able to know and do for whatever occupational path they choose to pursue; they are what distinguishes college education from vocational preparation; they define what it means to be a well-educated person.

Major Divisions of Knowledge and Subject Areas in the Liberal Arts Curriculum

The divisions of knowledge in today's liberal arts curriculum have expanded to include more subject areas than those included in the original curriculum devised by the ancient Greeks and Romans. These divisions and the courses that make up each division vary somewhat from campus to campus. Campuses also vary in terms of the nature of courses required within each of these divisions of knowledge and the variety of courses from which students can choose to fulfill their liberal arts requirements. On average, about one-third of a college graduate's course credits are required general education courses selected from the liberal arts curriculum (Conley, 2005).

Reflection 3.2

For someone to be successful in any major and career, what do you think that person should:

1. Know; and

2. Be able to do?

Despite campus-to-campus variation in the number and nature of courses required, the liberal arts curriculum on every college campus represents the areas of knowledge and the types of skills that all students should possess, no matter what their particular major may be. The breadth of this curriculum allows you to stand on the shoulders of intellectual giants from a range of fields and capitalize on their collective wisdom.

On most campuses today, the liberal arts curriculum typically consists of general divisions of knowledge and related subject areas similar to those listed in the sections that follow. As you read through these divisions of knowledge, highlight any subjects in which you've never taken a course.

Humanities

Courses in the humanities division of the liberal arts curriculum focus on the human experience and human culture, asking the important "big picture" questions that arise in the life of humans, such as "Why are we here?" "What is the meaning or purpose of our existence?" "How should we live?" "What is the good life?" and "Is there life after death?"

The following are the primary subject areas in the humanities:

- **English Composition.** Writing clearly, critically, and persuasively;
- **Speech.** Speaking eloquently and convincingly;
- **Literature.** Reading critically and appreciating the artistic merit of various literary genres (forms of writing), such as novels, short stories, poems, plays, and essays;
- **Languages.** Listening to, speaking, reading, and writing languages other than the student's native tongue;
- **Philosophy.** Thinking rationally, developing wisdom (the ability to use knowledge prudently), and living an ethically principled life; and
- **Theology.** Understanding how humans conceive of and express their faith in a transcendent (supreme) being.

"Never mistake knowledge for wisdom. One helps you make a living; the other helps you make a life."
—Sandra Carey, lobbyist to the California State Assembly

"Dancing is silent poetry."
—Simonides, ancient Greek poet

Fine Arts

Courses in the fine arts division focus largely on the art of human expression, asking such questions as "How do humans express, create, and appreciate what is beautiful?" and "How do we express ourselves aesthetically (through the senses) with imagination, creativity, style, and elegance?"

The primary subject areas of the fine arts are as follows:

© Ekaterina Pokrovskaya, 2013. Under license from Shutterstock, Inc.

- **Visual Arts.** Creating and appreciating human expression through visual representation (drawing, painting, sculpture, photography, and graphic design);
- **Musical Arts.** Appreciating and creating rhythmical arrangements of sounds; and
- **Performing Arts.** Appreciating and expressing creativity through drama and dance.

Mathematics

Courses in this division of the liberal arts are designed to promote skills in numerical calculation, quantitative reasoning, and problem solving.

The primary subject areas comprising mathematics for general education include:

- **Algebra.** Mathematical reasoning involving symbolic representation of numbers in a language of letters that vary in size or quantity;
- **Statistics.** Mathematical methods for summarizing quantitative data, estimating probabilities, representing and understanding numerical information depicted in graphs, charts, and tables, and drawing accurate conclusions from statistical data; and
- **Calculus.** Higher mathematical methods for calculating the rate at which the quantity of one entity changes in relation to another and calculating the areas enclosed by curves.

"The universe is a grand book which cannot be read until one learns to comprehend the language and become familiar with the characters of which it is composed. It is written in the language of mathematics."
—Galileo Galilei, 17th-century Italian physicist, mathematician, astronomer, and philosopher

Natural Sciences

Courses in this division of the liberal arts curriculum are devoted to systematic observation of the physical world and the explanation of natural phenomena, asking such questions as "What causes physical events that take place in the natural world?" "How can we predict and control these events?" and "How do we promote mutually productive interaction between humans and the natural environment that contributes to the survival and development of both?"

The following are the primary subject areas of the natural sciences division:

© Yuri Arcurs, 2013. Under license from Shutterstock, Inc.

The natural sciences division of the liberal arts curriculum focuses on the observation of the physical world and the explanation of natural phenomena.

- **Biology.** Understanding the structure and underlying processes of all living things;
- **Chemistry.** Understanding the composition of natural and synthetic (manmade) substances and how these substances may be changed or developed;
- **Physics.** Understanding the properties of physical matter and the principles of energy, motion, electrical, and magnetic forces;
- **Geology.** Understanding the composition of the earth and the natural processes that have shaped its development; and
- **Astronomy.** Understanding the makeup and motion of celestial bodies that comprise the universe.

Social and Behavioral Sciences

"We cannot defend these [democratic] ideals or protect the vitality of our institutions, including our institutional government, unless we understand their origins and how they evolved over time."

—David Boren, president of the University of Oklahoma and longest-serving chairman of the U.S. Senate Intelligence Committee

"Science is an imaginative adventure of the mind seeking truth in a world of mystery."

—Cyril Herman Hinshelwood, Nobel Prize-winning English chemist

"Man, the molecule of society, is the subject of social science."

—Henry Charles Carey, 19th-century American economist

Courses in the division of social and behavioral sciences focus on the observation of human behavior, individually and in groups, asking such questions as "What causes humans to behave the way they do?" and "How can we predict, control, or improve human behavior and human interaction?"

This division of the liberal arts curriculum is composed primarily of the following subject areas:

- **History.** Understanding past events, their causes, and their influence on current events;
- **Political Science.** Understanding how societal authority is organized and how this authority is exerted to govern people, make collective decisions, and maintain social order;
- **Psychology.** Understanding the human mind, its conscious and subconscious processes, and the underlying causes of human behavior;
- **Sociology.** Understanding the structure, interaction, and collective behavior of organized social groups, institutions, and systems that comprise human society (e.g., families, schools, and social services);
- **Anthropology.** Understanding the cultural and physical origin, development, and distribution of the human species;

- **Geography.** Understanding how the places (physical locations) where humans live influence their cultural and societal development and how humans have shaped (and been shaped) by their surrounding physical environment; and
- **Economics.** Understanding how the monetary needs of humans are met through allocation of limited resources and how material wealth is produced and distributed.

Physical Education and Wellness

Courses in the physical education and wellness division of the liberal arts curriculum focus on the human body, how to best maintain health, and how to attain peak levels of human performance. They ask such questions as "How does the body function most effectively?" and "What can we do to prevent illness, promote wellness, and improve the physical quality of our lives?"

These primary subject areas fall under this division:

- **Physical Education.** Understanding the role of human exercise for promoting health and performance;
- **Nutrition.** Understanding how the body uses food as nourishment to promote health and generate energy;
- **Sexuality.** Understanding the biological, psychological, and social aspects of sexual relations; and
- **Drug Education.** Understanding how substances that alter the body and mind affect physical health, mental health, and human behavior.

Most of your liberal arts requirements will be fulfilled during your first two years of college. Don't be disappointed if some of these required courses seem similar to courses you recently had in high school, and don't think you'll be bored because these are subjects you've already studied. College courses are not videotape replays of high school courses; you will examine these subjects in greater depth and breadth and at a higher level of thinking (Conley, 2005). Research shows that most of the thinking gains that students make in college take place during their first two years—the years when they're taking most of their liberal arts courses (Pascarella & Terenzini, 2005). Although you will specialize in a particular field of study in college (your major), "real-life" issues and challenges are not neatly divided and conveniently packaged into specialized majors. Important and enduring issues, such as effective leadership, improving race relations, and preventing international warfare, can neither be fully understood nor effectively solved by using the thinking tools of a single academic discipline. Approaching such important, multidimensional issues from the perspective of a single, specialized field of study would be to use a single-minded and oversimplified strategy to tackle complex and multifaceted problems.

> "To eat is a necessity, but to eat intelligently is an art."
> —La Rochefoucauld, 17th-century French author

Reflection **3.3**

Look back at the liberal arts subject areas in which you've never taken a course. Which of these courses strike you as particularly interesting or useful?

Why?

Acquiring Transferable Skills That Last a Lifetime

A liberal arts education promotes success in your major, career, and life by equipping you with a set of lifelong learning skills with two powerful qualities:

"Intellectual growth should commence at birth and cease only at death."

—Albert Einstein, Nobel Prize–winning physicist

- **Transferability.** Skills that can be transferred and applied to a range of subjects, careers, and life situations.
- **Durability.** Skills that are enduring and can be continually used throughout life.

To use an athletic analogy, what the liberal arts do for the mind is similar to what cross-training does for the body. Cross-training engages the body in a wide range of different exercises to promote total physical fitness and a broad set of physical skills (e.g., strength, endurance, flexibility, and agility), which can be applied to improve performance in any sport or athletic endeavor. Similarly, the liberal arts and diversity engage the mind in a wide range of subject areas (e.g., arts, sciences and humanities) and multiple cultural perspectives, which develop a wide range of mental skills that can be used to improve performance in any major or career.

"You know you've got to exercise your brain just like your muscles."

—Will Rogers, Native American humorist and actor

There's a big difference between learning factual knowledge and learning transferable skills. A transferable skill can be applied to different situations or contexts. The mental skills developed by the liberal arts are transportable across academic subjects you'll encounter in college and work positions you'll assume after college. It could be said that these lifelong learning skills are mental gifts that keep on giving throughout life.

"If you give a man a fish, you feed him for a day. If you teach a man how to fish, you feed him for life."

—Author unknown

> **Remember**
>
> *The liberal arts not only provide you with academic skills needed to succeed in your chosen major, they also equip you with skills to succeed in whatever career or careers you decide to pursue. Don't underestimate the importance of these transferable and durable skills. Work hard at developing them, and take seriously the liberal arts courses designed to promote their development. The broad-based knowledge and general, flexible skills developed by the liberal arts will multiply your career options, opening up more career doors for you after college graduation and providing you with greater career mobility throughout your professional life.*

The transferable skills developed by the liberal arts are summarized in Snapshot Summary 3.1. As you read each of them, rate yourself on each of the skills using the following scale:

4 = very strong, 3 = strong, 2 = needs some improvement,
1 = needs much improvement

Snapshot Summary

3.1   Transferable Lifelong Learning Skills Developed by the Liberal Arts

One way the liberal arts "liberate" you is by equipping you with skills that are not tied to any particular subject area or career field, but which can be transferred freely to different learning situations and contexts throughout life. Some key forms of these versatile, durable skills are listed below.

1. **Communication skills.** Accurate comprehension and articulate expression of ideas. Five particular types of communication skills are essential for success in any specialized field of study or work:

   - **Written communication skills.** Writing in a clear, creative, and persuasive manner;
   - **Oral communication skills.** Speaking concisely, confidently, and eloquently;

Student Perspective

> "I intend on becoming a corporate lawyer. I am an English major. The reason I chose this major is because while I was researching the educational backgrounds of some corporate attorneys, I found that a lot were English majors. It helps with writing and delivering cases."
>
> —College sophomore

   - **Reading skills.** Comprehending, interpreting, and evaluating the literal meaning and connotations of words written in various styles and subject areas;
   - **Listening skills.** Comprehending spoken language accurately and sensitively; and
   - **Technological communication skills.** Using computer technology to communicate effectively.

2. **Information literacy skills.** Accessing, retrieving, and evaluating information from various sources, including in-print and online (technology-based) systems.

3. **Computation skills.** Accurately calculating, analyzing, summarizing, interpreting, and evaluating quantitative information or statistical data.

4. **Higher-level thinking skills.** Thinking at a more advanced level than simply acquisition and memorization of factual information.

> "Ability to recognize when information is needed and have the ability to locate, evaluate, and use it effectively."
>
> —Definition of *information literacy*, American Library Association Presidential Committee on Information Literacy

Students often see general education as something to "get out of the way" or "get behind them" so they can get into their major and career (AAC&U, 2007). Don't buy into the belief that general education represents a series of obstacles along the way to a degree. Instead, "get into" general education and take away from it a set of powerful skills that are *portable*— "travel" well across different work situations and life roles— and *stable*—will remain relevant across changing times and stages of life.

Remember

You may forget the facts you learn in college, but you will remember the ways of thinking, the habits of mind, and the communication skills for the rest of your life.

Reflection 3.4

Reflect on the four skill areas developed by a liberal arts education (communication, information literacy, computation, and higher-level thinking). Which one do you think is most important or most relevant to your future success?

Write a one-paragraph explanation of why you chose this skill.

Remember

When you acquire lifelong learning skills, you're also acquiring lifelong learning skills.

Remember

The earning potential you acquire after college will depend on the learning potential you develop in college.

Student *Perspective*

"They asked me during my interview why I was right for the job and I told them because I can read well, write well and I can think. They really liked that because those were the skills they were looking for."

—English major hired by a public relations firm

"At State Farm, our [employment] exam does not test applicants on their knowledge of finance or the insurance business, but it does require them to demonstrate critical thinking skills and the ability to calculate and think logically. These skills plus the ability to read for information, to communicate and write effectively need to be demonstrated."

—Edward B. Rust Jr., chairman and chief executive officer of State Farm Insurance Companies (AAC&U, 2007)

The skills developed by a liberal arts education are strikingly similar to the types of skills that employers seek in new employees. In numerous national surveys and in-depth interviews, employers and executives in both industry and government consistently report that they seek employees with skills that fall into the following three categories:

1. **Communication skills.** Listening, speaking, writing, and reading (Business-Higher Education Forum, 1999; National Association of Colleges & Employers, 2007; Peter D. Hart Research Associates, 2006). "There is such a heavy emphasis on effective communication in the workplace that college students who master these skills can set themselves apart from the pack when searching for employment." —Marilyn Mackes, executive director of the National Association of Colleges and Employers (Mackes, 2003, p. 1).

2. **Thinking skills.** Problem solving and critical thinking (Business-Higher Education Forum, 1999; Peter D. Hart Research Associates, 2006; Education Commission of the States, 1995). "We look for people who can think critically and analytically. If you can do those things, we can teach you our business." —Paul Dominski, store recruiter for the Robinson-May Department Stores Company.

3. **Lifelong learning skills.** Learning how to learn and how to continue learning throughout life (Conference Board of Canada, 2000). "Employers are virtually unanimous that the most important knowledge and skills the new employee can bring to the job are problem solving, communication, and 'learning to learn' skills (SECFHE, 2006). The workers of the future need to know how to think and how to continue to learn." —David Kearns, former chief executive officer for the Xerox Corporation.

The remarkable resemblance between the work skills sought by employers and the academic skills developed by a liberal arts education isn't surprising when you think about the typical duties or responsibilities of working professionals. They need good communication skills because they must listen, speak, describe, and explain ideas to co-workers and customers. They are required to read and critically interpret written and statistical reports and write letters, memos, and reports. They also need highly developed thinking skills to analyze problems, construct well-organized plans, generate innovative ideas and solutions to problems (creative thinking), and evaluate whether their plans and strategies are effective (critical thinking).

The Liberal Arts Promote Employability

The transferable skills developed by the liberal arts have become more and more sought out by employers. In fact, colleges and universities are hearing from employers that these transferable skills are the very abilities their new staff members need to be successful in today's workplace and to effectively take on "real-life" issues. Given the complexity of today's world, this isn't surprising. The 21st century has increased our interconnectedness with many different countries and cultures. At the same time, the 21st century also has brought with it many new global challenges that were not present even 20 years ago. These changes necessitate that college graduates bring with them the knowledge, experience, and abilities to step into the world they will encounter upon graduating. In fact, according to a recent survey of employers (Peter

D. Hart Research Associates, 2010, p. 5), new employees are expected to do the following to a much greater degree today than in the past:

- Take on more responsibilities and use a broader set of skills
- Work harder to coordinate with other departments
- Address challenges that are more complex
- Use higher levels of thinking and a wider range of knowledge

Clearly, as the world itself has changed in the 21st century, so has the world of work. Given these changes, it makes sense that employers are seeking new hires with a distinct set of knowledge, values, and skills.

So what are employers looking for in the people they hire? They are seeking workers who that can problem-solve and manage projects. They want employees with effective interpersonal skills who can work well with groups. They also want their new hires to be able to adapt to a variety of environments and be skilled communicators. Students develop these qualities while in college through a well-rounded education that balances the curriculum of the liberal arts and their major. In a study conducted by the American Association of State Colleges and Universities (2007, p. 2) employers stated that this curricular balance is ideal since it produces the following highly valued outcomes in students and prepares them for the world of work:

- Integrative learning
  - The ability to apply knowledge and skills to real-world settings
- Knowledge of human cultures and the physical and natural world
  - Concepts and new developments in science and technology
  - Global issues and developments and their implications for the future*
  - The role of the United States in the world
  - Cultural values and traditions in America and other countries*
- Intellectual and practical skills
  - Teamwork skills and the ability to collaborate with others in diverse group settings*
  - The ability to effectively communicate orally and in writing
  - Critical thinking and analytical reasoning skills
  - The ability to locate, organize, and evaluate information from multiple sources
  - The ability to be innovative and think creatively
  - The ability to solve complex problems
  - The ability to work with numbers and understand statistics
- Personal and social responsibility
  - Teamwork skills and the ability to collaborate with others in diverse group settings*
  - Global issues and developments and their implications for the future
  - A sense of integrity and ethics
  - Cultural values and traditions in America and other countries*

*Three items are shown in two learning outcome categories because they apply to both.

Author's Experience I graduated from college with a BA in political science and sociology. Many of my friends asked me, "What are you going to do with such majors? What kind of job will you get offered?" As it turned out, I received a position in corporate management training after I graduated and spent the next many years working in corporate America. I quickly became aware of the knowledge these liberal arts degrees and my general education bestowed on me. I understood how organizations worked. I could communicate well, orally and written. I understood people and their uniqueness. I could problem solve. I got these degrees in the 20th century and these are the skills still in most demand in the 21st century.

— Aaron Thompson

"As times goes on, the technical and practical skills vocational majors learn in college become less important to continued success. Such abilities as communication skills, human relations, creativity, and 'big picture thinking' matter more."

—Derek Bok, president emeritus, Harvard University

This study's results further demonstrate the important contributions made by the liberal arts toward your college success and your marketability upon graduation. When you work with your advisor on your academic plan and map out the courses you'll take to complete your degree, think of your liberal arts requirements as courses that will complement the learning you'll do in your major courses. Delve into both! By doing so, you be will be investing in your academic success and future employability.

A Liberal Arts Education Is Preparation for Your Major

For most college students, choosing a major and choosing a career are not decisions made at the same time because their major doesn't turn into their career. It is this belief that leads some students to procrastinate about choosing a major; they think they're making a lifelong decision and are afraid they'll make the "wrong" choice and get stuck doing something they hate for the rest of their life.

The truth is that the trip from your college major to your eventual career(s) is less like climbing a pole and more like climbing up a tree. As illustrated in Figure 3.1, you begin with the tree's trunk (the foundation provided by the liberal arts), which leads to separate limbs (choices for college majors), which, in turn, leads to different branches (different career paths or options).

FIGURE 3.1

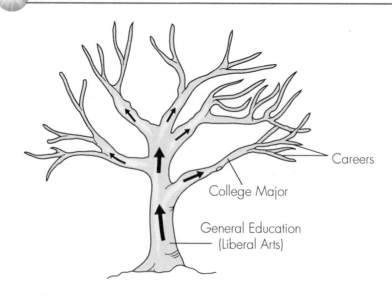

© Kendall Hunt

The Relationship between General Education (Liberal Arts), College Majors, and Careers

Note that the different sets of branches (careers) grow from the same major limb. So, too, do different sets of careers or "career families" grow from each major. For example, an English major will often lead to careers that involve use of the written language (e.g., editing, journalism, or publishing), while a major in art will often lead to careers that involve use of visual media (e.g., illustration, graphic design, or art therapy).

Don't assume that liberal arts courses you're taking as general education requirements have nothing to do with your specialized field of interest. Liberal arts courses provide a relevant foundation for success in your major. Recall our story at the start of the chapter about Laura, the first-year student with a business major who questioned why she had to take a course in philosophy. Laura needed to take philosophy because she would encounter topics in her business major that related either directly or indirectly to philosophy. In her business courses, she would likely encounter philosophical issues relating to (1) the logical assumptions and underlying values of capitalism, (2) business ethics (e.g., hiring and firing practices), and (3) business justice (e.g., how profits should be fairly or justly distributed to workers and shareholders). Philosophy would equip her with the fundamental logical thinking and ethical reasoning skills to understand these issues deeply and respond to them humanely.

"Virtually all occupational endeavors require a working appreciation of the historical, cultural, ethical, and global environments that surround the application of skilled work."

—Robert Jones, "Liberal Education for the Twenty-First Century: Business Expectations"

The same is true for careers other than business. For example, historical and ethical perspectives are needed for all fields because all of them have a history and none of them are value-free.

Keep in mind that the career path of most college graduates does not run like a straight line directly from their major to their career. For instance, most physics majors do not become physicists, most philosophy majors do not become philosophers, and most history majors do not become historians. It is this mistaken belief that may account for the fact that business continues to be the most popular major among college students (Zernike, 2009). Students (and their parents) see that most college graduates are employed in business settings and think that if you want to get a job in business after graduation, you'd better major in business.

Reflection 3.5

During your college experience, you might hear students say that they need to get their general education (liberal arts) courses out of the way so that they can get into courses that relate to their major and career. Would you agree or disagree with this argument?

Why?

"The unexamined life is not worth living."

—Socrates, classic Greek philosopher and one of the founding fathers of Western philosophy

The academic skills developed by a liberal arts education are also practical skills that contribute to successful performance in any career.

The Liberal Arts Promote Self-Awareness and Development of the Whole Person

One of the most emphasized goals of a liberal arts education is to "know thyself" (Cross, 1982; Tubbs, 2011). Fully educated people look inward to learn about themselves just as they look outward to learn about the world around them. The ability to turn inward and become aware of ourselves has been referred to as intrapersonal

FIGURE 3.2

© Kendall Hunt

Key Elements of Holistic (Whole-Person) Development

intelligence (Gardner, 1999, 2006). Self-knowledge represents the key first step in any quest toward personal growth and fulfillment.

To become self-aware requires awareness of all elements that comprise the self. As illustrated in Figure 3.2, the human self is composed of multiple dimensions that join together to form the whole person.

Key Dimensions of the Self

Each of the following elements of self plays an influential role in promoting human health, success, and happiness:

1. **Intellectual.** Knowledge, multiple perspectives, and different ways of thinking;
2. **Emotional.** Awareness of feelings, self-esteem, emotional intelligence, and mental health;
3. **Social.** Interpersonal relationships;
4. **Ethical.** Values, character, and moral convictions;
5. **Physical.** Bodily health and wellness;
6. **Spiritual.** Beliefs about the meaning or purpose of life and the hereafter;
7. **Vocational.** Economic well-being and career success; and
8. **Personal.** Identity, self-concept, and self-management.

Research strongly suggests that quality of life depends on attention to and development of all elements of the self. It's been found that people who are healthy (physically and mentally) and successful (personally and professionally) are those who attend to and integrate dimensions of the self, enabling them to lead well-rounded and well-balanced lives (Covey, 1990; Goleman, 1995; Heath, 1977).

In Figure 3.2, these diverse dimensions of the self are joined or linked to represent how they are interrelated, working together to promote personal development and well-being (Love & Love, 1995). The dimensions of self are discussed separately in this chapter to keep them clear in your mind. In reality, they do not operate independent of one another; instead, they interconnect and influence each other. (This is why the elements of the self in Figure 3.2 are depicted as links in an interconnected chain.) Thus, the self is a diverse, multidimensional entity that has the capacity to develop along various interdependent dimensions.

Student
Perspective

"I want to see how all the pieces of me come together to make me, physically and mentally."

—College sophomore

One of the primary goals of the liberal arts is to provide a well-rounded education that promotes development and integration of the whole person (Kuh, Shedd, & Whitt, 1987). Research on college students confirms that their college experience affects them in multiple ways and promotes the development of multiple dimensions of self (Bowen, 1997; Feldman & Newcomb, 1994; Pascarella & Terenzini, 1991; 2005).

Since wholeness is essential for wellness, success, and happiness, read carefully the following descriptions and skills associated with each of the eight elements of holistic development. As you read the skills and qualities listed beneath each of the eight elements, place a checkmark in the space next to any skill that is particularly important to you. You may check more than one skill within each area.

Skills and Qualities Associated with Each Element of Holistic (Whole-Person) Development

1. **Intellectual development.** Acquiring knowledge and learning how to learn deeply and think at a higher level.
   Goals and skills:
   ☑ Becoming aware of your intellectual abilities, interests, and learning styles
   ☑ Maintaining attention and concentration
   ☑ Improving your ability to retain and apply knowledge
   ☑ Moving beyond memorization to higher levels of thinking
   ☑ Acquiring effective research skills for accessing information from various sources and systems
   ☑ Viewing issues from multiple angles or viewpoints (psychological, social, political, economic, etc.) to attain a balanced, comprehensive perspective
   ☑ Evaluating ideas critically in terms of their truth and value
   ☑ Thinking creatively or imaginatively
   ☑ Responding constructively to differing viewpoints or opposing arguments
   ☑ Detecting and rejecting persuasion tactics that appeal to emotions rather than reason

2. **Emotional development.** Strengthening skills for understanding, controlling, and expressing emotions.
   Goals and skills:
   ☑ Dealing with personal emotions in an honest, non-defensive manner
   ☑ Maintaining a healthy balance between emotional control and emotional expression
   ☑ Responding with empathy and sensitivity to emotions experienced by others
   ☑ Dealing effectively with depression
   ☑ Dealing effectively with anger
   ☑ Using effective stress-management strategies to control anxiety and tension
   ☑ Responding effectively to frustrations and setbacks
   ☑ Overcoming fear of failure and lack of self-confidence
   ☑ Accepting feedback in a constructive, non-defensive manner
   ☑ Maintaining optimism and enthusiasm

3. **Social development.** Enhancing the quality and depth of interpersonal relationships.
   Goals and skills:
   ☑ Developing effective conversational skills
   ☑ Becoming an effective listener
   ☑ Relating effectively to others in one-to-one, small-group, and large-group situations

Student *Perspective*

"Being successful is being balanced in every aspect of your life."
—First-year college student

"The research portrays the college student as changing in an integrated way, with change in any one area appearing to be part of a mutually reinforcing network or pattern of change in other areas."
—Ernest Pascarella and Pat Terenzini, *How College Affects Students*

"It's not stress that kills us, it is our reaction to it."
—Hans Selye, Canadian endocrinologist and author of *Stress Without Distress*

"Chi rispetta sara rippetato."
("Respect others and you will
be respected.")

—Italian proverb

☑ Collaborating effectively with others when working in groups or teams
☑ Overcoming shyness
☑ Establishing meaningful and intimate relationships
☑ Resolving interpersonal conflicts assertively, rather than aggressively or passively
☑ Providing feedback to others in a constructive and considerate manner
☑ Relating effectively with others from different cultural backgrounds and lifestyles
☑ Developing leadership skills

4. **Ethical development.** Developing a clear value system for guiding life choices and decisions, building moral character, making ethical judgments, and demonstrating consistency between convictions (beliefs) and commitments (actions). Goals and skills:
☑ Gaining deeper self-awareness of personal values and ethical assumptions
☑ Making personal choices and life decisions based on a meaningful value system
☑ Developing the capacity to think and act with personal integrity and authenticity
☑ Using technology in an ethical and civil manner
☑ Resisting social pressure to act in ways that are inconsistent with personal values
☑ Treating others in an ethical manner
☑ Knowing how to exercise individual freedom without infringing on the rights of others
☑ Demonstrating concern and commitment for human rights and social justice
☑ Developing the courage to confront those who violate the rights of others
☑ Becoming a responsible citizen

5. **Physical development.** Applying knowledge about how the human body functions to prevent disease, preserve wellness, and promote peak performance. Goals and skills:
☑ Maintaining awareness of your physical condition and state of health
☑ Applying knowledge about exercise and fitness training to promote physical and mental health
☑ Understanding how sleep patterns affect health and performance
☑ Maintaining a healthy balance of work, recreation, and relaxation
☑ Applying knowledge of nutrition to reduce the risk of illness and promote optimal performance
☑ Becoming knowledgeable about nutritional imbalances and eating disorders
☑ Developing a positive physical self-image
☑ Becoming knowledgeable about the effects of drugs and their impact on physical and mental well-being
☑ Being knowledgeable about human sexuality and sexually transmitted diseases
☑ Understanding how biological differences between the sexes affect male-female relationships and gender orientation

6. **Spiritual development.** Searching for answers to the big questions, such as the meaning or purpose of life and death, and exploring nonmaterial issues that transcend human life and the physical world.

"The moral challenge is simply to abide by the knowledge we already have."

–Søren Kierkegaard, 19th-century Danish philosopher and theologian

"If you don't stand for something you will fall for anything."

—Malcolm X, African American Muslim minister, public speaker, and human rights activist

"A man too busy to take care of his health is like a mechanic too busy to take care of his tools."

—Spanish proverb

Student
Perspective

"You may think I'm here, living for the 'now' . . . but I'm not. Half of my life revolves around the invisible and immaterial. At some point, every one of us has asked the Big Questions surrounding our existence: What is the meaning of life? Is my life inherently purposeful and valuable?"

—College student (Dalton, Eberhardt, Bracken, & Echols, 2006)

Goals and skills:

☑ Developing a personal philosophy or worldview about the meaning and purpose of human existence

☑ Appreciating what cannot be completely understood

☑ Appreciating the mysteries associated with the origin of the universe

☑ Searching for the connection between the self and the larger world or cosmos

☑ Searching for the mystical or supernatural—that which transcends the boundaries of the natural world

☑ Being open to examining questions relating to death and life after death

☑ Being open to examining questions about the possible existence of a supreme being or higher power

☑ Being knowledgeable about different approaches to spirituality and their underlying beliefs or assumptions

☑ Understanding the difference and relationship between faith and reason

☑ Becoming aware and tolerant of religious beliefs and practices

7. **Vocational development.** Exploring career options, making career choices wisely, and developing skills needed for lifelong career success.

   Goals and skills:

   ☑ Understanding the relationship between college majors and careers

   ☑ Using effective strategies for exploring and identifying potential careers

   ☑ Selecting career options that are consistent with your personal values, interests, and talents

   ☑ Acquiring work experience in career fields that relate to your occupational interests

   ☑ Developing an effective resume and portfolio

   ☑ Using effective strategies for identifying personal references and acquiring letters of recommendation

   ☑ Acquiring effective job-search strategies

   ☑ Using effective strategies for writing letters of inquiry and applications to potential employers

   ☑ Developing strategies for performing well in personal interviews

   ☑ Acquiring effective networking skills for connecting with potential employers

8. **Personal development.** Developing positive self-beliefs, personal attitudes, and personal habits.

   Goals and skills:

   ☑ Developing a strong sense of personal identity and a coherent self-concept (e.g., "Who am I?")

   ☑ Finding a sense of purpose or direction in life (e.g., "Who will I become?")

   ☑ Developing self-respect and self-esteem

   ☑ Increasing self-confidence

   ☑ Developing self-efficacy, or the belief that events and outcomes in life are influenced or controlled by personal initiative and effort

   ☑ Setting realistic personal goals and priorities

   ☑ Developing self-motivation and self-discipline

   ☑ Developing personal resiliency and perseverance to persist to completion of long-range goals

   ☑ Acquiring practical skills for managing personal affairs effectively and efficiently

   ☑ Becoming independent and self-reliant

"Everyone is a house with four rooms: a physical, a mental, an emotional, and a spiritual. Most of us tend to live in one room most of the time but unless we go into every room every day, even if only to keep it aired, we are not complete."

—Native American proverb

"Your work is to discover your work and then with all your heart to give yourself to it."

—Hindu Prince Gautama Siddhartha, a.k.a. Buddha, founder of the philosophy and religion of Buddhism

"Remember, no one can make you feel inferior without your consent."

—Eleanor Roosevelt, UN diplomat and humanitarian

"I'm a great believer in luck and I find the harder I work, the more I have of it."

—Thomas Jefferson

The Co-Curriculum: Using the Whole Campus to Develop the Whole Person

The power of a liberal arts education is magnified when you take advantage of the total college environment. This includes not only taking advantage of the courses in the college curriculum; it also includes learning experiences that are available to you outside the classroom—referred to as the *co-curriculum*. Co-curricular experiences include all educational discussions you have with your peers and professors outside the classroom, as well as your participation in the various events and programs offered on your campus. As mentioned in Chapter 3, research clearly indicates that out-of-class learning experiences are equally important to your personal development and professional success as the course curriculum (Kuh, 2005; Kuh et al., 1994; 1995; Pascarella & Terenzini, 2005); hence, these experiences are referred to as the *co-curriculum*.

Reflection **3.6**

Look back and count the number of checkmarks you've placed by each of the eight areas of self-development. Did you find that you placed roughly the same number of checkmarks in all eight areas, or were there large discrepancies across the different areas?

Based on the checkmarks that you placed in each area, would you say that your interests in self-development are balanced across elements of the self, or do they suggest a strong interest in certain dimensions of yourself, with little interest in others?

Do you think you will eventually develop a more balanced set of interests across these different dimensions of self-development? Why?

Learning that takes place in college courses is primarily vicarious—that is, you learn from or through somebody else, by listening to professors in class and by reading outside of class. This type of academic learning is valuable, but it needs to be complemented by experiential learning (i.e., learning directly through firsthand experiences). For example, you don't learn to be a leader solely by listening to lectures and reading books about leadership. To fully develop your leadership skills, you need to have leadership experiences, such as experiences involving "leading a [discussion] group in class, holding office in student government or by being captain of a sports team" (AAC&U, 2002, p. 30). Capitalizing on experiential learning opportunities enables you to take advantage of your whole college to develop yourself as a whole person.

Listed in Snapshot Summary 3.2 are some programs and services included in a co-curriculum, accompanied by the primary dimensions of the self that they are designed to develop.

"To educate liberally, learning experiences must be offered which facilitate maturity of the whole person. These are goals of student development and clearly they are consistent with the mission and goals of liberal education."

—Theodore Berg, "Student Development and Liberal Education"

Snapshot Summary

3.2 **Dimensions of Holistic (Whole-Person) Development Promoted by Different Co-Curricular Programs and Services**

Intellectual Development
- Academic advising
- Learning center services
- College library
- Tutoring services
- Information technology services
- Campus speakers
- Academic workshops
- Concerts, theater productions, and art shows

Social and Emotional Development
- Student activities
- Student clubs and organizations
- Multicultural Center
- International student programs
- Counseling services
- Peer counseling
- Peer mentoring
- Residential life programs
- Commuter programs

Ethical Development
- Judicial Review Board
- Student government
- Integrity committees and task forces

Physical Development
- Student health services
- Wellness programs
- Campus athletic activities and intramural sports

Spiritual Development
- Campus ministry
- Peer ministry
- Religious services

Vocational Development
- Career development services
- Internships programs
- Service learning experiences
- Work-study programs
- Major and career fairs

Personal Development
- Financial aid services
- Campus workshops on self-manage-ment (e.g., managing time or money)
- Student development workshops and retreats

Note: This list represents just a sample of the total number of programs and services that may be available on your campus. As you can see from the list's length, colleges and universities are organized to promote your development in multiple ways. The power of the liberal arts is magnified when you combine coursework and co-curricular experiences to create a college experience that contributes to your development as a whole person.

Remember

A liberal arts education includes both the curriculum and the co-curriculum; it involves strategic use of the total college environment, both inside and outside the classroom.

Broadening Your Perspective of the World around You

Learn about things that go beyond yourself—learn about the world around you. A liberal arts education helps you move beyond yourself and expands your perspective to include the wider world around you (Braskamp, 2008). The components of this larger perspective are organized and illustrated in Figure 3.3.

In Figure 3.3, the center circle represents the self. Fanning out to the right of the self is a series of arches that encompasses the *social–spatial perspective*; this perspective includes increasingly larger social groups and more distant places, ranging from the narrowest perspective (the individual) to the widest perspective (the universe). The liberal arts liberate you from the narrow tunnel vision of a self-centered (egocentric) perspective, providing a panoramic perspective of the world that enables you to move outside yourself and see yourself in relation to other people and other places.

To the left of the self in Figure 3.3 are three arches labeled the *chronological perspective*. This perspective includes the three dimensions of time: past (historical), present (contemporary), and future (futuristic). The liberal arts not only widen your perspective, but also lengthen it by stretching your vision beyond the present,

Student Perspective

"College was not something I deemed important in order to be really rich later on in life. It was something I considered fundamental to learning about myself and the world around me."

—First-year college student (Watts, 2005)

FIGURE 3.3

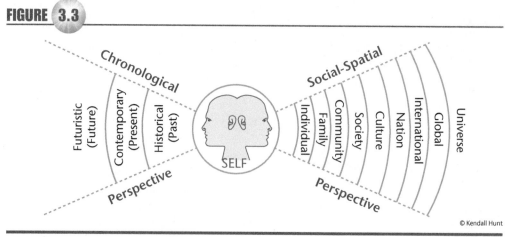

Multiple Perspectives Developed by the Liberal Arts

enabling you to see yourself in relation to humans who've lived before you and will live after you. The chronological perspective gives you hindsight to see where the world has been, insight into the world's current condition, and foresight to see where the world may be going.

It could be said that the chronological perspective provides you with a mental time machine for flashing back to the past and fast-forwarding to the future, while the social-spatial perspective provides you with a conceptual telescope for viewing people and places that are far away. Together, these two broadening perspectives of the liberal arts enable you to appreciate the experiences of humans living in different places and different times.

The specific elements comprising each of these broadening perspectives are discussed next.

> "A quality liberal education leads students to reflect on their place in the world and locate themselves historically and socially."
>
> —Nancy Thomas, "In Search of Wisdom: Liberal Education for a Changing World"

Elements of the Social-Spatial Perspective

The Family Perspective

Moving beyond the perspective of yourself as individual, you are part of a larger social unit—a family. The people with whom you were raised have almost certainly influenced the person you are today and how you got to be that way. Moreover, you influence your family. For example, your decision to go to college may make your parents and grandparents proud and may influence the decision of other members of your family to attend college. In addition, if you have children, graduating from college will have a positive influence on their future welfare; as mentioned in the introduction to this book, children of college graduates experience improved intellectual development, better physical health, and greater economic security (Bowen, 1977, 1997; Pascarella & Terenzini, 1991; 2005).

The Community Perspective

> "Think globally, act locally."
>
> —Patrick Geddes, Scottish urban planner and social activist

Moving beyond the family, you are also a member of a larger social unit—your community. This wider social circle includes friends and neighbors at home, at school, and at work. These are communities where you can begin to take action to improve the world around you. If you want to make the world a better place, this is the place to start—through civic engagement in your local communities.

Civically engaged people demonstrate civic commitment by stepping beyond their narrow self-interests to selflessly volunteer time and energy to help members of their community, particularly those in need. They demonstrate their humanity by being humane—they show genuine compassion for others who are less fortunate than themselves—and by being humanitarian—they work to promote the welfare of other human beings.

The Societal Perspective

Moving beyond your local communities, you are also a member of a larger *society*—a group of people organized under the same social system. Societies include subgroups divided into different regions (e.g., north, south, east, west), different population densities (e.g., urban, suburban, rural), and different socioeconomic classes (e.g., level of income, education, and job status). Within a society, there are typically subgroups that are stratified (layered) into different social classes with unequal levels of economic resources.

In human societies, groups of people are typically stratified into social classes with unequal levels of resources, such as monetary wealth.

> "[Liberal arts education] shows you how to accommodate yourself to others, how to throw yourself into their state of mind, how to come to an understanding of them. You are at home in any society; you have common ground with every class."
> —John Henry Newman

The Cultural Perspective

Culture can be broadly defined as a distinctive pattern of beliefs and values that are learned by a group of people who share the same social heritage and traditions. In short, culture is the whole way in which a group of people has learned to live (Peoples & Bailey, 2008); it includes their customary style of speaking (language), fashion, food, art, music, values, and beliefs.

Reflection **3.7**

What would you say is the factor that is most responsible for poverty in human societies?

Intercultural awareness is one of the outcomes of a liberal arts education (Center of Inquiry, 2011). Being able to step outside of your own culture and see issues from a broader worldview enables you to perceive reality and evaluate truth from the vantage points of different cultural groups. This makes your thinking more comprehensive and less ethnocentric (centered on your own culture).

> "It is difficult to see the picture when you are inside the frame."
> —Author unknown

The National Perspective

Besides being a member of society, you're also a citizen of a nation. The privilege of being a citizen in a free nation brings with it the responsibility of participating in your country's governance through the process of voting. As a democracy, the United States is a nation that has been built on the foundation of equal rights and freedom of opportunity guaranteed by its constitution.

Exercise your right to vote, and when you do vote, be mindful of political leaders who are committed to ensuring equal rights, social justice, and political freedom. When the personal rights and freedom of any of our fellow citizens are threatened, the political stability and survival of our democratic nation is threatened.

The International Perspective

Moving beyond your particular country of citizenship, you are also a member of an international world that includes close to 200 nations (Rosenberg, 2009). Communication and interaction among citizens of different nations is greater today than at any other time in world history, largely because of rapid advances in electronic technology (Dryden & Vos, 1999; Friedman, 2005). The World Wide Web is making today's world a small world after all, and success in this smaller world requires an international perspective. Our lives are increasingly affected by events beyond our national borders; boundaries between nations are breaking down as a result of international travel, international trading, and multinational corporations. By learning from and about different nations, you become more than a citizen of your own country: you become cosmopolitan—a citizen of the world. Moreover, employers of today's college graduates value employees with international knowledge and foreign language skills (Bok, 2006; Fixman, 1990; Office of Research, 1994).

The Global Perspective

Even broader than the international perspective is the global perspective. It extends beyond the relations among citizens of different nations to include all life forms that inhabit planet earth and the relationships between these diverse life forms and the earth's natural resources (minerals, air, and water). Humans share the earth and its natural resources with approximately 10 million animal species (Myers, 1997) and more than 300,000 forms of vegetative life (Knoll, 2003). As inhabitants of this planet and global citizens, we have a responsibility to address environmental issues that require balancing our industrial-technological progress with the need to sustain the earth's natural resources and preserve the life of our planet's cohabitants.

The Universal Perspective

Beyond the global perspective is the broadest of all perspectives—the universal. The earth is just one planet that shares a solar system with seven other planets and is just one celestial body that shares a galaxy with millions of other celestial bodies, including stars, moons, meteorites, and asteroids (Encrenaz et al., 2004).

Just as we should guard against being ethnocentric (thinking that our culture is the center of humanity), we should guard against being geocentric (thinking that our planet is at the center of the universe). All heavenly bodies do not revolve around the earth; our planet revolves around them. The sun doesn't rise in the east and set in the west; our planet rotates around the sun to produce our earthly experiences of day and night.

Elements of the Chronological Perspective

The Historical Perspective

A historical perspective is critical for understanding the root causes of our current human condition and world situation. Humans are products of both their social and natural history. Don't forget that the earth is estimated to be more than 4.5 billion years old and our human ancestors date back more than 250,000 years (Knoll, 2003). Thus, our current lives represent one very short time frame in a very long chronological reel. Every modern convenience we now enjoy reflects the collective efforts

"A liberal [arts] education frees a person from the prison-house of class, race, time, place, background, family, and nation."

—Robert Hutchins, former dean of Yale Law School and president of the University of Chicago

"Treat the Earth well. It was not given to you by your parents. It was loaned to you by your children."

—Kenyan proverb

"In astronomy, you must get used to viewing the earth as just one planet in the larger context of the universe."

—Physics professor (Donald, 2002)

"The sun, with all those planets revolving around it and dependent on it, can still ripen a bunch of grapes as if it had nothing else in the universe to do."

—Galileo Galilei

and cumulative knowledge of diverse human groups that have accumulated over thousands of years of history. By studying the past, we can build on our ancestors' achievements and avoid making their mistakes. For instance, by understanding the causes and consequences of the Holocaust, we can reduce the risk that an atrocity of that size and scope will ever happen again.

Reflection 3.8

Look back at the broadening perspectives developed by a liberal arts education. What college course would develop each perspective? If you're unsure or cannot remember whether a course is designed to develop any of these perspectives, look at the course's goals described in your college catalog (in print or online).

The Contemporary Perspective

The contemporary perspective focuses on understanding the current world situation and the events that comprise today's news. One major goal of a liberal arts education is to increase your understanding the contemporary human condition so that you may have the wisdom to improve it (Miller, 1988; Harris, 2010). For example, despite historical progress in the nation's acceptance and appreciation of different ethnic and racial groups, the United States today remains a nation that is deeply divided with respect to culture, religion, and social class (Brookings Institution, 2008).

The current technological revolution is generating new information and new knowledge at a faster rate than at any other time in human history (Dryden & Vos, 1999). When there is rapid creation and communication of new information, knowledge quickly becomes obsolete (Naisbitt, 1982). Workers in the today's complex, fast-changing world need to continually update their skills to perform their jobs and advance in their careers (Niles & Harris-Bowlsbey, 2002). This creates a demand for workers who have learned how to learn—a hallmark of the liberal arts.

The Futuristic Perspective

The futuristic perspective allows us to flash forward and envision what our world will be like years from now. This perspective focuses on such questions as "Will we leave the world a better or worse place for humans who will inhabit after our departure, including our children and grandchildren?" and "How can humans living today avoid short-term, shortsighted thinking and adopt a long-range vision that anticipates the consequences of their current actions on future generations of humans?"

To sum up, a comprehensive chronological perspective brings the past, present, and future into focus on a single screen. It enables us to see how the current world is a single segment of a temporal sequence that has been shaped by events that preceded it and how it will shape the events of the future.

> **Remember**
>
> *By embracing the perspectives of different times, places, and people, you're embracing the diversity promoted by a liberal arts education. These diverse perspectives liberate or emancipate you from the here and now and empower you to see things long ago and far away.*

"Those who cannot remember the past are damned to repeat it."
—George Santayana, Spanish-born American philosopher

"Yesterday is gone. Tomorrow has not yet come. We have only today. Let us begin."
—Mother Teresa of Calcutta, Albanian Catholic nun and winner of the Nobel Peace Prize

"The only person who is educated is the one who has learned how to learn and change."
—Carl Rogers, humanistic psychologist and Nobel Peace Prize nominee

"In times of change, learners inherit the Earth . . . [they] find themselves beautifully equipped to deal with a world that no longer exists."
—Eric Hoffer, author of *The Ordeal of Change* and recipient of the Presidential Medal of Freedom

"The future is literally in our hands to mold as we like. But we cannot wait until tomorrow. Tomorrow is now."
—Eleanor Roosevelt

"We all inherit the past. We all confront the challenges of the present. We all participate in the making of the future."
—Ernest Boyer and Martin Kaplan, *Educating for Survival*

The Synoptic Perspective: Integrating Diverse Perspectives into a Unified Whole

A liberal arts education helps you not only appreciate multiple perspectives but also how to integrate them into a meaningful whole (King, Brown, Lindsay, & Van-Hencke, 2007). Understanding of how the perspectives of time, place, and person interrelate to form a unified whole is referred to as a *synoptic* perspective (Cronon, 1998; Heath, 1977). The word derives from a combination of two roots: *syn*, meaning "together" (as in the word *synthesize*), and *optic*, meaning "to see." Thus, a synoptic perspective literally means to "see things together" or "see the whole." Said in another way, it enables you to see how all the trees come together to form the forest.

"A truly great intellect is one which takes a connected view of old and new, past and present, far and near, and which has an insight into the influence of all these on one another, without which there is no whole, and no center."

—John Henry Newman, *The Idea of a University* (1852)

Reflection 3.9

In light of the information you've read how would you interpret the following statement: "We can't know where we're going until we know where we've been"?

A liberal arts education helps you step beyond yourself to see the wider world and connects you with it. By seeing yourself as an integral part of humankind, you become integrated with the whole of humanity; you're able to see how you, as an individual, fit into the big picture—the larger scheme of things (Cuseo & Thompson, 2010). When we view ourselves as nested within a web of interconnections with other places, cultures, and times, we become aware of the common humanity we all share. This increased sense of connection with humankind decreases our feelings of personal isolation or alienation (Bellah, Madsen, Sullivan, Swidler, & Tipton, 1985). In his book, *The Perfect Education*, Kenneth Eble (1966) skillfully describes this benefit of a liberal arts education:

"Without exception, the observed changes [during college] involve greater breadth, expansion, and appreciation for the new and different. These changes are eminently consistent with values of a liberal [arts] education, and the evidence for their presence is compelling."

—Ernest Pascarella and Pat Terenzini, How College Affects Students

> *It can provide that overarching life of a people, a community, a world that was going on before the individual came onto the scene and that will continue on after [s]he departs. By such means we come to see the world not alone. Our joys are more intense for being shared. Our sorrows are less destructive for our knowing universal sorrow. Our fears of death fade before the commonness of the occurrence.*

Remember

A liberal arts education launches you on a quest for two forms of wholeness: (1) an inner wholeness in which elements of your "self" become connected to form a whole person, and (2) an outer wholeness in which you become connected to the whole world. This inner and outer quest will enable you to lead a richer, more fulfilling life that's filled with greater breadth, balance, and wholeness.

Educating You for Life

Research shows that the primary reasons students go to college are to prepare for a career and get a better job (Pryor et al., 2012). While these are important reasons and your career is an important element of your life, a person's vocation or occupation represents just one element of the self. It also represents just one of many roles or responsibilities that you are likely to have in life.

Reflection 3.10

In light of the knowledge you've acquired thus far in this chapter, what points or arguments would you make to counter the claim that the liberal arts are impractical?

"The finest art, the most difficult art, is the art of living."

—John Albert Macy, American author, poet, and editor of Helen Keller's autobiography

Similar to global issues, personal issues and challenges you face as an individual in your everyday life are multidimensional, requiring perspectives and skills that go well beyond the boundaries of a single academic field or career specialization. Your occupational role represents just one of many roles you will assume in life, which in-

Author's Experience One life role that a liberal arts education helped prepare me for was the role of parent. Courses that I took in psychology and sociology proved to be useful in helping me understand how children develop and how a parent can best support them at different stages of their development. Surprisingly, however, there was one course I had in college that I never expected would ever help me as a parent. That course was statistics, which I took to fulfill a general education requirement in mathematics. It was not a particularly enjoyable course; some of my classmates sarcastically referred to it as "sadistics" because they felt it was a somewhat painful or torturous experience. However, what I learned in that course became valuable to me many years later when my 14-year-old son (Tony) developed a life-threatening disease, leukemia, which is a form of cancer that attacks blood cells. Tony's form of leukemia was a particularly perilous one because it had only a 35 percent average cure rate; in other words, 65 percent of those who develop the disease don't recover and eventually die from it. This statistic was based on patients that received the traditional treatment of chemotherapy, which was the type of treatment that my son began receiving when his cancer was first detected.

Another option for treating Tony's cancer was a bone-marrow transplant, which involved using radiation to destroy all of his own bone marrow (that was making the abnormal blood cells) and replace it with bone marrow donated to him by another person. My wife and I got opinions from doctors at two major cancer centers—one from a center that specialized in chemotherapy, and one from a center that specialized in bone-marrow transplants. The chemotherapy doctors felt strongly that drug treatment would be the better way to treat and cure Tony, and the bone-marrow transplant doctors felt strongly that his chances of survival would be much better if he had a transplant. So, my wife and I had to decide between two opposing recommendations, each made by a respected group of doctors.

To help us reach a decision, I asked both teams of doctors for research studies that had been done on the effectiveness of chemotherapy and bone-marrow transplants for treating my son's particular type of cancer. I read all of these studies and carefully analyzed their statistical findings. I remembered from my statistics course that when an average is calculated for a general group of people (e.g., average cure rate for people with leukemia), it tends to lump together individuals from different subgroups (e.g., males and females or young children and teenagers). Sometimes, when separate statistics are calculated for different subgroups, the results may be different from the average statistic for the whole group. So, when I read the research reports, I looked for any subgroup statistics that might have been calculated. I found two subgroups of patients with my son's particular type of cancer that had a higher rate of cure with chemotherapy than the general (whole-group) average of 35 percent. One subgroup included people with a low number of abnormal cells at the time when the cancer was first diagnosed, and the other subgroup consisted of people whose cancer cells dropped rapidly after their first week of chemotherapy. My son belonged to both of these subgroups, which meant that his chance for cure with chemotherapy was higher than the overall 35 percent average. Furthermore, I found that the statistics showing higher success rate for bone-marrow transplants were based only on patients whose body accepted the donor's bone marrow and did not include those who died because their body rejected the donor's bone marrow. So, the success rates for bone-marrow patients were not actually as high as they appeared to be, because the overall average did not include the subgroup of patients who died because of transplant rejection. Based on these statistics, my wife and I decided to go with chemotherapy and not the transplant operation.

Our son has now been cancer-free for more than five years, so we think we made the right decision. However, I never imagined that a statistics course, which I took many years ago to fulfill a general education requirement, would help me fulfill my role as a parent and help me make a life-or-death decision about my own son.

Joe Cuseo

Remember

A liberal arts education not only prepares you for a career but also prepares you for life.

clude the roles of family member, friend, co-worker, community member, citizen, and possibly mother or father. A liberal arts education provides you with the breadth of knowledge and the variety of skills needed to successfully accommodate the multiple roles and responsibilities you will encounter throughout life.

Summary and Conclusion

The liberal arts represent the foundation of a college education, upon which all academic majors are built. They promote success in any major and career by supplying students with a set of lifelong learning skills that can be applied in multiple settings and that can be continually used throughout life.

The liberal arts also promote your development as a whole person (intellectual, emotional, social, physical, spiritual, etc.) and broadens your perspective on the world by expanding (1) your social-spatial perspective to include increasingly larger social groups and more distant places, ranging from micro (the individual) to macro (the universe), and (2) your chronological perspective, ranging from the past to the present to the future.

Despite popular beliefs to the contrary, the liberal arts have many practical benefits, including promoting career mobility and career advancement. Most importantly, a liberal arts education prepares you for life roles other than an occupation, including roles such as family member, community member, and citizen. In short, a liberal arts education prepares you for more than a career: it prepares you for life.

Learning More through the World Wide Web

Internet-Based Resources for Further Information on Liberal Arts Education

For additional information related to the ideas discussed in this chapter, we recommend the following Web sites:

Liberal Arts Education:

www.aacu.org/resources/liberaleducation/index.cfm

Liberal Arts Resources:

www.iseek.org/education/liberalarts.html

3.1 Planning Your Liberal Arts Education

Since general education is an essential component of your college experience, it should be intentionally planned. This exercise will leave you with a flexible plan that capitalizes on your educational interests while ensuring that your college experience has both breadth and balance.

1. Use your course catalog (bulletin) to identify the general education requirements at your college. The requirements should be organized into general divisions of knowledge similar to those discussed in this chapter (humanities, fine arts, natural sciences, etc.). Within each of these liberal arts divisions, there will be specific courses listed that fulfill the general education requirements for that particular division. (Catalogs can sometimes be difficult to navigate; if you encounter difficulty or doubt about general education requirements, seek clarification from an academic advisor on campus.)

2. You'll probably have some freedom to choose courses from a larger group of courses that fulfill general education requirements within each division. Use your freedom of choice to select courses whose descriptions capture your curiosity or pique your interest. You can take liberal arts courses not only to fulfill general education requirements, but also to test your interest and talent in fields that you may end up choosing as a college major or minor.

3. Highlight the courses in the catalog that you plan to take to fulfill your general education requirements in each division of the liberal arts, and use the form on the following page to pencil in the courses you've chosen. (Use pencil because you will likely make some adjustments to your plan.) Remember that the courses you're taking this term may be fulfilling certain general education requirements, so be sure to list them on your planning form.

3.2 General Education Planning Form

Division of the Liberal Arts Curriculum: _____

General education courses you're planning to take to fulfill requirements in this division (record the course number and course title):

_____   _____

_____   _____

_____   _____

Division of the Liberal Arts Curriculum: _____

General education courses you're planning to take to fulfill requirements in this division (record the course number and course title):

_____   _____

_____   _____

_____   _____

Assignment – Left Footprint*

1. Write inside of the left footprint what you have chosen to be your major, and why you have chosen this particular major.

2. Write in the footprint the goals you would like to accomplish by the end of your freshman year and your senior year in your chosen major.

3. Write in the footprint how you plan to achieve these goals.

4. Ask yourself if the goals you have chosen are realistic, and write in the footprint why you feel they are or are not realistic.

5. After the second week of classes, write in the footprint if you feel you have chosen the right or wrong major. Explain why. If you feel you have chosen the wrong major, write down your plan for implementing a process to select an appropriate major for yourself, but still maintaining a passing Grade Point Average (GPA) in your current major until the next semester begins.

6. Write the study habits that you plan to use and implement this semester. At the end of the third week of classes, ask yourself if they are working for you. If they are not working for you, go back and devise another way to study. Write it down.

7. Community Service work is very important at Hampton University. Write down three community service projects you would like to complete by the end of your freshman year and why.

8. Write what it means to you to be a Hamptonian?

9. What legacy would you like to leave at Hampton after you graduate?

10. Make a check list of everything that you do that is significant during your first semester.

11. At the end of the first semester, go through your check list, see if you have accomplished everything you set out to do. Write down the things that you feel need to be tweaked.

12. When the second semester begins, use the right footprint and use question numbers (2, 3, 4, 6, and 7). At the end of the semester, look at what you have written in both footprints. Ask yourself if you have accomplished what you set out to do your freshman year.

13. Continue this process every class year. At the end of your senior year, look at all 8 footprints. Ask yourself, did I achieve what I set out to do on the first day I entered Hampton University, and what legacy have I left for others to follow.

*Contributed by Joan Wickham. Copyright © Kendall Hunt Publishing Company

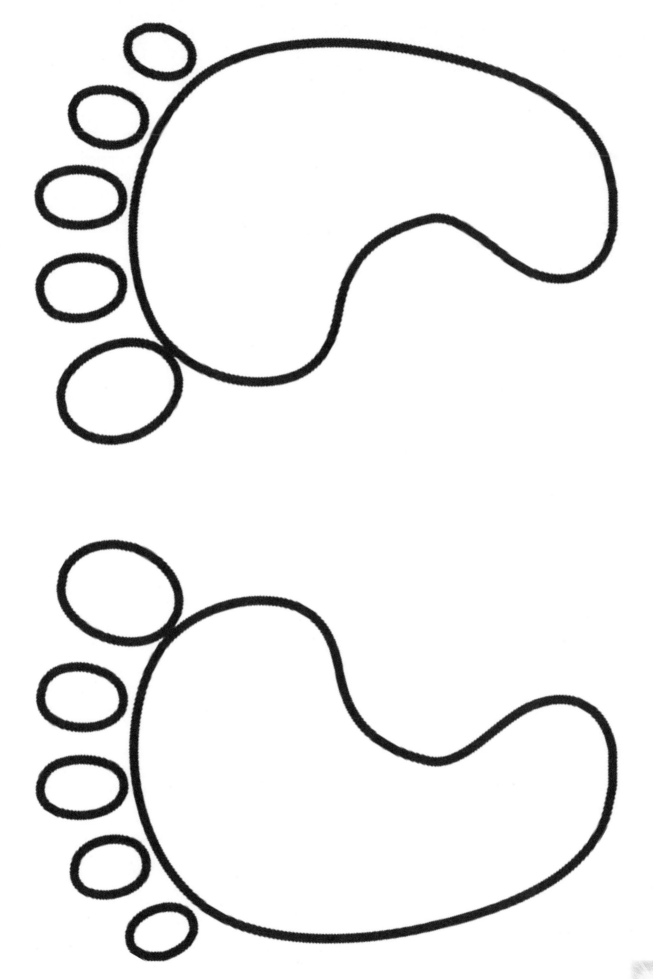

Dazed and Confused: General Education versus Career Specialization

Joe Tech was really looking forward to college because he thought he would have freedom to select the courses he wanted and the opportunity to get into the major of his choice (computer science). However, he's shocked and disappointed with his first-term schedule of classes because it consists mostly of required general education courses that do not seem to relate in any way to his major. He's frustrated further because some of these courses are about subjects that he already took in high school (English, history, and biology). He's beginning to think he would be better off quitting college and going to a technical school where he could get right into computer science and immediately begin to acquire the knowledge and skills he'll need to prepare him for his intended career.

Reflection and Discussion Questions

1. Can you relate to Joe, or do you know of students who feel the same way Joe does?

2. If Joe decides to leave college for a technical school, how do you see it affecting his future (1) in the short run and (2) in the long run?

3. Do you see any way Joe might strike a balance between pursuing his career interest and obtaining his college degree so that he could work toward achieving both goals at the same time?

Hampton Helped Me!

Elise Preston

Photo courtesy of Hampton University

Elise Preston joined the News Channel 3 team in October, 2011. Elise reports during the week, and co-anchors report during weekend and daybreak. Previously, she was a reporter for the CBSaffiliate, KFDA in Amarillo, Texas. Before covering wildfires in the Texas panhandle, Elise worked as an assignment editor at WVEC in Norfolk, VA. Elise is a proud alumna of Hampton University in Hampton, Virginia.

She earned a Bachelor of Arts degree in broadcast journalism from the Scripps Howard School of Journalism and Communications.

The Columbus, Ohio, native is a member of the National Association of Black Journalists and Delta Sigma Theta Sorority, Inc. Her HU Activities include Gamma Iota Chapter of Delta Sigma Theta Sorority Inc., Greer Dawson Wilson Student Leadership Program, and Show Host for WHOV 88.1FM

Hampton Helped Me!

Lewis Myers III

Photo courtesy of Hampton University

Lewis Myers III was born and raised in Durham, North Carolina, and attended Hampton University in the fall of 2003 where he became a distinguished member ofthe 5-year MBA program.

As a freshman, Myers joined the Hampton University Men's Golf Team and was named a unanimous scholar athlete all 4 years.

CHAPTER 4
Goal Setting, Motivation, Character and Ethics

"The price of success is hard work, dedication to the job at hand, and the determination that whether we win or lose, we have applied the best of ourselves to the task at hand."

—Vince Lombardi

Upon completion of this chapter, you will be able to:

- **Set** and strive for meaningful goals
- **Maintain** motivation to reach goals
- **Examine** three chapter traits
- **Set** positive goals
- **Develop** a time management plan

Goal Setting, Motivation, Character and Ethics

Moving from Dreams to Plans to Action

How would you define the word "successful"?

_____

_____

_____

LEARNING GOAL

To help you set and strive for meaningful goals and maintain your motivation to reach those goals.

What Does Being "Successful" Mean to You?

"Achieving a desired outcome" is how *success* is commonly defined. The word *success* derives from the Latin root *successus*, meaning "to follow or come after" (as in the word *succession*). Thus, by definition, success involves an order or sequence of actions that lead to a desired outcome. The process starts with identifying an end (goal) and then finding a means (sequence of steps) to reach that goal (achieving success). Goal setting is the first step in the process of becoming successful because it gives you something specific to strive for and ensures that you start off in the right direction. Studies consistently show that setting goals is a more effective self-motivational strategy than simply telling yourself that you should try hard and do your best (Boekaerts, Pintrich, & Zeidner, 2000; Locke & Latham, 1990).

By setting goals, you show initiative—you initiate the process of gaining control of your future and taking charge of your life. When you take initiative, you demonstrate what psychologists call an *internal* locus of control: you believe that the locus (location or source) of control for events in your life is inside of you, rather than being *external*, or outside of you and beyond your control—for instance, determined by such factors as innate ability, luck, chance, or fate (Rotter, 1966; Carlson, Buskist, Heth, & Schmaltz, 2007). They believe that success is influenced more by attitude, effort, commitment, and preparation than by natural ability or inborn intelligence (Jernigan, 2004).

Research has revealed that individuals with a strong internal locus of control display the following characteristics:

1. Greater independence and self-direction (Van Overwalle, Mervielde, & De Schuyer, 1995);
2. More accurate self-assessment (Hashaw, Hammond, & Rogers, 1990);

Student Perspective

"Stopping a long pattern of bad decision-making and setting positive, productive priorities and goals."

—College sophomore's answer to the question "What does being successful mean to you?"

"I'm a great believer in luck, and I find the harder I work the more I have of it."

—Thomas Jefferson, third president of the United States

From *Thriving in College and Beyond: Research-Based Strategies for Academic Success and Personal Development* by Cuseo et al. Copyright © 2013 by Kendall Hunt Publishing Company. Reprinted by permission.

"The future is literally in our hands to mold as we like. But we cannot wait until tomorrow. Tomorrow is now."

—Eleanor Roosevelt, UN diplomat and humanitarian

"What lies behind us and what lies in front of us are small matters compared to what lies within us."

—Ralph Waldo Emerson, 19th-century American essayist and lecturer

"Nothing ever comes to one that is worth having, except as a result of hard work."

—Booker T. Washington, born-in-slavery Black educator, author, and advisor to Republican presidents

Student *Perspective*

"Accomplishing something hard to do. Not something that has just been handed to me."

—First-year student's response to the question: "What does being successful mean to you?"

"Control your own destiny or someone else will."

—Jack Welch, chemical engineer, author, and successful CEO of the General Electric Company

"The price of greatness is responsibility."

—Winston Churchill, British prime minister during World War II and Nobel Prize winner in literature

"Man who stand on hill with mouth open will wait long time for roast duck to drop in."

—Confucius, Chinese philosopher who emphasized sincerity and social justice

"You miss 100 percent of the shots you never take."

—Wayne Gretzky, Hall of Fame hockey player, nicknamed "The Great One" and considered by many to be the greatest hockey player of all time.

3. Higher levels of learning and achievement (Wilhite, 1990); and
4. Better physical health (Maddi, 2002; Seligman, 1991).

An internal locus of control also contributes to the development of another positive trait that psychologists call *self-efficacy*—the belief that you have power to produce a positive effect on the outcomes of your life (Bandura, 1994). People with low self-efficacy tend to feel helpless, powerless, and passive; they allow things to happen to them rather than taking charge and making things happen for them. College students with a strong sense of self-efficacy believe they're in control of their educational success and can take control of their future, regardless of their past or current circumstances.

People with a strong sense of self-efficacy initiate action, exert effort, and sustain that effort until they reach their goals. If they encounter setbacks or bad breaks along the way, they don't give up or give in; they persevere or push on (Bandura, 1986; 1997). They don't have a false sense of entitlement—that they're entitled to or owed anything; they believe success is something that's earned and the harder they work at it, the more likely they'll get it.

Students with a strong sense of *academic* self-efficacy have been found to:

1. Put considerable effort into their studies;
2. Use active-learning strategies;
3. Capitalize on campus resources; and
4. Persist in the face of obstacles (Multon, Brown, & Lent, 1991; Zimmerman, 1995; 2000).

Reflection 4.2 ────────────────────

You are not required by law or by others to attend college; you've made the decision to continue your education. Do you believe you are in charge of your educational destiny?

Why or why not?

Students with a stronger sense of self-efficacy also possess a strong sense of personal responsibility. As the breakdown of the word *responsible* implies, they are "response" "able"—that is, they believe they are able to respond effectively to personal challenges, including academic challenges.

For example, studies show that students who convert their college degrees into successful careers have two common characteristics: personal initiative and a positive attitude (Pope, 1990). They don't take a passive approach and assume good positions will fall into their laps; nor do they believe they are owed a position simply because they have a college degree or credential. Instead, they become actively involved in the job-hunting process and use various job-search strategies (Brown & Krane, 2000).

Strategies for Effective Goal Setting

Motivation begins with goal setting. Studies show that people who neglect to set and pursue life goals are prone to feelings of "life boredom" and a belief that their lives are meaningless (Bargdill, 2000). Goals may be classified into three general categories: long-range, mid-range, and short-range, depending on the length of time it takes to reach them and the order in which they are to be achieved. Short-range goals need to be completed before a mid-range goal can be reached, and mid-range goals must be reached before a long-range goal can be achieved. For example, if your long-range goal is a successful career, you must complete the courses required for a degree (mid-range goal) that will allow you entry into a career; to reach your mid-range goal of a college degree, you need to successfully complete the courses you're taking this term (short-range goal).

This process is called means-end analysis, which involves working backward from your long-range goal (the end) and identifying the order and timing of the mid-range and short-range subgoals (the means) that need to be taken to reach your long-range goal (Brooks, 2009; Newell & Simon, 1959).

Setting Long-Range Goals

Setting effective long-range goals involves a process that has two components: (1) self-awareness, or self-insight into who you are now, and (2) self-projection, or a vision of what you want to become. When you engage in both of these processes, you're able to see a connection between your short-range and long-range goals.

Long-range goal setting enables you to take an approach to your future that is proactive—acting beforehand to anticipate and control your future life rather than putting it off and being forced to react to it without a plan. Research shows that people who neglect to set goals for themselves are more likely to experience boredom with life (Bargdill, 2000). Setting long-range goals and planning ahead also helps reduce feelings of anxiety about the future because when you give forethought to your future, you gain greater power to control it—i.e., you develop a stronger sense of self-efficacy. As the old saying goes, "To be forewarned is to be forearmed."

Reflection **4.3**

In what area or areas of your life do you feel that you've been able to exert the most control and achieve the most positive results?

In what area or areas do you wish you had more control and were achieving better results?

What strategies have you used in those areas of your life where you've taken charge and gained control? Could you apply the same strategies to those areas in which you need to gain more control?

Remember that setting long-range goals and developing long-range plans doesn't mean you can't adjust or modify them. Your goals can undergo change as you change, develop skills, acquire knowledge, and discover new interests or talents. Finding yourself and discovering your path in life are among the primary purposes of a college education. Don't think that the process of setting long-range goals means you are locking yourself into a premature plan and reducing your options. Instead, long-range goal setting just gives you a map that provides you with some sense of direction about where you're going, which can also provide you with the ignition and motivation to get going.

"What keeps me going is goals."

—Muhammad Ali, philanthropist, social activist, and Hall of Fame boxer crowned "Sportsman of the 20th Century" by *Sports Illustrated*

"To fail to plan is to plan to fail."

—Robert Wubbolding, internationally known author, psychologist, and teacher

"You've got to be careful if you don't know where you're going because you might not get there."

—Yogi Berra, Hall of Fame baseball player

"There is perhaps nothing worse than reaching the top of the ladder and discovering that you're on the wrong wall."

—Joseph Campbell, American professor and writer

Steps in the Goal-Setting Process

Effective goal setting involves a four-step sequence:

> 1. **Awareness of yourself.** Your personal interests, abilities and talents, and values;

↓

> 2. **Awareness of your options.** The range of choices available to you;

↓

> 3. **Awareness of the options that best fit you.** The goals that are most compatible with your personal abilities, interests, values, and needs;

↓

> 4. **Awareness of the process.** The steps you need to take to reach your chosen goal.

Discussed in the next sections are strategies for taking each of these steps in the goal-setting process.

Step 1. Self-Awareness

The goals you choose to pursue say a lot about who you are and what you want from life. Thus, self-awareness is a critical first step in the process of goal setting. You must know yourself before you can choose the goals you want to achieve. While this may seem obvious, self-awareness and self-discovery are often overlooked aspects of the goal-setting process. Deepening your self-awareness puts you in a better position to select and choose goals and to pursue a personal path that's true to who you are and what you want to become.

> **Remember**
>
> *Self-awareness is the first and most important step in the process of making any important life choice or decision. Good decisions are built on a deep understanding of one's self.*

No one is in a better position to know who you are, and what you want to be, than *you*. One effective way to get to know yourself more deeply is through self-questioning. You can increase self-awareness by asking yourself questions that can stimulate your thinking about your inner qualities and priorities. Effective self-questioning launches you on an inward quest or journey to self-insight and self-discovery, which is the essential first step to effective goal setting. For example, if your long-range goal is career success, you can launch your voyage toward achieving this goal by asking yourself thought-provoking questions related to your personal:

- **Interests.** What you like to do;
- **Abilities and talents.** What you're good at doing; and
- **Values.** What you believe is worth doing.

The following questions are designed to sharpen your self-awareness with respect to your interests, abilities, and values. As you read each question, briefly note what thought or thoughts come to mind about yourself.

"You have brains in your head. You have feet in your shoes. You can steer yourself any direction you choose."

—Theodore Seuss Giesel, a.k.a. Dr. Seuss, author of children's books including *Oh, the Places You'll Go!*

"Know thyself, and to thine own self be true."

—Plato, ancient Greek philosopher

"In order to succeed, you must know what you are doing, like what you are doing, and believe in what you are doing."

—Will Rogers, Native American humorist and actor

Your Personal Interests

1. What tends to grab your attention and hold it for long periods of time?
2. What sorts of things are you naturally curious about and tend to intrigue you?
3. What do you enjoy and do as often as you possibly can?
4. What do you look forward to or get excited about?
5. What are your favorite hobbies or pastimes?
6. When you're with friends, what do you tend to talk most about or spend most of your time doing?
7. What has been your most stimulating or enjoyable learning experience?
8. If you've had previous work or volunteer experience, what jobs or tasks did you find most enjoyable or stimulating?
9. When time seems to fly by for you, what are you usually doing?
10. When you choose to read, what topics do you read about?
11. When you open a newspaper or log on to the Internet, where do you tend to go first?
12. When you find yourself daydreaming or fantasizing about your future life, what's going on or what are you doing?

Reflection 4.4

From your responses to the preceding questions, identify one long-range goal you could pursue that's compatible with your personal interests. In the space that follows, write down the goal and your interests that are compatible with it.

Your Personal Abilities and Talents

1. What seems to come easily or naturally to you?
2. What would you say is your greatest personal strength or talent?
3. What do you excel at when you apply yourself and put forth your best effort?
4. What are your most advanced or well-developed skills?
5. What would you say has been the greatest accomplishment or achievement in your life thus far?
6. What about yourself are you most proud of, or what do you take the most pride in doing?
7. When others come to you for advice or assistance, what is it usually for?
8. What would your best friend or friends say is your best quality, trait, or characteristic?
9. When you had a strong feeling of being successful after you had done something, what was it that you did?
10. If you've received awards or other forms of recognition, what did you do to earn them?
11. In what types of learning tasks or activities have you experienced the most success?
12. In what types of courses do you tend to earn the highest grades?

"Never desert your line of talent. Be what nature intended you for and you will succeed."

—Sydney Smith, 18th-century English writer and defender of the oppressed

Reflection 4.5

From your responses to the preceding questions, identify a long-range goal you could pursue that's compatible with your personal abilities and talents. In the space that follows, write down the goal and your abilities and talents that are compatible with it.

Your Personal Values

"Do what you value; value what you do."

—Sidney Simon, author of *Values Clarification* and *In Search of Values*

"Success is getting what you want. Happiness is wanting what you get."

—Dale Carnegie, author of the bestselling book *How to Win Friends and Influence People* (1936) and founder of the Dale Carnegie Course, a worldwide program for business based on his teachings

1. What matters most to you?
2. If you were to single out one thing you stand for or believe in, what would it be?
3. What would you say are your highest priorities in life?
4. What makes you feel good about what you're doing when you're doing it?
5. If there were one thing in the world you could change, improve, or make a difference in, what would it be?
6. When you have extra spending money, what do you usually spend it on?
7. When you have free time, what do you usually spend it on?
8. What does "making it big in life" mean to you?
9. How would you define success? (What would it take for you to feel that you were successful?)
10. How would you define happiness? (What would it take for you to feel happy?)
11. Do you have any heroes or anyone you admire, look up to, or believe has set an example worth following? If yes, who and why?
12. Which of the following four personal qualities would you want to be known for? Rank them in order of priority to you (1 = highest, 4 = lowest).

   _____ Smart

   _____ Wealthy

   _____ Creative

   _____ Caring

Reflection 4.6

From your responses to the preceding questions, identify a long-range goal you could pursue that's compatible with your personal values. In the space that follows, write down the goal and your values that are compatible with it.

"Students [may be] pushed into careers by their families, while others have picked one just to relieve their anxiety about not having a career choice. Still others may have picked popular or lucrative careers, knowing nothing of what they're really like or what it takes to prepare for them."

—Lee Upcraft, Joni Finney, and Peter Garland, student development specialists

Step 2. Awareness of Your Options

The second critical step in the goal-setting process is to become aware of your options for long-range goals. For example, to effectively choose a career goal, you need to be aware of the career options available to you and have a realistic understanding of the types of work performance required by these careers. To gain this knowledge, you'll need to capitalize on available resources by doing the following:

1. Reading books about different careers
2. Taking career development courses
3. Interviewing people in different career fields
4. Observing (shadowing) people working in different careers

Step 3. Awareness of Options That Best "Fit" You

A third key step in the goal-setting process is becoming aware of the full range of options available to you as potential goals. For instance, in college you have multiple courses and majors from which to choose. To deepen your awareness of whether a field may be a good fit for you, take a course in that field to test out how well it matches your interests, values, talents, and learning style. Ideally, you want to select a field that closely taps into, or builds on, your strongest skills and talents. Choosing a field that's compatible with your strongest abilities will enable you to master the skills required by that field more deeply and efficiently. You are also more likely to succeed or excel in a field that draws on your talents, and the success you experience will, in turn, strengthen your self-esteem, self-confidence, and drive to continue with it. You've probably heard of the proverb "If there's a will, there's a way"—when you're motivated, you're more likely to succeed. It's also true that "If there's a way, there's a will"—when you know how to do something well, you're more motivated to do it.

Step 4. Awareness of the Key Steps Needed to Reach Your Goal

This is the fourth and final step in an effective goal-setting process. For example, if you've set the goal of achieving a college degree in a particular major, you need to be aware of the courses you need to complete to reach that major. Similarly, with a career goal, you need to know what major or majors lead to that career; some careers may require a specific major, but many careers may be reached through a variety of different majors.

Reflection **4.7**

Think about a major you've chosen or are considering and answer the following questions:

1. Why are you considering this major? What led or caused you to become interested in this choice? Why or why not?

2. Would you say that your interest in this major is motivated primarily by intrinsic factors—i.e., factors "inside" of you, such as your personal abilities, interests, needs, and values? Or is your interest in the career motivated more heavily by extrinsic factors—i.e., factors "outside" of you, such as starting salary or meeting the expectations of parents?

The word motivation derives from the Latin *movere*, meaning "to move." Success comes to those who overcome inertia—they first initiate momentum to start moving them toward their goal; then they maintain motivation until their goal is reached. Goal setting only creates the potential for success; it takes motivation to turn this potential into reality by converting intention into action. You can have the best-planned goals and all the knowledge, strategies, and skills to be successful, but if you don't have the will to succeed, there's no way you will succeed. Studies show that without a strong personal commitment to achieve a goal, that goal will be not be achieved, no matter how well designed the plan is to reach it (Locke, 2000; Locke & Latham, 1990).

> "Mere knowledge is not power; it is only possibility. Action is power; and its highest manifestation is when it is directed by knowledge."
>
> —Francis Bacon, English philosopher, lawyer, and champion of modern science

> "You can lead a horse to water, but you can't make him drink."
>
> —Author unknown

Remember

The process of effective goal setting applies to more than just educational goals. It's a strategic process that can and should be applied to any goal you set for yourself in life, at any stage of your life.

Snapshot Summary

4.1   **The SMART Method of Goal Setting**

A popular mnemonic device for remembering the key components of a well-designed goal is the acronym "SMART" (Doran, 1981; Meyer, 2003).

A SMART goal is one that is:

Specific: States exactly what the goal is and what will be done to achieve it.

Example: I'll achieve at least a "B" average this term by spending 25 hours per week on my course work outside of class and by using the effective learning strategies described in this book. (As opposed to the non-specific goal, "I'm really going to work hard.")

Meaningful (and Measurable): A goal that really matters to the individual, for which progress can be steadily measured or tracked.

Example: I will achieve at least a "B" average this term because it will enable me to get into a field that I really want to pursue as a career, and I will measure my progress toward this goal by keeping track of the grades I'm earning in all my courses throughout the term.

Actionable: Identifies the concrete actions or behaviors that will be engaged in to reach the goal.

Example: I will achieve at least a "B" average this term by (1) attending all classes, (2) taking detailed notes in all my classes, (3) completing all reading assignments before their due dates, and (4) avoiding cramming by studying in advance of all my major exams.

Realistic: A goal capable of being achieved or attained.

Example: Achieving a "B" average this term will be a realistic goal for me because my course load is manageable and I will not be working at my part-time job for more than 15 hours per week.

Timed: A goal that is broken down into a timeline that includes short-range, mid-range, and long-range steps.

Example: To achieve at least a "B" average this term, first I'll acquire the information I need to learn by taking complete notes in class and on my assigned readings (short-range step). Second, I'll study the information I've acquired from my notes and readings in short study sessions held in advance of major exams (mid-range step). Third, I'll hold a final review session for all information previously studied on the day before my exams, and after exams I'll review my test results as feedback to determine what I did well and what I need to do better in order to maintain at least a "B" average (long-range step).

Note: The strategy for setting SMART goals is a transferable process that can be applied to reaching goals in any aspect or dimension of your life, including health-related goals such as losing weight, social goals such as meeting new people, and fiscal goals such as saving money. The SMART goal-setting strategy can help you achieve goals for any and all elements of holistic (whole-person) development described in Chapter 4.

Strategies for Maintaining Motivation and Progress toward Your Goals

Reaching your goals requires will and energy; it also requires skill and strategy. Listed here are strategies for maintaining your motivation and commitment to reaching your goals.

Visualize reaching your long-range goal. Create mental images of being successful. For example, if your goal is to achieve a college degree, imagine a crowd of cheering family, friends, and faculty at your graduation. Visualize how you'll be able to cherish and carry this proud memory with you for the rest of your life, and how the benefits of a college degree will last your entire lifetime. Imagine yourself in the career that your college degree enabled you to enter. Visualize your typical workday going something like this: You wake up in the morning and hop out of bed enthusiastically, looking forward to your day at work. When you're at work, time flies by, and before you know it, the day's over. When you return to bed that night and look back on your day, you feel good about what you did and how well you did it.

Put your goals in writing. When you put your goals in writing, you remain aware of them and remember them. This can stimulate your motivation to pursue your plan into action by serving almost like a written contract that holds you accountable to following through on your commitment. Place your written goals where you see them regularly. Consider writing them on sticky notes and posting them in multiple places that you encounter on a daily basis (e.g., your laptop, refrigerator, and bathroom mirror). If you keep them constantly in sight, you'll keep them constantly in mind.

Map out your goals. Lay out your goals in the form of a flowchart to show the steps you'll be taking to move from your short-range to mid-range to long-range goals. Visual diagrams can help you "see" where you want to go, enabling you to connect where you are now and where you want to be. Diagramming can also be energizing because it gives you a sneak preview of the finish line and a map-like overview of how to get there.

Keep a record of your progress. Research indicates that the act of monitoring and recording progress toward goals can increase motivation to continue pursuing them (Locke & Latham, 2005; Matsui, Okada, & Inoshita, 1983). The act of keeping records of your progress probably increases your motivation by giving you frequent feedback on your progress and positive reinforcement for staying on track and moving toward your target (long-range goal) (Bandura & Cervone, 1983; Schunk, 1995). For example, mark your accomplishments in red on your calendar, or keep a journal of the goals you've reached; your entries will keep you motivated by supplying you with concrete evidence of your progress and commitment. You can also chart or graph your progress, which provides a powerful visual display of your upward trends and patterns. Keep the chart where you can see it on a daily basis so you can use it as an ongoing source of inspiration and motivation. You can add musical inspiration by playing a motivational song in your head to keep you going (e.g., "We Are the Champions" by Queen).

Develop a skeletal resume of your career goals. Include your goals as separate sections or categories that will be fleshed out as you complete them. Your to-be-completed resume can provide a framework or blueprint for organizing, building, and tracking progress toward your goals. It can also serve as a visual reminder of the things you plan to accomplish and eventually showcase to potential employers. Furthermore, every time you look at your growing resume, you'll be reminded of your past accomplishments, which can energize and motivate you to reach your goals. As you fill in and build up your resume, you will see (literally) how much you have achieved, which boosts your self-confidence and motivation to continue achieving. **Reward yourself for making steady progress toward your long-range goal.** Reward is already built into reaching your long-range goal because it represents the end of your trip: it lands you at your desired destination. However, short- and mid-range goals may not be desirable ends in themselves; often, they are merely the means to a desirable end (your long-range goal). Consequently, you need to intentionally reward yourself for landing on these smaller stepping stones up the path to your long-range goal. When you complete these short- and mid-range goals, record and reward your accomplishments (e.g., celebrate your successful completion of midterms or finals by treating yourself to something you enjoy).

Like any other habit, the habit of perseverance and persistence through all intermediate steps needed to reach a long-range goal is more likely to continue if it's followed by a reward (positive reinforcement). The process of setting small goals,

Remember
The next best thing to accomplishing something immediately is immediately writing down your intention to do it!

"Life isn't a matter of milestones but of moments."

—Rose Fitzgerald Kennedy, philanthropist and mother of John F. and Robert F. Kennedy

"Willpower is the personal strength and discipline, rooted in strong motivation, to carry out your plans. 'Waypower' is the exertion of willpower that helps you find resources and support."

—Jerry Pattengale, history professor and author of *The Purpose-Guided Student: Dream to Succeed*

"Develop an inner circle of close associations in which the mutual attraction is not sharing problems or needs. The mutual attraction should be values and goals."

—Denis Waitley, former mental trainer for U.S. Olympic athletes and author of *Seeds of Greatness*

moving steadily toward them, and rewarding yourself for reaching them is a simple but powerful strategy. It helps you maintain motivation over the extended period needed to reach your long-range goal.

Capitalize on available campus resources that can help you stay on track and moving toward your goal. Research indicates that college success results from a combination of what students do for themselves (personal responsibility) and what students do to capitalize on resources available to them—i.e., their resourcefulness (Pascarella & Terenzini, 1991, 2005). Successful college students are resourceful students; they seek out and take advantage of college resources to help them reach their goals.

For example, a resourceful student who is having trouble deciding what field of study to pursue for a degree will seek assistance from an academic advisor on campus. A resourceful student who is interested in a particular career but is unclear about the best educational path to take toward that career will use the Career Development Center as a resource.

Use your social resources. Ask yourself, "Who can help me stick to my plan and complete the steps needed to reach my goal?" The power of social support groups for helping people achieve personal goals is well documented by research in various fields (Brissette, Cohen, & Seeman, 2000; Ewell, 1997). You can use the power of people by surrounding yourself with peers who are committed to successfully achieving their educational goals and by avoiding "toxic" people who are likely to poison your plans or dampen your dreams.

Find supportive, motivated friends and make a mutual pact to help each other reach your respective goals. This step could be taken to a more formal level by drawing up a "social contract" whereby you and your partner are "co-witnesses" or designated social-support agents whose role is to help each other stay on track and moving toward long-range goals. Studies show that making a public commitment to a goal increases your commitment to it, probably because it becomes a matter of personal pride and integrity that's seen not only through your own eyes but also through the eyes of others (Hollenbeck, Williams, & Klein, 1989; Locke, 2000).

Convert setbacks into comebacks. The type of thoughts you have after experiencing a setback can affect your emotional reaction to the setback and the action you take in response to it. What you think about a poor performance (e.g., a poor test grade) can affect your emotional reaction to that grade and what action, or lack of action, you take to improve it. You can react to the poor grade by knocking yourself down with a putdown ("I'm a loser") or by building yourself back up with a positive pep talk ("I'm going to learn from my mistakes on this test and rebound with a stronger performance on the next one").

It's noteworthy that the root of the word *failure* is *fallere*, which means to "trip or fall," while the root word for *success* is *successus*, which means "to follow or come after." Thus, when we fail at something, it doesn't mean we've been defeated: it just means we've stumbled and fallen. Success can still be achieved after the fall by getting up, not giving up, and continuing to take the succession of steps need to successfully reach our goal.

Reflection 4.8

What would you say is the biggest setback or obstacle you've overcome in your life thus far?

How did you overcome it? (What enabled you to get past it or prevented you from being blocked by it?)

If a poor past performance is seen not as a personal failure but as a learning opportunity, the setback may be turned into a comeback. Here are some notable people who turned early setbacks into successful comebacks:

- Louis Pasteur, famous bacteriologist, who failed his admission test to the University of Paris;
- Albert Einstein, Nobel Prize–winning physicist, who failed math in elementary school;
- Thomas Edison, prolific inventor, who was once expelled from school as "uneducable";
- Johnny Unitas, Hall of Fame football player, who was cut twice from professional football teams early in his career.

In response to their early setbacks, these successful professionals didn't get discouraged. Getting mad or sad about a setback is likely to make you stressed or depressed and leave you focused on a past event that you can no longer control. By reacting optimistically to a poor performance and using the results as feedback to improve your future performance, you gain control of it. You put yourself in the position to bounce back from the setback and turn a liability into an opportunity.

> **Remember**
> *Don't let past mistakes bring you down emotionally or motivationally, but don't ignore or neglect them. Instead, inspect them, reflect on them, and correct them so that they don't happen again.*

Maintain positive expectations. Just as your thoughts in reaction to something that's already taken place can affect your motivation, thoughts about what you expect to happen next can affect what will occur. Your expectations of things to come can be either positive or negative. For example, before a test you could think, "I'm poised, confident, and ready to do it." Or you could think, "I know I'm going to fail this test; I just know it."

Expectations can lead to what sociologists and psychologists have called a self-fulfilling prophecy—a positive or negative expectation leads you to act in a way that is consistent with your expectation, which, in turn, makes your expectation come true. For instance, if you expect you're going to fail an exam ("What's the use? I'm going to fail anyway."), you're less likely to put as much effort into studying for the test. During the test, your negative expectation is likely to reduce your test confidence and elevate you test anxiety; for example, if you experience difficulty with the first item on a test, you may get anxious and begin to think you're going to have difficulty with all remaining items and flunk the entire exam. All of this negative thinking is likely to increase the probability that your expectation of doing poorly on the exam will become a reality.

Reflection **4.9**

Would you consider yourself to be an optimist or a pessimist?

In what situations are you more likely to think optimistically and pessimistically?

Why?

"What happens is not as important as how you react to what happens."
—Thaddeus Golas, *Lazy Man's Guide to Enlightenment*

"When written in Chinese, the word 'crisis' is composed of two characters. One represents danger, and the other represents opportunity."
—John F. Kennedy, 35th president of the United States

"Whether you think you can or you can't, you're right."
—Henry Ford, founder of Ford Motor Company

"A pessimist sees the difficulty in every opportunity; an optimist sees the opportunity in every difficulty."

—Winston Churchill

In contrast, positive expectations can lead to a positive self-fulfilling prophecy: If you expect to do well on an exam, you're more likely to demonstrate higher levels of effort, confidence, and concentration, all of which combine to increase the likelihood that you'll earn a higher test grade. Research shows that learning and practicing positive self-talk serves to promote hope—belief in one's ability to reach goals and the ability to actually reach them (Snyder, 1994).

Keep your eye on the prize. Don't lose sight of the long-term consequences of your short-term choices and decisions. Long-range thinking is the key to reaching long-range goals. Unfortunately, however, humans are often more motivated by short-range thinking because it produces quicker results and more immediate gratification. It's more convenient and tempting to think in the short term ("I like it. I want it. I want it now."). Many years of research reveal that the later consequences follow a decision, the less likely people are to consider those consequences of their decisions (Ainslie, 1975; Elster & Lowenstein, 1992; Goldstein & Hogarth, 1997). For example, choosing to do what you feel like doing instead of doing work that needs to be done is why so many people procrastinate, and choosing to use a credit card to get something now instead of saving money to buy it later is why so many people pile up credit-card debt.

"You've got to think about 'big things' while you're doing small things, so that all the small things go in the right direction."

—Alvin Toffler, American futurologist and author who predicted the future effects of technology on our society

To be successful in the long run, you need to keep your focus on the big picture—your dream. At the same time, you need to focus on the details—the due dates, to-do lists, and day-to-day duties that require perspiration but keep you on track and going in the right direction.

Setting meaningful life goals and steadily progressing toward them require two focus points. One involves a narrow-focus lens that allows you to focus in on the details immediately in front of you. The other is a wide-angle lens that gives you a big-picture view of what's further ahead of you (your long-range goal). Success involves your ability to see and make connections between small, short-term chores and challenges (e.g., completing an assignment that's due next week) and the large, long-range picture (e.g., college graduation and a successful future). Thus, you need to switch back and forth from the wide-angle lens that gives you a vision of the bigger, more distant picture (your dream) to a narrow-focus lens that shifts your attention to completing the smaller tasks immediately ahead of you and keeping on the path to your dream.

"Whoever wants to reach a distant goal must take many small steps."

—Helmut Schmidt, former chancellor of West Germany

Author's Experience

When I was coaching a youth soccer team, I noticed that many of the less successful players tended to make one of two mistakes when they were trying to move with the ball. Some spent too much time looking down, focusing on the ball at their feet, and trying to be sure that they did not lose control of it. By not lifting their heads and looking ahead periodically, they often missed open territory, open teammates, or an open goal. Other unsuccessful players made the opposite mistake: They spent too much time with their heads up, trying to see where they were headed. By not looking down at the ball immediately in front of them, they often lost control of the ball, moved ahead without it, or sometimes stumbled over it and fell flat on their faces. The successful soccer players on the team developed the habit of shifting their focus between looking down to maintain control of the ball immediately in front of them and lifting their eyes to see where they were headed.

The more I thought about how the successful players alternated between handling the ball in front of them and viewing the goal farther ahead, it struck me that this was a metaphor for success in life. Successful people alternate between both of these perspectives so that they don't lose sight of how the short-range tasks immediately in front of them connect with the long-range goal that's far ahead of them.

Joe Cuseo

Remember

Keep your future dreams and current tasks in clear focus. Integrating these two perspectives will produce an image that provides you with the inspiration to complete your college education and the determination to complete your day-to-day tasks.

The Importance of Personal Character

Reaching your goals depends on acquiring and using effective strategies, but it takes something more. Ultimately, success emerges from the inside out; it flows from positive qualities or attributes found within you, which, collectively, form your personal character.

We become effective and successful human beings when our actions and deeds become a natural extension of who we are and how we live. At first, developing the habits associated with achieving success and leading a productive life may require substantial effort and intense concentration because these behaviors may be new to us. However, if these actions occur consistently enough, they're transformed into natural habits.

When you engage in effective habits regularly, they become virtues. A virtue may be defined as a characteristic or trait that is valued as good or admirable, and someone who possesses a collection of important virtues is said to be a person of character (Peterson & Seligman, 2004). There are three key character traits or virtues that typify highly motivated people:

1. Drive
2. Discipline
3. Determination

Drive

Drive is the force within you that supplies you with the energy needed to initiate action. Much like shifting into the drive gear is necessary to move your car forward, it takes personal drive to move forward and toward your goals. People with drive are not just dreamers: they are also doers. They take the action needed to convert their dreams into reality; they hustle—they go all out and give it their all, all of the time, to achieve their goals. College students with drive approach college with passion and enthusiasm. They don't hold back and work halfheartedly; they give 100 percent by putting their whole heart and soul into it. Studies show that individuals with dedication—who are deeply committed to what they do—are more likely to report that they are healthy and happy (Csikszentmihalyi, 1990; Maddi, 2002; Myers, 1993).

Discipline

Discipline includes such positive qualities as commitment, devotion, and dedication. These personal qualities enable us to keep going and moving toward our long-range goals over an extended period of time. Successful people think big but start small; they take all the small steps and diligently do all the little things that need to be done, which, in the long run, add up to a big accomplishment—achievement of their long-range goal.

People who are self-disciplined accept the day-to-day sweat, toil, and perspiration needed to attain their long-term aspirations. They're willing to tolerate short-term strain or pain for long-term gain. They have the self-control and self-restraint

"If you do not find it within yourself, where will you go to get it?"

—Zen saying (Zen is a branch of Buddhism that emphasizes seeing deeply into the nature of things and ongoing self-awareness)

"We are what we repeatedly do. Excellence, then, is not an act, but a habit."

—Aristotle, ancient Greek philosopher

"Sow an act and you reap a habit; sow a habit and you reap a character; sow a character and you reap a destiny."

—Frances E. Willard, 19th-century American educator and women's rights activist

Student *Perspective*

"Why is it so hard when I *have* to do something and so easy when I *want* to do something?"

—First-year college student

"Self-discipline is the ability to make yourself do the thing you have to do, when it ought be done, whether you like it or not."

—Thomas Henry Huxley, 19th-century English biologist

Remember

Sometimes you've got to do what you have to do in order to get to do what you want to do.

needed to resist the impulse for instant gratification or the temptation to do what they feel like doing instead of what they need to do. They're willing to sacrifice their immediate needs and desires in the short run to do what is necessary to put them where they want to be in the long run.

Reflection 4.10

Think about something that you do with drive, effort, and intensity. What thoughts, attitudes, and behaviors do you display when you do it?

Do you see ways in which you could apply the same approach to achieving your goals in college?

"I long to accomplish some great and noble task, but it is my chief duty to accomplish small tasks as if they were great and noble."

—Helen Keller, seeing- and hearing-impaired author and activist for the rights of women and the handicapped

The ability to delay short-term (and shortsighted) gratification is a distinctively human characteristic that differentiates people from other animals. As you can see in Figure 4.1, the upper frontal part of the brain that's responsible for long-range planning and controlling emotions and impulses is much larger in humans than it is in one of the most intelligent and humanlike animals, the chimpanzee.

FIGURE 4.1

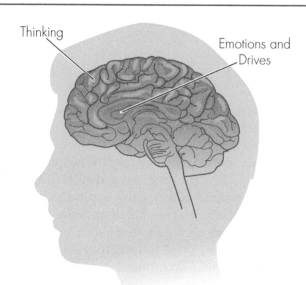

Thinking

Emotions and Drives

© Kendall Hunt

The part of the brain responsible for long-range planning and controlling emotions and impulses is much larger in humans than in other animals, including the highly intelligent chimpanzee.

Where Thoughts, Emotions, and Drives Are Experienced in the Brain

Author's Experience When I entered college in the mid-1970s, I was a first-generation student from an extremely impoverished background. Not only did I have to work to pay for part of my education, but I also needed to assist my family financially. I stocked grocery store shelves at night during the week and waited tables at a local country club on the weekends. Managing my life, time, school, and work required full-time effort. However, I always understood that my purpose was to graduate from college and all of my other efforts supported that goal. Thus, I went to class and arrived on time even when I did not feel like going to class. One of my greatest successes in life was to keep my mind and body focused on the ultimate prize of getting a college education. That success has paid off many times over.

— *Aaron Thompson*

© Kendall Hunt Publishing Company

> **Remember**
> *Sacrifices made for a short time can bring benefits that last a lifetime.*

The ability to postpone immediate wants or needs is a key characteristic of self-discipline.

Determination

People who are determined pursue their goals with a relentless tenacity. They have the fortitude to persist in the face of frustration and the resiliency to bounce back after setbacks. If they encounter something on the road to their goal that's hard to do, they work harder and longer to do it. When they encounter a major bump or barrier, they don't let it stand in their way by giving up or giving in; instead, they dig deeper and keep going.

People with determination are also more likely to seek out challenges. Research indicates that people who continue to pursue opportunities for personal growth and self-development throughout life are more likely to report feeling happy and healthy (Maddi, 2002; Myers, 1993). Rather than remaining stagnant and simply doing what's safe, secure, or easy, they stay hungry and display an ongoing commitment to personal growth and development; they keep striving and driving to be the best they can possibly be in all aspects of life.

"SUCCESS is peace of mind which is a direct result of self-satisfaction in knowing you made the effort to become the best that you are capable of becoming."

—John Wooden, college basketball coach and creator of the "Pyramid of Success"

Studies of highly successful people, whether they are scientists, musicians, writers, chess masters, or basketball stars, consistently show that achieving high levels of skill and success requires dedicated practice (Levitin, 2006). This is true even of people whose success is thought to be due to natural gifts or talents. For example, during the Beatles' first four years as a band and before they burst into musical stardom, they performed live an estimated 1,200 times, and many of these performances lasted five or more hours a night. They performed (practiced) for more hours during those first four years than most bands perform during their entire careers. Similarly, before Bill Gates became a computer software giant and creator of Microsoft, he logged almost 1,600 hours of computer time during one seven-month period alone, averaging eight hours a day, seven days a week (Gladwell, 2008). What these extraordinary success stories show is that success takes dedication to putting in the time and practice to be successful. Reaching long-range goals means making small steps; they aren't achieved in one quick, quantum leap; it requires patience, persistence, and practice.

In addition to drive, discipline, and determination, three other character traits or virtues typify successful people:

> "As gold which he cannot spend will make no man rich, so knowledge which he cannot apply will make no man wise."
>
> —Dr. Samuel Johnson, famous English literary figure and original author of the *Dictionary of the English Language* (1747)

1. Wisdom
2. Integrity
3. Civility

Wisdom

> "Be as smart as you can, but remember that it is always better to be wise than smart."
>
> —Alan Alda, visiting professor at the State University of New York at Stony Brook and six-time Emmy Award and Golden Globe Award winner, best known for his role as Hawkeye Pierce in the TV series *M*A*S*H*

You demonstrate wisdom when you use the knowledge you acquire to guide you toward becoming an effective and successful human being (Staudinger & Baltes, 1994). For instance, if you apply the knowledge you've acquired in this chapter about goal setting and motivation to guide your behavior in college and beyond, you are exhibiting wisdom.

Reflection **4.11**

Thus far in your college experience, which of the following four principles of success have you put into practice most effectively? (Circle one.)

active involvement   resourcefulness   collaboration   reflection

Which of the four principles do you think will be the most difficult for you to put into practice? (Circle one.)

active involvement   resourcefulness   collaboration   reflection

Why?

Integrity

The word *integrity* comes from the same root as the word integrate, which captures a key characteristic of people with integrity: their outer selves are integrated or in harmony with their inner selves. "Outer-directed" people decide on their personal standards of conduct by looking outward to see what others are doing (Riesman, Glazer,

& Denney, 2001). In contrast, individuals with integrity are "inner-directed"—their actions reflect their inner qualities and are guided by their consciences.

People of character are not only wise, they're ethical. They don't pursue success at any ethical cost. They have a strong set of personal values that steer them in the right moral direction. Besides doing things effectively and successfully, they do what's good and right. For instance, college students with integrity don't cheat and then rationalize that their cheating is acceptable because "others are doing it." They don't look to other people to determine their goals and values, and they don't conform to the norm if the norm is wrong; instead, they look inward, use their consciences as their guides, and self-determine their goals.

Civility

People of character are personally and socially responsible. They model what it means to live in a civilized community by demonstrating civility—they respect the rights of other members of their community, including members of their college community. In exercising their own rights and freedoms, they don't step (or stomp) on the rights and freedoms of others. They treat other members of their community in a sensitive and courteous manner and are willing to confront others who violate the rights of their fellow citizens. They are model citizens whose actions visibly demonstrate to others that they oppose any attempt to disrespect or interfere with the rights of fellow members of their community.

Student Perspective

"To achieve success through deceitful actions is not success at all. In life, credibility is more important than credentials, and if honesty is not valued personally, others will not value you. Lack of self-respect results in lack of respect from others."

—First-year college student's reflection on an academic integrity violation

"There is no pillow as soft as a clear conscience."

—French proverb

"Our character is what we do when we think no one is looking."

—Henry David Thoreau, American philosopher and lifelong abolitionist who championed the human spirit over materialism and conformity

Snapshot Summary

4.2

Violating Civility: Insensitive Use of Personal Technology in the Classroom

Behavior that interferes with the rights of others to learn or teach in the college classroom represents a violation of civility. Listed below are behaviors illustrating classroom incivility that involve student use of personal technology. These behaviors are becoming more common in college, as is the anger of college instructors and college students who witness them. Be sure to avoid them.

Using Cell Phones

Keeping a cell phone on in class is a clear example of classroom incivility, because if it rings, it will interfere with the right of others to learn. In a study of college students who were exposed to a cell phone ringing during a class session and were later tested for their recall of information presented in class, they scored approximately 25 percent worse when attempting to recall information that was presented at the time a cell phone rang. This attention loss occurred even if the material was covered by the professor prior to the cell phone ringing and if it was projected on a slide during the call. The study also showed that classmates are further distracted when classmates frantically search through handbags or pockets to find and silence a ringing (or vibrating) phone (Shelton, Elliot, Eaves, & Exner, 2009). These findings clearly suggest that the civil thing to do is turn your cell phone off before entering the classroom, or keep it out of the classroom altogether.

"The right to do something does not mean that doing it is right."

—William Safire, American author, journalist, and presidential speechwriter

Text Messaging

Answering a cell phone during class represents a violation of civility because it interferes with the learning of other members of the classroom community, and so does text messaging. It can distract or disturb classmates who see you messaging instead of listening and learning. It's also discourteous or disrespectful to instructors when you put your head down and turn your attention away from them while they're trying to speak to the class.

Reflection 4.12

Have you observed an example of incivility that you thought was exceptionally admirable or particularly despicable? What was the situation and what uncivil behavior was displayed?

Summary and Conclusion

Goal setting is the key to igniting motivation; maintaining motivation after it has been ignited requires use of effective self-motivational strategies, such as:

- Visualizing reaching your long-range goals;
- Putting goals in writing;
- Creating a visual map of your goals;
- Keeping a record of your progress;
- Rewarding yourself for progress toward long-range goals;
- Converting setbacks into comebacks by using positive self-talk and maintaining positive expectations; and
- Keeping your eye on the long-term consequences of your short-term choices and decisions.

Remember

Success isn't a short-range goal: it's not a sprint but a long-distance run that takes patience and perseverance to complete. What matters most is not how fast you start but where you finish. Goal setting will get you going and motivation will keep you going until you cross the finish line.

Successfully setting and reaching goals also depends on personal character. The following character traits or virtues typify highly motivated and successful people:

- **Drive.** The internal force that provides energy to overcome inertia and initiate action.
- **Discipline.** Commitment, devotion, and dedication that enable you to sustain your effort over time.
- **Determination.** The capacity to relentlessly pursue your goals, persist in the face of frustration, and bounce back after any setback.
- **Wisdom.** Using knowledge to guide effective behavior and action.
- **Integrity.** Doing what's right, good, or ethical.
- **Civility.** Respecting the rights of other members of the community.

Learning More through the World Wide Web

Internet-Based Resources for Further Information on Liberal Arts Education

For additional information related to the ideas discussed in this chapter, we recommend the following Web sites:

Goal Setting:
www.siue.edu/SPIN/activity.html

Self-Motivational Strategies:
www.selfmotivationstrategies.com

Developing Personal Character: Who's Watching? Character and Integrity in the 21st Century:
www.calea.org/calea-update-magazine/issue-100who-s-watching-character-and-integrity-21st-century

Chapter 4 Exercises

4.1 Prioritizing Important Life Goals

Consider the following life goals. Rank them in the order of their priority for you (1 = highest, 5 = lowest).

___ Emotional well-being

___ Spiritual growth

___ Physical health

___ Social relationships

___ Rewarding career

Self-Assessment Questions

1. What were the primary reasons behind your first- and last-ranked choices?
2. Have you established any short- or mid-range goals for reaching your highest-ranked choice? If yes, what are they? If no, what could they be?

4.2 Setting Goals for Reducing the Gap between Your Ideal Future and Your Current Reality

Think of an aspect of your life where there is a gap between what you hoped it would be (the ideal) and what it is (the reality). On the lines that follow, identify goals you could pursue to reduce this gap.

Long-range goal: _____

Mid-range goal: _____

Short-range goal: _____

Use the form that follows to identify strategies for reaching each of these three goals. Consider the following areas for each goal:

* Actions to be taken:
* Available resources:
* Possible roadblocks:
* Potential solutions to roadblocks:

Long-range goal: _____

* Actions to be taken:
* Available resources:
* Possible roadblocks:
* Potential solutions to roadblocks:

Mid-range goal: _____

* Actions to be taken:
* Available resources:
* Possible roadblocks:
* Potential solutions to roadblocks:

Short-range goal: _____

- Actions to be taken:
- Available resources:
- Possible roadblocks:
- Potential solutions to roadblocks:

4.3 Converting Setbacks into Comebacks: Transforming Pessimism into Optimism through Positive Self-Talk

In *Hamlet*, Shakespeare wrote, "There is nothing good or bad, but thinking makes it so." His point was that experiences have the potential to be positive or negative, depending on how people interpret them and react to them.

Listed here is a series of statements representing negative, motivation-destroying interpretations and reactions to a situation or experience:

1. "I'm just not good at this."
2. "There's nothing I can do about it."
3. "Nothing is going to change."
4. "This always happens to me."
5. "Everybody is going to think I'm a loser."

For each of the preceding statements, replace the negative statement with a statement that represents a more positive, self-motivating interpretation or reaction.

No Goals, No Direction

Amy Aimless decided to go to college because it seemed like that was what she was expected to do. All of her closest friends were going and her parents had talked to her about going to college as long as she could remember.

Now that she's in her first term, Amy isn't sure she made the right decision. She has no educational or career goals, nor does she have any idea about what her major might be. None of the subjects she took in high school and none of the courses she's taking in her first term of college have really sparked her interest. Since she has no goals or sense of purpose, she's beginning to think that being in college is a waste of time and money, so she's considering withdrawing at the end of her first term.

Reflection and Discussion Questions

1. What advice would you give Amy about whether she should remain in college or withdraw?

2. What suggestion would you have for Amy that might help her find some sense of educational purpose or direction?

3. How could you counter Amy's claim that no subjects interest her as possible college majors?

4. Would you agree that Amy is currently wasting her time and her parents' money? Why?

5. Would you agree that Amy shouldn't have begun college in the first place? Why?

Mary Jackson

Credit: NASA

Mary Jackson earned bachelors' degrees in mathematics and physical science from Hampton Institute—now Hampton University—in 1942. She was a member of Alpha Kappa Alpha and a noted student leader.

Jackson spent 34 years at NASA, most of them as an engineer in several divisions. She attained the most senior title in the engineering department. Serving as both the Federal Women's Program Manager in the Office of Equal Opportunity Programs and as the Affirmative Action Program Manager, she strived to shape the career paths of female NASA employees holding STEM positions. She continued to work at NASA until her retirement in 1985.

Jackson was married with two children and died on February 11, 2005, at age 83.

The 2016 film *Hidden Figures* depicts her career at NASA along with that of Katherine Johnson and Dorothy Vaughan, with a particular focus on their Project Mercury efforts during the Space Race.

Actress Janelle Monáe portrays Jackson in the film.

CHAPTER 5
Time Management

*"Don't spend time; it's very precious -
utilize it constructively."*

—Amit Abraham

Upon completion of this chapter, you will be able to:

- **Identify** elements of a comprehensive time management plan
- **Develop** strategies for managing time
- **Avoid** procrastination
- **Develop** a personal time management plan

Time Management

Preventing Procrastination and Promoting Self-Discipline

ACTIVATE YOUR THINKING | *Reflection* **5.1** | **LEARNING GOAL**

Complete the following sentence with the first thought that comes to your mind:

For me, time is . . .

> **LEARNING GOAL**
>
> To help you appreciate the significance of managing time and supply you with a powerful set of time-management strategies that can be used to promote your success in college and beyond.

The Importance of Time Management

Reaching goals requires managing time because it takes time to successfully complete the series of steps that lead to those goals. For first-year college students, time management is especially essential for achieving their goals because the beginning of college brings with it the challenge of independent living and managing their newfound freedom. Even for first-year students who have lived on their own for some time, managing time remains a crucial skill because they will be juggling multiple responsibilities, including school, family, and work.

In addition, the academic calendar and class scheduling patterns in college differ radically from high school. There's less "seat time" in class each week and more "free time" outside of class, which leaves you with a lot more personal time to manage. Your time is not as closely monitored by school authorities or family members, and you are expected to do more academic work on your own outside of class. Personal time-management skills grow in importance when one's time is less structured and controlled by others, leaving the individual with more decision-making power about how to spend personal time. Thus, it's not surprising that research shows the ability to manage time effectively plays a crucial role in college success (Erickson, Peters, & Strommer, 2006).

Simply stated, college students who have difficulty managing their time have difficulty managing college. In one study, college sophomores who had an outstanding first year (both academically and personally) were compared to another group of sophomores who struggled during the prior year. Interviews conducted with these students revealed one key difference between the two groups: The sophomores who experienced a successful first year repeatedly brought up the topic of time during the interviews. The successful students said they had to think carefully about how they spent their time and that they needed to budget their time because it was a scarce resource. In contrast, the sophomores who experienced difficulty in their first year of

Student *Perspective*

> "The major difference [between high school and college] is time. You have so much free time on your hands that you don't know what to do for most of the time."
>
> —First-year college student (Erickson & Strommer, 1991)

From *Thriving in College and Beyond: Research-Based Strategies for Academic Success and Personal Development* by Cuseo et al. Copyright © 2013 by Kendall Hunt Publishing Company. Reprinted by permission.

Student
Perspective

"I cannot stress enough that you need to intelligently budget your time."

—Advice to new college students from a first-year student

college hardly talked about the topic of time during their interviews, even when they were specifically asked about it (Light, 2001).

Studies also indicate that managing time plays a pivotal role in the lives of working adults. Setting priorities and balancing multiple responsibilities (e.g., work and family) that compete for limited time and energy can be a stressful juggling act for people of all ages (Harriott & Ferrari, 1996). Thus, good time management serves as good stress management.

For these reasons, time management should be viewed not only as a college-success strategy but also as a life-management and life-success skill. Studies show that people who manage their time well report they are more in control of their lives and are happier (Myers, 1993; 2000). In short, when you gain greater control of your time, you become more satisfied with your life.

Author's
Experience   I started the process of earning my doctorate a little later in life than other students. I was a married father with a preschool daughter (Sara). Since my wife left for work early in the morning, it was always my duty to get up and get Sara's day going in the right direction. In addition, I had to do the same for me—which was often harder than doing it for my daughter. Three days of my week were spent on campus, in class or in the library. (We did not have quick access to research on home computers then as you do now.) The other two days of the workweek and the weekend were spent on household chores, family time, and studying.

I knew that if I was going to have any chance of finishing my Ph.D. in a reasonable amount of time and have a decent family life, I had to adopt an effective schedule for managing my time. Each day of the week, I held to a strict routine. I got up in the morning, drank coffee while reading the paper, took a shower, got Sara ready for school, and took her to school. Once I returned home, I put a load of laundry in the washer, studied, wrote, and spent time concentrating on what I needed to do to be successful from 8:30 a.m. to 12:00 p.m. every day. At lunch, I had a pastrami and cheese sandwich and a soft drink while rewarding myself by watching *Perry Mason* reruns until 1:00 p.m. I then continued to study until it was time to pick up Sara from school. Each night, I spent time with my wife and daughter and prepared for the next day. I lived a life that had a preset schedule. By following that schedule, I was able to successfully complete my doctorate in a decent amount of time while giving my family the time they needed. (By the way, I still watch *Perry Mason* reruns.)

Aaron Thompson

Strategies for Managing Time

Effective time management involves three key mental processes:

1. **Analysis.** Breaking down time into specific segments and work into smaller tasks;
2. **Itemizing.** Identifying all key tasks that need to be done and by what dates;
3. **Prioritizing.** Organizing and attacking tasks in order of their importance.

The following steps can help you apply these skills to find more time in your schedule and use this time more productively.

1. **Break time down into smaller units to become more aware about your time is being spent.** Have you ever asked yourself, "Where did all the time go?" or told yourself, "I just can't seem to find the time"? One way to find out where your time went is by taking a time inventory. Conduct a time analysis by tracking your time and recording what you do and when you do it. By mapping out how you spend time, you become more aware of how much total time you actually have and where it goes, including patches of wasted time during which you get little or nothing accomplished. You just need to do this time analysis for more than a week or two to see where your time is going and to get started on strategies for using your time more productively.

Reflection 5.2

Do you have time gaps between your classes this term? If you do, what have you been doing during those "free" periods between classes?

What would you say is your greatest time waster?

Do you see a need to stop or eliminate it?

If you don't, why not? If yes, what could you do to convert your wasted time into productive time?

2. **Identify the key tasks you need to accomplish and when you need to accomplish them.** People make lists to be sure they don't forget items they need from the grocery store or people they want to be sure are invited to a party. You can use the same list-making strategy for work tasks so that you don't forget to do them or forget to do them on time. Studies of effective people show that they are list makers; they write out lists not only for grocery items and wedding invitations, but also for things they want to accomplish each day (Covey, 2004).

    You can itemize the tasks on your lists by using the following time-management tools:

    - **Personal digital assistant (PDA) or cell phone.** You can use these to do a lot more than check social networking sites and send and receive text messages. Use the calendar tools in these devices to record due dates and set up the alert functions to remind you of these deadlines. Many PDAs and smartphones will also allow you to set up task or "to-do" lists and to set priorities for each item you enter.

    - **Small, portable planner.** List all your major assignments and exams for the term, along with their due dates. Putting all work tasks from different courses into one place makes it easier to keep track of what you have to do and when you have to do it.

    - **Large, stable calendar.** In the calendar's date boxes, record your major assignments for the academic term and when they are due. Place the calendar in a position or location where it's in full view and you can't help but see it every day (e.g., on your bedroom or refrigerator door). If you regularly and literally "look" at the things you have to do, you're less likely to "overlook" them, forget about them, or subconsciously push them out of your mind because you don't really want to do them.

© Gary Woodward, 2013. Under license from Shutterstock, Inc.

Using a personal planner is an effective way to itemize your academic commitments.

3. **Rank your tasks in order of their importance.** Once you've itemized your work by listing all tasks you need to do, prioritize them—determine the order in which you will do them. Prioritizing basically involves ranking your tasks in terms of their importance, with the highest-ranked tasks appearing at the top of your list to ensure that they are tackled first. How do you determine which tasks are most important and should be ranked highest? Two criteria or standards of judgment can be used to help determine which tasks should be your highest priorities:

    - **Urgency.** Tasks that are closest to their deadlines or due dates should receive high priority. For example, finishing an assignment that's due tomorrow should receive higher priority than starting an assignment that's due next month.

"Things that matter most
must never be at the mercy of
things that matter least."

— Johann Wolfgang von Goethe,
German poet, dramatist, and author
of the epic *Faust*

- **Gravity.** Tasks that carry the heaviest weight (count the most) should receive highest priority. For example, if an assignment worth 100 points and another worth 10 points are due at the same time, the 100-point task should receive higher priority. Just like investing money, you want to invest your time in tasks that yield the greatest dividends or payoff.

Author's Experience

My mom was the person who ensured I got up for school on time. Once I got to school, the bell would ring to let me know to move on to the next class. When I returned home, I had to do my homework and chores. My daily and weekly schedules were dictated by others.

When I entered college, I quickly realized that I needed to develop my own system for being organized, focused, and productive without the assistance of my mother. Since I came from a modest background, I had to work my way through college. Juggling schedules became an art and science for me. I knew the things that I could not miss, such as work and school, and the things I could miss—TV and girls. (OK, TV, but not girls.)

After college, I spent 10 years in business—a world where I was measured by being on time and a productive "bottom line." It was during this time that I discovered a scheduling book. When I became a professor, I had other mechanisms to make sure I did what I needed to do when I needed to do it. This was largely based on when my classes were offered. Other time was dedicated to working out and spending time with my family. Now, as an administrator, I have an assistant who keeps my schedule for me. She tells me where I am going, how long I should be there, and what I need to accomplish while I am there. Unless you take your parents with you or have the luxury of a personal assistant, it's important to determine which activities are required and to allow time in your schedule for fun. Use a planner!

— *Aaron Thompson*

Reflection 5.3

Do you have a calendar for the current academic term that you carry with you? What about an up-to-date to-do list?

If yes to either, why? If no to either, why not?

If you carry neither a calendar nor a to-do list, why do you think you don't?

Student Perspective

"I like to get rid of my stress by doing what I have to do first, like if it's a paper."

—First-year college student

One strategy for prioritizing your tasks is to divide them into A, B, and C lists (Lakein, 1973; Morgenstern, 2004). The A list is for *essential* tasks—what you *must* do now. The B list is for *important* tasks—what you *should* do soon. Finally, the C list is for *optional* tasks—what you *could* or *might* do if there is time remaining after you've completed the tasks on the A and B lists. Organizing your tasks in this fashion can help you decide how to divide your labor in a way that ensures you put first things first. Don't waste time doing unimportant things to deceive yourself into thinking that you're keeping busy and getting things done; in reality, all you're doing is taking time (and your mind) away from the more important things you should be doing.

At first glance, itemizing and prioritizing may appear to be rather boring chores. However, if you look at these mental tasks carefully, they require higher-level thinking skills, such as:

1. **Analysis.** Dividing time into component elements or segments and breaking down work into specific tasks;

2. **Evaluation.** Critically evaluating the relative importance or value of tasks; and
3. **Synthesis.** Organizing individual tasks into classes or categories based on their level of priority.

> **Remember**
>
> *Developing self-awareness about how your time is spent is more than a brainless, clerical activity. When it's done with thoughtful reflection, it becomes an exercise in higher-level thinking. It's also a good values-clarification exercise because it makes us aware of whether we're actually spending our time on those things that we say we really value.*

Develop a Time-Management Plan

Humans are creatures of habit. Routines help you organize and gain control of your lives. Doing things by design, rather than leaving them to chance or accident, is the first step toward making things happen for you rather than allowing them to happen. By developing an intentional plan for how you're going to spend your time, you're developing a plan to gain greater control of your life.

Don't buy into the myth that you don't have time to plan because it takes too much time that could be spent getting started and getting things done. Time-management experts estimate that the amount of time you spend planning your work reduces your total work time by a factor of three (Goldsmith, 2010; Lakein, 1973). In other words, for every one unit of time you spend planning, you save three units of work time. Thus, five minutes of planning time will typically save you 15 minutes of total work time, and 10 minutes of planning time will save you 30 minutes of work time. You save work time by engaging in planning time because you end up with a clearer understanding of what needs to be done and the order of steps you need to take to get it done. This clearer sense of direction reduces the likelihood of losing time to "false starts"—having to restart your work because you started off in the wrong direction. If you have no plan of attack, you're more likely to go off track; when you discover this at some point after you've started, you're then forced to retreat and start all over again.

As the proverb goes, "A stitch in time saves nine." Planning your time represents the "stitch" (unit of time) that saves you nine additional stitches (units of time). Similar to successful chess players, successful time managers plan ahead and anticipate their next moves.

"Time = Life. Therefore waste your time and waste your life, or master your time and master your life."

—Alan Lakein, international expert on time management and author of the bestselling book *How to Get Control of Your Time and Your Life*

"Failing to plan is planning to fail."

—Alan Lakein, author of *How to Get Control of Your Time and Your Life*

Elements of a Comprehensive Time-Management Plan

Once you've accepted the notion that taking the time to plan your time saves you time in the long run, you're ready to design a time-management plan. The following are elements of a comprehensive, well-designed plan for managing time.

1. **A good time-management plan includes short, mid- and long-range time frames.** For instance, a good academic time-management plan for the term should include:
   - A *long-range* plan for the entire term that identifies deadline dates for reports and papers that are due toward the end of the term;
   - A *mid-range* plan for the upcoming month and week; and
   - A *short-range* plan for the following day.

Here's how you can put this three-stage plan into action this term:

- Review the *course syllabus (course outline)* for each class you are enrolled in this term, and highlight all major exams, tests, quizzes, assignments, and papers and the dates on which they are due.

Remember

College professors are more likely than high school teachers to expect you to rely on your course syllabus to keep track of what you have to do and when you have to do it.

- Obtain a *large calendar* for the academic term (available at your campus bookstore or learning center) and record all your exams, assignments, and so on, for all your courses in the calendar boxes that represent their due dates. To fit this information within the calendar boxes, use creative abbreviations to represent different tasks, such as E for exam and TP for term paper (not toilet paper). When you're done, you'll have a centralized chart or map of deadline dates and a potential master plan for the entire term. Get in the habit of not only doing short-range academic planning and calendaring for the upcoming day or week, but long-range planning for the academic semester or term.
- Activate the calendar and task lists functions on your PDA or cell phone. Enter your schedule, important dates, deadlines, and set alert reminders. Since you carry your PDA or cell phone with you regularly, you will always have this information at your fingertips.

Work backward from this long-range plan to:

- Plan your week.
  a. Make a map of your *weekly schedule* that includes times during the week when you are in class, when you typically eat and sleep, and if you are employed, when you work.
  b. If you are a full-time college student, find *at least 25 total hours per week* when you can do academic work outside the classroom. (These 25 hours can be pieced together in any way you like, including time between daytime classes and work commitments, evening time, and weekend time.) When adding these 25 hours to the time you spend in class each week, you will end up with a 40-hour workweek, similar to any full-time job. If you are a part-time student, you should plan on spending at least two hours on academic work outside of class for every hour that you're in class.
  c. Make good use of your *free time between classes* by working on assignments and studying in advance for upcoming exams. See **Do It Now! 5.1** for a summary of how you can use your out-of-class time to improve your academic performance and course grades.

- Plan your day.
  a. Make a *daily to-do list.*

Remember

If you write it out, you're less likely to block it out and forget about it.

Student *Perspective*

"The amount of free time you have in college is much more than in high school. Always have a weekly study schedule to go by. Otherwise, time slips away and you will not be able to account for it."

—Advice to new college students from a first-year student (Rhoads, 2005)

"In high school we were given a homework assignment every day. Now we have a large task assigned to be done at a certain time. No one tells [us] when to start or what to do each day."

—First-year college student (Rhoads, 2005)

b.   Attack daily tasks in *priority order*.

Remember

"First things first." Plan your work by placing the most important and most urgent tasks at the top of your list, and work your plan by attacking tasks in the order in which you have listed them.

- Carry a *small calendar, planner, or appointment book* at all times. This will enable you to record appointments that you may make on the run during the day and will allow you to jot down creative ideas or memories of things you need to do—which can sometimes pop into your mind at the most unexpected times.
- Take *portable work* with you during the day that you can carry with you and do in any place at any time. This will enable you to take advantage of "dead time" during the day. For example, carry material with you that you can read while sitting and waiting for appointments or transportation, allowing you to resurrect this dead time and convert it to "live" work time. (Not only is this a good time-management strategy, it's a good stress-management strategy because it puts you in control of "wait time," enabling you use it to save time later and reducing the likelihood that you'll feel frustrated, anxious, or bored.)
- Wear a *watch* or carry a cell phone that can accurately and instantly tell you what time it is and what date it is. You can't even begin to manage time if you don't know what time it is, and you can't plan a schedule if you don't know what date it is. (Try setting the time on your watch or cell phone slightly ahead of the actual time to help ensure that you arrive to class, work, or meetings on time.)

Reflection 5.4

Do you make a to-do list of things you need to get done each day? (Circle one.)

never   seldom   often   almost always

If you circled "never" or "seldom," why don't you?

2.   **A good time-management plan includes planning reserve time to take care of the unexpected.** Always hope for the best, but always be prepared for the worst. Your time-management plan should include a buffer zone or safety net of extra time in case you encounter unforeseen developments or unexpected emergencies. Just as you should plan to have extra funds in your account to pay for unexpected costs (e.g., an auto repair), you should plan to have extra time in your schedule for unexpected events (e.g., a random emergency).

Student Perspective

"I was constantly missing important meetings during my first few weeks because I did not keep track of the dates and times. I thought I'd be told again when the time was closer, just as had been done in high school. Something I should have done to address that would have been to keep a well-organized planner for reference."

—College sophomore (Walsh, 2005)

"Only boring people get bored."

—Graffiti appearing in a bathroom stall at the University of Iowa, circa 1977

"Always expect the unexpected."

—Margaret Thatcher, first female prime minister of England and subject of the popular movie *The Iron Lady*

Murphy's Laws:
1. Nothing is as simple as it looks.
2. Everything takes longer than it should.
3. If anything can go wrong, it will.

—Author unknown (Murphy's Laws were named after Captain Edward Murphy, naval engineer)

5.1

Making Productive Use of Free Time Outside the Classroom

Unlike in high school, homework in college often does not involve turning things in to your instructor daily or weekly. The academic work you do outside the classroom may not even be collected and graded. Instead, it is done for your own benefit to help prepare yourself for upcoming exams and major assignments (e.g., term papers or research reports). Rather than formally assigning work to you as homework, your professors expect that you will do this work on your own and without supervision. Listed below are strategies for working independently and in advance of college exams and assignments. These strategies will increase the quality of your time management in college and the quality of your academic performance.

Working Independently in Advance of Exams

Use the following strategies to use out-of-class time wisely to prepare for exams:

● **Complete reading assignments** relating to lecture topics before the topic is discussed in class. This will make lectures easier to understand and will prepare you to participate intelligently in class (e.g., ask meaningful questions of your instructor and make informed comments during class discussions).

● **Review your class notes** between class periods so that you can construct a mental bridge from one class to the next and make each upcoming lecture easier to follow. When reviewing your notes before the next class, rewrite any class notes that may be sloppily written the first time. If you find notes related to the same point all over the place, reorganize them by combining them into one set of notes. Lastly, if you find any information gaps or confusing points in your notes, seek out the course instructor or a trusted classmate to clear them up before the next class takes place.

● **Review information** you highlighted in your reading assignments to improve your retention of the information. If certain points are confusing to you, discuss

them with your course instructor during office hours or with a fellow classmate outside of class.

● **Integrate key ideas** in your class notes with information that you have highlighted in your assigned reading, which relates to the same major point or general category. In other words, put related information from your lecture notes and your reading in the same place (e.g., on the same index card).

● **Use a part-to-whole study method** whereby you study material from your class notes and assigned reading in small pieces during short, separate study sessions that take place well in advance of the exam; then make your last study session before the exam a longer review session during which you restudy all the small parts together as a whole. It's a myth that studying in advance is a waste of time because you'll forget it all anyway by test time. Information studied in advance of an exam remains in your brain and is still there when you later review it. Even if you cannot recall the previously studied information when you first start reviewing it, you will relearn it faster than you did the first time, thus proving that some memory of it was retained from your earlier study sessions.

Work Independently Well in Advance of Due Dates for Term Papers and Research Reports

Work on large, long-range assignments by breaking them into the following smaller, short-term tasks:

1. Search for and select a topic.
2. Locate sources of information on the topic.
3. Organize the information obtained from these sources into categories.
4. Develop an outline of the report's major points and the order or sequence in which you plan to discuss them.
5. Construct a first draft of the paper (and, if necessary, a second draft).
6. Write a final draft of the paper.
7. Proofread the final draft of your paper for minor mechanical mistakes, such as spelling and grammatical errors, before submitting it to your instructor.

3. **A good time-management plan should balance work and recreation.** Don't only plan work time: plan time to relax, refuel, and recharge. Your overall time-management plan shouldn't turn you into an obsessive-compulsive workaholic. Instead, it should represent a balanced blend of work and play, including activities that promote your mental and physical wellness, such as relaxation, recreation, and reflection. If your schedule makes room for the things you like to do, you're more likely do to the things you have to do. You could also arrange your schedule of work and play as a self-motivation strategy by using your play time to reward completion of your work time. A good time-management plan includes a balanced blend of time planned for both work and recreation.

Reflection 5.5

What activities do you engage in for fun or recreation?

What do you do to relax or relieve stress?

Do you build these activities into your daily or weekly schedule?

> **Remember**
>
> *A good time-management plan should help you stress less, learn more, and earn higher grades while leaving you time for other important aspects of your life. A good plan not only enables you to get your work done on time, but also enables you to attain and maintain balance in your life.*

4. **A good time-management plan has some flexibility.** Some students are immediately turned off by the idea of developing a schedule and planning their time because they feel it over-structures their lives and limits their freedom. It's only natural for you to prize your personal freedom and resist anything that appears to restrict your freedom in any way. However, a good time-management plan doesn't limit freedom: it preserves freedom by helping you get done what you must do and reserves free time to do what you want and like to do.

A good time-management plan shouldn't enslave you to a rigid work schedule. The plan should be flexible enough to allow you to occasionally bend it without breaking it. Just as work commitments and family responsibilities can crop up unexpectedly, so, too, can opportunities for fun and enjoyable activities. Your plan should allow you the freedom to modify your schedule so that you can take advantage of these enjoyable opportunities and experiences. However, you should plan to make up the work time you lost. In other words, you can borrow or trade work time for play time, but don't "steal" it; plan to pay back the work time you borrowed by substituting it for play time that was planned for another time. If you can't do something you planned to do, the next best thing is to re-plan when you'll do it.

> **Remember**
>
> *When you create a personal time-management plan, remember that it is* your *plan—you own it and you run it. It shouldn't run you.*

Student Perspective

"It is important to allow time for things you enjoy doing because this is what will keep you stable."

—Advice to new college students from a first-year student

"Some people regard discipline as a chore. For me, it is a kind of order that sets me free to fly."

—Julie Andrews, Academy Award-winning English actress who starred in the Broadway musicals *Mary Poppins* and *The Sound of Music*

Converting a Time-Management Plan into an Action Plan

Once you've planned the work, the next step is to work the plan. A good action plan is one that enables you to (1) preview what you intend to accomplish and (2) review what you actually accomplished. You can begin to implement an action plan by constructing a daily to-do list, bringing that list with you as the day begins, and checking off items on the list as you get them done throughout the day. At the end of the day, review your list and identify what was completed and what still needs to be done. The uncompleted tasks should become high priorities for the next day.

Reflection **5.6**

By the end of a typical day, how often do you find that you accomplished most of the important tasks you hoped to accomplish? (Circle one.)

never   seldom   often   almost always

Why?

At the end of the day, if you find many unchecked items remain on your daily to-do list, this may mean that you're spreading yourself too thin by trying to do too many things in a day. You may need to be more realistic about the number of items you can accomplish per day by shortening your daily to-do list.

Being unable to complete many of your intended daily tasks may also mean that you need to modify your time-management plan by adding more work time or subtracting activities that are drawing time and attention away from your work (e.g., responding to phone calls and text messages during your planned work times).

Dealing with Procrastination

Procrastination Defined

The word *procrastination* derives from two roots: *pro* (meaning "forward") plus *crastinus* (meaning "tomorrow"). As these roots suggest, procrastinators don't abide by the proverb "Why put off to tomorrow what can be done today?" Their philosophy is just the opposite: "Why do today what can be put off until tomorrow?" Adopting this philosophy promotes a perpetual pattern of postponing what needs to be done until the last possible moment, forcing a frantic rush to finish the job in time, which results in a product of poorer quality (or not finishing the product at all).

Research shows that 80–95 percent of college students procrastinate (Steel, 2007) and almost 50 percent report that they procrastinate consistently (Onwuegbuzie, 2000). Furthermore, the percentage of people reporting that they procrastinate is on the rise (Kachgal, Hansen, & Nutter, 2001).

Procrastination is such a serious issue for college students that some colleges and universities have opened "procrastination centers" to provide help exclusively for students who are experiencing problems with procrastination (Burka & Yuen, 2008).

Myths That Promote Procrastination

Before there can be any hope of putting a stop to procrastination, procrastinators need to let go of two popular myths (misconceptions) about time and performance.

"Many people take no care of their money 'til they come nearly to the end of it, and others do just the same with their time."

—Johann Wolfgang von Goethe, German poet, dramatist, and author of the epic *Faust*

Student *Perspective*

"I believe the most important aspect of college life is time management. DO NOT procrastinate because, although this is the easy thing to do at first, it will catch up with you and make your life miserable."

—Advice to new college students from a first-year student

List of Things To Do Today
1. Write Paper
2. Study for Math Test
3. Prepare Speech

List of Things Due Today
1. Turn in Paper
2. Take Math Test
3. Deliver Speech

Next time I'll start sooner!

A procrastinator's idea of planning ahead and working in advance often boils down to this scenario.

© Kendall Hunt Publishing Company

Myth 1. "I work better under pressure" (e.g., on the day or night before something is due). Procrastinators often confuse desperation with motivation. Their belief that they work better under pressure is often just a rationalization to justify or deny the reality that they *only* work when they're under pressure—that is, when they've run out of time and have no choice but to do it under the gun of the final deadline.

It's true that some people will only start to work and will work really fast when they're under pressure, but that does not mean they're working more *effectively* and producing work of better quality. Because they're playing "beat the clock," the procrastinator's focus is no longer is on doing the job *well* but is on doing the job *fast* so that it gets done before they run out of time. This typically results in a work product that turns out to be incomplete or inferior to what could have been produced if the work process began earlier.

Myth 2. "Studying in advance is a waste of time because you will forget it all by test time." The misconception that information learned early will be forgotten is commonly used to justify procrastinating with respect to preparing for upcoming exams. Studying that is distributed (spread out) over time is more effective than massed (crammed) studying. Furthermore, last-minute studying that takes place the night before exams often results in lost sleep time resulting from pulling "late-nighters" or "all-nighters." This fly-by-night strategy interferes with retention of information that has been studied and elevates test anxiety because of lost dream sleep (a.k.a. rapid eye movement, or REM) that the brain needs to store memories and manage stress (Hobson, 1988; Voelker, 2004). Research indicates that procrastinators experience higher rates of stress-related physical disorders, such as insomnia, stomach problems, colds, and flu (McCance & Pychyl, 2003).

Working under time pressure adds to performance pressure because procrastinators are left with no margin of error to correct mistakes, no time to seek help on

"Haste makes waste."
—Benjamin Franklin

© Elena Elisseeva, 2013. Under license from Shutterstock, Inc.

Although you may work quickly under pressure, you are probably not working better.

their work, and no chance to handle random catastrophes that may arise at the last minute (e.g., an attack of the flu or a family emergency).

Psychological Causes of Procrastination

Sometimes, procrastination has deeper psychological roots. People may procrastinate for reasons that do not relate directly to poor time-management habits but to emotional issues. For instance, studies show that procrastination is sometimes used as a psychological strategy to protect self-esteem. Referred to as *self-handicapping* (Rhodewalt & Vohs, 2005), this strategy is used, either consciously or unconsciously, by some procrastinators to give themselves a "handicap" or disadvantage. Thus, if their performance turns out to be less than spectacular, they can conclude (rationalize) that it was because they were performing under a handicap—lack of time rather than lack of ability (Chu & Cho, 2005).

Reflection 5.7

Do you tend to put off work for so long that getting it done turns into an emergency or panic situation?

If your answer is yes, why do you think you find yourself in this position? If your answer is no, what is it that prevents this from happening to you?

"We didn't lose the game; we just ran out of time."

—Vince Lombardi, football coach

"Procrastinators would rather be seen as lacking in effort than lacking in ability."

—Joseph Ferrari, professor of psychology and procrastination researcher

For example, if they receive a low grade on a test or paper, they can "save face" (self-esteem) by concluding that it was because they waited until the last minute and didn't put much time or effort into it. In other words, they had enough ability or intelligence to earn a high grade; they just didn't have enough time. Better yet, if they happened to luck out and get a good grade—despite doing it at the last minute—they can think it proves just how smart they are because they were able to get that good grade without putting in much time at all! Thus, self-handicapping creates a fail-safe or win-win scenario that's guaranteed to protect the procrastinator's self-image. If the work performance or product is less than excellent, it can be blamed on external factors (e.g., lack of time); if it happens to earn them a high grade, they can attribute the result to themselves—their extraordinary ability enabled them to do so well despite working at the last minute.

In addition to self-handicapping, other psychological factors have been found to contribute to procrastination, including the following:

- **Fear of failure.** The procrastinator feels better about not completing the work on time than doing it and experiencing failure (Burka & Yuen, 2008; Solomon & Rothblum, 1984);
- **Perfectionism.** Having unrealistically high personal standards or expectations, which leads to the procrastinator's belief that it's better to postpone work or not do it than to risk doing it less than perfectly (Kachgal et al., 2001);
- **Fear of success.** Fearing that doing well will show others that the procrastinator has the ability to achieve success and will lead others to expect the procrastinator

to maintain those high standards in the future (Beck, Koons, & Milgram, 2000; Ellis & Knaus, 2002)

- **Indecisiveness.** The procrastinator has difficulty making decisions, including decisions about what to do first, when to do it, or whether to do it (Anderson, 2003; Steel, 2007);
- **Thrill seeking.** The procrastinator enjoys the adrenaline rush triggered by hurrying to get things done just before a deadline (Szalavitz, 2003).

> "Striving for excellence motivates you; striving for perfection is demoralizing."
> —Harriet Braiker, psychologist and bestselling author

Reflection 5.8

How often do you procrastinate? (Circle one.)

rarely   occasionally   frequently   consistently

When you do procrastinate, what's the usual cause?

If these underlying psychological issues are at the root of procrastination, they must be dealt with before procrastination can be overcome. Because they have deeper roots, it may take some time and professional assistance to uproot them. A good place to get such assistance is the Counseling Center on campus, where there are counseling psychologists who are professionally trained to deal with emotional issues, including those that may be contributing to procrastination.

Self-Help Strategies for Beating the Procrastination Habit

Once inaccurate beliefs or emotional issues underlying procrastination have been identified and dealt with, the next step is to take direct action on the procrastination habit itself. What follows are seven key strategies for minimizing or eliminating the procrastination habit.

1. **Continually practice effective time-management strategies.** If effective time-management practices, such as those previously cited in this chapter, are implemented consistently, they can turn into a habit. When people repeatedly practice effective time-management strategies, these practices gradually become part of their routine and develop into habits. For instance, when procrastinators repeatedly practice effective time-management strategies with respect to tasks that they procrastinate on, their procrastination tendencies begin to fade and are gradually replaced by good habits of good time management (Ainslie, 1992; Baumeister, Heatherton, & Tice, 1994).

> "Just do it."
> —Commercial slogan of Nike, the athletic equipment company named after the Greek goddess of victory

2. **Make the start of work as inviting or appealing as possible.** Getting started can be a stumbling block for many procrastinators. They experience what's called "start-up stress"—when they're about to begin a task, they start to experience negative feelings about the task being unpleasant, difficult, or boring (Burka & Yuen, 2008). If you have trouble starting your work, one way to give yourself a jump-start is to arrange your work tasks in an order that allows you to start with tasks that you're likely to find most interesting or to succeed in. Once you overcome the initial inertia and get going, you can ride the momentum you've created to attack other tasks that you find less appealing or more daunting.

Student Perspective

"Did you ever dread doing something, then it turned out to take only about 20 minutes to do?"

—Conversation between two college students overheard in a coffee shop

You're also likely to discover that the dreaded work wasn't as difficult, boring, or time-consuming as it appeared to be. When you sense that you're making some

"The secret to getting ahead is getting started."

—Mark Twain (Samuel Clemens), American humorist and author of *The Adventures of Huckleberry Finn* (1885), often called "the Great American Novel"

progress toward getting work done, your anxiety begins to decline. As with many experiences in life that are feared and avoided, the anticipation of the event turns out to be worse than the event itself. Research on students who hadn't started a project until it was about to be due indicates that they experienced anxiety and guilt about delaying their work, but once they begin working these negative emotions subsided and were replaced by more positive feelings of progress and accomplishment (McCance & Pychyl, 2003).

© marekuliasz, 2013. Under license from Shutterstock, Inc.

For many procrastinators, getting started is often their biggest obstacle.

"To eat an elephant, first cut it into small pieces."

—Author unknown

3. **Make the work manageable.** Work becomes less overwhelming and less stressful when it's handled in small chunks or pieces. You can conquer procrastination for large tasks by using a "divide and conquer" strategy: divide the large task into smaller, more manageable units, and then attack and complete them one at a time.

Don't underestimate the power of short work sessions. They can be more effective than longer sessions because it's easier to maintain momentum and concentration for shorter periods of time. If you're working on a large project or preparing for a major exam, dividing your work into short sessions will enable you to take quick jabs and poke small holes in it, reducing its overall size with each successive punch. This approach will also give you the sense of satisfaction that comes with knowing that you're making steady progress toward completing a big task—by continually jabbing at it in short strokes and gradually reducing the pressure associated with having to go for a big knockout punch right before the final bell (deadline).

Author's Experience

The two biggest projects I've had to complete in my life were writing my doctoral thesis and writing this textbook. The strategy that enabled me to keep going until I competed both of these large tasks was to make up short-term deadlines for myself (e.g., complete 5–10 pages each week). I psyched myself into thinking that these make-believe due dates were real, drop-dead deadlines and if I didn't meet them by completing these smaller tasks on time, I was going to fall so far behind that I'd never get the whole thing done. I think these self-imposed deadlines worked for me because they gave me smaller, more manageable tasks to work on that allowed me to make steady progress toward my larger, long-term goal. It was as if this strategy enabled me to take a huge, hard-to-digest meal and break it into small, bite-sized pieces that I could easily swallow and gradually digest over time—as opposed to trying to devour and digest a monstrous-sized meal right before bedtime (the final deadline).

Joe Cuseo

4. **Organization matters.** Research indicates that disorganization is a factor that contributes to procrastination (Steel, 2007). How well you organize your workplace and manage your work materials can reduce your risk of procrastination. Ask yourself, "Can I just go in and do it?" Having the right materials in the right place at the right time can make it easier to get to your work and get going on your work. Once you've made a decision to start working, you don't want to delay acting on that decision by looking for the tools you need to get started. For procrastinators, this time delay may be just the amount of time they need to change their minds and decide not to start working!

Remember

The less time and effort it takes to start doing something, the more likely you are to do it.

One simple but effective way to organize your college work materials is to develop your own file system. You can begin to create an effective academic file system by filing (storing) materials from different courses in different-colored folders or notebooks. This will allow you to keep all materials related to the same course in the same place, giving you direct and immediate access to the materials you need as soon as you need them. Such a system helps you get organized, reduces stress associated with having things all over the place, and reduces the risk of procrastination by reducing the time it takes for you to start working.

5. **Location matters.** Where you choose to work can influence whether you work. Research on procrastinators demonstrates that distraction is a factor that can contribute to procrastination (Steel, 2007). Thus, you can reduce your risk of procrastinating by working in an environment whose location and arrangement prevent distraction and promote concentration.

Reflection 5.9

List your two most common sources of distraction while working. Next to each distraction, identify a strategy that you might use to reduce or eliminate it.

Source of Distraction   Strategy for Reducing This Distraction

1.

2.

Distractions tend to come in two major forms: social distractions, e.g., people nearby who are not working, and media distractions, e.g., cell phones, e-mails, text messages, CDs, and TV. Research on college students indicates that the number of hours per week they spend watching TV is *negatively* associated with success: more TV leads to lower grade point averages, less likelihood of graduating with honors, and lower levels of personal development (Astin, 1993).

Remember

Select a workplace and arrange your workspace to minimize distraction from people and media. Try to remove everything from your work site that's not relevant or directly related to your work.

You can arrange your work environment in a way that not only disables distraction but also enables concentration. Your concentration is easier to maintain when you work in an environment that allows you easy access to (1) work support materials, e.g., class notes, textbooks, and a dictionary, and (2) social support networks, e.g., a group of motivated students who will help you stay focused, on task, and on track toward completing your work.

6. **Arrange the order or sequence of work tasks to intercept procrastination at times when you're most likely to experience it.** While procrastination often involves difficulty starting work, it can also involve difficulty continuing and

Student Perspective

"To reduce distractions, work at a computer on campus rather than using one in your room or home."

—Advice to new college students from a first-year student

Student
Perspective

"I'm very good at starting
things but often have trouble
keeping a sustained effort."

—First-year college student

completing work (Lay & Silverman, 1996). As previously mentioned, if you have trouble starting work, it might be best to first do the tasks that you find most interesting or easiest. However, if you have difficulty maintaining or sustaining your work until it's finished, you might try to schedule work tasks that you find easier and more interesting *in the middle or toward the end* of your planned work time. If you perform tasks of greater interest and ease at a time when you typically lose interest or energy, you may be able to restore or revive your interest and energy. Also, doing your most enjoyable and easiest tasks later can provide an incentive or reward for completing your less enjoyable tasks first.

7. **If you're close to completing a task, don't stop until you complete it.** It's often harder to restart a task than it is to finish a task that you've already started because you've overcome the initial inertia needed to get started can ride the momentum you've created until you finish. Furthermore, finishing a task can give you a sense of *closure*—the feeling of personal accomplishment and self-satisfaction that comes from knowing that you "closed the deal." Placing a checkmark next to a completed task can serve as a source of positive self-reinforcement that increases your motivation to complete other tasks on your to-do list.

Summary and Conclusion

To manage time effectively, you need to:

- **Analyze.** Break down time and become aware of how you spend it;
- **Itemize.** Identify the tasks you need to accomplish and their due dates; and
- **Prioritize.** Tackle your tasks in their order of importance.

Developing a comprehensive time-management plan for academic work involves long-, mid-, and short-range components that include:

- Planning the total term (long-range);
- Planning your week (mid-range); and
- Planning your day (short-range).

A good time-management plan also has the following features:

- It sets aside time to take care of unexpected developments;
- It takes advantage of your natural peak periods and down times;
- It balances work and recreation; and
- It gives you the flexibility to accommodate unforeseen opportunities.

The enemy of effective time management is procrastination, which is often rooted in the following myths:

- Better work occurs on the day or night before something is due.
- Studying in advance is a waste of time because everything you study will be forgotten by test time.

Effective strategies for beating the procrastination habit include the following:

- Start with the work that is the most inviting or appealing.
- Divide large tasks into smaller, more manageable units.

- Organize your work materials to make it easy and convenient for you to start working.
- Organize your work place or space so that you work in a location that minimizes distractions and temptations not to work.
- Intentionally arrange your work tasks so that you're working on more enjoyable or stimulating tasks at times when you're vulnerable to procrastination.
- If you're close to finishing a task, finish it, because it's often harder to restart a task than to complete one you've already started.

Mastering the skill of managing time is critical for success in college and beyond. Time is one of our most powerful personal resources; the better we manage it, the more likely we are to achieve our goals and gain control of our lives.

"Dost thou love life? Then do not squander time, for that is the stuff life is made of."

—Benjamin Franklin, 18th-century inventor, newspaper writer, and signer of the *Declaration of Independence*

Learning More through the World Wide Web

Internet-Based Resources for Further Information on Time Management

For additional information related to the ideas discussed in this chapter, we recommend the following Web sites:

Time-Management Strategies for All Students:

www.studygs.net/timman.htm

www.pennstatelearning.psu.edu/resources/study-tips/time-mgt

Time-Management Strategies for Adult Students:

www.essortment.com/lifestyle/timemanagement_sjmu.htm

Beating Procrastination:

www.mindtools.com

Chapter 5 Exercises

5.1 Term at a Glance

Term _____, Year _____

Review the syllabus (course outline) for all classes you're enrolled in this term, and complete the following information for each course.

Course ↓	Professor ↓	Exams ↓	Projects & Papers ↓	Other Assignments ↓	Attendance Policy ↓	Late & Makeup Assignment Policy ↓

Self-Assessment Questions

1. Is the overall workload what you expected? Are your surprised by the amount of work required in any particular course or courses?

2. At this point in the term, what do you see as your most challenging or demanding course or courses? Why?

3. Do you think you can handle the total workload required by the full set of courses you're enrolled in this term?

4. What adjustments or changes could you make to your personal schedule that would make it easier to accommodate your academic workload this term?

5.2 Taking a Personal Time Inventory

On the blank Week-at-a-Glance Grid that follows, map out your typical or average week for this term. Start by recording what you usually do on these days, including when you have class, when you work, and when you relax or recreate. You can use abbreviations (e.g., J for job and R&R for rest and relaxation) or write tasks out in full if you have enough room in the box. List the abbreviations you created at the bottom of the page so that your instructor can follow them.

If you're a *full-time* student, find 25 *hours* in your week that you could devote to homework (HW). These 25 hours could be found between classes, during the day, in the evenings, or on the weekends. If you can find 25 hours per week for homework (in addition to the time you spend in class), you'll have a 40-hour workweek for coursework, which research has shown to result in good grades and success in college.

If you're a *part-time* student, find two *hours* you could devote to homework *for every hour* that you're in class (e.g., if you're in class nine hours per week, find 18 hours of homework time).

Week-at-a-Glance Grid

	Sunday	Monday	Tuesday	Wednesday	Thursday	Friday	Saturday
7:00 a.m.							
8:00 a.m.							
9:00 a.m.							
10:00 a.m.							
11:00 a.m.							
12:00 p.m.							
1:00 p.m.							
2:00 p.m.							
3:00 p.m.							
4:00 p.m.							
5:00 p.m.							
6:00 p.m.							
7:00 p.m.							
8:00 p.m.							
9:00 p.m.							
10:00 p.m.							
11:00 p.m.							

1. Go to the following Web site: pennstatelearning.psu.edu/resources/study-tips/time-mgt
    Click on the link for the "time-management exercise."

2. Complete the time-management exercise at this site. The exercise asks you to estimate the hours per day or week that you spend doing various activities (e.g., sleeping, employment, and commuting). As you enter the amount of time you engage in these activities, the total number of remaining hours available in the week for academic work will be automatically computed.

3. After completing your entries, look at your Week-at-a-glance Grid and answer the following questions (or provide your best estimate).

   a. How many hours per week do you have available for academic work?

   b. Do you have two hours available for academic work outside of class for each hour you spend in class?

   c. What time wasters do you detect that might be easily eliminated or reduced to create more time for academic work outside of class?

Procrastination: The Vicious Cycle

Delilah has a major paper due at the end of the term. It's now past midterm and she still hasn't started to work on her paper. She tells herself, "I should have started sooner."

However, Delilah continues to postpone starting her work on the paper and begins to feel anxious and guilty about it. To relieve her growing anxiety and guilt, she starts doing other tasks instead, such as cleaning her room and returning e-mails. This makes Delilah feel a little better because these tasks keep her busy, take her mind off the term paper, and give her the feeling that at least she's getting something accomplished. Time continues to pass; the deadline for the paper is growing dangerously close. Delilah now finds herself in the position of having lots of work to do and little time in which to do it.

Source: Burka & Yuen, *Procrastination: Why you do it, and what to do about it.*

Reflection and Discussion Questions

1. What do you predict Delilah will do at this point?

2. Why did you make the above prediction?

3. What grade do you think Delilah will receive on her paper?

4. What do you think Delilah will do on the next term paper she's assigned?

5. Other than starting sooner, what recommendations would you have for Delilah (and other procrastinators like her) to break this cycle of procrastination and prevent it from happening repeatedly?

Hampton Helped Me!

Allister Primo

Photo courtesy of Hampton University

Allister Primo attended Hampton University during 2002–2006. At Hampton, he majored in computer and electrical engineering. He was a member of the marching band, an RA, a member of the student leader organization and Omega Psi phi fraternity.

Upon graduating from Hampton on the dean's list, Allister migrated to Washington to work at the Patent and Trademark Office.

In Washington, Allister was also able to start his own promotional company Primo-Events, which is now one of the most recognized companies in the DMV area.

CHAPTER 6
Relationships and Stress

"We need to build a relationship of trust, not just within a firm, but within a society. By trust, I mean the recognition of a mutual purpose for which we work together and in which we all benefit. It is a Stakeholder Economy in which all opportunity is available to all, advancement is through merit, and from which no group or class is set apart or excluded."

—Tony Blair

Upon completion of this chapter, you will be able to:

- **Acquire** social and emotional knowledge skills to enhance the quality of your interpersonal relationships and mental health
- **Recognize** symptoms of distress
- **Develop** strategies for preventing and managing stress

Relationships and Stress

Relating to Others and Regulating Our Emotions

ACTIVATE YOUR THINKING

When you think about someone who's "intelligent," what personal characteristics come to mind? Why?

LEARNING GOAL

To acquire social and emotional knowledge and skills to enhance the quality of your interpersonal relationships and mental health.

Social intelligence (a.k.a. interpersonal intelligence) refers to the ability to communicate and relate effectively to others (Gardner, 1993, 1999). It's a major type of human intelligence, which research indicates is a better predictor of personal and professional success than intellectual ability (Goleman, 2006). *Emotional intelligence* refers to the ability to identify and monitor our emotions and to remain aware of how our emotions affect our thoughts and actions (Salovey & Mayer, 1990). Emotional intelligence has been found to be a better predictor of personal and occupational success than performance on intellectual intelligence tests (Goleman, 1995). These two important elements of human intelligence and personal success are the focus points of this chapter.

Social Intelligence

Our interpersonal relationships may be a source of social support that promotes success, or they may serve as a source of social conflict that distracts us from focusing on and achieving your personal goals. As a new college student, you may find yourself surrounded by multiple social opportunities. One of the college adjustments you'll need to make is finding a healthy middle ground between too much and too little socializing, as well as forming solid interpersonal relationships that support rather than sabotage your educational success.

Studies show that people with stronger social support networks have a longer life expectancy (Giles, Glonek, Luszcz, & Andrews, 2005) and are more likely to report being happy (Myers, 1993, 2000). Development of a strong social support system is particularly important in today's high-tech world of virtual reality and online (vs. in-person) communication, both of which make it easier to avoid direct contact, neglect connections with others, and increase the risk of isolation, loneliness, and social avoidance (Putman, 2000).

"The most important single ingredient in the formula of success is knowing how to get along with people."

—Theodore (Teddy) Roosevelt, 26th president of the United States and winner of the Nobel Peace Prize

"I will pay more for the ability to deal with people than any other ability under the sun."

—John D. Rockefeller, American industrialist and philanthropist and once the richest man in the world

Student *Perspective*

"I have often found conflict in living a balanced academic and social life. I feel that when I am enjoying and succeeding in one spectrum, I am lagging in the other."

—First-year college student

From *Thriving in College and Beyond: Research-Based Strategies for Academic Success and Personal Development* by Cuseo et al. Copyright © 2013 by Kendall Hunt Publishing Company. Reprinted by permission.

Student *Perspective*

"The Internet supposedly increases communication and brings humanity closer together. Instead, in my generation, I'm noticing quite the opposite. There seems to be less face-to-face communication. Everyone is hooked on social networking websites. We cowardly avoid interaction where there are no facial expressions or tones."

—First-year college student

The quality of our interpersonal relationships rests on two types of personal skills: our communication skills, or how well we send and receive information when interacting with others (verbally and nonverbally), and our human relations skills, or how well we relate to and treat others (i.e., people skills).

Following are our top recommendations for strengthening your interpersonal communication skills. Some strategies may appear to be very basic, but they're also very powerful. It may be that because they are so basic, people overlook them or forget to use them consistently. Don't be fooled by the seeming simplicity of the following suggestions, and don't underestimate their impact on your social interactions and relationships.

Reflection 6.2

Who are the people in your life that you tend to turn to for social support when you are experiencing stress or need personal encouragement?

Strategies for Improving the Quality of Interpersonal Communication

"We have been given two ears and but a single mouth in order that we may hear more and talk less."

—Zeno of Citium, ancient Greek philosopher and founder of Stoic philosophy

1. **Work hard at being a good listener.** When the term *communication* is used, the skills of speaking and writing usually come to mind. However, the etymological root of the word *communicate* is *communicare*, meaning "to share or divide out." The prefix *co* in communication implies that it's a two-way process that involves not only the art of delivering ideas, but also receiving them. In fact, studies show that listening is the most frequent human communication activity, followed, in order, by reading, speaking, and writing (Newton, 1990; Purdy & Borisoff, 1996). One study found that college students spend an average of 52.5 percent of each day listening (Barker & Watson, 2000). Being a good listener is one of the top characteristics mentioned by people when they cite the positive features of their best friends (Berndt, 1992). Listening is also one of the top skills employers look for when hiring and promoting employees (Maes, Weldy, & Icenogle, 1997; Winsor, Curtis, & Stephens, 1997).

> **Remember**
>
> *When you listen closely to those who speak to you, you send them the message that you respect their ideas and that they're worthy of your undivided attention.*

Human relations experts often recommend that we spend less time talking and more time listening and listening well (Nichols, 1995). Because we're not actively doing something while listening, it's easy to lapse into *passive listening*—we hear their words, but our mind isn't actively and fully processing the message because it's partially somewhere else. While listening, we need to remain aware of this natural tendency to drift off and actively combat it by devoting our full attention to others when they're speaking. Two key strategies for doing so are to: (1) focus your attention on what the speaker is saying rather than on what you're going to say next, and (2) actively engage with the speaker's message by occasionally asking questions or seeking clarification about what is being said.

"Give every man thine ear, but few thy voice."

—William Shakespeare, English poet, playwright, and the most quoted writer in the English-speaking world

2. **Remain conscious of the nonverbal messages you send while listening.** It's estimated that more than two-thirds of all communication is nonverbal because human body language often communicates stronger and truer messages than spoken language (Driver, 2010; Navarro, 2008).

When it comes to listening, body language may be the best way to communicate interest in the message, as well as interest in and respect for the speaker. Similarly, if you are speaking, awareness of your listeners' body language can provide you with important clues about whether you're holding or losing their interest.

A good mnemonic device (memory-improvement method) for the nonverbal signals you should send others while listening is the acronym SOFTEN, in which each letter stands for an effective nonverbal message:

S = **Smile.** Smiling suggests interest and acceptance, but do it periodically, not continually. (A permanent smile can come across as an artificial pose.)
Sit still. Fidgeting and squirming send the message that the speaker is making you feel anxious or bored.

O = **Open posture.** Avoid closed-posture positions, such as crossing your arms or folding your hands; they can send a message that you're not open to what the speaker is saying or passing judgment on what's being said.

F = **Forward lean.** Leaning back can send a signal that you're not "into" what the person is saying or evaluating (psychoanalyzing) the person saying it.
Face the speaker directly. Line up both shoulders with the speaker rather than turning one shoulder away, as if to give the speaker the cold shoulder.

T = **Touch.** A light touch on the arm or hand can be a good way to communicate warmth, but no rubbing, stroking, or touching in ways that could be interpreted as inappropriate intimacy (or sexual harassment).

E = **Eye contact.** Lack of eye contact sends the message that you're looking around for something more interesting or stimulating than the speaker. However, don't make continual or relentless eye contact, because that borders on staring or glaring. Instead, strike a happy medium by making *periodic* eye contact.

N = **Nod your head.** Slowly and periodically, not rapidly and repeatedly—this sends the message that you want the speaker to hurry up and finish up so you can start talking.

An interesting exercise you can use to gain greater awareness of your nonverbal communication habits is to choose a couple of people whom you trust, and who know you well, and ask them to imitate your body language. This is an exercise that can frequently be revealing (and occasionally entertaining).

3. **Be open to different topics of conversation.** Don't be a closed-minded or selective listener who listens to others like you're listening to a radio—selecting or tuning into only those stations that immediately capture your special interests and reinforce your opinions, but tuning out or turning off everything else.

> **Remember**
>
> *People learn most from others whose interests and viewpoints don't necessarily match or mimic their own. Ignoring or blocking out information and ideas about topics that don't immediately interest you or support your particular perspective is not only a poor social skill: it's also a poor learning strategy.*

If people express viewpoints that you don't agree with, you don't have to nod in agreement; however, you still owe them the courtesy of listening to what they have to say (rather than shaking your head, frowning, or interrupting them). This isn't just a matter of social etiquette: it's a matter of social ethics. Only after others finish expressing their point of view should you then feel free to express your own. Your informed opinions are worth expressing, as long as you don't express them in an opinionated way—stating them so strongly that it sounds like your viewpoints are the only rational or acceptable ones while all others are inferior or insane. Opinionated expression is likely to immediately end a potentially useful discussion or a possible future relationship.

"The most important thing in communication is to hear what isn't being said."

—Peter F. Drucker, Austrian author and founder of the study of "management"

Reflection 6.3

On what topics do you hold strong opinions?

When you express these opinions, how do others usually react to you?

Human Relations Skills (a.k.a. "People Skills")

In addition to communicating and conversing well with others, another aspect of social intelligence is how well you relate to and treat others. Here are three key strategies for strengthening your human relations skills.

1. **Remember the names of people you meet.** When you remember others' names, you acknowledge their uniqueness and individuality. It makes them feel less like anonymous faces in a crowd and more like special individuals with distinctive identities.

    You've likely heard people claim they don't have a good memory for names; however, there's no evidence that ability to remember names is a natural talent or inherited trait that people are born with or without. Instead, it's a habit and skill that can be developed through personal effort and consistent use of effective memory-improvement strategies.

    You can use the following strategies for remembering names:

    - Consciously pay attention to the name of each person you meet. Listen for the person's name rather than focusing on the impression you're making on that person, the impression that person is making on you, or what you're going to say next. When people say, "I forgot that person's name," what they really mean is they never *got* that person's name in the first place because they weren't paying attention to it when they first heard it.
    - Reinforce your memory of the person's name by saying it or rehearsing it within a minute or two after you first hear it. For instance, if your friend Gertrude has just introduced you to Geraldine, you might say: "Geraldine, how long have you known Gertrude?" By using a person's name soon after you've heard it, you intercept memory loss when forgetting is most likely to occur—immediately after information is first received and processed.
    - Strengthen your memory of an individual's name by associating it with other information, you've learned or know about the person. For instance, you can associate the person's name with (1) your first impression of the individual's personality, (2) a physical characteristic of the person, (3) your topic of conversation, (4) the place where you met, or (5) a familiar word that rhymes with the person's name. By making a mental connection between the person's name and some other piece of information, we make learning of the name more meaningful and memorable.
    - People write down things that they want to be sure to remember. We can do the same for remembering names by keeping a name journal that includes the names of new people we meet plus some information about them (e.g., what they do and what their interests are). Make it a goal to meet one new person every day or week and remember that person's name by recording it in a name journal, along with the situation or circumstances in which you met.

"We should be aware of the magic contained in a name. The name sets that individual apart; it makes him or her unique among all others. Remember that a person's name is to that person the sweetest and most important sound in any language."

—Dale Carnegie, author of the bestselling book *How to Win Friends and Influence People* and founder of The Dale Carnegie Course, a worldwide program for business based on his teachings

"When I joined the bank, I started keeping a record of the people I met and put them on little cards, and I would indicate on the cards when I met them, and under what circumstances, and sometimes [make] a little notation which would help me remember a conversation."

—David Rockefeller, prominent American banker, philanthropist, and former CEO of the Chase Manhattan Bank

> **Remember**
>
> *Developing the habit of remembering names is not only a social skill that can improve your social life and bring you friends, but also a powerful professional tool that can promote your career success in whatever field you may pursue.*

In business, remembering names can help recruit and retain customers; in politics, it can win votes; and in education, it can build effective teacher-student relationships that can increase learning.

2. **Refer to people by name when you greet and interact with them.** When you greet a person, be sure to use the person's name in your greeting. Saying, "Hi, Waldo," will mean a lot more to Waldo than simply saying "Hi" or "Hi, there," which sounds like you just detected somebody "out there," or addressing a letter "to whom it may concern" rather than using the name of an actual person. By continuing to use people's names after you've learned them, you continue to send them the message that you haven't forgotten who they are and you continue to strengthen your memory for their names.

"If we obey this law, [it] will bring us countless friends. The law is this: Always make the person feel important."
—Dale Carnegie, *How to Win Friends and Influence People*

3. **Show interest in others by remembering information about them.** Ask people questions about their personal interests, plans, and experiences. Listen closely to their answers, especially to what seems most important to them, what they care about, or what interests them, and use this information as topics of conversation with them. For one person that topic may be politics, for another it may be sports, and for another it may be relationships.

When you see that person again, ask about something that was brought up in your last conversation. Try to get beyond the standard, generic questions that people routinely ask after they say "Hello" (e.g., "What's going on?"). Instead, ask about something specific you discussed with them last time you spoke (e.g., "How did that math test go that you were worried about last week?"). This sends a clear message to others that you remember them and care about them. Our memories often reflect our priorities—we're likely to remember what's important to us. When we remember people's names and something about them, it lets them know that they're a high priority to us.

"You can make more friends in two months by becoming interested in other people than you can in two years by trying to get other people interested in you."
—Dale Carnegie, *How to Win Friends and Influence People*

Furthermore, you're likely to find that others start showing more interest in you after you show interest in them. When you ask questions that show interest in others, you're also likely to discover another surprising thing may happen: You'll hear people say that you're an excellent listener, a great conversationalist, and a good friend.

Strategies for Meeting People and Forming Friendships

An important aspect of the college experience is meeting new people, learning from them, and forming lifelong friendships. Here are some practical strategies for increasing the quantity and variety of the people you meet and the quality of friendships you form.

1. **Place yourself in situations and locations where you will come into regular contact with others.** Social psychologists have found that the origin of friendships is physical propinquity—people are more likely to become friends if they continually find themselves in the same place at the same time (Latané, Liu, Nowak, Bonevento, & Zheng, 1995). You can apply this principle by spending as much time on campus as possible and spending time in places where others are likely to be present (e.g., by eating your meals in the student cafeteria and studying in the college library). If you have the opportunity to live on campus, do so;

studies show that it helps students make social connections and increases their satisfaction with the college experience (Pascarella & Terenzini, 2005; Tinto, 1993). If you are a commuter student, try to make your college experience as similar as possible to that of a residential student: for example, try to spend more than just class time on campus by spending study time and social time on campus (e.g., attending campus social or cultural events).

2. **Put yourself in social situations where you're likely to meet people who have similar interests, goals, and values.** Research supports the proverb, "Birds of a feather flock together." People tend to form friendships with others who share similar interests, values, or goals (AhYun, 2002). When two people have something in common, they're more likely to become friends because they're more likely to enjoy spending time together doing things that relate to their common interests. They're also more likely to get along with each other because they reinforce or validate each other's personal interests and values (Festinger, 1954; Suls, Martin, & Wheeler, 2002).

An important aspect of the college experience is meeting new people and forming lasting friendships.

One straightforward way to find others with whom you have something in common is by participating in clubs and organizations on campus that reflect your interests and values. If you cannot find one, start one of your own. Also, regularly check your college newspaper, posted flyers on campus, and the Student Information Desk in your Student Activities Center to keep track of social events that are more likely to attract others who share your interests, values, or goals.

3. **Meeting others through a social website.** Facebook and other social websites are another type of venue through which you can network with other college students. You can use this electronic medium to meet new people, join groups on campus, and check for announcements of parties or other social events. However, be careful about the people you respond to, and be careful about what you post on your page or "wall." Reports indicate that both schools and employers are checking students' Facebook entries and using that information to help them decide whether to accept or reject applicants (Palank, 2006).

Student
Perspective

"I have observed different kinds of people. There are the ones that party and flunk, then there are the kind that party rationally and don't flunk, and the kinds that just don't party."

—First-year college student

Reflection **6.4**

Have you been to college parties on or off campus?

If yes, what were they like?

If no, are there any reasons you have not gone?

Dating and Romantic Relationships

Romantic relationships begin through the process of dating. Research shows that college students take different approaches to dating, ranging from not dating at all to dating with the intent of exploring or cementing long-term relationships. Listed below is a summary of the major forms or purposes of college dating.

Snapshot Summary

6.1

Approaches to Dating

Postpone dating. Students who adopt this approach feel that the demands of college work and college life are too time-consuming to take on the additional social and emotional burden of dating while in college.

Student Perspectives

"Relationships take time and patience, and in college, both of these can be very limited."
—College student quoted in Kucewicz (2001)

"It's hard enough to have fun here with all the work you have to do. There's no reason to have the extra drama [of dating] in your life."
—College sophomore quoted in Sax (2003)

Hooking up. Students who prefer this approach believe that formal dating is unnecessary; they feel that their social and sexual needs are better met more casually by associating with friends and acquaintances. Instead of going out on one-on-one dates, they prefer to first meet and connect with romantic partners in larger group settings, such as college parties.

"Now all a guy has to do to hook up on a Saturday night is to sit on the couch long enough at a party. Eventually a girl will plop herself down beside him . . . he'll make a joke, she'll laugh, their eyes will meet, sparks will fly, and the mission is accomplished. And you want me to tell this guy to call a girl, spend $100 on dinner and hope for a goodnight kiss."
—College student quoted in Beckett (2003)

Casual dating. Students taking this approach go out on dates primarily for the purpose of enjoying themselves, but not getting "tied down" to any particular person. These "casual daters" prefer to go out on a series of successive dates with different partners, and they may date different individuals at the same time. Their primary goal is to meet new people and discover what characteristics they find attractive in others.

Exclusive dating. Students adopting this approach prefer to date only one person for an extended period of time. Although marriage is not the goal, exclusive dating takes casual dating one step further. This form of dating may help the partners develop a clearer idea of what characteristics they may seek in an ideal spouse or long-term mate.

Courtship. This form of dating is intended to continue the relationship until it culminates in marriage or a formal, long-term commitment.

Source: Adapted from research reviewed by Seirup (2004).

The different approaches to dating described in Snapshot Summary 6.1 don't always occur separately or independently: they may be blended or combined. Romantic relationships may also evolve or grow into different stages with the passage of time. Following are the characteristics of two major stages that often take place in the evolution or maturation of romantic love.

Reflection **6.5**

How would you define love?

Would you say that love is a feeling? An action? Both?

What do you think are the best signs that two people are "in love"?

What would you say are the most common reasons why people "fall out of love"?

Romantic Relationships

Research on romantic love indicates that it comes in two major stages (Bassham, Irwin, Nardone, & Wallace, 2005; Ruggiero, 2004; Wade & Tavris, 1990).

Stage 1. Passionate Love (Infatuation)

This represents the very first stage of a romantic relationship, and it's often characterized by the following features.

- Heavy emphasis placed on physical elements of the relationship. Lots of attention is focused on the partner's physical appearance or attractiveness, and the partners experience a high level of physical arousal and passion—they experience "erotic love" in which lust and love are closely connected.
- Impulsive: Partners quickly or suddenly "fall" into love or are "swept off their feet"—i.e., "love at first sight."
- Obsessive: Partners can't stop thinking about each other ("madly in love").
- Intense emotion characterized by a "rush" of chemical changes in the body, similar to a drug-induced state—namely:
  a. Release of the hormone adrenaline, which triggers faster heartbeat and breathing, and
  b. Increased production of the brain chemical dopamine, which triggers feelings of excitement, euphoria, joy, and general well-being (Bartels & Zeki, 2000).

The intensity of this emotional and chemical experience decreases with the passage of time, typically leveling off within a year after the couple has been together. The leveling off of emotional intensity experienced by romantic partners after their relationship continues for an extended period of time is similar to the buildup of tolerance to a drug after the drug continues to be used for an extended period of time (Fisher, 2004; Peele & Brodsky, 1991).

- **Idealism.** The partner and the relationship are perceived as "perfect." The partners may say things like "We're perfect for each other," "Nobody else has a relationship like ours," "We'll be together forever." This is the stage where love can be

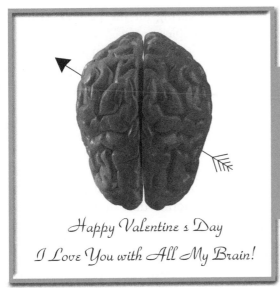

Happy Valentine's Day
I Love You with All My Brain!

© Kendall Hunt Publishing Company

> Despite expressions like "I love you with all my heart," romantic love takes place in the human brain and is accompanied by major changes in the production of brain chemicals.

"blind"—the partners may not "see" each other's obvious flaws and weaknesses. As in the psychological defense mechanism of *denial*, the partner's personal shortcomings, or any problems that may threaten the security of the relationship, are pushed out of consciousness.

- **Attachment and dependency.** The lover feels insecure without the partner and cannot bear being separated from him or her (e.g., "I can't live without him"). This type of attachment and dependence follows the principle "I love you because I am loved" and "I love you because I need you." Thus, it may be difficult to determine whether the person is in love with the other person or is in love with the process of being in love or the feeling of being loved (Fromm, 1970).

- **Possessiveness and jealousy.** The lover feels that he or she has exclusive rights to the partner and may become very suspicious of the partner's fidelity, or very jealous of those who interact with the partner in a friendly or affectionate manner, which can be totally illogical or irrational ("insanely jealous"): the lover may suspect the partner is "cheating" when there's no real evidence that any cheating is taking place.

- **"Love sickness."** If the relationship breaks up, intense depression or "love withdrawal" may follow the breakup, similar to the feeling of withdrawing from a pleasure-producing drug. Studies show that the most common cause of despair or depression among college students is a romantic breakup (Foreman, 2009).

Stage 2. Mature Love

At this more advanced stage of the relationship, the partners gradually "fall out" of first-stage (puppy) love, and gradually grow into a more mature stage of love that has the following characteristics.

- The partners become less selfish and self-centered (egocentric), and become more selfless and other-centered (altruistic). Love moves beyond being just a noun, an emotion or feeling within the person (e.g., "I am in love"), and becomes an action verb, a way in which the partners act toward one another (e.g., "we love each other"). More emphasis is placed on caring for the partner, rather than being cared for. Mature love follows two principles:

1. "I am loved because I love"—not "I'm in love because I am loved" and
2. "I need you because I love you"—not "I love you because I need you." (Fromme, 1980)

- There's less of an emotional high experienced at this stage than during early stages of the relationship. For example, the mad rush of hormones and mass production of euphoria-producing brain chemicals is replaced by feelings of emotional serenity (mellowness) and emotional evenness (versus the emotional "ups and downs" of early-stage love). The love "rush" is replaced by a less intense, but more consistently pleasant emotional state characterized by slightly elevated levels of different brain chemicals (endorphins, rather than dopamine). Unlike infatuation or early-stage love, this pleasant emotional state doesn't decline with time: in fact, it may actually grow stronger as the partners' relationship continues and matures (Bartels & Zeki, 2000).

- Physical passion decreases. The "flames of the flesh" don't burn as intensely as in first-stage love, but a romantic afterglow continues. This afterglow is characterized by more emotional intimacy or psychological closeness between the partners, greater self-disclosure, mutual trust, and interpersonal honesty, which enhances both the physical and psychological quality of the relationship (Viorst, 1998).

At this more advanced stage of love, interest is focused broadly on the partner as a whole person, rather than narrowly on the partner's physical qualities. Each partner has a realistic (not idealistic) view of the other: their respective strengths and weaknesses are recognized and accepted. The partners genuinely like one another as individuals and consider each other to be their "best" or "closest" friend.

- The partners have mutual trust and confidence in each other's commitment and aren't plagued by feelings of suspicion, distrust, or petty jealousy. Each partner continues to have interests and close friends outside the relationship without the other becoming jealous (Hatfield & Rapson, 1993; Hatfield and Walster, 1985).

- The partners have mutual concern for each other's growth and fulfillment. Rather than being envious or competitive, they take joy in each other's personal success and accomplishments.

- The partners maintain a balanced blend of independence and interdependence in their relationship—sometimes referred to as the "paradox (contradiction) of love"—both partners maintain their independence and individuality yet feel more complete and fulfilled when they're together. The partners maintain their own sense of personal identity and self-worth; however, together, their respective identities become more complete.

Student *Perspective*

"I learned love and I learned you. I learned that, in order to love someone, you must be blind to the physical and the past. You must see their emotional and mental strengths and weaknesses, passions and dislikes, hobbies and pastimes."

—Letter written by first-year student

"Two become one, yet remain one."

—Erich Fromm, in the book *The Art of Loving*

Reflection 6.6

Rate your degree of agreement or disagreement with the following statements:

"All you need is love."

strongly agree   agree   not sure   disagree   strongly disagree

Reason for rating:

"Love is just a four-letter word."
   strongly agree   agree   not sure   disagree   strongly disagree

Reason for rating:

"Love stinks."
   strongly agree   agree   not sure   disagree   strongly disagree

Reason for rating:

Unhealthy Relationships

When a relationship becomes unhealthy, there are often clear warning signs telling you it's time to end things for your own well-being. If you are feeling disrespected or controlled, or you are concerned for your safety, it's essential that you acknowledge and act upon these signals. Relationship violence—whether emotional, psychological, physical, or sexual—is *never* appropriate or acceptable. Neither is it an effective means for dealing with a dating conflict. If you are in such a situation, or you have a friend who is, addressing the violence immediately is of primary importance.

Sometimes victims and perpetrators don't recognize that they are in fact in a violent relationship because they don't identify the behaviors as abusive. Behaviors that characterize relationship violence include, but are not limited to, degrading language, dominating or dictating a partner's actions, and physical and/or sexual assault (Murray & Kardatzke, 2007). Without such recognition, victims and perpetrators are likely to remain in their current relationships or have relationships that are more violent in the future (Miller, 2011).

Unfortunately, this type of violence is highly common among college-aged women and men. In fact, recent studies have reported that 13 to 42 percent of college students have experienced and/or perpetrated physical relationship violence (Beyers, Leonard, Mays, & Rosen, 2000; Luthra & Gidycz, 2006; Miller, 2011; Perry & Fromuth, 2005; Shook, Gerrity, Jurich, & Segrist, 2000). In another study, 88 percent of females and 81 percent of males reported being victims and/or perpetrators of psychological and/or emotional relationship violence (White & Koss, 1991). Also important to note is that relationship violence occurs among all segments of the college-aged population. When looking at the demographics of victims and perpetrators, studies show comparable rates among men and women and among members of all races, ethnicities, and socioeconomic groups (Malik, Sorenson, & Aneshensel, 1997). Comparable levels of occurrence have also been found among victims and perpetrators who are gay, bisexual, and straight (Freedner, Freed, Yang, & Austin, 2002). Taken together, these data highlight the unfortunate fact that relationship violence is all too common. Furthermore, they emphasize the need for such cases to be stopped before they escalate to even more dangerous levels.

Since victims of relationship violence often experience distress, and perhaps even trauma, it is critical that they seek help. Victims tend to be reluctant to do so however for fear of embarrassment or retribution. If you find yourself in a violent relationship, it is important that you tell someone what is going on and get support. Don't let fear immobilize you. Talking to a trusted friend who has your health and safety in mind is a good place to start. Also, connecting with your college's Counseling Center is especially helpful so that you can get the trained assistance you might need. Counseling Centers are often staffed with professionals who have experience working with victims—and perpetrators—of relationship violence and will explain to you your rights as a victim. If the center on your campus is not staffed with such experienced professionals, they are likely to help connect you to a center in your community that is.

Snapshot Summary

6.2 Examples of Emotional, Psychological, Physical, and Sexual Abuse and Violence

This list explains various forms of abuse and violence experienced by both men and women. Note that these examples are not just physical or sexual in nature; emotional and psychological violence can be just as harmful to victims.

Sexual Harassment

Sexual harassment may be defined as unwelcome sexual advances or requests for sexual favors in exchange for a grade, job, or promotion. Harassment can take the following forms:

- Verbal (e.g., sexual comments about your body or clothes; sexual jokes or teasing)
- Nonverbal (e.g., staring or glaring at your body or obscene gestures)
- Physical (e.g., contact by touching, pinching, or rubbing up against your body)

Recommendations for Dealing with Sexual Harassment

- Make your objections clear and firm. Tell the harasser directly that you are offended by the unwanted behavior and that you consider it sexual harassment.
- Keep a written record of any harassment. Record the date, place, and specific details about the harassing behavior.
- Become aware of the sexual harassment policy at your college, which is likely to be found in the Student Handbook or may be available from the Office of Human Resources on your campus.
- If you're unsure about whether you are experiencing sexual harassment or what to do, seek help from the Counseling Center on campus.

Abusive Relationships

Abusive relationships may be described as relationships in which one partner abuses the other sexually, physically, verbally, psychologically, or emotionally. Abusive individuals are often dependent on their partners for a sense of self-worth. They commonly have low self-esteem and fear their partners will abandon them, so they attempt to prevent this abandonment by over-controlling their partners. Frequently, abusers feel powerless or weak in other areas of life and overcompensate by attempting to gain and exert power and personal strength over their partners.

Potential Signs of Abuse

- Abuser tries to dominate or control all aspects of the partner's life
- Abuser frequently yells, shouts, intimidates, or makes physical threats
- Abuser constantly checks up on the partner
- Abuser constantly puts down the partner and damages the partner's self-esteem
- Abuser displays intense and irrational jealousy
- Abuser demands affection or sex when the partner is not interested
- The abused partner behaves differently and is more inhibited when the abuser is around
- The abused partner fears the abuser
- The abuser blames the partner for their abusive behavior

Strategies for Avoiding or Escaping Abusive Relationships

- Avoid isolation by continuing to maintain social ties with others outside the relationship.
- To help you see your relationship more clearly, ask friends for feedback on how they see it (love can sometimes be "blind"; it's possible to be in denial about the abusive relationship and not see what's really going on).
- Speak with a professional counselor on campus to help you see your relationship more objectively and to help you cope or escape from any relationship that you sense is becoming abusive.

Sexual Violence and Sexual Assault

Rape is a form of sexual assault, which is legally defined as "the penetration, no matter how slight, of the vagina or anus with any body part or object, or oral penetration by a sex organ of another person, without the consent of the victim" (Office of Public Affairs, 2012). Rape occurs in two major forms:

1. **Stranger Rape:** When a total stranger forces sexual intercourse on the victim.
2. **Acquaintance Rape or Date Rape:** When the victim knows or is dating the person who forces unwanted sexual intercourse. It's estimated that 63 percent of completed rapes against women in 2008 were committed by perpetrators known to the victims (Bureau of Justice Statistics, 2009). Alcohol is frequently associated with acquaintance rapes because it lowers the rapist's inhibitions and reduces the victim's ability to judge whether he or she is in a potentially dangerous situation. (Most acquaintance rape is committed by men against women; however, men are also victims of acquaintance rape.) Since the victim is familiar with the offender, he or she may feel at fault or conclude that what happened is not sexual assault.

Recommendations to Reduce the Risk of Rape and Sexual Assault

- Don't drink to excess or associate with others who drink to excess.
- Go to parties with at least one friend so you can keep an eye out for each other.
- Clearly and firmly communicate your sexual intentions and limits (e.g., if you say no, make absolutely sure that the other individual knows that you mean what you say and you say what you mean).
- Distinguish lust from love. If you just met someone who makes sexual advances toward you, that person lusts for you but doesn't love you.
- Take a self-defense class.
- Carry Mace or pepper spray.

Recommendations for Men

- Don't assume a woman wants to have sex just because she's:
  - Very friendly
  - Dressed in a certain way
  - Drinking alcohol
- If a woman says no, don't assume that she really means yes.
- Don't interpret sexual rejection as personal rejection.

Sources: Evans (2010); Smith & Segal (2012);

Handling Interpersonal Conflict

Disagreement and conflict among people are inevitable aspects of social life. Research shows that even the most happily married couples don't live in continual marital bliss: they have occasional disagreements and conflicts (Gottman, 1994, 1999). Thus, conflict is something you cannot expect to escape or eliminate; you can only hope to contain it, defuse it, and prevent it from reaching unmanageable levels. The interpersonal communication and human relations skills already discussed in this chapter can help minimize conflicts. In addition to these general social skills, the following specific set of strategies may be used to handle interpersonal conflict constructively and compassionately.

1. **Pick the right place and time to resolve the conflict.** Don't discuss sensitive issues when you're fatigued, in a fit of anger, or in a hurry (Daniels & Horowitz, 1997). Also, don't discuss them in front of others: deal with them only with the person involved. As the expression goes, "Don't air your dirty laundry in public." Criticizing someone in public is akin to a public stoning; it's likely to embarrass or humiliate the person and will cause him or her to resist or resent you.

2. **Decompress yourself before you express yourself.** When you have a conflict with a person, your ultimate objective should be to solve the problem, not unload your anger and enjoy an emotionally cathartic experience. Impulsively dumping on the other person and saying the first thing that comes to your mind may give you an immediate sense of relief, but it's not likely to produce permanent improvement in the other person's attitude or behavior toward you. Instead

Remember
Sometimes things are better left unsaid until you find the right time and place to say them.

of unloading, take the load off—cool down and give yourself a little downtime to reflect rationally before you react emotionally. For example, count to 10 and give your emotions time to settle down and your rational mind time to reflect on what you're going to say before you say it. Pausing for reflection also communicates to the other person that you've given careful thought and focused attention to the matter, rather than blasting away randomly like a loose cannon.

If the conflict is so intense that you're feeling incensed or enraged, it may be a good idea to slow things down by writing out your thoughts ahead of time before you confront the person. This strategy supplies you with time to organize and clarify your ideas by first talking silently to yourself (on paper) before talking out loud to the other person (in person).

3. **Give the person a chance to respond.** Just because you're angry doesn't mean that the person you're angry with must forfeit the right to free speech and self-defense. Giving the other person a chance to speak and be heard increases the likelihood that you'll receive a cooperative response to your request. It will also prevent you from storming in, jumping the gun, and pulling the trigger before being sure you've got all the facts straight.

After listening to the other person's response, check your understanding by summarizing it in your own words (e.g., "What I hear you saying is . . ."). This is an important first step in the conflict resolution process because conflicts often revolve around a simple misunderstanding, a failure to communicate, or a communication breakdown. Sometimes just taking the time to hear where the other person is coming from before launching into a full-scale complaint or criticism can reduce or resolve the conflict.

4. **Acknowledge the person's perspectives and feelings.** After listening to the person's response, if you disagree with it, don't dismiss or discount the person's feelings. For instance, don't say, "That's ridiculous," or "You're not making any sense." Instead, say, "I see how you might feel that way, but . . ." or "I feel bad that you are under pressure, but . . ."

5. **If things begin to get nasty, call for a time-out or cease-fire and postpone the discussion to allow both of you time to cool off.** When emotion and adrenaline run high, logic and reason tend to run low. This can result in one person saying something during a fit of anger that triggers an angry response from the other person; then the anger of both combatants continues to escalate and turns into an intense volley of verbal punches and counterpunches. For example, an emotionally heated conversation may end up going something like this:
Person A: "You're way out of control."
Person B: "I'm not out of control; you're the one that's overreacting."
Person A: "*I'm* overreacting? You're the one who's acting like a jerk!"
Person B: "I might be acting like a jerk but *you're* a real jerk!"

Blow-by-blow exchanges such as these are likely to turn up the emotional heat to a level so high that focusing on the issue and resolving the conflict take a back seat to winning the argument. Both fighters need to back off, retreat to their respective corners, cool down, and try again later when neither one of them is ready to throw a knockout punch.

6. **Make your point assertively (not passively, aggressively, or passive-aggressively).** When you're passive, you don't stand up for your personal rights: you allow others to take advantage of you and push you around. You say nothing when you should say something. You say yes when you want to say no. People who handle conflict passively tend to become angry, anxious, or resentful about doing nothing and keeping it all inside (Alberti & Emmons, 2001).

"Seek first to understand, then to be understood."

—Stephen Covey, international bestselling author of *The Seven Habits of Highly Effective People*

When you're aggressive, you stand up for your rights, but you also violate the rights of the other person by threatening, dominating, humiliating, or bullying that person. You use intense, emotionally loaded words to attack the person (e.g., "You spoiled brat" or "You're a sociopath"). You may manage to get what you want, but at the other person's expense and at the risk of losing a friend. Later, you tend to feel guilty about overreacting or coming on too strong (e.g., "I knew I shouldn't have said that").

Remember

Your goal is reconciliation, not retaliation.

When you're passive-aggressive, you get back at or get even with the other person by either (1) withholding or taking away something (e.g., not speaking to the other person or withdrawing all attention and affection), or (2) indirectly hinting that you're angry (e.g., by making cynical comments or using sarcastic humor).

In contrast, when you're assertive, you strike a happy medium between being too aggressive or too passive. You handle conflict in a way that protects or restores your rights without taking away or stepping on the rights of the other person. You approach conflict in an even-tempered way rather than in an angry or agitated manner; you speak in a normal volume rather than yelling or screaming; and you communicate at a normal distance rather than getting up close and into the face of the other person involved in the conflict. You can resolve conflicts assertively by using the following strategies.

- **Focus on the specific behavior causing the conflict, not the person's general character.** Avoid labeling the person as "selfish," "mean," "inconsiderate," etc. For instance, if you're upset because your roommate doesn't do his share of cleaning, stay away from aggressive labels such as "slacker" or "lazy bum." Attacking others with such negative labels does to the other person just what it sounds like: It makes the person feel like he's being verbally assaulted. This is likely to put him on the defensive and provoke a counterattack aimed at one of your personal characteristics. Before you know it, you're likely to find yourself in a full-out war of words and mutual character assassinations that has escalated well beyond a small-scale skirmish about the specific behavior in question.

  Rather than focusing on the person's general character, focus on the action that's causing the problem (e.g., failing to do the dishes or leaving dirty laundry around the room). This will enable the other person to know exactly what behavior needs to be changed to resolve the conflict. Furthermore, it's much easier to change a specific behavior than it is to change one's entire character, which would require a radical change in personality (or frontal lobotomy surgery).

- **Use "I" messages to focus on how the other person's behavior or action affects you.** "I" messages focus on what you're perceiving and feeling, which sends a message that's less accusatory and threatening to the other person. In contrast, "you" messages are more likely to make the other person defensive and put that person on the offensive—ready to retaliate rather than cooperate (Bippus & Young, 2005).

  Suppose you've received a course grade that's lower than what you think you earned or deserved and you decide to question your instructor about it. Don't begin by saying to the instructor, "You made a mistake," or "You gave me the wrong grade." These messages are likely to make your professor immediately ready to defend the grade you received. Your professor will be less threatened and more likely to listen to and consider your complaint if you initiate the conversation with an "I" statement, such as "I don't believe I received the correct grade" or "I think an error may have been made in my final grade."

"I" messages are less aggressive because you're targeting an issue, not a person (McKay, Davis, & Fanning, 2009). Saying, "I feel angry when . . ." rather than "You make me angry when . . . " sends the message that you're taking responsibility for the way you feel rather than guilt-tripping the individual for making you feel that way (perhaps without the person even being aware of how you feel). When using "I" messages:

a. Be specific about what emotion you're experiencing. For example, saying, "I feel neglected when you don't write or call" identifies what you're feeling more specifically than saying, "I wish you'd be more considerate." Describing what you feel in specific terms increases the persuasive power of your message and reduces the risk that the other person will misunderstand or discount it.

b. Be specific about what you're requesting of the other person to resolve the conflict. For example, "I would like for you to call me at least once a day" is more specific than "I want you to keep in touch with me."

c. Express what you want the other person to do in the form of a firm request rather than a demand or ultimatum. For example, saying, "I would like you to . . ." is less likely to put the person on the defensive than saying, "I insist . . ." or "I demand . . ."

7. **Avoid absolute judgments or blanket statements.** Compare the following three pairs of statements:

a. "You're no help at all" versus "You don't help me enough"

b. "You never try to understand how I feel" versus "You don't try hard enough to understand how I feel"

c. "I always have to clean up" versus "I'm doing more than my fair share of the cleaning"

The first statement in each of the preceding pairs is an absolute statement that covers all times, situations, and circumstances: it leaves no room for any possible exceptions. Such extreme, blanket criticisms are likely to put the criticized person on the defensive because they suggest the person is totally lacking or deficient with respect to the behavior in question (a character flaw). The second statement in each pair states the criticism in terms of degree or amount, which is less likely to threaten the person's self-esteem (and is probably closer to the truth).

Reflection 6.7

Your teammates aren't carrying their weight on a group project that you're all supposed to be working on together, and you're getting frustrated and angry because you're doing most of the work.

Construct an "I" message you could use to communicate your concern in a non-threatening way.

8. **Focus on solving the problem, not winning the argument.** Don't approach conflict with the attitude that you're going to get even or prove that you're right. Winning the argument but not persuading the person to change the behavior that's causing the conflict is like winning a battle but losing the war. Instead, approach conflict resolution as a problem to be solved in a way that allows both parties to win—i.e., both of you can end up with a better relationship in the long run.

"Precision of communication is important, more important than ever, in our era of hair-trigger balances, when a false or misunderstood word may create as much disaster as a sudden thoughtless act."

—James Thurber, U.S. author, humorist, and cartoonist

"Don't find fault. Find a remedy."

—Henry Ford, founder of Ford Motor Company and one of the richest people of his generation

9. **Conclude your discussion of the conflict on a warm, constructive note.** End on a positive note by ensuring that there are no hard feelings, and let the person know you're optimistic that the conflict can be resolved and your relationship improved.

10. **If the conflict is resolved because of some change made by the other person, express your appreciation for the individual's effort.** Even if your complaint was legitimate and your request was justified, the person's effort to accommodate your request shouldn't be taken for granted. At the least, you shouldn't react to a positive change in behavior by rubbing it in with sarcastic comments such as "That's more like it" or "It's about time!"

Expressing appreciation to the other person for making a change in response to your request is not only a socially sensitive thing to do but also a self-serving thing to do. By recognizing or reinforcing the other person's changed behavior, you increase the likelihood that the positive change in behavior will continue and you'll continue to benefit from the change.

"To keep your marriage brimming with love . . . when you're wrong, admit it; when you're right, shut up."

—Ogden Nash, American poet

Emotional Intelligence

Research shows that college students who score higher on tests of emotional intelligence, such as the ability to identify their emotions and moods, are (1) less likely to experience boredom (Harris, 2006) and (2) more able to focus their attention and get absorbed (in the zone) when completing challenging tasks (Wiederman, 2007). Excelling in college is a challenging task that will test your emotional strength and your ability to persist to task completion (graduation).

Research also indicates that experiencing positive emotions, such as optimism and excitement, promotes learning by increasing the brain's ability to take in, store, and retrieve information (Rosenfield, 1988). In one study involving nearly 4,000 first-year college students, it was found that students' level of optimism or hope for success during their first term on campus was a more accurate predictor of their first-year grades than was their SAT score or high school grade point average (Snyder, Harris, Anderson, Holleran, Irving, Sigmon, et al., 1991). In contrast, negative emotion—such as anxiety and fear—can interfere with the brain's ability to (1) store and retrieve memories, and (2) engage in higher-level thinking (Caine & Caine, 1991; Hertel & Brozovich, 2010).

Following are research-based strategies for minimizing the impact of negative emotions that sabotage success, as well as strategies for maximizing the impact of positive emotions that promote success.

Stress and Anxiety

Among the most common emotions that humans must monitor, manage, and regulate is stress. Students report experiencing higher levels of stress in college than they did in high school (Bartlett, 2002; Sax, 2003).

What exactly is stress? The biology of stress originates from the fight-or-flight reaction that's been wired into your body for survival purposes. This automatic reaction prepares us to handle danger or threat by flooding our bodies with chemicals (e.g., adrenaline) in the same way that ancient humans had to handle threats by engaging in fight or flight (escape) when confronted by life-threatening predators. The word *stress* derives from a Latin root that means "to draw tight." Thus, stress isn't necessarily bad; in the right amount, it can actually be productive. For example, a tightened guitar string generates better sound than a string that's too lax or loose, a tightened bow delivers a more powerful arrow shot, and a tightened muscle provides more strength or speed. Such productive stress is sometimes referred to as *eustress*—deriving from the root *eu* meaning "good" (as in the words *euphoria*, meaning a good mood, and *eulogy*, meaning good words).

If you keep college stress at a moderate level, it can be a productive emotion that promotes learning and personal development. Moderate stress can improve your:

1. Physical performance (e.g., strength and speed);
2. Mental performance (e.g., attention and memory); and
3. Mood (e.g., hope and optimism).

Reflection 6.8

Can you think of a situation in which you performed at a higher level because you were slightly nervous or experienced a moderate amount of stress?

However, if stress becomes extreme and continues for a prolonged period, it moves from being productive to destructive. Using the guitar string as an analogy, if it's strung too tightly, the string is likely to snap or break, which isn't productive. Unproductive stress is often referred to as *distress*—from the root *dis* meaning "bad" (as in the words *discomfort* and *disease*). Extreme stress can create the negative feeling of anxiety and contribute to anxiety disorders (e.g., panic attacks). If stress persists at a high level for a prolonged period, it can trigger psychosomatic illnesses—tension-induced bodily disorders (from *psyche*, meaning "mind," and *soma*, meaning "body"). For instance, prolonged distress can trigger indigestion by increasing secretion of stomach acids or contribute to high blood pressure, a.k.a. hypertension. Prolonged stress can also suppress the immune system, leaving you more vulnerable to flu, colds, and other infectious diseases. Studies show that the immune systems of college students are suppressed (produce fewer antibodies) at stressful times during the

Research indicates that college students' stress levels tend to rise when they are experiencing a wave of exams, such as midterms and finals.

© Kendall Hunt Publishing Company

academic term, such as during midterms and finals (Bosch, de Geus, Ring, & Nieuw-Amerongen, 2004; Deinzer, Kleineidam, Stiller-Winkler, Idel, & Bachg, 2000).

Excess stress interferes with mental performance because anxious feelings and thoughts begin to preoccupy our mind, taking up valuable space in our working memory, leaving it with less capacity to process information we're trying to learn and retain. Studies also show that students experiencing higher levels of academic stress and performance anxiety are more likely to use ineffective surface approaches to learning that rely on memorization (Biggs & Tang, 2007; Ramsden, 2003) rather than effective deep-learning strategies that involve seeking meaning and understanding. Furthermore, high levels of test anxiety are more likely to interfere with memory for information that's been studied and to result in careless concentration errors on exams—e.g., overlooking key words in test questions (Tobias, 1985, 1993). Although considerable research points to the negative effects of excess stress, you still need to keep in mind that stress can work either for or against you: you can be either energized or sabotaged by stress depending on its level of intensity and the length of time it continues. You can't expect to stop or eliminate stress completely, nor should you want to: you can only hope to contain it and maintain it at a level where it's more productive than destructive. Many years of research indicate that personal performance is best when it takes place under conditions of moderate stress because this creates a sense of challenge. On the other hand, too much stress creates performance anxiety, and too little stress results in loss of intensity or indifference (Sapolsky, 2004; Yerkes & Dodson, 1908). (See Figure 6.1.)

Reflection 6.9

How would you rate your level of anxiety in the following situations?

1. Taking tests or exams	high	moderate	low
2. Interacting in social situations	high	moderate	low
3. Making decisions about the future	high	moderate	low

FIGURE 6.1

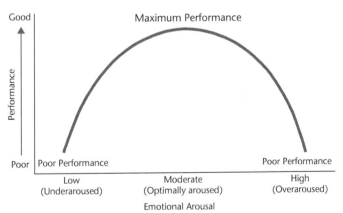

Moderate challenge that produces moderate stress typically promotes maximum (peak) performance.

Source: Williams, Landers, & Boutcher (1993).

Relationship between Arousal and Performance

Snapshot Summary 6.3 provides a short summary of the signs or symptoms of extreme stress that indicate stress has climbed to a level where it's creating distress or anxiety. If these symptoms are experienced for an extended period (e.g., longer than a week), deliberate action should be taken to reduce them.

Snapshot Summary

6.3 High Anxiety: Recognizing the Symptoms (Signs) of Distress

- Jitteriness or shaking, especially in the hands
- Accelerated heart rate or heart palpitations: irregular heartbeat
- Muscle tension: tightness in the chest or upper shoulders or a tight feeling (lump) in the throat (the expressions "uptight" and "choking" stem from these symptoms of upper-body tension)
- Body aches: heightened muscle tension leading to tension headaches, backaches, or chest pain (in extreme cases, it can feel as if a heart attack is taking place)
- Sweating, especially sweaty (clammy) palms
- Cold, pale hands or feet, symptoms that have led to the expressions "white knuckles" and "cold feet" to describe someone who is very anxious
- Dry mouth: decreased production of saliva (leading to the expression

"cotton mouth" and the need for very nervous speakers to have water nearby)
- Stomach discomfort or indigestion due to increased secretion of stomach acid (the expression "feeling butterflies in my stomach" relates to this symptom)
- Gastrointestinal discomfort, e.g., stomach cramps, constipation, or diarrhea
- Feeling faint or dizzy due to constriction of blood vessels that decreases oxygen flow to the brain
- Weakness and fatigue: a sustained (chronic) state of arousal and prolonged muscle tension becomes tiring
- Menstrual changes: missing or irregular menstrual periods
- Difficulty sleeping: insomnia or interrupted (fitful) sleep
- Increased susceptibility to colds, flu, and other infections due to suppression of the body's immune system

---

Effective Methods for Managing Stress

Student Perspective

"My stress has caused me to lose a lot of weight; my appetite is cut in half. My sleep pattern is off; I have trouble falling/staying asleep. No matter how stressed I was in high school, this never happened [before]. What can I do to de-stress?"

—First-term college student

If you perceive your level of stress to be reaching a point where it's beginning to interfere with the quality of your academic performance or personal life, you need to take steps to reduce it. Listed here are three stress-management methods whose positive effects have been well documented by research in psychology and biology (Benson & Klipper, 1990; Lehrer et al., 2007).

Deep (Diaphragmatic) Breathing

The type of breathing associated with excessive stress is hyperventilation—fast, shallow, and irregular breathing through the mouth rather than the chest. Breathing associated with relaxation is just the opposite—slow, deep, and regular breathing that originates from the stomach.

Breathing is something you usually do automatically (involuntarily) without conscious awareness. However, with some concentration and effort, you can gain voluntary control of your breathing by controlling your diaphragm—the muscle that enables you to expand and contract your lungs. By voluntarily controlling the diaphragm muscle, you can slow your breathing rate, which, in turn, can bring down your stress level.

Progressive Muscle Relaxation

This is a stress-management method similar to stretching exercises that are used to relax and loosen muscles before and after physical exercise. Total body (head-to-toe) muscle relaxation can be achieved by progressively tensing and releasing the five sets of muscles listed below. For each muscle area listed, hold the tension for about five seconds and then release it slowly.

1. Wrinkle your forehead muscles, then release them.
2. Shrug your shoulders up as if to touch your ears, then drop them.
3. Make a fist with each hand, then open both.
4. Tighten your stomach muscles, then release them.
5. Tighten your toes by curling them under your feet, and then raise them as high as you can.

Student
Perspective

"To relax, I like to stretch a lot."

—First-year college student

To help tense your muscles before releasing them, imagine using your muscles to push or lift a heavy object. When relaxing your muscles, take a deep breath and think or say, "Relax." By breathing deeply and thinking or hearing "Relax" each time you release your muscles, you come to associate the word with your muscles becoming relaxed. Thus, if you find yourself in a stressful situation, you can take a deep breath, think or say, "Relax," and immediately reduce tension because your muscles have been conditioned to relax in response to that word. You can do this at any time and in any place: for example, when you're stuck in traffic, waiting in line, or waiting to take a test.

Mental Imagery

Create visual images to generate relaxation. You can create your own relaxing mental movie or imaginary DVD by visually placing yourself in a calm, comfortable, and soothing setting. Visualize images such as ocean waves, floating clouds, sitting in a warm sauna, or any sensory experience that tends to relax you. The more senses you use, the more real the scene will seem and the more powerful its relaxing effects will be (Fezler, 1989). Try to use all of your senses—not only to see it, but try to hear it, smell it, touch it, and feel it. You can also use musical imagination to create calming background music that accompanies your visual image.

Author's Experience My wife, Mary, is a kindergarten teacher. Whenever her young students start misbehaving and the situation becomes stressful (e.g., during lunchtime when the kids are running wildly, arguing vociferously, and screaming at maximum volume), Mary "plays" relaxing songs in her head. She reports that her musical imagination always works to soothe her nerves, enabling her to remain calm and even-tempered when she must confront children who need to be scolded or disciplined.

— *Joe Cuseo*

Reflection 6.10

What are your most common sources or causes of stress?

What strategies do you use to cope with stress?

Would you say that you cope with stress well?

Simple Stress-Reduction Strategies and Habits

In addition to formal stress-management techniques of diaphragmatic breathing, progressive muscle relaxation, and mental imagery, stress may be managed by simpler strategies and habits, such as those discussed below.

1. **Exercise.** Exercise reduces stress by increasing release of serotonin—a mellowing brain chemical that reduces feelings of tension (anxiety) and depression. Studies also show that people who exercise regularly tend to report feeling happier (Myers, 1993). Exercise also elevates mood by improving people's sense of self-esteem because it gives them a sense of accomplishment by improving their physical self-image. It is for these reasons that counselors and psychotherapists recommend exercise for patients experiencing milder forms of anxiety or depression (Johnsgard, 2004).

2. **Keep a journal of feelings and emotions.** Writing about our feelings in a personal journal can serve as an effective way to identify our emotions (one form of emotional intelligence) and provide a safe outlet for releasing steam and coping with stress. Writing about our emotions also enables us to become more aware of them, reducing the risk that we'll deny them and push them out of consciousness.

3. **Take time for humor and laughter.** Research on the power of humor for reducing tension is clear and convincing. In one study, college students were suddenly told they had to deliver an impromptu (off the top of their head) speech. This unexpected assignment caused students' heart rate to elevate to an average of 110 beats per minute during delivery of the speech. However, students who watched humorous episodes of sitcoms before delivering their impromptu speeches had an average heart rate during the speech that was significantly lower (80–85 beats per minute), suggesting that humor reduces anxiety (O'Brien, as cited in Howard, 2000). Research also shows that if our immune system is suppressed or weakened by stress, humor strengthens it by blocking the body's production of the stress hormone cortisol—a biochemical responsible for suppressing our immune system when we're stressed (Berk, as cited in Liebertz, 2005b).

> "There are thousands of causes for stress, and one antidote to stress is self-expression. That's what happens to me every day. My thoughts get off my chest, down my sleeves, and onto my pad."
>
> —Garson Kanin, American writer, actor, and film director

> "The arrival of a good clown exercises a more beneficial influence upon the health of a town than the arrival of twenty asses laden with drugs."
>
> —Thomas Sydenham, 17th-century physician

Depression

Along with anxiety, depression is the emotional problem that most commonly afflicts humans and needs to be managed. Depression may be succinctly described as an emotional state characterized by loss of optimism, hope, and energy. As the term implies, when we're depressed, our mood is lowered or pushed down (like depressing the accelerator in a car). In contrast to anxiety, which typically involves worrying about something that is currently happening or is about to happen (e.g., experiencing test anxiety before an upcoming exam), depression more often relates to something that has already happened. In particular, depression is often related to a loss, such as a lost relationship (e.g., a departed friend, a broken romance, or the death of a family member) or a lost opportunity (e.g., losing a job, failing a course, or failing to be accepted into a major) (Bowlby, 1980; Price, Choi, & Vinokur, 2002). It is natural and normal to feel dejected after losses such as these. However, if dejection reaches a point where we can't concentrate and complete our day-to-day tasks, and if this continues for an extended period, we may be experiencing what psychologists call *clinical depression*—i.e., depression so serious that it requires professional help.

Research indicates that depression is a significant predictor of lower college GPA and higher probability of withdrawing from college, even among highly motivated and academically well-prepared students (Eisenberg, Golberstein, & Hunt, 2009).

6.1

Recognizing the Symptoms (Signs) of Depression

- Feeling low, down, dejected, sad, or blue
- Pessimistic feelings about the future (e.g., expecting failure or feeling helpless or hopeless)
- Decreased sense of humor
- Difficulty finding pleasure, joy, or fun in anything
- Lack of concentration
- Loss of motivation or interest in things previously found to be exciting or stimulating
- Stooped posture (e.g., hung head or drawn face)
- Slower and softer speech rate
- Decreased animation and slower bodily movements
- Loss of energy
- Changes in sleeping patterns (e.g., sleeping more or less than usual)
- Changes in eating patterns (e.g., eating more or less than usual)
- Social withdrawal
- Neglect of physical appearance
- Consistently low self-esteem (e.g., thinking "I'm a loser")
- Strong feelings of worthlessness or guilt (e.g., thinking "I'm a failure")
- Suicidal thoughts (e.g., thoughts such as "I can't take it anymore," "People would be better off without me," or "I don't deserve to live")

Do It Now! 6.1 provides a summary of symptoms or signs of depression. If these symptoms continue to occur for two or more weeks, action should be taken to relieve them.

> **Remember**
> There is a difference between feeling despondent or down and being depressed. When psychologists use the word **depression**, they're usually referring to clinical depression—a mood state so low that it's interfering with a person's ability to cope with day-to-day life tasks, such as getting to school or going to work.

Reflection 6.11

Have you, or a member of your family, ever experienced clinical depression?

What do you think was the primary cause or factor that triggered it?

Strategies for Coping with Depression

Depression can vary widely in intensity. Moderate and severe forms of depression often require professional counseling or psychotherapy, and their cause often lies in genetic factors that involve inherited imbalances in brain chemistry.

The following strategies are offered primarily for milder cases of depression that are manageable through self-help and self-control. These strategies may also be used in conjunction with professional help or psychiatric medication to reduce the intensity and frequency of depression.

1. **Focus on the present and the future, not the past.** We should consciously fight the tendency to dwell on past losses or failures, because we can no longer change or control them. Instead, focus on things you can still control, which are occurring now and will occur in the future. This can be a challenging task because when you have an experience, your response to it passes through emotional areas of the brain before it reaches areas of the brain involved in rational thinking and reasoning (LeDoux, 1998, 2003). (See Figure 6.2.)

   Thus, your brain reacts to events emotionally before it does rationally. If an experience triggers intense emotions (e.g., anger, anxiety, or sadness after receiving a bad test grade), your emotional reaction has the potential to short-circuit or wipe out rational thinking. Thus, if you find yourself beginning to feel overwhelmed by negative emotions following a setback, you need to consciously and quickly block them with rational thoughts (e.g., thinking or saying to yourself, "Before I get carried away emotionally, let me think this through rationally"). This involves more than simply saying, "I have to stay positive." Instead, you should develop a set of specific counter-thinking strategies ready to use as soon as you begin to think negatively.

2. **Increase effort to engage in positive or emotionally uplifting behavior.** If our behavior is upbeat, our mind (mood) often follows suit. "Put on a happy face" may be an effective depression-reduction strategy because smiling induces certain changes in our facial muscles, which, in turn, trigger changes in brain chemistry that improve our mood (Liebertz, 2005a). In contrast, frowning activates a different set of facial muscles that tend to reduce production of mood-elevating brain chemicals (Myers, 1993).

3. **Continue to engage in activities that are fun and enjoyable.** Falling into the downward spiral of withdrawing from doing the things that bring you joy because you're too down to do them will bring you even lower by taking away the very things that bring you up. You should continue to socialize with friends and engage in your usual recreational activities. Interestingly, the root of the word *recreation* means "to re-create" (create again), which suggests that recreation can revive, restore, and renew us—physically and emotionally.

4. **Continue trying to get things done.** By staying busy and getting things done when we're feeling down, helps boost our mood because we experience a sense of accomplishment that boosts our self-esteem. Doing things for others less fortunate than yourself can be a particularly effective way to elevate your mood because it helps you realize that your issues are often far less serious and more manageable than the problems faced by others.

> "Yesterday is gone. Tomorrow has not yet come. We have only today. Let us begin."
>
> —Mother Teresa of Calcutta, Albanian Catholic nun and winner of the Nobel Peace Prize

> "The best way to cheer yourself up is to try to cheer somebody else up."
>
> —Samuel Clemens, a.k.a. Mark Twain, writer, lecturer, and humorist

FIGURE 6.2

Information passes through the emotional center of the brain (lower, shaded area) before reaching the center responsible for rational thinking (upper area). Thus, people need to counteract their tendency to respond emotionally and irrationally to personal setbacks by making a conscious attempt to respond rationally and positively.

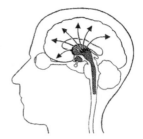

© Kendall Hunt

The Human Brain First Processes Information Emotionally before It Reaches Higher Areas of Rational Thinking

5. **Intentionally seek out humor and opportunities to laugh.** In addition to reducing anxiety, laughter can lighten and brighten a dark mood. In addition, humor improves memory (Nielson, as cited in Liebertz, 2005a), which is an important benefit because depression tends to impair concentration and memory. Research supporting the benefits of humor for the body and mind is so well established that humor has become a legitimate academic field of study known as *gelontology*—the study of laughter (from the Greek word *gelos* for "laughter" and *ology*, meaning "study of").

"If you can laugh at it, you can survive it."
—Bill Cosby, American comedian, actor, and activist

6. **Make a conscious effort to focus on your personal strengths and accomplishments.** Another way to drive away the blues is by keeping track of the positive developments in your life. You can do this by keeping a positive events journal in which you note the good experiences in your life, including things you're grateful for, as well as your accomplishments and achievements. Positive journal entries will leave you with a visible uplifting record that you can review any time you're feeling down. Furthermore, a positive events journal can provide a starting point for developing a resume, portfolio, and personal strengths sheet, which can be provided to those who serve as your personal references and those who write letters of recommendation for you.

7. **If you're unable to overcome depression on your own, seek help from others.** Compared to previous generations, today's college students are more likely to seek professional help if they're feeling depressed (Kadison & DiGeronimo, 2004). This is good news because it suggests that seeking help is no longer viewed as a source of embarrassment or a sign of personal weakness: instead, college students are more willing to share their feelings with others and improve the quality of their emotional life.

One strategy for coping with depression is to write down the positive events in your life in a journal.

In some cases, students may be able to help themselves overcome emotional problems through personal effort and effective coping strategies. This is particularly true if they experience depression or anxiety in milder forms and for limited periods. However, overcoming more serious and long-lasting episodes of clinical depression or anxiety isn't as simple as people make it out to be when they glibly and insensitively say, "Just deal with it," "Get over it," or "Snap out of it." More serious cases of depression and anxiety are often strongly associated with genetic factors, which are not completely within the person's ability to control.

Reflection 6.12

If you thought you were experiencing a serious episode of anxiety or depression, would you feel comfortable seeking help from a professional?

If yes, why? If no, why not?

Summary and Conclusion

The quality of our interpersonal relationships is strengthened by communication skills (verbal and nonverbal) and human relations (people) skills. We can improve our interactions and relationships by working hard at remembering the names and interests of people we meet, being good listeners, and being open to different topics of conversation.

Interpersonal conflict is an inevitable aspect of social life; we can't completely eliminate it, but we can minimize and manage it with effective strategies that enable us to resolve conflicts assertively rather than aggressively, passively, or passive–aggressively.

Today's college students report higher levels of stress than students in years past. Strategies for reducing excess stress include formal stress-management techniques (e.g., diaphragmatic breathing and progressive muscle relaxation), good physical habits (e.g., exercising and reducing intake of caffeine or other stimulants), and positive ways of thinking (e.g., focusing on the present and the future, rather than the past, and making a conscious effort to focus on our personal strengths and accomplishments).

Intellectual ability is only one form of human intelligence. Social and emotional intelligence are at least as important for being successful, healthy, and happy. The strategies discussed in this chapter are not merely "soft skills": they're actually "hardcore" skills essential for success in college and beyond.

Learning More through the World Wide Web

Internet-Based Resources for Further Information on Social and Emotional Intelligence

For additional information related to the ideas discussed in this chapter, we recommend the following Web sites:

Social Intelligence and Interpersonal Relationships:

www.articles911.com/Communication/Interpersonal_Communication/hodu.com/ECS-Menu1.shtml

Emotional Intelligence and Mental Health:

www.eqi.org/eitoc.htm

www.nimh.nih.gov/health/publications/index.shtml (National Institute of Mental Health)

www.activeminds.org (national, student-run organization that supports mental health awareness)

6.1 Identifying Ways of Handling Interpersonal Conflict

Think of a social situation or relationship that's currently causing the most conflict in your life. Describe how this conflict could be approached in each of the following ways:

1. Passively:
2. Aggressively:
3. Passive-aggressively:
4. Assertively:

(See pp. 172–173 for descriptions of each of these four approaches.)

Practice the assertive approach by role-playing it with a friend or classmate and consider applying it to the actual situation or relationship in your life that's currently causing you the most conflict.

6.2 College Stress: Identifying Potential Sources and Possible Solutions

Read through the following 29 college stressors and rate them in terms of how stressful each one is for you on a scale from 1 to 5 (1 = lowest, 5 = highest):

Potential Stressors	Stress Rating				
Tests and exams	1	2	3	4	5
Assignments	1	2	3	4	5
Class workload	1	2	3	4	5
Pace of courses	1	2	3	4	5
Performing up to expectations	1	2	3	4	5
Handling personal freedom	1	2	3	4	5
Time pressure (e.g., not enough time)	1	2	3	4	5
Organizational pressure (e.g., losing things)	1	2	3	4	5
Living independently	1	2	3	4	5
The future	1	2	3	4	5
Decisions about a major or career	1	2	3	4	5
Moral and ethical decisions	1	2	3	4	5
Finding meaning in life	1	2	3	4	5
Emotional issues	1	2	3	4	5
Physical health	1	2	3	4	5
Social life	1	2	3	4	5
Intimate relationships	1	2	3	4	5
Sexuality	1	2	3	4	5

Family responsibilities	1	2	3	4	5
Family conflicts	1	2	3	4	5
Family pressure	1	2	3	4	5
Peer pressure	1	2	3	4	5
Loneliness or isolation	1	2	3	4	5
Roommate conflicts	1	2	3	4	5
Conflict with professors	1	2	3	4	5
Campus policies or procedures	1	2	3	4	5
Transportation	1	2	3	4	5
Technology	1	2	3	4	5
Safety	1	2	3	4	5

Review your ratings and write down three of your top (highest-rated) stressors. Identify: (1) a coping strategy you may use on your own to deal with each source of stress, and (2) a campus resource you could use to obtain help with each source of stress.

Stressor: _____

Personal coping strategy:

Campus resource:

Stressor: _____

Personal coping strategy:

Campus resource:

Stressor: _____

Personal coping strategy:

Campus resource:

6.3 Transforming Pessimistic Thought into Optimistic Thoughts

In *Hamlet*, Shakespeare wrote, "There is nothing good or bad, but thinking makes it so." His point was that our experiences have the potential to be positive or negative, depending on how we interpret them and react to them.

Listed below is a series of statements representing negative interpretations and reactions to a bad situation or personal setback.

1. "I'm just not good at this."

2. "There's nothing I can do about it."

3. "Things will never be the same."

4. "This always happens to me."

5. "This is unbearable."

6. "Everybody is going to think I'm a loser."

For each of the above statements, replace the negative statement with a statement that reflects a more positive interpretation or reaction—i.e., one that would decrease anxiety and increase the person's sense of optimism or hope.

Caught between a Rock and a Hard Place: Romantic versus Academic Commitments

Lauren has been dating her boyfriend (Nick) for about two months. She's convinced this is the real thing and that she's definitely in love. Lately, Nick has been asking her to skip class to spend more time with him. He tells Lauren, "If you really love me, you would do it for our relationship." Lauren feels that Nick truly loves her and wouldn't do anything to hurt her or interfere with her goals. So she figures that skipping a few classes to spend time with her boyfriend is the right choice. However, Lauren's grades soon start to slip; at the same time, Nick starts to demand that she spend even more time with him.

Reflection and Discussion Questions

1. What concerns you most about Lauren's behavior?

2. What concerns you most about Nick's behavior?

3. Would you agree with Lauren's decision to start skipping classes?

4. What might Lauren do to keep her grades up and still keep her relationship with Nick strong?

5. If you were Lauren's friend, what advice would you give her?

6. If you were Nick's friend, what advice would you give him?

Hampton Helped Me!

Jack Manning III

Photo courtesy of Hampton University

Jack Manning III has been doing art all of his life and photography since the age of 13. Jack began his matriculation at Hampton University in 1994 as an engineering major. During his second year, Jack changed his major to Graphic Design and started taking an introduction to photography class. After developing his first print in the darkroom of Armstrong-Slater, he was hooked!

Upon graduating from Hampton University, Jack decided to turn his hobby into something greater. He has been published in Ebony, Sister Sister, Billboard, Jet and Essence Magazines, and his work has been featured in O Magazine, on the Own network, Buzzfeed, Source, ABC's Good Morning America and many more. Jack has also had the honor of being a commencement photographer and photographing the President of the United States, Barack Obama in 2010.

For the past ten years, Jack has enjoyed a schedule that affords him the opportunity to photograph friends and family from Hampton University as well as a mix of celebrity, fashion, corporate, commercial, and industrial clients, in addition to weddings. Jack currently resides in Atlanta, Georgia with his wife, Tene (Taper) Manning, HU class of 2001, and their two daughters, Kaylee and Devi. Jack hopes to continue to grow his business and eventually move into film and directing.

Hampton Helped Me!

Robi Reed

Photo © Derek Blanks, D. Blanks Studio

Denzel Washington, Halle Berry, Rosie Perez and Queen Latifah all have something in common with Emmy Award-winning casting director Robi Reed. Her magic touch landed them major roles in their careers. Blessed with an eye for talent and a gift for spotting a diamond in the rough, her career has spanned over 27 years. Reed has had a hand in the careers of many and is known for taking the ordinary and creating the extraordinary. Her ability to match a role with the perfect choice has made household names out of Jamie Foxx, who she discovered at a local comedy club in Los Angeles, and Mekhi Phifer, who she plucked from an open casting call. Reed has more than 50 films to her credit, including blockbusters *Soul Food*, *The Best Man*, *For Colored Girls*, *Love Jones*, *Set It Off* and *Antwone Fisher*, in which she cast Derek Luke in his first leading role. Her first studio film came with Spike Lee's *School Daze*. She went on to cast Lee's *Do The Right Thing*, *Mo' Better Blues*, *Crooklyn*, *Clockers* and *Jungle Fever*, breaking out two of Hollywood's biggest stars, Samuel L. Jackson and Halle Berry.

Reed holds a Bachelor of Science degree in Speech Communication and Theatre from Hampton University. She recently received the National Hampton Alumni Association, Inc. *Legacy Award*. Reed is a member of Delta Sigma Theta Sorority, Inc. She is also the proud mother of college freshman Noah and high school junior Summer Humes.

CHAPTER 7
Financial Literacy

"An investment in knowledge pays the best interest… When it comes to investing, nothing will pay off more than educating yourself. Do the necessary research, study and analysis before making any investment decisions."

—Alan Lakein

Upon completion of this chapter, you will be able to:

- **Acquire** knowledge of the financial planning process
- **Identify** pitfalls to financial literacy
- **List** your financial strengths and weaknesses
- **Review** 5 Cs of Credit
- **Develop** and use a budget to manage and control spending

Financial Literacy

7

Where Does All the Money Go?

As would happen, two of our students stopped by on the very same day a few years after their graduation and talked about their school loans. The first student was excited. She had paid off her school loans in just three short years and now was ready to buy her first home. The financial planning process she learned in class helped her track her everyday expenditures and put some additional money toward paying off her school loans. She paid off $28,000 in three years rather than the ten it usually takes.

The second student was not as happy. He was looking for advice on how he could better manage his expenses. He had never implemented a financial plan or even created a cash flow statement and was having trouble making his school loan payment.

The difference between these two students is big. What did our first student do that allowed her to pay off her school loan so quickly that our second student did not do?

Financial Planning Process

Ask this question: "Do I have enough money, or would I like to have more?" Everyone who understands that money is what it takes to buy more stuff wants more of it. It does not mean you are being greedy. In fact, maybe you would like to have more money because there are so many great things you would like to do with that money, such as build a shelter for abandoned animals or sponsor cancer research for children. Businesses always want more money, but so do nonprofit organizations. You may even be part of a group on campus that tries to raise money for various projects or causes. No matter how noble the intentions, everyone focuses on getting more money.

But more money is not the answer. That is the fallacy that most people buy into. The purpose of this chapter is not to help you earn more money, but to help you learn the financial competencies necessary to make the most of whatever money you do earn. Financial success is not about how much you make, it's about how much you spend.

If you think financial success is tied to income, look at Michael Jackson. When he passed away, he was preparing for his "This Is It" tour. He wasn't going back on the road because he missed the crowds and adulation. "This Is It" was happening because *he was broke*. Reportedly worth $400 million at one time, Michael's home (Neverland Ranch) had been taken from him, and he was on the verge of bankruptcy.

Michael Jackson is not an isolated example. It was rumored for several years that Lindsey Lohan was broke. She had allegedly gone through over $7 million. She had to sell her apartments in Los Angeles and New York to help cover expenses, which included 24-hour chauffeur service, $1,200-night stays at the Chateau Marmont, tanning and salon services, and clothing and partying, which also led to several stints at rehab clinics.

If people who have a seven-figure income going back to their early childhood can go broke, what hope is there for the rest of us? You cannot outearn financial ignorance.

From *Life Skills for Student Success: Achieving Financial Literacy* by William Pratt, Mark Weitzel, and Len Rhodes. Copyright © 2011 by William Pratt, Mark Weitzel, and Len Rhodes. Reprinted by permission of Kendall Hunt Publishing Company.

You have heard the term *financial literacy*. The term tends to get thrown around quite often these days. You hear teachers, parents, news reporters, and even members of congress use the phrase. So what is financial literacy anyway? Is it reading the *Wall Street Journal?* Do you have to get up every morning and sip a cup of coffee, browse the paper, and repeat phrases such as "commodity futures are down and the euro has gained on the dollar," all while spilling jam on your pressed, white shirt? Perhaps financial literacy is simply the ability to make more money? We discussed careers in the previous chapter with hints and tips on how to be successful in your field. Maybe just being able to understand your credit card bill makes you financially literate. Or maybe financial literacy can be demonstrated by making sound financial decisions.

Although many people may have a slightly different definition of financial literacy, most would agree that a combination of all the above would make for a strong case of financial literacy. So why is it so important to increase your financial literacy? Everyone knows that literacy is important because if you cannot read and write, it will be difficult to get a decent job. But why is *financial literacy* so important? Before we can answer that question, we have to understand the pitfalls of poor financial literacy.

Pitfalls of Poor Financial Literacy

Every day people walk onto car lots and believe everything the car salesperson tells them and drive off the lot with a brand new car. In the process we break nearly every rule about smart car shopping, and the worst part is we feel good about it. When we buy our first home, we make the same mistakes. Instead of doing it the right way and protecting our finances, we do it the way an industry wants us to, much to the demise of our own financial health.

What you will learn throughout this book is that entire industries are designed to take advantage of your financial illiteracy. They will not do anything illegal, unethical, or immoral, but they will separate you from as much of your money as they possibly can. You will drive off a car dealer's lot paying $5,000 less than the sticker price. You will think you got a good deal but did you really? Do you know what you should have paid? Do you know that the dealer, the salesperson, the insurance agent, and the bank all want you to get that new car? It must be nice to have so many people on your side. But why are they on your side all of a sudden? Is it in your best interest that you buy the car today or is it in *their* best interest? It is all in the way that they are compensated.

Even before the most recent financial crisis that resulted in high unemployment and skyrocketing home foreclosure rates, Americans were averaging nearly 1.5 million personal bankruptcies per year. You might be thinking that bankruptcies are like the reset button on your Xbox or Wii. If you just reset it before you lose, then that game does not count. That could not be farther from the truth. You hear that bankruptcies stay on your record for seven years and then go away. What record are they talking about? Are they referring to your credit score or your public record? Bankruptcies continue to affect you well beyond the seven years that it stays on your credit report. Bankruptcy is a public admission of failure. It is a very emotional process, and the feelings that go with declaring bankruptcy stay with you for the rest of your life.

After graduation, you start a full-time job. Your first couple of days on the job involve filling out a lot of paperwork. Much of that paperwork affects your wealth, your ability to retire, your health insurance, and more. If you do not understand the paperwork, you are likely to make some serious financial mistakes that will have lifelong consequences.

It is too easy to get ripped off if you do not have a firm grasp of basic personal financial principles. Financial "experts" give all kinds of advice, and it is up to you to discern what advice is good and what is bad. For instance, one financial "expert" says not to buy disability insurance while you are healthy. Well, who in their right mind is going to sell disability insurance to you once you become sick or disabled? That would be like selling car insurance to you right after your car is totaled. Investment "experts" sell seminars and software to teach you how to get rich with no money down or how to get rich as a day trader. If it was really that easy to be a day trader, then everyone would already be doing it. What they fail to explain to you is that although you can achieve annualized returns of 300% in the short term, there are high costs involved as well as high risk that could lead to losses of 300% or more. They also fail to include the high costs of brokerage commissions, tax consequences, and the fact that you will be a nervous wreck as you are constantly watching the ups and downs of the stock market by the minute. If it was easy to make $5,000 per month from home working part time, then why would anyone work outside the home full time at a job for less than $5,000 per month? As you begin to understand the basics of personal finance, you will be able to know the right questions to ask to determine who is right and who is simply misleading you for their own personal gain.

Poor financial decisions spill over into our personal lives as well. For instance, nearly half of all marriages end in divorce. The number one reason marriages fail is not infidelity but money issues and arguments. It is not the lack of money that causes the problems, otherwise only the poor would get divorced, whereas the wealthy would have long happy marriages. It is the disagreement and stress involving money that can contribute to a failing marriage. In many cases the wealthy are at greater risk. In some cases one spouse is a spender and one is a saver, and instead of talking about money, they simply work against each other until the resentment builds up to the point that the two just cannot stand each other anymore. After all, we talk more openly about sex in our society than we do about money. A couple who understands personal finance can work together, even if one is a saver and one is a spender, because they know how to communicate with each other and let their strengths complement each other.

Goals

So how do we achieve personal financial success? We set goals. If we do not have any goals, then how can we ever determine if we are heading in the right direction? The key is to set realistic goals. Do not set a goal of making one million dollars your first month of summer vacation unless you have a real plan on how to accomplish it. Think about a sports team that comes in last place. The very next season they are going to set new goals to improve their record, but if the coach simply says the team is going to go from last place to winning the national championship in one season without a plan, nobody on the team will be able to get behind the goal because it is not realistic. On the other hand, if the coach says they are going to rebuild and have a winning record the next season and work their way to the national championship over the next four years, then that is a realistic goal that the fans and the players can support and believe. You want to set realistic, achievable goals. For instance, your goal may be to graduate in four years or to make a certain amount of money within two or three years after graduation. The key is to give some thought to your goals because this is the very first step in your financial plan.

Timelines

Our goals can be short term, mid range, or long term. Although there is no exact cutoff point, short-term goals tend to be less than three years, mid-range goals three to five years, and long-term goals five years or longer. A short-term goal may be to save enough money over the summer to cover your expenses during the next school year. A mid-range goal may be to have enough money for a good down payment on a car in three or four years. A long-term goal may be to purchase a home within the next ten years or save enough money so you can retire when you choose.

SMART Goals

Now that we can differentiate between the different time periods for our goals, we need to make sure we are choosing the correct types of goals. The easiest way to remember how to set goals is to use the acronym SMART. SMART refers to goals that are Specific, Measurable, Attainable, Relevant, and Time framed.

Specific: Avoid general terms such as, "I plan to graduate from college." Instead, choose something specific such as "I plan to graduate from this university with a Bachelor of Science degree in Biology."

Measurable: Emphasize how much. For instance, "I will have a very good semester," is not measurable. Instead use something measurable such as, "I will get three As and one B this semester."

Achievable: Your goal must be realistic and achievable for you or your organization. You need to be able to look at the goal and say, "I can do that." For instance, if you start a new organization on campus and your goal is to have every student on campus join your organization, not only is that highly improbable, but you will also have a difficult time motivating the other members in your group. Instead, choose a more realistic goal, such as getting a certain percentage of the campus to join each semester over the next few semesters until a reasonably sized group has been achieved.

Relevant: The goal must be relevant to you. It needs to be yours and not your parents' goal for you. If the goal is your own, then you are more likely to succeed. If your parents' goal for you is to become a lawyer, and you want to be a school-teacher, you will be hard pressed to really do what is necessary to be a successful lawyer because it is not your goal.

Time Framed: You need a time frame in which to measure progress. For instance, if your goal is simply to obtain a college degree, then you could take one class every other semester for the next ten years or more. On the other hand if your goal is to earn your degree within the next five years, you can now measure your progress each semester by seeing how close you are to your goal and how well you are doing to keep yourself on pace to achieve it. The time-framed concept is one of the reasons why milestone birthdays are so difficult for some people if they have not achieved certain goals. For instance, most of us make goals or promises for ourselves such as "I want to have my first novel written by age 30," or "I want to own my own business by age 35."

Good Goals for Everyone

Although everyone has different goals based on their own personal situations, goal setting may be new to you. To help get you started, here are some goals that are good for just about everyone.

- *Build an emergency fund*—An emergency fund is a reserve or cushion to get you through the hard times, whether it is a period of unemployment or unexpected repairs for your car. Building an emergency fund may be your first SMART goal after college.
- *Save for retirement*—Time is on your side. The sooner you start saving for retirement, the less you will be required to save to reach your goal.
- *Save for a house*—Homeownership is the American dream, but it does not come cheap.
- *Save for big purchases*—If you make all of your large purchases on credit instead of saving ahead of time everything that you buy will be significantly more expensive.

- *Pay off school loans*—The sooner you pay off your loan balance, the sooner you have more money left at the end of the month.

Net Worth

Assume for a moment that you are going on a trip. You know exactly where you want to go, so you go to Google Maps and type in your destination. If you click on 'Driving Directions,' Google does not plot out your plan for travel right away. Google cannot tell you how to get to where you want to go without first knowing your starting point. If Google cannot do it, then it is probably safe to assume that we cannot do it either. We cannot plan how we want to reach a destination without first knowing our starting point. The same logic is true with our personal financial situation. We just finished discussing setting our financial goals. That is our destination. To understand how we are going to get there, we first have to know where we are. It is our net worth statement that tells us where we are now.

Your net worth is the difference between your assets and your liabilities—the difference between what you own and what you owe. The net worth statement is a snapshot of a moment in time. The snapshot may occur at the end of the year, quarter, or month. The important point here is that we always choose the same moment in time. We don't calculate our net worth as of the end of the month one time and the middle of the month the next. Our objective is to track our net worth over time to see if we are moving toward achieving our financial goals. One common mistake is to include our monthly bills on our net worth statement; after all we "owe" that money. But regular monthly bills do not belong on your net worth statement unless you fall behind and end up owing a past due amount. We will account for our monthly bills on another financial statement.

Net Worth Statement Worksheet

Assets	
Cash on Hand	$ _____
Checking Account Balance	$ _____
Savings Account Balance	$ _____
Money Market Account Balance	$ _____
Market Value of Your Home	$ _____
Estimated Value of Household Items	$ _____
Market Value of Other Real Estate (i.e., investment, rental property, timeshare, vacation home)	$ _____
Investment Accounts (Outside Retirement)	$ _____
Market Value of Vehicles	$ _____
Current Value of Retirement Accounts	$ _____
Estimated Value of Personal Items	$ _____
Total Assets	$ _____
Liabilities	
1st Mortgage	$ _____
Home Equity Loan or Line of Credit	$ _____
Other Real Estate Loans	$ _____
Auto Loan	$ _____
Credit Card Balances	$ _____

continued

Student Loans	$ _____
Personal Unsecured Loans	$ _____
Other Liabilities	$ _____
Total Liabilities	$ _____
NET WORTH (Assets minus Liabilities)	$ _____

Can your net worth be negative? Absolutely. Many college graduates, especially those who graduate with professional degrees such as attorneys and medical doctors, will graduate with a large amount of debt and little or no assets. That is okay for now because it is related to your student loans. However, it should be a temporary situation because the purpose of acquiring the debt was to earn a degree that allows you to earn more money. Over time, you will reduce what you owe (your liabilities) and increase what you own (your assets) until you eventually have a positive net worth.

What is important is that you use your net worth to track your progress toward achieving your goals. You can regularly track your progress using a net worth statement. If your net worth is increasing on a regular basis it is a good indication that your financial plan is working. On the other hand, if your net worth is decreasing, then you know you need to make some changes in your financial plan to reverse that trend.

Keep in mind there is absolutely no connection between your net worth and your worth as a person. Just think about the number of wealthy people who have committed crimes against other people. Meanwhile, teachers, social workers, and volunteers with very little, if any, net worth, do good for their communities and other people. Just think about Mother Theresa, the humanitarian nun with no net worth, compared to Bernie Madoff, the billionaire who ran a pyramid scheme and robbed thousands of people of their entire life savings. It should not be about comparing your net worth to somebody else's net worth. It should be about tracking your net worth over time to make sure you are on pace to achieve your goals.

Cash Flow

Many times the changes on our net worth statement are directly affected by our cash flow statement.

So now we need to focus on cash flow, which deserves a rather lengthy explanation. That is because most of our short-term monthly or weekly actions are driven by our monthly or weekly cash flow. The cash flow statement allows you to look at what you make compared to what you spend.

Most of us have some bills that we need to pay. If you do not have any bills yet, do not worry because your time will come. Cash flow statements show us how our money moves in and out of our banking account over a period of time, whereas net worth statements show us how much we actually have at any one point in time. A personal cash flow statement typically spans a month because most bills are due monthly. Car payments, student loan payments, cell phone bills, and rent are all due monthly. To understand if we make enough money to cover all of our expenses, we generally look at how much money we make during a month and compare that to how much we have in expenses during the month. We need to track every dollar that comes in and goes out the door.

A real eye-opener for most people is to fill out a projected cash flow statement and then compare it to reality. In other words, first fill out a cash flow statement based on where you believe you spend all your money each month. Then the next month fill out your statement as you actually spend the money so you can compare your projection to where you actually spent your money. The purpose of doing this comparison is actually to point out where you spend your money so you can make positive changes. The earlier you take corrective action, the easier it will be to get back on track toward achieving your financial goals.

Cash flow analysis consists of looking at your income and expenses. We mentioned at the beginning of the chapter that financial success is achieved by controlling your expenses, not by increasing your income. Thus, we will spend most of our time with cash flow statements focusing on understanding our expenses.

Cash Flow Statement
For Period Ending
MM/DD/YY

Monthly Income		**TRANSPORTATION:**		
Net Wages (His)	$_____	Car Payments	$_____	
Net Wages (Hers)	$_____	Gasoline/Oil	$_____	
Bonuses	$_____	Auto Repairs/Maintenance/Fees	$_____	
Investments	$_____	Other Transportation (Bus, Taxis)	$_____	
Alimony	$_____	**DEBT PAYMENTS:**		
Child Support	$_____	Credit Cards	$_____	
Gift	$_____	Student Loans	$_____	
Other	$_____	Other Loans	$_____	
Total Income	$_____	**ENTERTAINMENT:**		
		Cable TV/Videos/Movies	$_____	
Monthly Expenses		Computer Expense	$_____	
HOME:		Hobbies	$_____	
Mortgage or Rent	$_____	Subscriptions and Dues	$_____	
Homeowners/Renters Insurance	$_____	Vacations	$_____	
Property Taxes	$_____	**PETS:**		
Home Repair/Maintenance/ HOA Dues	$_____	Food	$_____	
UTILITIES:		Grooming, Boarding, Vet	$_____	
Water and Sewer	$_____	**CLOTHING:**	$_____	
Natural Gas or Oil	$_____	**INVESTMENTS AND SAVINGS:**		
Telephone (Land, Cell)	$_____	401K or IRA	$_____	
FOOD:		Stocks/Bonds/Mutual Funds	$_____	
Groceries	$_____	College Fund	$_____	
Eating Out, Lunches, Snacks	$_____	Savings	$_____	
FAMILY OBLIGATIONS:		Emergency Fund	$_____	
Child Support	$_____	**MISCELLANEOUS:**		
Alimony	$_____	Toiletries, Household Products	$_____	
Day Care, Babysitting		Gifts/Donations	$_____	
HEALTH AND MEDICAL:		Grooming (Hair, Make-up, Other)	$_____	
Insurance (Medical, Dental, Vision)	$_____	Miscellaneous Expense	$_____	
Unreimbursed Medical Expenses, Copays	$_____	**Total Investments and Expenses**	$_____	
Fitness (Yoga, Massage, Gym)	$_____	Surplus or Shortage (Spendable Income minus Total Expenses and Investments)	$_____	

Income

As you can see from the cash flow statement, the income portion is the easiest to complete because, unfortunately, most of us have few sources of income. Make sure you only include the net amount of your paycheck because we want to track the dollars you actually receive, not the dollars you earn. It is important to include all sources of income. Perhaps certain months each year you get a bonus or extra hours at work or maybe money for your birthday. You have to include these extra sources of income for those months they are received to track how you spend the extra money. If you do not include these extra sources of income, you will not truly understand your finances. Ultimately we want to know how much we get and when we get it.

Expenses

At some point everyone asks, "Where did my money go?" There are many ways that money seems to leak out of your budget. For instance, if you have a monitored security alarm, you may pay around $50 to $75 per month. In addition, you may have a home telephone line, which could cost $15 to $45 per month. Perhaps you have a magazine subscription or a gym membership that you do not use. Cable expenses can easily jump to more than $100 per month if you have high-speed Internet and HDTV. Add a few premium channels, and you could be up to $150 per month. In addition to recurring monthly payments, you will also find that your income is attacked by impulse purchases, hunger, and time restraints all at the same time.

Expenses: Home

Be sure to track your rent or mortgage payment. In addition, any other expenses incurred for your home in a particular month should be included in this category. For instance, if you have to call a plumber to fix the toilet, you would list the plumber's bill under home repairs.

Expenses: Utilities

Most utilities are covered for students living on campus and in many private student housing complexes. However, some of you may be paying utilities (electricity, water, trash removal, etc.) now or at least a portion of them, and the rest of you will be paying them soon enough. Some of your expenses are the same amount every month (such as your cell phone bill) and others vary from month to month (such as your electricity bill).

Expenses: Food

People under age 25 spend nearly 8% on prepared foods outside the home. For someone making $30,000 per year, that translates to $200 per month. That is why it is a good idea to separate your food category into groceries and dining out. As we will see later, adjusting how often you eat out is one of the easiest ways to reduce your expenses. In addition, do not forget to account for those small stops to buy bread and milk throughout the month, which usually result in picking up a few other items as well. Many adults will tell you that the average bread and milk trip to the grocery store costs around $25 to $40.

Expenses: Family Obligations

Although most of you may not be thinking about this category at the moment, it is important to consider these expenses once they become relevant to your life. This includes things like alimony and child support.

Expenses: Health and Medical

Even if you are young and healthy and on your parents' health insurance you still have medical expenses. Any time you pay copayments for doctor office visits or prescriptions, make sure to include these expenses.

Expenses: Transportation

The obvious expense that should be included in transportation is your car payment. Do not forget to include other expenses related to your car including gasoline, oil changes, and other maintenance costs, as well as potential repair bills. Another transportation-related expense includes auto insurance. If you pay monthly, then include your monthly payment amount in this category. If your payments are every six months, then be sure to include the insurance amount in the month you pay it.

Other transportation costs should be considered as well. If you take public transportation, such as a subway, bus, or train, this is part of your transportation expense. If you have to pay for a monthly parking garage permit or a parking pass, then include these expenses in the transportation category as well.

Expenses: Debt Payments

Include all your debt payments, except for your mortgage and your car payment, because those are included in other categories. For now you want to include the amount you actually pay toward your debt.

Included in this category are credit card payments, student loan payments, and any other debt you may have acquired. Perhaps you have a personal loan, or you owe some money on unpaid utility bills. If you have any accounts that are in collections and you are making payments, then those expenses should also be included in this category.

Expenses: Entertainment/Recreation

Include your cable or satellite television service, the amount you spent on movies during the month, which could include subscriptions to services such as NetFlix. Your computer-related expenses, such as high-speed Internet (which may be part of your cable bill) or other related subscription services, should be included. If you have any hobbies that have a cost to them, include those expenses as well. Include all your subscriptions or dues to magazines, clubs, or other organizations. You may want to include your gym memberships under medical or you can include them here, whichever you decide.

Expenses: Pets

Although pets may come to you for free or for a very small fee from a shelter, there are costs associated with caring for a pet. The obvious expense for all pets is food. Whether you have a dog, a cat, a hamster, goldfish or some other animal, you have to feed it. Taking good care of your pets' health is also a must, so you must include the costs for trips to the veterinarian's office. You need to consider other expenses such as grooming, litter for your cat, or bedding for your hamster.

Expenses: Clothing

Although you may not buy clothing every month, you will spend money on clothes sometime during the year. Do not forget to account for shoe purchases in your clothing category.

Expenses: Investments and Savings

Money that you set aside for your personal savings, a college fund, an emergency fund, a retirement account or other investments should all be included in this category. Keep in mind, just like with medical expenses, if you already accounted for your retirement account through work, which lowered your net income, then do not repeat it again in this category. You may ask why investments are listed as an expense. You should remember to pay yourself first. You are going to be working really hard for the next several years, and as you can see, there are a lot of expenses that are draining your income. If you do not make it a priority to pay yourself first, then you are unlikely to ever have enough left over for you.

Expenses: Miscellaneous

What else was missed? Where else do you spend your money? You may include gifts or donations in this category. Think about how many birthdays and anniversaries you help celebrate. During the first few years after graduation, you will likely be invited to several weddings or you may actually be part of the wedding party. Do not forget about haircuts, hair coloring, and other grooming activities, such as manicures, etc. You will probably have toiletry expenses and other household product expenses as well. Any other expenses that were not accounted for at this point should be included in this category. If your miscellaneous category begins to grow to a significant portion of your overall budget, then you may want to split some of the expenses out and create a new category.

What Do the Numbers Mean?

Now you will need to add up all your expenses and subtract that number from your total income. You will have one of three results. If your number ends up at zero, then your budget is very tight because you have absolutely no wiggle room. If your number is positive then you have a surplus. A surplus means that you have extra money you can redistribute to your expense categories (including savings). If your number is negative then you have a problem because you have a shortage that must be covered. A shortage means you either went into debt this month to cover some expenses or you reduced your savings account. If the shortage was due to a one-time event that was covered by your savings account, then you are probably okay. Replenish the savings account over the next few months. If the shortage was due to a one-time event that you covered with debt, then you need to save more in the future to avoid going into debt. If, however, the shortage was not due to a one-time event or emergency, then you need to make some adjustments to your spending as you go forward. Understanding your cash flow statement allows you to identify areas that you can immediately save on to take corrective measures before you completely destroy your finances.

Now we can use what we have tracked in the past to project our future income and expenses. This is the real power of the cash flow statement. We can begin to align our cash flow statement to our financial goals.

Over time you can take the average of the bills that vary month to month. For instance, you can estimate your monthly fuel expenses, utility bills, and so forth. By setting aside the average amount each month, you will have extra money from the cheaper months to use to pay the bills during the more expensive months.

Set aside money for unanticipated or nonmonthly expenses as well. This will help you avoid running up large amounts of debt each time one occurs. For instance, you probably do not change your oil every month, but if you treat it as a monthly expense, then you would set aside a small portion each month to cover it instead of having to come up with the full amount every three months or so. Another example is six-month insurance premiums. For six-month insurance premiums, you need to put aside one-sixth of your premium each month to avoid getting hit with a large bill every six months that you cannot afford. For instance, if your 6-month premium is $600, then your monthly expense is $100 ($600 / 6 = $100). In this example you should put $100 in your savings account each month so you will have the full $600 available when the payment comes due.

What about unknown future expenses such as clothing, veterinary bills, gifts for birthdays and holidays, or vacations? For some items you average the actual expenses you tracked, such as clothing, gifts, and vet visits. For other items, such as vacations or spring break, you simply need to decide how much you want to spend and divide that amount by the number of months remaining until your vacation or spring break begins. You should save that amount each month so you can afford your trip without going into debt.

Surplus

The great news is that a surplus on your cash flow statement can lead to an increase in your net worth every month. You can choose where to allocate your surplus by going through the categories and deciding what areas are your greatest priorities. Perhaps you want to focus on getting out of debt first, which will quickly increase your net worth and lead to additional surpluses in the future as you eliminate some monthly debt expenses. On the other hand you may want to save more for retirement, educational expenses, or other investment or savings. Increasing the investment and savings categories will also quickly increase your net worth. Another option is to increase funds to areas such as entertainment or clothing, which will give you a little more money to work with. The key is that having a surplus at the end of your cash flow gives you more options and choices.

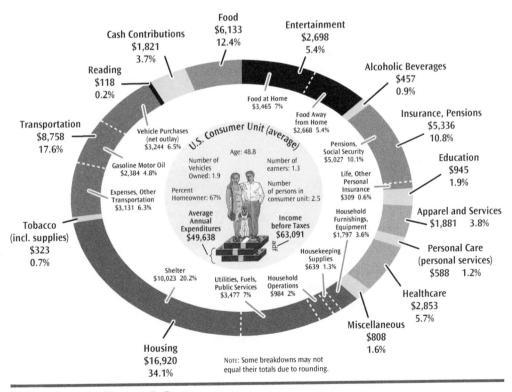

Where Does the Money Go?

Shortage

If your cash flow statement indicates you have a shortage, which means your expenses are greater than your income, you will have to make some adjustments. You have two options; you can increase your income or you can decrease your expenses. Because increasing your income may be more desirable, yet less likely to be done quickly and easily, we will focus on decreasing your expenses. For the time being, ignore fixed expenses that cannot be adjusted such as your current rent or mortgage payment, health insurance, child support, and other fixed expenses. Now look at the remaining categories, such as telephone, eating out, subscriptions, grooming, etc. You will have to start looking for opportunities to save in some of these categories. If you can, reduce your utility expenses by making adjustments to your habits such as turning off your electric water heater when you are not home, or adjusting your thermostat. The point is that you cannot bury your head in the sand and hope everything will somehow work out. We have a word for people who try to live that way: Bankrupt.

Financial Planning Is a Process

Because you want to avoid the fate of the celebrities we discussed at the beginning of the chapter (at least the part where they went bankrupt), then you want to follow the financial planning process. The process is really a cycle—do it and review it!

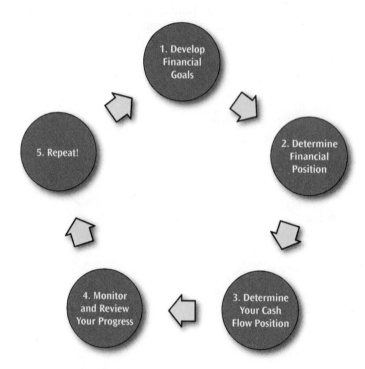

Develop your financial goals—Remember to use SMART goals and include short-term, mid-range and long-term goals.

- *Determine your financial position*—Use the net worth statement and take an assessment of your current situation, including your education, marriage, and family plans.
- *Determine your cash flow position*—Use the cash flow statement to cover your expenses and properly allocate any leftover dollars.

- *Monitor and review your progress*—Track your increased net worth and your progress toward achieving your goals. If you are on track, then keep on doing what you are doing. If you are not, then look to see what you can do to improve your situation.
- *Repeat*—The financial planning process is a cycle. As you achieve your goals, replace them with new ones and begin the cycle again.

Why Do Most Financial Plans Fail?

Now we have these great financial tools available to us. If we use all of these tools the way we are supposed to, then why do financial plans still fail? That can be summed up in one simple phrase: life happens. More importantly, we can use the acronym L.I.F.E.

L—Listed expenses are underestimated

I—Impulse buying

F—Forgotten bills

E—Emergencies

Listed expenses are underestimated: It is one thing to guess how much you spend on grooming, gifts, and clothing, but it is another thing to guess correctly. Most people do not realize how much they actually spend on each category until they really start to pay attention to where their money goes. You may come up shorter each month than you realize simply because you have underestimated how much you actually spend on certain categories. This highlights the importance of accurately tracking your expenses for several months so that your future estimates are based on a period of actual spending.

Impulse buying: Grocery stores place candy bars right at the checkout line. Department stores place their magazines, batteries, and other impulse items near the registers. Even an innocent evening where you plan to just "go out" can result in hundreds of dollars of items that were on sale or clearance that you had not planned to purchase. The point is that impulse buying is when you make purchases that you had not planned and particularly ones that were not taken into account on your cash flow statement.

Forgotten bills: Because most people do not put together a cash flow statement for each month, they may forget to take into account bills that do not come due every month. For instance, many automobile insurance policies are due every six months. It is much easier to set aside $100 per month to make your insurance payment than it is to come up with $600 at one time when the statement arrives in the mail three weeks before the due date. Other forgotten bills could include tax bills, homeowner's association annual dues, or other annual or semiannual dues. Without accounting for these irregular payments, you may think you are achieving your financial goals when in fact you are falling short.

Emergencies: Perhaps you have been very responsible with your money and you never spend more than you make. What happens when your transmission goes out on your car, the refrigerator breaks, or you have a medical emergency? Keep in mind almost all insurances require you to pay a deductible up front. That means you could be responsible for the first $500 or even $2,500. Establishing an emergency fund and setting aside some money for medical expenses will protect you from these situations.

Does Money Buy Happiness?

It would seem from our conversation so far that it is all about the money. The real trick, however, is that it is not about the money. It is about getting to the point where you can stop focusing on the money and start focusing on those things that really matter. A good financial plan means you no longer have to be stressed when you are spending money because you don't have to wonder if you are spending too much.

Does money buy happiness? After asking this question in class, a student responded by saying, "No, but it sure makes for a good down payment." As funny as that is, he missed the point. Think about some of the best moments in your life. What you will find is that the people in your life, including family and friends, are what determine your happiness, not how much money you spend. Even if you spend a lot of money to have a family reunion or go on an expensive trip, you have the most fun when you are not alone. It is all about the people and the relationships, not the money. Money should be seen as a tool or as a way to provide choices and options. Debt takes away your choices. On the flip side, money gives you choices.

Once you understand that money is a tool and not a goal, you can keep the accumulation of wealth in perspective. If you simply build your wealth for the sake of building your wealth, then you missed the point entirely.

When trying to balance our cash flow statement, most people only focus on making more money. The problem is that expenses rise to meet or exceed our new, higher income. Think about the fact that there are plenty of people making $50,000 per year who seem to be just a few hundred dollars short every month from being able to comfortably balance their cash flow statement and save enough for retirement. On the other hand, there are also plenty of people making $60,000 per year who seem to be just a few hundred dollars short every month from being able to comfortably balance their cash flow statement and save enough for retirement. Continuing this illustration, there are plenty of people making $75,000 per year who seem to be just a few hundred dollars short every month. As you can see, we find a way to buy more expensive homes and more expensive cars and so forth as our income rises, so we continue to outspend our income by a few hundred dollars each month. Remember, you cannot out earn financial ignorance.

The Cost of Financial Ignorance

The real power of the financial planning process is that it forces you to write down your goals and gives you a concrete way to track your progress toward achieving them. Once you see it on paper (or computer), it is easy to spot specific things you can do to reach any goal. Ask any person you know how they achieved any of their goals. Their answer will not be that they are smarter than you or that they started with more money than you did, but their answer will be that they clearly identified their goals and wrote them down.

That was the difference between our two students at the beginning of the chapter. The first student had paid off her school loans way early and now was ready to start shopping for her first house. She followed the financial planning process she learned while in class. She developed clear SMART goals and created a cash flow statement to identify expenses she could eliminate or reduce and put the savings toward paying off her school loans. That's how she paid off $28,000 in school loans in just three years. Without a financial plan in place, our hapless second student will continue to barely make his loan payments and take the entire 10 years to pay off the debt.

By focusing her efforts on one goal and putting a plan in place, our first student saved a lot of money. At the typical student loan rate of 5.1%, by paying off her loan in three years it saved her $18,000 in interest expense over the student that was taking the entire 10 years to pay it off.

Total cost of student loan payments over ten years	$48,000
Total cost of student loan payments over three years	$30,000
Total Cost of Financial Ignorance	**$18,000**

So What is Credit?

For most of you, right now, you are borrowing money to attend college. In fact, you may have borrowed money just to buy this book! Whether you took out student loans, personal loans, or used a credit card, you are using credit. Credit is simply money that belongs to others that they are willing to let you use for a period of time. When dealing with credit, the fee is usually listed as an interest rate, which is a percentage. There may be other fees attached to various types of credit, such as loan origination fees, late fees, and so forth, but for the most part we are referring to the percentage that you must pay in interest charges.

Credit is important to our economy as businesses use credit to invest, expand, and hire employees. Consumers use credit to make large purchases such as houses, cars, or a college education. If every student had to go out and earn $20,000 before they could attend college, either the enrollment on campuses would decrease dramatically or the average age of a college student would be much older. If everyone had to save up and pay cash for their car, then the automobile industry would look different than it does today. If people had to save up enough money to buy homes with cash then the housing market would be much smaller, homes would have very few amenities, and the American dream may be reduced to a pitch tent.

If credit helps an economy grow as consumers can spend money on large purchases that keep businesses running, and businesses can then use credit to expand operations to build more big items that consumers can buy, then why would we not want everyone to use as much credit as possible? The more credit we use, the more debt we accumulate. Debt allows an economy to appear very large but debt also creates more risk in an economy. Think about it from an individual level. Suppose you make $2,000 per month and have $100 in debt payments. Then your boss cuts your salary by 20%. Your income would only be $1,600 per month, but you would still be able to make your $100 per month debt payment. Now imagine if you have $1,500 in debt payments every month. You would just barely be able to make your debt payments, but you would not have any money left over for your other expenses such as food. Now imagine that you have $1,800 in debt payments every month. A reduction in salary means that you could not even make your minimum payments. As you can see, there is an upside and a downside to credit, so the key is to balance it at the appropriate level where you are not increasing your risk too much, but you are using credit the right way and for the right types of purchases.

What Lenders Want

At this stage in your life, you are likely to need credit over the next several years. Because credit is offered by businesses, generally banks, they have the right to make sure you are a worthy customer. They cannot base your worthiness on demographics such as race, religion, ethnicity, and so forth, but they can base it on how likely and willing you are to pay them back, with interest. The financial industry has come up with some standard ways to evaluate whether you can and will pay back your loans. They can use these measurements to determine how much credit they are willing to extend to you and how much they will charge you to borrow their money.

What Lenders Measure

Lenders want to make sure that you have the ability to repay your loans and that you are willing to use your resources to do so. Both factors are important to a lender because any money you do not pay back results in a loss for the lender. Large losses could cost some people their jobs, could result in higher fees and rates for those who do pay their loans, or could even cause the lender to go bankrupt.

Although you may be the most honest person on the planet, have every intention of repaying a loan, and can even demonstrate your honesty to the bank, if you simply do not have any income they will not lend you money. Or maybe they will lend you money, but they simply will not lend you as much as you want. They have to make sure you have the ability to pay the loan back before they are willing to give you their money.

On the other hand, maybe you make lots of money and definitely have the ability to repay the loan without too much problem. Now the lender will need to make sure that you are *willing* to pay back the loan. Not everyone who has money is responsible with it. If you have a history of missing or late payments, then lenders may decide either to not lend any money to you or to lend it to you at a higher interest rate.

The Five Cs of Credit

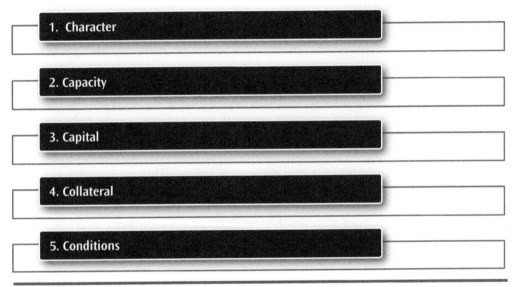

1. Character

2. Capacity

3. Capital

4. Collateral

5. Conditions

Five Cs of Credit

Character has to do with your willingness to pay your bills on time. Your credit history is the key here. Late payments may be an indication that you are not as serious about your financial obligations as you should be. Most creditors won't report a late payment until it is more than 30 days late. So any late payments will give you a "red flag" to lenders and could impede your ability to get the loan or increase the rate that you have to pay.

Capacity deals with your ability to pay the loan. Do you have the financial resources to pay the loan when it is due? Typically this comes from your income. Lenders usually do not like to see your debt payments (home, car, credit cards, and other loans) exceed roughly 36% of your gross monthly income. A debt payment ratio in excess of 36% may be a sign that you won't have the resources to pay the loan on time, even though you may have the desire.

Capital looks at your assets (the things you own) and your net worth (the difference between what you own and what you owe). In looking at your assets, the creditor is trying to see if you could sell anything to satisfy the loan in a worst-case scenario. Closely related to this, your net worth helps the creditor understand if over time you are moving in the right financial direction. A negative net worth is not necessarily a bad thing. It depends on the circumstances. A college graduate at age 22 who has a negative net worth of $15K from student loans is in much better shape than a 45-year-old with a small positive net worth.

Collateral is something that you own of value that is pledged to the lender that can be taken away by the lender and sold to satisfy the debt if you don't pay the loan. You can typically receive better loan terms when you provide collateral like your house or your car.

Conditions take into account the big picture. What economic conditions, typically beyond your control, could affect your ability to repay the loan? Are you working in an industry that is currently downsizing? Did you leave your last job of ten years to go to work for a dot.com company? Do you move or change jobs frequently?

The five Cs of credit take into account both your willingness and your ability to repay your loans. So how exactly can the lenders use these five Cs to make their determination? Put another way, what exactly do the lenders look at or use to determine how much, if any, money they are willing to lend and at what interest rate?

What Lenders Consider

Almost every lender looks at your credit score. Your credit score is derived from information gathered from your credit reports. Your credit reports are literally reports from credit bureaus or reporting agencies. Although there are several reporting agencies, the three most utilized are Equifax, Experian, and TransUnion. The information that is gathered for your credit reports come from credit and banking agencies voluntarily reporting information about you and your credit habits to one or more of the agencies. In addition, some public record information about you is collected, as well such as any judgments or liens.

Credit reports are like report cards about your financial life. Your name, address, and Social Security number are all collected, which should "hopefully" keep your information from being mixed up with someone else's. In addition, the reports collect your loan amounts, your payment history including on-time and late payments, and when your accounts were opened. In addition, some utility companies may choose to report your information, particularly if you begin to fall behind on your payments.

Because the reporting of your information is technically voluntary, your three credit reports may actually look somewhat different from each other, as not all financial companies report to all three major credit bureaus. It is important, as a consumer, that you check all three credit reports at least once per year to make sure the information is up to date and correct. You can get access to each report for free once per year by going to www.annualcreditreport.com. Although numerous commercials advertise access to free credit reports or free credit scores, the only way to get the reports for free is through the annual credit report Web site. The advertisements are for credit monitoring services to which you pay a monthly or annual fee to use, and as part of your payment, they will provide a report or a score for free. In addition, anytime you are denied credit due to information gathered from a credit report, you have the right to see your credit report to ensure that it is accurate. Please note that you can get free access to your credit reports, but if you want to see your actual credit score, you will have to pay a fee.

The difference between your credit report and your credit score is a credit report has some public information available about you as well as information reported by various financial companies, whereas your credit score is based on a formula that is owned by a private company. The most common credit score used is the FICO score. The score is called FICO because it was created by a company called Fair Isaac

Corporation. Your FICO credit score consists of five main pieces of information: your payment history, the amounts owed, the length of credit history, new credit, and types of credit.

Your payment history represents 35% of your score and includes past due items, how long they are past due, and any delinquencies or judgments that are a result of paying late or simply never paying them at all. That is why it is important that if you borrow money, make sure you have the ability to pay it back on time. A credit card is considered delinquent when you are more than 30 days late on your payment and will likely show up on your credit report.

The amounts you owe represent 30% of your score. That means multiple loans and credit cards with large amounts owed can hurt your score even if you are making all the payments on time. Banks understand that the more debt you have, the harder it will be for you to make your payments if something goes wrong, such as the loss of a job or a major unexpected emergency . They also look at the proportion of your credit that is being used. That means if you have two credit cards with a $1,000 credit limit and one card is maxed out and the other is not being used, you are using 50% of your available credit. Some people mistakenly close the unused card, but if you close the unused card, you would now be using 100% of your available credit, and your score will go down.

The length of history represents 15% of your score. Keep in mind you must have credit that is reported for at least six months to even have a credit score. The length of history looks at the time since you opened your accounts and the time since you last had activity on them. Ask yourself would you rather have a surgeon who has 10 years of experience or one who just graduated from medical school? The same concept applies to credit. From the perspective of a bank, if they are going to loan you money, the longer history you have of proving you will repay your debt, the less risky you seem. On the other hand, having never missed a payment over only one year of credit history you have only proven that you can make payments for a short period of time. You may not have had a chance to go through life's ups and downs while still maintaining your payments.

New credit represents 10% of your score. It looks at the number of new accounts and how many times you have asked for credit recently. If you have five accounts, but they are all new, then all that says is that you are either just starting out, or you suddenly found yourself in need to borrow more. This only makes you appear more of a risk to lenders. Each time you apply for credit (loan, credit card, etc.) it is tracked. If you do it too frequently, then it looks like you are desperate for credit, which makes you look like a poor credit risk.

The remaining 10% of your score is made up of the types of credit you have. A mix of different types of credit is good. For example, if you only have four credit cards and nothing else, you only have one type of credit, which is revolving credit. On the other hand, if you have a loan and a credit card then you have at least two types of credit; a revolving loan and a fixed-term loan. This will improve your score as you can demonstrate that you are able to handle different types of debt.

Most lending institutions go through a process called underwriting. During the underwriting process, they are essentially trying to make a decision about how risky you are as a borrower to determine if they will lend any money to you, how much they are willing to lend, and at what rate. During this process they look at your credit score as one of their main sources of information. However, they do consider other elements as well, as demonstrated by the Five Cs of credit such as what industry you work in and whether that industry is stable or not. They will also consider how much available credit you have relative to your income. In other words, if you want to lower your credit utilization ratio by opening up several credit cards, it could help your credit score, but the bank will look at this ratio outside your credit score and may still find that you are too risky.

The point is that banks, credit card companies, and other lending institutions take a look at your financial situation to make sure you are someone they want to lend money. The better you take care of your money to minimize your debt, spend responsibly, and pay your bills on time, the better chance you will have to get a loan at favorable (low) interest rates.

Credit Cards

Credit cards are a very controversial financial product. Some experts say you should avoid credit cards at all cost. Others say that you should definitely have credit cards for various reasons. Sometimes it is difficult to know whose advice to use. The key to understanding credit cards is to understand how they work, what purpose they serve, and when you should and should not use them.

Credit cards are not evil by themselves. In fact, credit cards are simply a tool. You can use that tool to build or destroy. Going one step further, credit cards are really more like power tools. In high school, when you take a shop class, you are not allowed to use the power tools until you receive the proper training and are supplied with the proper safety equipment such as goggles and gloves. You are not allowed to drive a car, which is a powerful machine, without first receiving training and being issued a license. Yet, we allow people to use a credit card without providing any of the necessary warnings, safety training, or basic instructions. Although credit cards will not hurt you, misusing your credit card will.

Currently, 84% of the overall student population have at least one credit card. For undergraduates, 76% have credit cards and an average credit card debt of $2,200. Half of all undergraduates actually have four or more credit cards. With so many students carrying credit cards, and many carrying debt, it is essential to understand how to properly use the cards. The misuse of credit is not easily resolved after college students graduate and begin to increase their income. In fact, the issue only gets worse as credit limits increase with increased income. The average credit card debt per household is $15,788. Although many adults begin to use credit cards in college, the lack of education on how to properly use them results in more debt issues after graduation.

Historically, credit card companies or their vendors would visit college campuses and college events and offer freebies to students who applied for a credit card. While most students opened credit cards through solicitations received in their mail, the on-campus booths were the most visible form of solicitation. As a result, many students found themselves in financial difficulty within their first few years of college. These direct appeals to college students were outlawed in the 2009 Credit Card Accountability, Responsibility, and Disclosure Act (the Credit CARD Act).

The Credit CARD Act also made it more difficult for college students to open credit cards before the age of 21. Anyone under the age of 21 must have a cosigner or be able to prove their ability to make the payments. Other changes under the law include the elimination of practices such as universal default and two-cycle billing, requiring credit card bills to be sent at least 21 days before the payment is due, allowing payments to be received up to 5 p.m. on the due date, and several other restrictions on fees and rates.

The changes were designed to provide greater consumer protection. The biggest gap in the law was that interest rates were not capped, which means credit card companies are still free to charge whatever rate they want, particularly for adjustable rate credit cards. You do have to be notified at least 45 days before your rate will change if it is a fixed rate card or if your variable rate card will be increased for any reason other than the movement of the index attached to the rate.

All of these practices were used by credit card companies in the past to increase their revenues. They looked for behaviors that occurred frequently and could be used to make money. Although there is certainly nothing wrong with an industry finding ways to make more money, it is only fair if the consumer understands what is happening.

Credit card companies employ PhDs in finance and economics, as well as attorneys, who try to find ways to charge you and to keep you from understanding what they are charging! Now that the laws have changed, it is even more important that you do your research and be aware of what is going on as credit card companies will be looking for new ways to earn more profits off you such as new fees, increased rates, or other approaches that have not yet been discovered.

Advantages of Credit Cards

There are several advantages to using credit cards. You will not need to carry cash if you make your purchases with credit cards. Whether you are making large purchases or several small purchases, it is difficult to carry large amounts of cash with you. Using your credit card instead of cash means that you will not have to estimate how much cash you will need to carry to go shopping. You have the ability to buy now and pay later. If you do not have enough money in the bank, but find something that is on sale or that you really want to buy, you can make the purchase now and then pay off the card as you earn future income. Your bookkeeping will be much easier because you can always use your monthly credit card statement to see where you spent your money during the previous month. In addition, you are more protected from fraud and poor business practices when you use your credit card compared to when you use cash. If you make a purchase with cash, it may be difficult to return to the store or company that did not deliver what was promised and demand your money back. With most credit cards, you may be able to stop the payment so you will not be charged or defrauded. Perhaps the key advantage to credit cards is that they are simply more convenient.

Disadvantages of Credit Cards

There are several disadvantages to credit cards as well. The biggest disadvantage is they are simply more convenient. Yes, the key advantage of credit cards is also their key disadvantage. Due to their convenience, you are able to obligate your future income very easily. Your ability to buy now and pay later could mean that you could buy too much now and have too much to pay later and may find it difficult to make your minimum payments. Using credit cards can result in you losing lots of money in high interest rates and other hidden costs. Using a credit card actually results in spending more money. The convenience of having a credit card could result in purchasing items on the spot that you would have otherwise had time to think about and reconsider. In other words, if you have time to go home, get the cash, and think about whether you really needed the item, you may change your mind and not make the purchase. If you have a credit card, you could just make the purchase that instant without giving yourself time to really think about it.

Because interest rates are not capped, you could find yourself paying rates well over 20%, particularly on department store cards. If you are more than 60 days late on your payment your rates could easily go above 30%. Late payment fees and over the limit fees could easily reach as high as $25 or $35 if it is not your first offense (the fees reached $39 before the recent Credit CARD Act). Grace periods (the time between when you make your purchase and when you will be charged interest) are nonexistent if you already carry a balance on your credit card.

Credit cards may offer you to transfer your balance from another card to their card. However, they usually charge a 4% fee, which means if you transfer a $1,000 debt you will now owe $1,040. If the offer came with a 0% introductory rate, it will most likely be for only six months. That means you get 0% for six months, you had to pay 4% to transfer the amount, and then the rate goes to whatever the standard rate is for that card. If you repeated that process again in six months, you would have effectively paid an 8% fee (interest rate) for the 0% interest rate. In other words, you are not really getting much of a deal at all. What can you do?

Let us recap how the financial system works. To get any significant type of loan, such as for a car or a mortgage, the lender will want to look at your credit report. To have a credit report you need to already have credit for at least six months. The longer your credit history, the better your credit score. The better your credit score, the lower your interest rate. Therefore, it makes sense for college students to get a credit card while they are still in college, so their credit score will have a chance to increase before they need their first big loan. If it is in your best interest to get a credit card, yet we have already discussed the disadvantages of credit cards and the warnings about how the credit card companies operate, what can you do to protect yourself?

You need to carefully select the credit card that is best for you. Cards come in all varieties with different interest rates, rules, annual fees, reward points, and so forth. You want to shop around using sites such as www.CardWeb.com. You can look for college student credit cards and see what offers are available from the various carriers or you can see if you are eligible for other credit cards besides those specifically for students.

You should read the offer (which is the contract) to see if there are any restrictions or fees that you do not want. There is a box that summarizes most of the key points of the contract, including the annual fee, the interest rate, the grace period, and other fees.

Once you have a credit card you can always try to negotiate better terms. The first time you are late on a payment you may be able to have the late fee waived. If you make a habit of late payments you will end up paying a lot of money in late fees, see your interest rate rise, damage your credit score, and the credit card company will be very unlikely to work with you. You can also ask for a lower rate at any time as well. Again, if you are in good standing you have a much better chance of getting better terms from the credit card company than if you abuse or misuse your credit.

To keep your credit score high and your rates low make sure you make your payments on time. Use automatic direct draft from your bank account if it is available to you. If not, then make your payments manually online. Rarely, if ever, will you have to mail paper checks to a credit card company. If you do use an automatic direct draft, be aware that your minimum payment may change as your balance changes so you will still want to monitor your card and the payments to make sure you always pay at least the minimum. Keep your e-mail confirmation or print the confirmation page for your files as verification you made your payment. In the event that a credit card company tries to argue that you did not pay on time, you have proof. If they try to do anything you feel is unethical or illegal such as not counting your payments and you are not able to resolve the issue directly with your credit card issuer, then you can make a complaint to the office of the attorney general for your state. You can find your attorney general's contact information at www. naag.org.

Debt

After all the discussion about credit cards and debt, you may be convinced that debt is bad. In fact, debt in and of itself is not bad. All debt is risky, but risk is not necessarily bad. Some debt is considered good debt, whereas other debt is considered bad debt. Your job is to first distinguish between the two and then focus on minimizing your bad debt.

Good Debt

So what is good debt? Good debt can be identified by three common characteristics. Keep in mind, all three characteristics must be present, not just one.

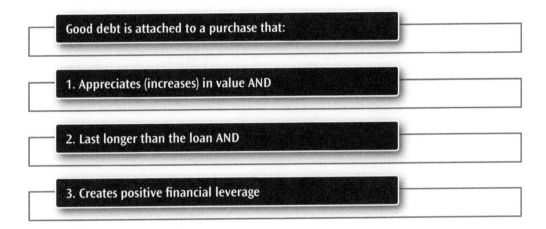

Good debt is attached to a purchase that:

1. Appreciates (increases) in value AND

2. Last longer than the loan AND

3. Creates positive financial leverage

A purchase does not always have to be an actual product. For instance, are college loans a good debt? It depends. First, if you borrow money to attend college, but never complete your degree, then it immediately breaks rule #3. Any education will last longer than your loan, but you are unlikely to leverage some college education to get a substantially better job. On the other hand, if you complete your degree, you may very well have made a great investment. Of course, if you borrow $100,000 to become a public schoolteacher making less than $30,000 per year, then it may actually create negative leverage because you are unlikely to earn enough money to comfortably repay your loans. On the other hand, if you borrow $25,000 to become a civil engineer, then you may have made an investment that will result in a great income for years to come.

Bad Debt

Because you can now identify good debt, it should be simple to identify bad debt. Although good debt had to display all three characteristics, bad debt only has to demonstrate one of the following three characteristics as it relates to the purchase.

When you borrow money to purchase a car, you have immediately bought an item that depreciates in value. A car is worth less each year, even if you bought it used. The good news is that cars will generally last longer than the loan, although new cars will likely lose their warranty during the last year or two of your payments. Even so, it does not matter because it only has to meet one of the rules to be considered bad debt.

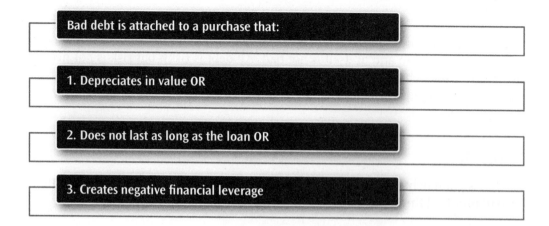

As a reminder, all debt is risky. Any time you are in debt, you are taking on some level of risk, even if your only debt is good debt. The main reason debt is risky is because it takes away your choices. If you buy a car your last year in college, and then decide you would like to spend three months in Europe after graduation before starting a full-time job, you may not be able to make that choice because you have a car payment. Maybe you borrowed $100,000 to get a medical degree so you could become a doctor. Arguably, borrowing for a medical degree is a good debt. However, if you decide you do not want to practice medicine, or you would rather open a free clinic to help the economically disadvantaged, you may not have that option because you have to make the payments on the $100,000 you borrowed.

When you borrow money, you are essentially making purchases on credit. Credit purchases come in many different varieties, such as mortgages, car loans, personal loans, and credit cards. The real danger is if you fail to understand what it really means to borrow money and fail to understand how much you could end up paying for the privilege of borrowing that money including interest payments and any additional fees.

Credit Costs

By referencing your cash flow statement you can calculate your own bad debt ratio. First, add up all your bad debt payments and divide that total by your total income. Any ratio greater than 25% is an indication that you could be in financial difficulty, and you could possibly find yourself in financial trouble. As your ratio exceeds the 25% threshold, it may limit your ability to handle short-term obligations, such as paying the utility bill or making a credit card payment. Remember the more risk we present to the lender, the more debt will cost us. It is the same concept that insurance companies use to justify how much they charge us in premiums. A person who gets into fender benders every couple of years is more risky than someone who has never been in an accident. Likewise, someone who misses a few payments or even someone whose financial picture indicates they are likely to miss a few payments, is more risky than someone who is in a much better cash position and can easily make their payments.

As you are able to lower your risk to the lender, the lender is willing to lower the cost of your credit. On the flip side, as you increase your risk to the lender, the lender will increase the cost of your credit. So, the lender's risk and your cost (interest rate) move in the same direction. A lender may ask two different people to pay two different interest rates for the exact same loan. As long as they are asking the riskier person to pay more than the stable person, they are not discriminating and they are not break-ing any laws. They are simply employing smart business practices.

Risky behavior will have ripple effects across your finances. For example, it will end up costing you in credit costs when you borrow money. It could also cost you in insurance costs because automobile insurance rates can be adjusted based on credit scores. Of course, how much credit will cost you only matters if you have credit or if you plan to borrow any money in the future. Because it is unreasonable to think that you will not have some type of debt at some point in time, especially within the first few years after graduation, you need to consider the consequences of debt and inter-est rates. Even if you do not plan to borrow any money, you have to be realistic and assume you will at least borrow if you plan to purchase a house or if you plan to buy a car as well.

Shopping for Car Loans

For car loans, you want to keep the financing portion separate from the price of the car and the value of your trade-in. Keeping the pieces separate will allow you to truly achieve the best rate possible for your circumstances. It is critical that you shop around for rates, as the dealership may not necessarily offer the best rate. A 1% dif-ference on a $25,000 car loan would be $12 per month for a total of $720. Another way to look at it is 1% difference equates to an extra 1.5 monthly payments. For someone making $30,000 per year, you would have to work more than one hour per month just to pay the interest on the extra 1%. If your favorite restaurant kept over-charging you by $12 every time you visited, you would likely complain and stop eat-ing at the restaurant.

While shopping for a car loan, keep in mind that everything is subject to negoti-ation. Maybe the used car needs new tires so you can negotiate for the tires to be replaced at the current negotiated price. If there is any part of the contract you do not understand, make sure you get clarification. For example, you want to make sure there is no prepayment penalty. You do not want to be charged an extra fee just for paying off your car loan early.

When it comes to financing a car, anything longer than five years is too long. If you need to finance longer you are buying too much car. You should step down in the type of car price or switch from buying new to used. With a longer loan you will be upside down on the loan much longer, which could get you into financial trouble. Being upside down on the loan means that you owe more than your car is worth. You should try to pay off the loan before the warranty on the car ends if at all possible. Otherwise you could find yourself in the tough financial position of making car pay-ments and huge repair bills at the same time.

Shopping for Mortgages

At some point in the not-too-distant future you will need to shop for a mortgage. You may not want to consider buying a house immediately after graduation so you can remain mobile in your career. After a few years of getting comfortable in your career and your location, then you can settle down and purchase a home.

Home loans, or mortgages, come in two major varieties; fixed rate and adjustable rate mortgages (ARMs). You need to consider the risks and the rewards with each, depending on your situation. ARMs have lower rates during the early months or years of the loan, then adjust upward periodically at predetermined times and a pre-determined percent in some instances. ARMs were really designed by the marketing departments of mortgage companies and banks as a way to lure buyers in with low teaser interest rates that would adjust to a specified financial index. They were designed during periods of high interest rates so banks could take less risk and they could offer lower rates.

The issue with ARMs is evident in the present financial crisis. One of the contributors to the housing crisis was the number of home buyers who held ARMs that began adjusting upward. The problem was that the home buyers could just barely afford the payments based on the low teaser rates, so when the rates increased (as everyone knew they would), causing the monthly payment to increase by hundreds of dollars in many instances, the home owner simply could not afford the payments. The home owners originally planned to simply refinance their mortgage into a new fixed-rate loan when the ARM began adjusting; however, once housing prices dropped and the home owners owed more than their house was worth, the banks would not lend them money to refinance. Now the home owners were stuck with mortgages they could not afford and a house that had decreased in value that would not cover the mortgages if they sold it.

The other problem home owners experienced was the fact that they were buying ARMs with low teaser rates during a period of time when rates were at historic lows. If rates were already at historic lows and a person held a rate that adjusted, then the only place the rate could go was up! ARMs rarely make sense today unless we find ourselves in another period of high interest rates, such as what happened in the 1970s. Of course, if you do get an ARM, then at least make sure there is still room in your budget in the event the rate creeps upward and your monthly payment increases along with it. Otherwise you could end up losing your home to foreclosure.

Points

When purchasing a mortgage you may have the option to pay points. Points are nothing more than prepaid interest. One point is equal to 1% of the loan value. Most mortgage rates are quoted with the assumption of one or two points paid up front.

(All the Wrong) Reasons We Get into Debt

Because debt takes away our choices and we know there is such a thing as bad debt, why are so many people in debt? What causes us to get into debt? There are seven key reasons why people get into the kind of debt that destroys personal finances.

#1   Keeping up with the Joneses.

It is human nature to compare ourselves to those who are better off than we are. If you were in a room with 100 other people and you were better off than 75 of them, your only focus would be on the five people who had more than you. No one person can have everything. You cannot expect to have the best house, the best car, the best deck, the best pool, the best clothes, the best furniture, and the best vacations compared to everyone else in your neighborhood. One person may have the best car, while another may have the best clothes. Even if you do not have the best of anything, it does not mean you are failing in some way. You do not know your neighbor's financial situation. Maybe they are living off a family trust fund, receiving structured settlement payments from a medical injury, or perhaps they simply have large amounts of debt and all of the stress that goes along with it.

#2 The use of money to punish.

Couples have a tendency to use money to punish each other. It is easy to go spend money that your spouse does not want you to spend to punish him or her. For instance, if your husband is saving to buy a new truck and he makes you mad, it is easy to go on a shopping spree causing him to not have enough money for his truck. Of course, he may buy the truck now out of spite, taking on larger monthly payments than the two of you had originally agreed on. As you can see, this spiteful spending can lead to a vicious cycle that will eventually lead to bankruptcy or divorce or both.

#3 Emotional problems.

The need for instant gratification is a huge part of our debt crisis. We are unwilling to simply wait and save until we can afford an item. We also use spending as a means to celebrate happy occasions (such as a new job or an anniversary) as well as a way to elevate our mood during sad occasions (such as a bad day at work or after a marital fight). The point is that we use shopping and spending as a way to mask the symptoms of a deeper emotional issue.

#4 Unrealistic expectations of young couples.

Most young couples who come from a home with means expect to start their first home with the same level of amenities as their parents' homes. For example, you may expect that your first home must have a dining room. Now you have to buy a dining room set and a china hutch to fit into that dining room. Of course, if you have a china hutch then you are going to need china. At the end of the day you have a small monthly payment for your china hutch, a small monthly payment for your dining room table, a small monthly payment for the china, a small monthly payment for that new big screen 3-D LED high-definition television, and a small monthly payment for all the curtains you had to buy to cover the windows. Although each small monthly payment is affordable to the young couple, the combination of them all is too much for their finances to handle. You cannot expect to start off where your parents left off. Your parents have had 20+ years to earn income, get pay raises, pay off debt, and learn a little about their finances. Your parents should have a nicer car, nicer vacations, and nicer stuff in general than you. You should hope that you will have nicer stuff in 20 years as well!

#5 Lack of communication among family members.

When a couple is not communicating about their finances and goals, they are likely to overspend significantly and usually by accident. For instance, if the couple receives a tax refund or a bonus paycheck, both spouses may make a joint spending decision based on the extra money that was deposited into their checking account. However, if both spouses spend the same money independently from one another you could end up even further in debt.

#6 The amount of finance charges is too high.

As you continue to borrow more money or take on additional loans, your minimum monthly payments become higher and higher, which makes it that much harder to make ends meet. Add to that a missed credit card payment, which results in increased interest rates and more of your money will be used just to pay the interest with very little being applied to the actual balance. In addition, an interest rate spike will cause your minimum monthly payment to increase as well, which could further cause you to slip behind.

#7   Overindulgence of children.

Babies only require and desire three things: to be loved, fed, and changed. Any indulgence above those three are really for the parents and not the child. Do you really think a baby knows what brand of shoe he or she is wearing? Does a child really need 80 boxes of Christmas gifts under the tree? Most parents experience a January hangover when the credit card bills arrive and they realize how much they spent. Sadly, the payments last longer than most of the toys.

The Cost of Financial Ignorance

The young woman at the beginning of the chapter with $3,000 of credit card debt wanted to buy a used car. She found a three-year-old car in great shape and needed a loan of almost $12,000. She did not realize that because of the balance on her credit card, the car loan would put her at the maximum total debt any lender would consider safe. It wasn't that she could not get a car for the loan, but because of the additional credit card debt the loan would be more expensive. Lenders would lend her the money, but at a higher interest rate.

Car loan with the credit card debt	$12,000, 8.6%, 5 years	= Total Interest $2,807
Car loan without the credit card debt	$12,000, 6.9%, 5 years	= Total Interest $2,223
Total Cost of Financial Ignorance		$ 584

Hampton Helped Me!

Steven Plater

Photo courtesy of Hampton University

Steven Plater graduated from Hampton University in 2007 with a BA/MT in Music Education (Voice). Immediately following graduation, Steven moved to New York City to pursue his dreams of entertainment. Not long after, he was performing on the high seas for Royal Caribbean, International. Upon returning to the states, Steven continued to perform in Off-Broadway musicals and became a member of the Broadway Inspirational Voices, an ensemble comprised of past and present Broadway performers. In addition to his music career, Steven has modeled extensively across the country in major cities including Los Angeles, Miami, Atlanta, Palm Springs, and of course his home, New York City where he is the current cover model for Odyssey Magazine New York. On February 28, 2014, he released his debut EP on iTunes entitled "The Crowned One: Still Standing." Steven continues to allow his life to do the singing!

CHAPTER 8

Educational Planning and Academic Decision Making

"Planning is bringing the future into the present so that you can do something about it now."

Upon completion of this chapter, you will be able to:

- **Review** the decision making process
- **Develop** effective strategies for exploring different academic fields
- **Choose** an educational path that best enables you to achieve your personal and occupational goals
- **Develop** a graduation plan

Educational Planning and Academic Decision Making

Making Wise Choices about College Courses and a College Major

---

ACTIVATE YOUR THINKING | *Reflection* **8.1** | **LEARNING GOAL**

At this point in your college experience, are you decided or undecided about your major?

If you're undecided, what subjects might be possibilities?

If you're decided:

1. What is your choice?

2. How sure are you about your choice? (Circle one.)

    absolutely sure   fairly sure   not too sure   likely to change

To develop effective strategies for exploring different academic fields and for choosing an educational path that best enables you to achieve your personal and occupational goals.

To Be or Not to Be Decided about a College Major: What the Research Shows

Studies of student decisions about a college major show that:

- Less than 10 percent of new college students feel they know a great deal about the fields in which that they intend to major in.
- As students proceed through the first year of college, they grow more uncertain about the majors they chose when they began college.
- More than two-thirds of new students change their minds about their majors during the first year of college.
- Only one in three college seniors eventually major in the same field that they chose during their first year of college (Cuseo, 2005).

These findings demonstrate that the vast majority of students entering college are not certain about their college majors. Many students don't reach their final decision about a major *before* starting their college experience; instead, they make that decision *during* their college experience. Being uncertain about a major is nothing to be embarrassed about. Being "undecided" and "undeclared" doesn't mean that you're irresponsible, clueless, or lost. Beginning college students may be undecided for very good reasons. For instance, you may be undecided simply because you have interests

---

From *Thriving in College and Beyond: Research-Based Strategies for Academic Success and Personal Development* by Cuseo et al. Copyright © 2013 by Kendall Hunt Publishing Company. Reprinted by permission.

"Not all those who wander are lost."

—J. R. R. Tolkien, *The Lord of the Rings*

Student
Perspective

"The best words of wisdom that I could give new freshmen [are] not to feel like you need to know what you want to major in right away. They should really use their first two years to explore all of the different classes available. They may find a hidden interest in something they never would have considered. I know this from personal experience."

—Advice to new students from a college sophomore (Walsh, 2005)

Student
Perspective

"I see so many people switch [their] major like 4 or 5 times; they end up having to take loads of summer school just to catch up because they invest time and money in classes for a major that they end up not majoring in anyway."

—College sophomore (Walsh, 2005)

in various subjects; this is a healthy form of indecision because it shows that you have a range of interests and a high level of motivation to learn about different subjects. You may also be undecided simply because you're a careful, reflective thinker whose decision-making style is to gather more information before making a firm and final commitment.

In one study of students who were undecided about a major at the start of college, 43 percent had several ideas in mind but were not yet ready to commit to one of them (Gordon & Steele, 2003). These students were not lacking direction. In fact, they had some ideas but still wanted to explore them and keep their options open, which is an effective way to go about making decisions.

As a first-year student, it's only natural to be at least somewhat uncertain about your educational goals because you haven't yet experienced the variety of subjects and academic programs that make up the college curriculum, some of which you didn't know existed. In fact, one purpose of general education courses is to help new students develop the critical thinking skills needed to make wise choices and well-informed decisions, such as their choice of a college major. The liberal arts curriculum is designed to introduce you to various academic subjects, and as you progress through this curriculum, you may discover subjects that captivate you and capture your interest. Some of these subjects may represent fields of study that you never experienced before, and all of them represent possible choices for a college major.

As you gain experience with the college curriculum, you will also gain more self-awareness about your academic strengths and weaknesses. This is important knowledge to take into consideration when choosing a major, because you want to be sure to select a field that builds on your academic abilities and talents.

It's true that some people take too long and sometimes procrastinate when it comes to making important decisions. However, it's also true that they can make decisions too quickly, resulting in premature choices made without sufficient reflection and careful consideration of all options. Judging from the large number of students who end up changing their minds about a college major, it's probably safe to say that more students make the mistake of reaching a decision about a major too quickly rather than procrastinating indefinitely. "What's your major?" is a question that students hear over and over again, even before they've set foot on a college campus. You probably also saw this question on your college applications, and you're likely to hear it often during your very first term in college. Family members are also likely to ask you the same question, particularly if they're paying or helping to pay the high cost of a college education. They want assurance that their investment will pay off, and they're likely to feel more assured if they know you have a definite commitment to a major and are on your way to a self-supporting career.

Reflection **8.2**

If you've selected a major or are strongly considering one, what or who led you to select or consider this option?

If you're undecided and are feeling pressure to make an early decision, we encourage you to respectfully resist it until you've gain more self-knowledge and more experience with the college curriculum and co-curriculum. Even if you think you're sure about your choice of major, before you make a formal and final commitment to it, take a course or two in the major to test it and confirm whether it's a good fit for your personal interests, talents, and values.

When Should Students Reach a Firm Decision about a College Major?

It's okay to start off not knowing what your major will be and to give yourself some time and college experience before reaching a decision. You can take courses that will count toward your degree and stay on track for graduation, even if you haven't yet decided on or declared your college major. If you're undecided, you can still enjoy the educational journey even if you aren't completely sure about your final destination; however, at the same time, you want to make progress (not mark time).

If you've entered college with a major in mind, there's still time to change your mind without falling behind. If you realize that your first choice of a major isn't a good choice, don't think you're "locked in" to your original plan and your only option is to stick with it throughout college or drop out of college. Changing your original educational plans is not necessarily a bad thing. It may mean that you have discovered another field that's more interesting to you or that's more compatible with your personal interests and talents. Your college, however, may require you to declare a major by a certain point in your academic career, so be sure to check your college catalog and speak with your academic advisor.

The one drawback to changing your major is making that change *late* in your college experience. Late major-changing can lengthen your time to college graduation, and increase the cost of your college education, because you'll likely need to complete additional courses for your newly chosen major—particularly if it's in a very different field than your previous major. The key to preventing this scenario from happening late in your college experience is to engage in long-range educational planning *early* in your college experience.

Changing your major this close to graduation will add to the time it takes for you to earn your college degree; it will also add to the cost of your college education.

© Kendall Hunt Publishing Company

• **Remember**

As a general rule, you should reach a fairly firm decision about your major during your second (sophomore) year in college. However, to reach a good decision within this time frame, the process of exploring and planning should begin now—during your first term in college.

The Importance of Long-Range Educational Planning

"When you have to make a choice and don't make it, that is in itself a choice."

—William James, philosopher and one of the founders of American psychology

College allows you choices about courses to enroll in and fields to specialize in. By looking beyond your first year of college and developing a tentative long-range educational plan, you're able to get a sneak preview and big-picture overview of your college experience. In contrast, looking at and scheduling your classes one term at a time—just before each registration period when—limits the view your college to as a choppy series of short, separate snapshots that lacks continuity, connection, and direction.

Long-range educational planning also enables you to take a *proactive* approach to your education: you take charge by taking early and preemptive action that anticipates your future, rather than passively allowing the future to sneak up on you and taking a reactive approach—i.e., reacting to your future without a strategic plan of attack. As the old saying goes, "If you fail to plan, you plan to fail." Through advanced planning, you can actively take charge of your academic future and make it happen *for* you, rather than waiting and passively letting it happen *to* you.

"Education is our passport to the future, for tomorrow belongs to the people who prepare for it today."

—Malcolm X, African American Muslim minister, public speaker, and human rights activist

• **Remember**

Any long-range educational plan you develop is not set in stone: it can change depending on changes in your academic interests and future plans. The purpose of long-range planning is not to lock you into a rigid plan, but to free you from short-sightedness, procrastination, and denial about making decisions on your future.

Don't take the avoidance and denial approach to planning your educational future.

© Kendall Hunt Publishing Company

Factors to Consider When Choosing a Major

Self-awareness is the critical first step in making decisions about a college major, or any important personal decision. You must know yourself before you can know what choice is best for you. While this may seem obvious, self-awareness and self-discovery are often overlooked aspects of the decision-making process. In particular, when choosing a major you should be aware of:

- Your *interests*, what you like doing;
- Your *abilities*, what you're good at doing; and
- Your *values*, what you feel good about doing.

Research indicates that students are more likely to continue in college and graduate when they choose majors that reflect their personal interests and talents (Leuwerke, Robbins, Sawyer, & Hovland, 2004).

Reflection 8.3

In Chapter 5 (p.137), you answered self-awareness questions related to three elements of "self": interests, abilities (talents), and values. Review your answers to these questions. Do you notice any patterns across your answers suggesting that a certain major would provide a nice "fit" or "match" with your personal interests, abilities, and values?

Multiple Intelligences: Identifying Personal Abilities and Talents

One element of the self that you should be aware of when choosing a major is your mental strengths, abilities, or talents. Intelligence was once considered to be one general trait that could be detected and measured by a single intelligence test score. The singular word "intelligence" has now been replaced by the plural word "intelligences" to reflect the fact that humans can display intelligence (mental ability) in many forms other than performance on an IQ test.

Listed in Snapshot Summary 8.1 are forms of intelligence identified by Howard Gardner (1993, 1999, 2006) based on studies of gifted and talented individuals, experts in different lines of work, and various other sources. As you read through the types of intelligence, place a checkmark next to the type that you think represents your strongest ability or talent. (You can possess more than one type.) Keep your type(s) of intelligence in mind when you're choosing a college major, because different majors emphasize different thinking skills (Brooks, 2009). Ideally, you want to select an academic field that allows you to utilize your strongest skills and talents. Choosing a major that's compatible with your abilities should enable you to master the concepts and skills required by your major more easily and more deeply. If you follow your academic talents, you're also more likely to succeed or excel in what you do, which will bolster your academic self-confidence and motivation.

Snapshot Summary

8.1 Multiple Forms of Intelligence

- **Linguistic intelligence.** Ability to communicate through language—e.g., verbal skills in the areas of speaking, writing, listening, and reading.
- **Logical-mathematical intelligence.** Ability to reason logically and succeed in tasks that involve mathematical problem solving—e.g., making logical arguments and following logical reasoning, or ability to work well with numbers and make quantitative calculations.
- **Spatial intelligence.** Ability to visualize relationships among objects arranged in different spatial positions and the ability to perceive or create visual images—e.g., forming mental images of three-dimensional objects; detecting detail in objects or drawings; artistic talent for drawing, painting, sculpting, and graphic design; and skills related to sense of direction and navigation.
- **Musical intelligence.** Ability to appreciate or create rhythmical and melodic sounds—e.g., playing, writing, and arranging music.
- **Interpersonal (social) intelligence.** Ability to relate to others, to accurately identify others' needs, feelings, or emotional states of mind, and to effectively express emotions and feelings to others—e.g., interpersonal communication skills and ability to accurately read the feelings of others and meet their emotional needs.
- **Intrapersonal (self) intelligence.** Ability to introspect and understand one's own thoughts, feelings, and behavior—e.g., capacity for personal reflection, emotional self-awareness, and self-insight.
- **Bodily-kinesthetic (psychomotor) intelligence.** Ability to use one's own body skillfully and learn through bodily sensations or movements—e.g., skilled at tasks involving physical coordination, ability to work well with hands, mechanical skills, talent for building models, assembling things, and using technology.

"I used to operate a printing press. In about two weeks I knew how to run it and soon after I could take the machine apart in my head and analyze what each part does, how it functioned, and why it was shaped that way."

—Response of college sophomore to the questions "What are you really good at? What comes easily or naturally to you?"

- **Naturalist intelligence.** Ability to carefully observe and appreciate features of the natural environment—e.g., keen awareness of nature or natural surroundings, and ability to understand causes and consequences of events occurring in the natural world.
- **Existential intelligence.** Ability to conceptualize phenomena and experiences that require one to go beyond sensory or physical evidence, such as questions and issues involving the origin of the universe and human life, and the purpose of human existence.

Source: Gardner (1993, 1999, 2006).

Learning Styles: Identifying Your Learning Preferences

Your learning style is another important personal characteristic you should be aware of when choosing your major. Learning style refers to the way in which individuals prefer to perceive information (receive or take it in) and process information (deal with it after taking it in). Individuals may differ in terms of whether they prefer to take in information by reading about it, listening to it, seeing an image or diagram of it, or physically touching and manipulating it. Individuals can vary in terms of whether they like to receive information in structured and orderly formats or prefer more unstructured formats that allow them the freedom to explore, play with, and restructure it in their own way. Once information has been received, individuals may also differ in terms of how they prefer to process or deal with it mentally. Some might like to think about it on their own; others may prefer to discuss it with someone else, some prefer to outline it, while others may prefer to map it out or draw a diagram of it.

Reflection 8.4

Which type or types of intelligence listed in Snapshot Summary 8.1 represent your strongest area or areas?

Which majors or fields of study do you think may be the best match for your natural talents?

Author's Experience In my family, whenever there's something that needs to be assembled or set up (e.g., a ping-pong table or new electronic equipment), I've noticed that my wife, my son, and myself have different learning styles in terms of how we go about doing it. I like to read the manual's instructions carefully and completely before I even attempt to touch anything. My son prefers to look at the pictures or diagrams in the manual and uses them as models to find parts; then he begins to assemble those parts. My wife seems to prefer not to look at the manual at all! Instead, she likes to figure things out as she goes along by grabbing different parts from the box and trying to assemble those parts that look like they should fit together—piecing them together as if she were completing a jigsaw puzzle.

— *Joe Cuseo*

You can take specially designed tests to assess your particular learning style and how it compares with others. If you're interested in assessing your learning style, the Learning Center or Career Development Center are the two most likely sites on campus where you will be able to do so.

Probably the most frequently used learning styles test is the Myers-Briggs Type Indicator (MBTI), which is based on the personality theory of psychologist Carl Jung. The test consists of four pairs of opposing traits and assesses how people vary on a scale (low to high) for each of these four sets of traits. The four sets of opposing traits are illustrated in Figure 8.1.

As you read about the four pairs of opposite traits, place a mark along the line where you think you fall with respect to each set of traits. For example, place a mark in the middle of the line if you think you are midway between these opposing traits, or place a mark at the far left or far right if you think you lean strongly toward the trait listed on either end.

FIGURE 8.1

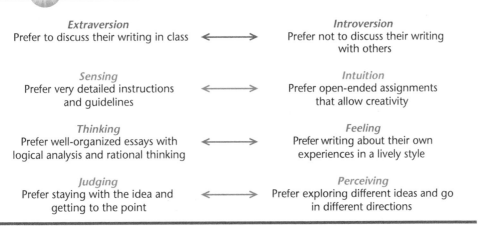

Extraversion
Prefer to discuss their writing in class ⟷ *Introversion*
Prefer not to discuss their writing with others

Sensing
Prefer very detailed instructions and guidelines ⟷ *Intuition*
Prefer open-ended assignments that allow creativity

Thinking
Prefer well-organized essays with logical analysis and rational thinking ⟷ *Feeling*
Prefer writing about their own experiences in a lively style

Judging
Prefer staying with the idea and getting to the point ⟷ *Perceiving*
Prefer exploring different ideas and go in different directions

Traits and Learning Styles Measured by the Myers-Briggs Type Indicator (MBTI)

Reflection 8.5

For each of the following four sets of opposing traits, make a note about where you fall—low, middle, or high.

MBTI Personality Traits	Low	Middle	High
Extraversion–Introversion			
Sensing–Intuition			
Thinking–Feeling			
Judging–Perceiving			

What majors or fields of study do you think are most compatible with your personality traits?

It's been found that college students who score high on the introversion scale of the MBTI are less likely to become bored than extroverts while engaging in mental tasks that involve repetition and little external stimulation (Vodanovich, Wallace, & Kass, 2005). Students who score differently on the MBTI also have different learning preferences when it comes to writing and types of writing assignments (Jensen & Ti Tiberio, as cited in Bean, 2001). These findings are depicted below.

FIGURE 8.2

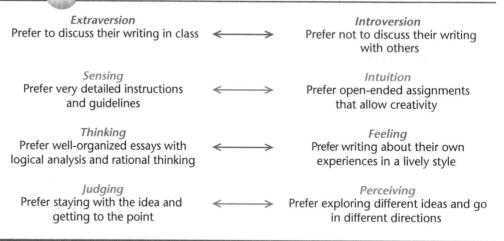

Extraversion Prefer to discuss their writing in class	⟷	**Introversion** Prefer not to discuss their writing with others
Sensing Prefer very detailed instructions and guidelines	⟷	**Intuition** Prefer open-ended assignments that allow creativity
Thinking Prefer well-organized essays with logical analysis and rational thinking	⟷	**Feeling** Prefer writing about their own experiences in a lively style
Judging Prefer staying with the idea and getting to the point	⟷	**Perceiving** Prefer exploring different ideas and go in different directions

Students with Each MBTI Learning Style Have a Preferred Style of Writing

These results clearly indicate that students have different learning styles, which, in turn, influence the type of writing assignments they feel most comfortable performing. This may be important to keep in mind when choosing your major because different academic fields emphasize different styles of writing. Some fields place heavy emphasis on writing that is structured and tightly focused (e.g., science and business), while other fields may encourage writing with personal style, flair, and creativity (e.g., English). How your writing style meshes with the style emphasized by an academic field may be an important factor to consider when making decisions about your college major.

Another popular learning styles test is the Learning Styles Inventory (Dunn, Dunn, & Price, 1990), originally developed by David Kolb, a professor of philosophy (Kolb, 1976, 1985). It's based on how individuals differ with respect to the following two elements of the learning process:

How Information Is *Perceived* (Taken in)

Concrete Experience
Learning through direct involvement
or personal experience

Reflective Observation
Learning by watching
or observing

How Information Is *Processed* (Dealt with after it has been taken in)

Abstract Conceptualization
Learning by thinking about things
and drawing logical conclusions

Active Experimentation
Learning by taking chances
and trying things out

When these two dimensions are crisscrossed to form intersecting lines, four sectors (areas) are created, each of which represents a different learning style, as illustrated in Figure 8.3. As you read the characteristics associated with each of these four areas (styles) in the figure, circle the style that you think reflects your most preferred way of learning.

FIGURE 8.3

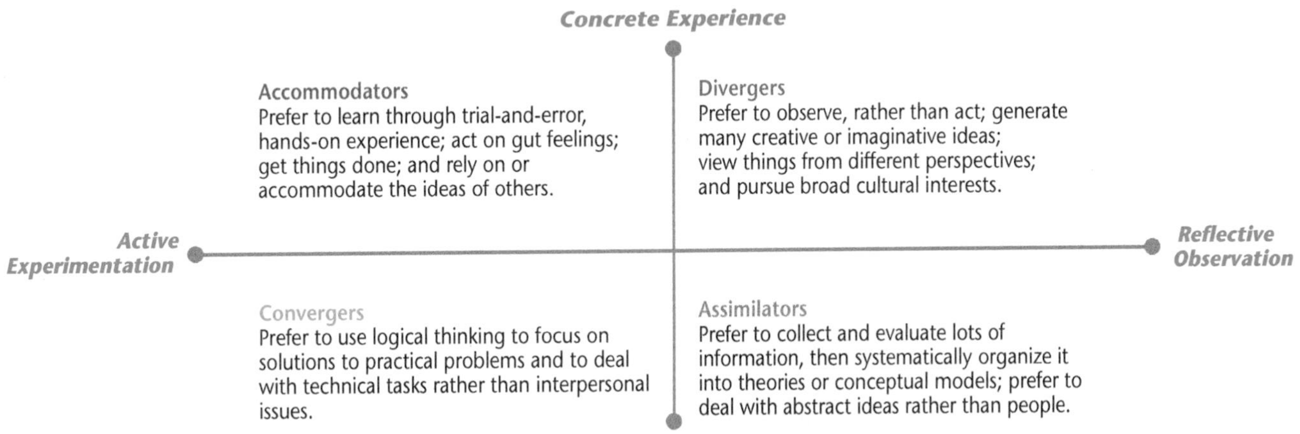

Concrete Experience

Accommodators
Prefer to learn through trial-and-error, hands-on experience; act on gut feelings; get things done; and rely on or accommodate the ideas of others.

Divergers
Prefer to observe, rather than act; generate many creative or imaginative ideas; view things from different perspectives; and pursue broad cultural interests.

Active Experimentation

Reflective Observation

Convergers
Prefer to use logical thinking to focus on solutions to practical problems and to deal with technical tasks rather than interpersonal issues.

Assimilators
Prefer to collect and evaluate lots of information, then systematically organize it into theories or conceptual models; prefer to deal with abstract ideas rather than people.

Learning Styles Measured by the Learning Styles Inventory (LSI)

Reflection 8.6

Which one of the four learning styles appears to most closely match your learning style? (Check one of the following boxes.)

☐ Accommodator

☐ Diverger

☐ Converger

☐ Assimilator

What majors or fields of study do you think would be a good match for your learning style?

Research indicates that students majoring in different fields tend to display differences in these four learning styles (Svinicki, 2004; Svinicki & Dixon, 1987). For instance, "assimilators" are more often found majoring in mathematics and natural sciences (e.g., chemistry and physics), probably because these subjects stress reflection and abstract thinking. In contrast, academic fields where "accommodators" tend to be more commonly found are business, accounting, and law, perhaps because these fields involve taking practical action and making concrete decisions. "Divergers" are more often attracted to majors in the fine arts (e.g., music, art, and drama), humanities (e.g., history and literature), or social sciences (e.g., psychology and political science), possibly because these fields emphasize appreciating multiple viewpoints and perspectives. In contrast, "convergers" are more often found in fields such as engineering, medicine, and nursing, probably because these fields focus on finding solutions to practical and technical problems (Kolb, 1976). These same clusters of fields are found when faculty are asked to classify academic fields in terms of what learning styles they emphasize (Biglan, 1973; Schommer-Aikins, Duell, & Barker, 2003).

The engineering and humanities majors settle their differences in the fine arts quad!

© Kendall Hunt Publishing Company

Since students have different learning styles and academic fields emphasize different styles of learning, it's important to consider how your learning style meshes with the style of learning emphasized by the field you're considering as a major. If the match seems to be close and compatible, then the marriage between you and that major could be one that leads to a satisfying and successful learning experience.

We recommend taking a trip to the Learning Center or Career Development Center on your campus to take a learning styles test, or you could try the learning styles inventory that accompanies this text (see the inside of the front cover for details). Even if the test doesn't help you choose a major, it will at least help you become more aware of your particular learning style. This alone could contribute to your academic success, because studies show that when college students gain greater self-awareness of their learning styles, their academic performance improves (Claxton & Murrell, 1987; Hendry et al., 2005).

Reflection 8.7

In addition to taking formal tests to assess your learning style, you can gain awareness of your learning style through some simple self-reflection. Take a moment to reflect on your learning style by completing the following statements:

I learn best if . . .

I learn most from . . .

I enjoy learning when . . .

Author's Experience I first noticed that students in different academic fields may have different learning styles when I was teaching a psychology course required for students majoring in nursing and social work. Some students seemed to lose interest (and patience) when we got involved in lengthy class discussions about controversial issues or theories, while others seemed to love it. On the other hand, whenever I lectured or delivered information for an extended period, some students seemed to lose interest (and attention), while others seemed to get "into it" and took great notes.

After one class period that involved quite a bit of class discussion, I thought about which students seemed most involved and which seemed to drift off or lose interest. I suddenly realized that the students who did most of the talking and seemed most enthused during the class discussion were the students majoring in social work. On the other hand, most of the students who appeared disinterested or a bit frustrated were the nursing majors. The more I thought about this, it dawned on me that the nursing students were accustomed to gathering factual information and learning practical skills in their major courses and were expecting to use that learning style in my psychology course. They felt more comfortable with structured class sessions in which they received lots of factual, practical information from the professor. On the other hand, the social work majors were more comfortable with unstructured class discussions because courses in their major often emphasized debating social issues and listening to different viewpoints.

As I left class that day, I wondered if the nursing and social work students had just become accustomed to learning in different ways because of the different teaching methods they were exposed to, or if they had chosen their majors because the teaching methods best matched their learning styles.

Joe Cuseo

"Minds differ still more than faces."

—Voltaire, 18th-century French author and philosopher

To sum up, the most important factors to consider when reaching decisions about a major are whether it is compatible with four characteristics of the self: (1) your learning style, (2) your abilities, (3) your personal interests, and (4) your values (see Figure 8.4). These four pillars provide the foundation for effective decision-making about a college major.

FIGURE 8.4

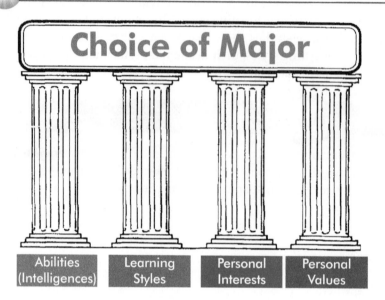

© Kendall Hunt

Personal Characteristics That Provide an Effective Foundation for Choice of a College Major

Reflection **8.8**

Consider the following statement: "Choosing a major is a life-changing decision because it will determine what you do for the rest of your life."

Would you agree or disagree with this statement?

Why?

Myths about the Relationship between Majors and Careers

Good decisions are based on accurate or valid information, rather than misconceptions or myths. Good decisions about a college major are built on accurate or valid information about the relationship between majors and careers. Unfortunately, numerous misconceptions exist about the relationship between majors and careers that often lead students to make uninformed or unrealistic choices of a college major. Following are four common myths about the major-career relationship that you should be aware of and factor into your decisions about a college major.

Myth 1. When you choose your major, you're choosing your career. While some majors lead directly to a particular career, most do not. Majors leading directly to specific careers are called pre-professional or pre-vocational majors; they include such fields as accounting, engineering, and nursing. However, the vast majority of college majors don't channel you straight to one particular career: instead, they leave you with a variety of career options. All physics majors don't become physicists, all philosophy majors don't become philosophers, all history majors don't become historians, and all English majors don't become Englishmen (or Englishwomen).

As we discussed and illustrated in Chapter 4, the truth is that the trip from your college major to your eventual career(s) is less like climbing a pole and more like climbing up a tree. You begin with the tree's trunk (the foundation provided by general education), which leads to separate limbs (choices for college majors), which, in turn, leads to different branches (different career paths or options). Just as a cluster of branches grow from the same limb, so does a "family" of related careers grow from the same major. For example, an English major typically leads to careers that involve use of the written language, such as editing, journalism, and publishing, while a major in art leads to careers that involve use of visual media, such as illustration, graphic design, and art therapy. (The Web site mymajors.com provides useful and free information on groups or families of jobs that tend to be related to different majors.)

Furthermore, different majors can also lead to the same career. For instance, a variety of majors can lead a student to law school and to an eventual career as a lawyer; there really isn't a law or pre-law major. Similarly, pre-med really isn't a major. Although most students interested in going into medical school graduate with a four-year degree in some field in the natural sciences (e.g., biology or chemistry), it's possible for students to go to medical school with majors in other fields, particularly if they take and do well in a cluster of science courses that are emphasized in medical school (e.g., general biology, general chemistry, organic and inorganic chemistry).

So, don't assume that your major *is* your career, or that your major automatically turns into your career field. It's this belief that can result in some students procrastinating about choosing a major; they think they're making a lifelong decision and fear that if they make the "wrong" choice, they'll be stuck doing something they hate for the rest of their lives. The belief that your major becomes your career may also account for the fact that 58 percent of college graduates major in a pre-professional or pre-vocational field—e.g., nursing, accounting, and engineering (Association of American Colleges and Universities, 2007). These majors have a career that's obviously connected to them, which reassures students (and their family members) that they will have a job after graduation. However, the truth is that students in pre-professional majors may be more likely to be hired *immediately* after graduation, but within six months after graduation, college graduates with other college majors are just as likely to have jobs and aren't any more likely to be unemployed (Pascarella & Terenzini, 2005).

> **Remember**
> *Don't assume that when you choose your college major, you're choosing what you'll be doing for the remainder of your working life.*

Additional research on college graduates indicates that they change careers numerous times, and the further they continue along their career paths, the more likely they are to work in fields unrelated to their college majors (Millard, 2004). Remember that the general education curriculum is an important and influential part of a college education. It allows students to acquire knowledge in diverse subjects and to develop durable, transferable skills (e.g., writing, speaking, organizing) that qualify

"Linear thinking can keep you from thinking broadly about your options and being open-minded to new opportunities."
—Karen Brooks, *You Majored in What?*

Student *Perspective*
"Things like picking majors and careers really scare me a lot! I don't know exactly what I want to do with my life."
—First-year student

them for a diversity of careers, regardless of what their particular majors happened to be. Thus, for the vast majority of college majors, students first make decisions about majors, and later, make decisions about careers. Although it's important to think about the relationship between your choice of major and your initial career choice, for most college students these are different choices made at different times. Both choices relate to your future goals, but they involve different timeframes: choosing your major is a more immediate or short-range goal, whereas choosing your career is an intermediate or long-range goal.

> **Remember**
>
> *Deciding on a major and deciding on a career are not identical decisions: they're often different decisions made at different times.*

Myth 2. If you want to continue your education after a bachelor's degree, you must continue in the same field as your college major. After college graduation, you have two main options or alternative paths available to you:

1. You can enter a career immediately, or
2. You can continue your education in graduate school or professional school. (See Figure 8.5 for a visual map of the signposts or stages in the college experience and the primary paths available to you after college graduation.)

Once you complete a bachelor's degree, it's possible to continue your education in a field that's not directly related to your college major. This is particularly true for students who are majoring in pre-professional careers that funnel them directly into a particular career after graduation (Pascarella & Terenzini, 2005). For example, if you major in English, you can still go to graduate school in a subject other than English, or go to law school, or get a master's degree in business administration. In fact, it's common to find that the majority of graduate students in master's of business administration (MBA) programs were not business majors in college (Dupuy & Vance, 1996).

Myth 3. You should major in business because most college graduates work in business settings. Studies show that college graduates with a variety of majors end up working in business settings. For instance, engineering majors are likely to work in accounting, production, and finance. Liberal arts majors are likely to move on to positions in business settings that involve marketing, human resources, or public affairs (Bok, 2006; Useem, 1989). So, don't restrict your choices of a major to business by believing in the myth that you must major in business to work for a business after graduation. Research shows that in the long run, the career mobility and career advancement of non-business majors in the business world are equal to those attained by business majors (Pascarella & Terenzini, 1991; 2005).

Myth 4. If you major in a liberal arts field, the only career available to you is teaching. Liberal arts majors are not restricted to teaching careers. Many college graduates with majors in liberal arts fields have proceeded to, and succeeded in, careers other than teaching. Among these graduates are such notable people as:

*   Jill Barad (English major), CEO, Mattel Toys
*   Steve Case (political science major), CEO, America Online
*   Brian Lamb (speech major), CEO, C-Span
*   Willie Brown (liberal studies major), mayor, San Francisco
    Source: Indiana University (2004).

FIGURE 8.5

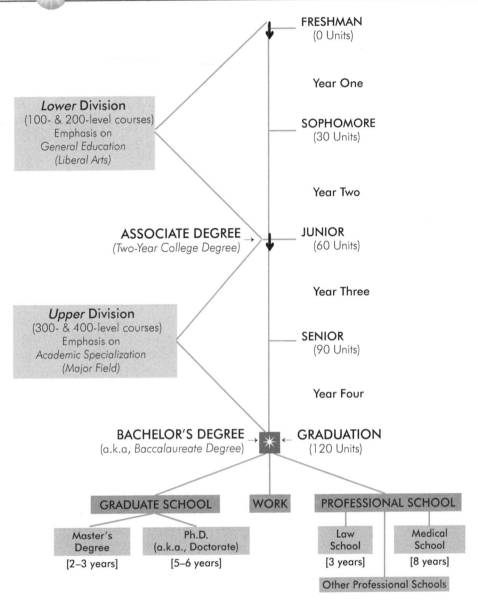

FRESHMAN
(0 Units)

Year One

Lower **Division**
(100- & 200-level courses)
Emphasis on
General Education
(Liberal Arts)

SOPHOMORE
(30 Units)

Year Two

ASSOCIATE DEGREE →
(Two-Year College Degree)

JUNIOR
(60 Units)

Year Three

Upper **Division**
(300- & 400-level courses)
Emphasis on
Academic Specialization
(Major Field)

SENIOR
(90 Units)

Year Four

BACHELOR'S DEGREE →   ← GRADUATION
(a.k.a, *Baccalaureate Degree*)   (120 Units)

GRADUATE SCHOOL   WORK   PROFESSIONAL SCHOOL

Master's   Ph.D.   Law   Medical
Degree   (a.k.a., Doctorate)   School   School

[2–3 years]   [5–6 years]   [3 years]   [8 years]

Other Professional Schools

Notes

1. The total number of *general education* units and the total number of units needed to **graduate** with a bachelor's degree may vary somewhat from school to school. Also, the total number of units required for a *major* will vary somewhat from major to major and from school to school.

2. It often takes college students longer than four years to graduate due to a variety of reasons, such as working part-time and taking fewer courses per term, needing to repeat courses that were failed or dropped, or making a late change to a different major and needing to fulfill additional requirements for the new major.

3. *Graduate* and *professional* schools are options for continuing to higher levels of education after completion of an undergraduate (college) education.

4. Compared to graduate school, *professional* school involves advanced education in more "applied" professions (e.g., pharmacy or public administration).

© Kendall Hunt

Timeline to the Future: A Snapshot of the College Experience and Beyond

In fact, studies show that college graduates with liberal arts majors are just as likely to advance to the highest levels of corporate leadership as graduates majoring in pre-professional fields, such as business and engineering (Pascarella & Terenzini, 2005). If you are considering a major in a liberal arts field, you shouldn't be dismayed or discouraged by those who may question your choice by asking, "What are you going to do with a degree in *that* major?" (Brooks, 2009).

Strategies for Discovering a Major That's Compatible with Your Interests, Talents, and Values

If you're undecided about a major, there's no need to feel anxious or embarrassed, because you're just beginning your college experience. Although you haven't officially declared a major, this doesn't mean you're a clueless procrastinator. Just be sure that you don't put all thoughts about your major on the back burner and simply drift along until you have no choice but to make a choice. Now is the time to start exploring and developing a game plan for narrowing down your options that will eventually lead to a well-informed choice of a college major.

Similarly, if you've already chosen a major, this doesn't mean that you'll never have to give any more thought to that decision or that you can just shift into cruise control and motor along a mindless ride in the major you've selected. Instead, you should continue the exploration process by carefully testing your first choice, making sure it's a choice that's compatible with your abilities, interests, and values. In other words, take the approach that this is your *current* choice. Whether it becomes your firm and *final* choice will depend on how well you perform (and how interested you are) in the first courses you take in the field.

Following are specific strategies for exploring and identifying majors that may be most compatible with your personal strengths and interests.

Reflect on successful and enjoyable learning experiences you've had in the past. Think about your high school courses and out-of-class learning experiences. If you have done well and continue to do well in a certain field of study, this may indicate that your natural abilities and learning style correspond well with the academic skills required by that particular field. This could translate into future success and satisfaction in the field if you decide to pursue it as a college major. As the old saying goes, "Nothing succeeds like success itself."

You can enter information about your academic performance in high school courses at mymajors.com, which will analyze it and provide you with college majors that may be a good match for you based on your experiences in high school.

Use your elective courses to test your interests and abilities in subjects that you might consider as a major. As its name implies, "elective" courses are those that you elect or choose to take. Your college electives come in two forms: free electives and restricted electives. *Free electives* are courses that you may elect (choose) to enroll in; they count toward your college degree but are not required for general education or your major. *Restricted electives* are courses that you must take, but you choose them from a restricted list of possible courses that have been specified by your college as fulfilling a requirement in general education or your major. For example, your campus may have a general education requirement in social or behavioral sciences that requires you to take two courses in this field, but you're allowed to choose what those two courses are from a menu of options in the field, such as anthropology, economics, political science, psychology, or sociology. If you're considering one of these subjects as a possible major, you can take an introductory course in that subject to test your interest in it while simultaneously fulfilling a general education requirement needed for graduation. This strategy will allow you to use general education as the main highway for travel toward your final destination (a college degree) while using your electives to explore side roads (potential majors) along the way. If you find one that's compatible with your talents and interests, you may have found yourself a major.

Naturally, you don't have to use all your electives for the purpose of exploring majors. Depending on your major, as many as one-third of your courses in college may be electives; this leaves you with a significant amount of freedom to shape your college experience that best meets your educational and personal goals. For suggestions on how to make the best use of your free electives, see Do It Now! 8.1.

8.1   DO IT NOW

Top 10 Suggestions for Making the Most of Your College Electives

Your elective courses give you some academic freedom and sense of personal control over your college coursework. Exercise this freedom responsibly and strategically by selecting electives in a way that enables you to make the most of your college experience and college degree.

Listed below are 10 recommendations for making effective use of your college electives. As you read them, identify three strategies that appeal most to you and that you'd most likely put into practice.

Electives may be used strategically for the following purposes.

1. **To complete a minor or build an area of concentration.** Your electives can complement and strengthen your major or allow you to pursue a field of interest other than your major.
2. **To help you choose a career path.** Just as you can use electives to test your interest in a college major, you can use them to test your interest in a career. For instance, you could enroll in:
   - career planning or career development courses; and
   - courses that include internships or service learning experiences in a field that you're considering as a possible career (e.g., health, education, or business).
3. **To strengthen your skills in areas that may appeal to future employers.** For example, courses in foreign language, leadership development, and argumentation or debate can develop skills that are attractive to future employers.
4. **To develop practical life skills that you can use now or in the near future.** Courses in managing personal finances, marriage and family, or child development can help you manage your money and your future family.
5. **To seek balance in your life and develop yourself as a whole person.** You can use your electives strategically to cover all key dimensions of self-development. For instance, you could take courses that promote your emotional development (e.g., stress management), social development (e.g., interpersonal relationships), mental development (e.g., critical thinking), physical development (e.g., nutrition, self-defense), and spiritual development (e.g., world religions or death and dying).

> **Remember**
> Choose courses that contribute not only to your particular major and career, but also to your overall quality of life.

6. **To make connections across different academic disciplines (subject areas).** Courses designed specifically to integrate two or more academic disciplines are referred to as interdisciplinary courses. For example, psychobiology is an interdisciplinary course that integrates the fields of psychology (focusing on the mind) and biology (focusing on the body), thus helping you see how the mind influences the body and vice versa. Making connections across subjects and seeing how they can be combined to create a more complete understanding of a personal

(continued)

or societal issue can be a stimulating mental experience. Furthermore, the presence of interdisciplinary courses on your college transcript may be attractive to future employers because responsibilities and issues in the work world are not neatly packaged into separate majors: they require the ability to combine skills acquired from different fields of study.

7. **To help you develop broader perspectives on the human condition and the world around you.** You can take courses that progressively widen your perspectives. For example, you could select courses that provide you with a societal perspective (e.g., sociology), a national perspective (e.g., political science), an international perspective (e.g., cultural geography), a global perspective (e.g., ecology), and a cosmological perspective (e.g., astronomy). These broadening perspectives widen your scope of knowledge and deepen your understanding of the world.

8. **To appreciate different cultural viewpoints and improve your ability to communicate with people from diverse cultural backgrounds.** You could take courses related to differences across nations (international diversity), such as international relations, and courses related to ethnic and racial differences in America (domestic diversity).

9. **To stretch beyond your familiar or customary learning style to experience different ways of learning and acquire new skills.** Your college curriculum is likely to include courses that were never previously available to you and that focus on skills you've never had the opportunity to test or develop. These courses can stretch your mind and allow you to explore new ideas and add to your repertoire of skills.

10. **To learn something you were always curious about or know little about.** For instance, if you've always been curious about how members of the other sex think and feel, you could take a course on the psychology of men and women. Or if you've always been fascinated by movies and how they are made, you might elect to take a course in filmmaking or cinematography.

"Try not to take classes because they fit neatly into your schedule. Start by identifying classes that are most important to you and fit your schedule to accommodate them."

—Karen Brooks, *You Majored in What?*

Remember

Your elective course in college will give you the opportunity to shape and create an academic experience that is uniquely your own. Seize this opportunity by exercising your freedom reflectively and responsibly. Don't make your elective choices randomly or merely on the basis of scheduling convenience (e.g., choosing courses to create a schedule with no early morning or late afternoon classes). Instead, make strategic choices of courses that will contribute most to your educational, personal, and professional development.

Choosing courses that best enable you to achieve your long-term educational and personal goals should take precedence over creating a schedule that leaves your Fridays free for three-day weekends.

© Kendall Hunt Publishing Company

Be sure you know what courses are required for the major you're considering. In college, students are expected to know the requirements for the majors they've chosen. These requirements vary considerably from one field to the next. Review your college catalog carefully to determine what courses are required for the major you're considering. College catalogs are often written in a technical and legalistic manner that can sometimes be hard to interpret. If you're having some trouble identifying and understanding the requirements for a major that you are considering, don't be embarrassed about seeking assistance from a professional in your school's Academic Advising Center.

Reflection 8.9

What three strategies on the list in **Do It Now! 8.1** most appealed to you and which are you most likely to implement?

Write a short explanation about why you chose each of these strategies.

Keep in mind that college majors often require courses in fields outside of the major that are designed to support the major. For instance, psychology majors are often required to take at least one course in biology, and business majors are often required to take calculus. If you're interested in majoring in a particular field, be sure you are fully aware of such outside requirements and are comfortable with them.

Once you've accurately identified all courses required for the major you're considering, ask yourself the following two questions:

1. Do the course titles and descriptions appeal to my interests and values?
2. Do I have the abilities or skills needed to do well in these courses?

Take a look at introductory textbooks in the field you're considering as a major. You can find introductory textbooks for all courses in your college bookstore, in the college library, or with a faculty member in that field. Review their tables of contents and read a few pages of each text to get some sense of the writing style used in the field and whether the topics are compatible with your educational interests and talents.

Speak with students majoring in the field you're considering and ask them about their experiences. Talk to several students in the field you're considering to get a different and balanced perspective on what the field is like. A good way to find students in the major you're considering is to visit student clubs on campus related to the major (e.g., psychology club or history club). You could also check the class schedule to see when and where classes in your major are meeting and then go to the rooms where these classes meet and speak with students about the major, either before or after class. The following questions may be good ones to ask students in a major that you're considering:

- What first attracted you to this major?
- What would you say are the advantages and disadvantages of majoring in this field?
- Knowing what you know now, would you choose the same major again?

Also, ask students about the quality of teaching and advising in the department. Studies show that different departments within the same college or university can vary greatly in terms of the quality of teaching, as well as their educational philosophy and attitude toward students (Pascarella & Terenzini, 1991; 2005).

Sit in on some classes in the field you're considering as a major. If the class you want to visit is large, you probably could just slip into the back row and listen. However, if the class is small, you should ask the instructor's permission. When visiting a class, focus on the content or ideas being covered rather than the instructor's personality or teaching style. Don't forget that you're trying to decide whether you'll major in the subject, not the teacher.

Discuss the major you're considering with an academic advisor. To get unbiased feedback about the pros and cons of majoring in that field, it's probably best to speak with an academic advisor who advises students in various majors, rather than someone who advises only students in that particular academic department or field.

Speak with faculty members in the department. Consider asking the following questions:

- What academic skills or qualities are needed for a student to be successful in your field?
- What are the greatest challenges faced by students majoring in your field?
- What do students seem to like most and least about majoring in your field?
- What can students do with a major in your field after graduation?
- What types of graduate programs or professional schools would a student in your major be well prepared to enter?

Surf the Web site of the professional organization associated with the field you're considering as a major. The Web site of a professional organization often contains useful information for students who are considering that field as a major. For example, if you're thinking about becoming an anthropology major, check out the Web site of the American Anthropological Association. If you're considering history as a major, look at the Web site of the American Historical Association. The Web site of the American Philosophical Association contains information about nonacademic careers for philosophy majors, and the American Sociological Association's Web site identifies various careers that sociology majors are qualified to pursue after college graduation. To locate the professional Web site of the field that you might want to explore as a possible major, ask a faculty member in that field or complete a search on the Web by simply entering the name of the field followed by the word "association."

Be sure you know whether the major you're considering is impacted or oversubscribed and whether it requires certain academic standards to be met before you can be admitted. Certain college majors may be "impacted" or "oversubscribed," meaning that more students are interested in majoring in these fields than there are openings for them. Some majors that are often oversubscribed are pre-professional fields that lead directly to a particular career (e.g., engineering, pre-med, nursing, or physical therapy). On some campuses, these majors are called "restricted" majors, meaning that departments control their enrollment by restricting the number of students they let into the major. For example, departments may restrict entry to their major by admitting only students who have achieved an overall GPA of 3.0 or higher in certain introductory courses required by the majors, or they may take all students who apply for the major, rank them by GPA, and then count down until they have filled their maximum number of available spaces.

If you intend to major in a restricted field of study, be sure to check whether you're meeting the acceptance standards of the major as you continue to complete courses and earn grades. If you find yourself failing to meet these standards, you may need to increase the amount of time and effort you devote to your studies and seek assistance from your campus Learning Center. If you're working at your maximum level of effort and are regularly using the learning assistance services available on your campus but are still not meeting the academic standards of your intended major, consult with an academic advisor to help you identify an alternative field that may be closely related to the restricted major you were hoping to enter.

Reflection 8.10

Do you think that the major you're considering is likely to be oversubscribed or restricted—i.e., a major in which there are more students trying to enter it than there are available openings?

Consider the possibility of a college minor in a field that complements your major. A college minor usually requires about half the number of credits (units) required for a major. Most campuses allow you the option of completing a minor with your major. Check the course catalog or consult with an academic advisor to see if your school offers a minor that interests you and what courses are required to complete it.

If you have strong interests in two different fields, a minor will allow you to major in one of these fields while minoring in the other. Thus, you can pursue two fields that interest you without having to sacrifice one for the other. Furthermore, a minor can usually be completed along with a major without delaying your time to graduation. In contrast, a double major is likely to lengthen your time to graduation because you must complete the separate requirements for both majors.

You can also pursue a second field of study in addition to your major without increasing your time to graduation by completing a "concentration" or "cognate area"—an academic specialization that requires fewer courses to complete than a minor (e.g., three to five courses vs. seven to eight courses). A concentration area may have even fewer requirements (only two to three courses).

Taking a cluster of courses in a field outside your major can be an effective way to strengthen your resume and increase your employment prospects; it demonstrates your versatility and enables you to develop skills and acquire knowledge in areas that may be missing or underemphasized in your major. For example, students majoring in the fine arts (e.g., music or theater) or humanities (e.g., English or history) may take a cluster of courses in the fields of mathematics (e.g., statistics), technology (e.g., computer science), or business (e.g., economics)—none of which are strongly emphasized by their majors and all of which are very likely to increase their prospects for employment after graduation.

Visit your Career Development Center. Ask if there's information available on college graduates who've majored in the field you're considering and what they've gone on to do with that major after graduation. This will give you an idea about the types of careers the major can lead to and what graduate or professional school programs students often enter after completing the major.

Summary and Conclusion

Here's a snapshot of the points that were made in this chapter:

Changing your educational goal is not necessarily a bad thing; it may represent your discovery of another field that's more interesting to you or more compatible with your personal interests and talents.

Two important characteristics to be aware of when choosing your major are:

1. Your intelligences, your mental strengths or talents, and
2. Your learning styles, your preferred ways of learning.

Several myths exist about the relationship between college majors and careers that need to be dispelled:

- Myth 1. When you choose your major, you're choosing your career.
- Myth 2. After a bachelor's degree, any further education must be in the same field as your college major.
- Myth 3. You should major in business because most college graduates work in business settings.
- Myth 4. If you major in a liberal arts field, the only career available is teaching.

Strategically select your college courses in a way that maximizes your educational, personal, and professional development. In particular, choose your elective courses with one or more of the following purposes in mind:

- To explore or confirm your choice of a college major.
- To acquire a minor or build a concentration to complement and augment your major.
- To broaden your perspectives on the world around you.
- To become a more balanced or complete person.
- To handle the practical life tasks that face you now and in the future.
- To strengthen your career development and employment prospects after graduation.

Compared to high school, higher education supplies you with more freedom of choice and greater opportunity to determine your own academic course of action. Enjoy and employ this freedom responsibly to make the most of your college experience and college degree.

Learning More through the World Wide Web

Internet-Based Resources for Further Information on Educational Planning and Decision Making

We recommend the following Web sites for additional information related to the ideas discussed in this chapter.

Identifying and Choosing College Majors:
www.mymajors.com
www.princetonreview.com/majors.aspx

Careers for Liberal Arts Majors:
http://www.bls.gov/opub/ooq/2007/winter/art01.pdf

Chapter (8) Exercises

8.1 Planning for a College Major

The point of this exercise is not to force you to commit to a major now, but to develop a tentative plan that will put you in a position to apply the knowledge you gain while completing this assignment to reach a well-informed final decision about your major. Even if you don't yet know what your final destination may be with respect to a college major, creating this educational plan will help keep you moving in the right direction.

1. Go to your college catalog and use its index to locate pages containing information related to the major you have chosen or are considering. If you're undecided, select a field that you might consider as a possibility. (To help you identify possible majors, peruse your catalog or go online and complete the short interview at the www.mymajors.com Web site.)

2. Once you've selected a major for this assignment, look at your college catalog and identify the courses that are required for the major you've selected. Use the form on the following page to list the number and title of each course required by the major.

    Note: You'll find that you must take specific courses for a major. For instance, all business majors are required to take microeconomics. You're also likely to discover that other required courses can be chosen from a menu or list of options (e.g., "choose any three courses from the following list of six courses"). Such courses are often called "major electives." When you find that you have a choice of electives in the major you've selected, read their course descriptions and choose those that most interest you now to include in your plan. Simply list the numbers and titles of these courses on the planning form. (You don't need to write down all choices listed in the catalog.)

    College catalogs can sometimes be tricky to navigate or interpret, so if you run into any difficulty, don't panic. Seek help from an academic advisor. Your campus may also have a degree audit program available, which allows you to track major requirements electronically. If so, take advantage of it.

College Major Planning Form

Major Selected:_____

Requirements in the Major
(Courses in your major that you must take)

Course #	Course Title	Course #	Course Title

Major Electives
(Courses required for your major that you choose to take from a specified list)

Course #	Course Title	Course #	Course Title

Self-Assessment Questions

1. Looking over the courses required for the major you've selected, would you still be interested in majoring in this field?

2. Were there courses required by the major that you were surprised to see or that you did not expect would be required?

3. Are there questions that you still have about this major?

8.2 Developing a Comprehensive Graduation Plan

A comprehensive, long-range graduation plan includes all three types of courses you need to complete a college degree:

1. General education requirements

2. Major requirements

3. Free electives

In Exercises 4.1 and 4.2 (pp.129–131) you planned for your required general education courses and required courses in your major. The third set of courses you'll take in college are called *free electives*—courses that are not required for general education or your major but that you freely choose from any of the courses listed in your college catalog. By combining your general education courses, major courses, and free elective courses, you can create a comprehensive, long-range graduation plan.

Use the "Long-Range Graduation Planning Form" to develop this complete educational plan. Use the slots to pencil in the general education courses you're planning to take to fulfill your general education requirements, your major requirements, and your free electives. (For ideas on choosing free electives, see Do It Now! 8.1 on pp. 223–224.) Since this may be a tentative plan, it's probably best to complete it in pencil or electronically, in case you need to modify it later.

Notes

1. If you haven't decided on a major, a good strategy might be to concentrate on taking liberal arts courses to fulfill your general education requirements during your first year of college. This will open more slots in your course schedule during your sophomore year. By that time, you may have a better idea of what you want to major in, and you can fill these open slots with courses required by your major. This may be a particularly effective strategy if you choose to major in a field that has many lower-division (first year and sophomore) requirements that must be completed before you can take upper-division (junior and senior) courses in the major. (These lower-division requirements are often referred to as *premajor requirements*.)

2. Keep in mind that the course number indicates the year in the college experience when the course is usually taken. Courses numbered in the 100s (or below) are typically taken in the first year of college, 200-numbered courses in the sophomore year, 300-numbered courses in the junior year, and 400-numbered courses in the senior year. Also, be sure to check whether the course you're planning to take has any *prerequisites*—courses that need to be completed *before* you can enroll in the course you're planning to take. For example, if you are planning to take a course in literature, it's likely that you cannot enroll in it until you have completed at least one prerequisite course in writing or English composition.

3. To complete a college degree in four years (approximately 120 units), you should complete about 30 credits each academic year.

> **Remember**
>
> *Unlike in high school, taking summer courses in college isn't something you do because you've failed or forgotten to do something during the "normal" school year (fall and spring terms). Instead, it's an additional term that you can use to make further progress toward your college degree and reduce the total time it takes to complete your degree. Adopt the attitude that summer term is a regular part of the college academic year, and make strategic use of it to keep you on a four-year timeline to graduation.*

4. Check with an academic advisor to see whether your college has developed a projected plan of scheduled courses that shows the academic terms when courses are scheduled to be offered (e.g., fall, spring, or summer) for the next two to three years. If such a long-range plan of scheduled courses is available, take advantage of it because it will enable you to develop a personal educational plan that includes not only

what courses you will take, but also *when* you will take them. This can be an important advantage because some courses you may need for graduation may not be offered every term. We strongly encourage you to inquire about and acquire any long-range plan of scheduled courses that may be available, and use it when creating your long-range graduation plan.

5. Don't forget to include out-of-class learning experiences as part of your educational plan, such as volunteer service, internships, and study abroad.

Your long-range graduation plan doesn't have to be set in stone and inflexible. Consider your plan to be built with clay, not concrete, so its shape may be molded and changed into final form as you gain more experience with the college curriculum. Your development of this initial plan provides the important blueprint for guiding the construction of your educational future. Once you've built slots into the educational plan for your general education requirements, your major courses, and your electives, you've created structures for all the three key categories of courses you need to graduate. If you need to make changes to your original plan, they can be easily accommodated by simply substituting different specific courses into the general slots you've already created.

Remember

Long-range educational planning shouldn't rigidly and prematurely lock you into a final product that you're not yet fully prepared or committed to. Instead, it's a process that supplies you with a telescope for viewing your educational future and a map for guiding you toward your educational goals.

Long-Range Graduation Planning Form

STUDENT: ID NO:

MAJOR: MINOR:

TERM		TERM		TERM		TERM	
Course	Units	Course	Units	Course	Units	Course	Units
TOTAL		TOTAL		TOTAL		TOTAL	

TERM		TERM		TERM		TERM	
Course	Units	Course	Units	Course	Units	Course	Units
TOTAL		TOTAL		TOTAL		TOTAL	

TERM		TERM		TERM		TERM	
Course	Units	Course	Units	Course	Units	Course	Units
TOTAL		TOTAL		TOTAL		TOTAL	

TERM		TERM		TERM		TERM	
Course	Units	Course	Units	Course	Units	Course	Units
TOTAL		TOTAL		TOTAL		TOTAL	

		Student Leadership & Development Experiences	Service Learning & Internship Experiences
Advisor's Signature:	Date:		
Student's Signature:	Date:		

Self-Assessment Questions

1. Do you think this was a useful assignment? Why or why not?

2. Do you see any way in which this assignment could be improved or strengthened?

3. Did completing this long-range graduation plan influence your educational plans in any way?

Whose Choice Is It Anyway?

Ursula, a first-year student, was in tears when she showed up at the Career Center. She had just returned from a weekend visit home, during which she informed her parents that she was planning to major in art or theater. When Ursula's father heard about her plans, he exploded and insisted that she major in something "practical," like business or accounting, so that she could earn a living after she graduates. Ursula replied that she had no interest in these majors, nor did she feel she had the skills needed to complete the level of math required by them, which included calculus. Her father shot back that he had no intention of "paying four years of college tuition for her to end up as an unemployed artist or actress!" He went on to say that if she wanted to major in art or theater, she'd "have to figure out a way to pay for college herself."

Reflection and Discussion Questions

1. What options (if any) do you think Ursula has at this point in her college experience?

2. If Ursula were your friend, what would you recommend she do?

3. Do you see any way(s) in which Ursula might pursue a major that she's interested in and, at the same time, ease her father's concern that she'll end up jobless after college graduation?

Hampton Helped Me!

Maurice Kuykendoll

Photo courtesy of Hampton University

Maurice Kuykendoll is the co-lead for Prudential's first filing of a resolution plan to the Federal Reserve Board and FDIC. He is also a member of the International Controller's Division where he coordinates financial reporting projects within Gibraltar Life.

Prior to his current role, Maurice was chief of staff to the CPO and supported the CFO in carrying out his responsibilities.

Maurice is a recent graduate of Harvard Business School where he earned the Master in Business Administration degree with Distinction. He earned a B.S. in Accounting from Hampton University with honors and is a Virginia certified public accountant. He also serves on the board of directors of the Gloucester Institute, and is active in Big Brothers, Big Sisters of America.

Part 2
EXPLORE

© Kendall Hunt Publishing Company

"I want to keep learning, keep exploring, keep doing things."

JESSYE NORMAN

"The day we stop exploring is the day we commit ourselves to live in a stagnant world, devoid of curiosity, empty of dreams."

—Neil deGrasse Tyson

CHAPTER 9

Introduction to English and African American Literature

"Literature adds to reality, it does not simply describe it. It enriches the necessary competencies that daily life requires and provides; and in this respect, it irrigates the deserts that our lives have already become."

—C. S. Lewis

Upon completion of this chapter, you will be able to:

- **Review** and discuss English literature
- **Read** and discuss Hamlet
- **Summarize** Edgar Allan Poe's Masque of the Red Death
- **Discuss** African American literature

Activate Your Thinking

1. What (or who) comes to mind when you think of English Literature?

   _____

   _____

   _____

   _____

   _____

2. What (or who) comes to mind when you think of African American Literature?

   _____

   _____

   _____

   _____

   _____

3. How do you think an exploration of English and African American literature will affect or impact your college experience?

   _____

   _____

   _____

   _____

   _____

Check this out: See the Hampton University Blackboard for additional information on English and African American literature.

Introduction to English and African American Literature

This University 101 course was designed to provide an introduction to English and African American literature. Generally, literature helps us to understand and make sense of the world in which we live. Literature develops the mind and allows us to see the world through different people and cultures. It can teach us life lessons, and it prepares us for further literature studies. Literature can come in the form of a novel, poem, short story or play.

English literature covers writings created hundreds of years ago. The writers do not have to be from England. Such literature is written in the English language. Common themes from this era include coming of age, love, sacrifices and death. Key authors whose work falls under this genre are William Shakespeare, Mark Twain, Robert Frost, Edgar Allen Poe, William Wordsworth, John Milton, William Blake and Jane Austin.

Unlike English literature, African American literature covers writings created by writers of African descent. Original writing classified as African American literature goes back to the late 18th century. The common themes of African American literature are freedom, equality and, of course, African American culture. Key authors whose work falls under this genre are Robert Hayden, Langston Hughes, Paul Dunbar, Phillis Wheatley, Alice Walker and Maya Angelou.

In order to gain a greater understanding of the literary principles at play, you will be required to read crucial selections, as well as associated supplemental resources, from these genres and complete post-test and reflection papers. The foundational materials in this course will effectively prepare you for a more comprehensive study of English, as well as African American, literature as you matriculate through your course work at Hampton University.

English Literature

Hamlet, William Shakespeare

Principal Characters

Claudius. Throughout the play Claudius is the king of Denmark, having succeeded his brother, King Hamlet, following King Hamlet's murder, a result of Claudius' doing, a central theme in the play. Within a month of King Hamlet's death, Claudius marries the late king's widow, Gertrude, Hamlet's mother, causing a problem throughout the play for Hamlet, her son and only child.

Gertrude. Queen Gertrude, Hamlet's mother, the queen to two kings, has a major role in the play, most of it being non-speaking. Hamlet and his mother never reconcile or come to peace over her hasty marriage to his uncle.

Hamlet. Hamlet is the prince of Denmark, the late King Hamlet's son, the current King Claudius' nephew. The marriage of Hamlet's mother, Gertrude, to her brother-in-law soon after the death of her husband is a major issue that Hamlet wrestles with throughout the play.   Shall we say, Hamlet has a complex **personality.** It seems he is always led by events, and is generally angry about things. He seems to wrestle with issues that don't surface in the play.

Horatio. Horatio remains a close friend and confidant to Hamlet throughout the play.

Laertes. Laertes is the son of Polonius and is Ophelia's brother. He spends much of his time in France, only to return late in the play as an accomplished swordsman and angry over the circumstances surrounding his father's "mysterious" death.

Ophelia. Ophelia is Laertes' sister and Polonius' daughter. She is also Hamlet's girlfriend, dropped abruptly late in the play by Hamlet, causing her, it seems, to fall into a depression that leads to her death, by drowning or by suicide. The reader gets to decide.

Polonius. Polonius is the father to both Laertes and Ophelia and was a friend and confidant to the late King Hamlet. He is well-meaning, but not young and not fully engaged in the events that swirl around him. But to his credit, Shakespeare uses him to provide wise counsel to his children.

The Play

- **Act 1, Scene 1**

- *The scene opens early in the morning on the walls of the castle at Elsinore, with Barnardo, a guard, about to relieve Francisco, another guard.*
  - BARNARDO
  - Get thee to bed, Francisco.
  - FRANCISCO
  - For this relief much thanks. 'Tis bitter cold.

- *Horatio and Marcellus enter; Horatio being Hamlet's friend, Marcellus a guard.*
  - FRANCISCO
  - Stand ho! Who is there?
  - HORATIO
  - Friends to this ground.
  - MARCELLUS
  - O farewell, honest soldier. Who hath relieved you?
  - FRANCISCO
  - Barnardo hath my place.

- *Francisco exits.*
  - HORATIO
  - What, has this thing appeared again tonight?
  - BARNARDO
  - I have seen nothing.
  - MARCELLUS
  - Horatio says 'tis but our fantasy and will not let belief take hold of him touching this dreaded sight twice seen of us. If again this apparition come, he may approve our eyes and speak to it.
  - HORATIO
  - Tush, tush, 'twill not appear.

- BARNARDO
- Sit down awhile, and let us once again assail your ears.
- HORATIO
- Well, sit we down, and let us hear Barnardo speak of this.

- *The Ghost enters.*
  - MARCELLAS
  - Look where it comes again.
  - BARNARDO
  - In the same figure like the King that's dead.
  - MARCELLAS
  - Thou art a scholar. Speak to it, Horatio.
  - HORATIO
  - It harrows me with fear and wonder.
  - MARCELLAS
  - Speak to it, Horatio.
  - HORATIO
  - What art thou that usurp'st this time of night. By heaven, I charge thee, speak.
  - MARCELLUS
  - It is offended.
  - HORATIO
  - I charge thee, speak!

- *The Ghost exits.*
  - BARNARDO
  - Horatio, you tremble and look pale. What think you on 't?
  - HORATIO
  - I might not this believe without the sensible and true avouch of mine own eyes.
  - MARCELLUS
  - Is it not like the King?
  - HORATIO
  - As thou art to thyself. 'Tis strange.
  - MARCELLUS
  - Thus twice before, and exactly at this dead hour. With martial stalk hath he gone by our watch.
  - HORATIO
  - In the scope of mine opinion this bodes some strange eruption tour state.
  - MARCELLUS
  - Good now, sit down, and tell me, he that knows, why this most observant watch so nightly toils the subject of the land. Who is 't that can inform me?
  - HORATIO
  - That can I.

- **Horatio to Marcellus and Barnardo**

- **Our last king, whose image here now appeared**
- **To us, was to fatal combat challenged**
- **By the daring and overconfident**
- **Fortinbras of Norway, a king who lacked**

- **Fighting skills, losing lands to our valiant**
- **Hamlet, who took the king's life, through a pact**
- **Sealed, against which lands pledged by our king would**
- **By bargain have gone to Fortinbras should**
- **He have been vanquisher. Young Fortinbras,**
- **We hear, hath drawn a list of poorly led**
- **Resolutes, himself without fear of loss,**
- **Determined to recover those foresaid**
- **Lands so by his father lost. I now take**
- **It, 'tis why this readiness we now make.**
- BARNARDO
- I think it be no other but e'en so.
- HORATIO
- A mote it is to trouble the mind's eye. The foreshadowing of feared events, as harbingers preceding still the fates and prologue to the omen coming on, unto our regions and countrymen.

- *The Ghost enters.*
  - HORATIO
  - But soft, behold! Lo, where it comes again!

- *It spreads its arms.*
  - HORATIO
  - If there be any good thing to be done that may to thee do ease and grace to me, speak to me. If thou art privy to thy country's fate, which happily foreknowing may avoid, O, speak!

- *The cock crows.*
  - HORATIO
  - Stay and speak! Stop it, Marcellus.

- *The Ghost exits.*
  - MARCELLUS
  - 'Tis gone. We do it wrong, begin so majestical, to offer it the show of violence, for it is as the air, invulnerable.
  - BARNARDO
  - It was about to speak when the cock crew.
  - HORATIO
  - And then it started like a guilty thing upon a fearful summons.
  - MARCELLUS
  - It faded on the crowing of the cock. Some say that ever 'gainst that season comes wherein our Savior's birth is celebrated. This bird of dawning singeth all night long. And then, they say, no spirit dare stir abroad, so hallowed and so gracious is that time.
  - HORATIO
  - But look, the morn in russet mantle clad walks o'er the dew of yon high eastward hill. Let us impart what we have seen tonight unto young Hamlet; for, upon my life, this spirit, dumb to us, will speak to him.
  - MARCELLUS
  - Let's do it.

- *They exit.*

- **Act 1, Scene 2**

- *At Elsinore, Claudius, the new King of Denmark, enters along with Queen Gertrude, Polonius, Laertes and Hamlet.*

- **Claudius to his court**

- **Though the memory of our dear brother's**
- **Death be green; befitting, his death transfers**
- **Our hearts to saddest grief, yet with wisest**
- **Sorrow, we must think with remembrance of**
- **Ourselves. Therefore, serving with what be best,**
- **We've taken this sometime sister we love**
- **As queen, in equal scale weighing delight**
- **And dole, thanking all, for you keep insight**
- **And wisdom. Young Fortinbras, holding you**
- **And I too weak in worth; our state to be**
- **Out of frame and disjoint, hath not failed to**
- **Pester us with message importing the**
- **Surrender of lands lost by his father,**
- **Within the law, to our valiant brother.**
- KING
- Now for ourself and for this time of meeting. We have here writ to Norway, uncle of young Fortinbras, who, bedrid, scarcely hears of this his nephew's purpose to suppress his further gait herein. We here dispatch you, good Cornelius, and you, Voltemand, for bearers of this greeting to old Norway.

- *He gives them a paper.*
  - CLAUDIUS
  - Farewell, and let your haste commend your duty.
  - CORNELIUS/VOLTEMAND
  - In that and all things will we show our duty.

- *Voltemand and Cornelius exit.*
  - KING
  - And now, Laertes, what's the news with you? You told us of some suit. What is 't, Laertes? What wouldst thou have, Laertes?
  - LAERTES
  - My lord, your leave and favor to return to France. My thoughts and wishes bend again toward France and bow them to your gracious leave and pardon.
  - KING
  - Have you your father's leave? What says Polonius?
  - POLONIUS
  - Upon his will I sealed my hard consent. I do beseech you give him leave to go.
  - KING
  - Take thy fair hour, Laertes. Time be thine, and thy best graces spend it at thy will. But now, my cousin Hamlet and my son.
  - HAMLET ASIDE
  - A little more than kin and less than kind.
  - QUEEN

- Good Hamlet, cast thy knighted color off, and let thine eye look like a friend on Denmark. Thou know'st 'tis common; all that lives must die, passing through nature to eternity.
- HAMLET
- Ay, madam, it is common.
- QUEEN
- If it be, why seems it so particular with thee?
- HAMLET
- "Seems," madam? Nay, it is. I know not "seems." These but the trappings and suits of woe.

- **Claudius to Hamlet**

- **Your nature is most commended, Hamlet,**
- **To give this mourning to your father, yet**
- **You must know your father lost a father,**
- **And that father, lost his. Each survivor**
- **Is bound to family grief, but to endure**
- **Obstinately is as if your heart bore**
- **A stubborn, openly defiant care**
- **For what must be. The world will note you're heir**
- **To this throne, and as the dearest father**
- **Bears to his son, I to you. It doth seem**
- **Strong grief for nature's fault; we can't defer**
- **This fault against the dead whose common theme**
- **Is death of fathers. Think of us as one**
- **Family, the comfort of our eye, our son.**
- QUEEN
- Let not thy mother lose her prayers, Hamlet. I pray thee, stay with us. Go not to Wittenberg.
- HAMLET
- I shall in all my best obey you, madam.
- KING
- Why, 'tis a loving and a fair reply. Be as ourself in Denmark. Madam, come. Come away.

- *All exit but Hamlet.*

- **Hamlet to himself, No. 1**

- **O, that this too, too sullied flesh would pale**
- **Into a dew. This world's uses seem stale,**
- **O God, possessed by all things gross and rank.**
- **That it should come to this. So loving this**
- **Kind king to my mother that he might bank**
- **The winds of heaven from her face. I miss**
- **Him, but must I remember? Why, she would**
- **Hang on him; yet within a month? How could**
- **She, before those shoes were old with which she**
- **Followed my father's poor body, marry**

- **My uncle, my father's brother, when he**
- **No more like my father than he to me.**
- **Ere an unweeded garden grows to seed,**
- **Ere tears in her flushed eyes dried, she married.**
- HAMLET
- It is not, nor it cannot come to good. But break, my heart, for I must hold my tongue.

- *Horatio, Marcellus and Barnardo enter.*
  - HORATIO
  - Hail to your lordship.
  - HAMLET
  - I am glad to see you well.
  - HORATIO
  - The same, my lord, and your poor servant ever.
  - HAMLET
  - But what, in faith, make you from Wittenberg? I know you are no truant. But what is your affair in Elsinore?
  - HORATIO
  - My lord, I came to see your father's funeral.
  - HAMLET
  - I prithee, do not mock me, fellow student. I think it was to see my mother's wedding.
  - HORATIO
  - Indeed, my lord, it followed hard upon.
  - HAMLET
  - Horatio! My father --- methinks I see my father.
  - HORATIO
  - Where, my lord?
  - HAMLET
  - In my mind's eye, Horatio.
  - HORATIO
  - My lord, I think I saw him yesternight.
  - HAMLET
  - The King my father? For God's love, let me hear!
  - HORATIO
  - Two nights together had these gentlemen, Marcellus and Barnardo, on their watch, been thus encountered: a figure like your father appears before them, whilst they, distilled almost to jelly with the act of fear, stand dumb and speak not to him. And I with them the third night kept the watch, where the apparition comes. I knew your father.
  - HAMLET
  - But where was this?
  - MARCELLUS
  - My lord, upon the platform where we watch.
  - HAMLET
  - Did you not speak to it?
  - HORATIO
  - My lord, I did, but answer made it none.
  - HAMLET
  - 'Tis very strange.
  - HORATIO

- As I do live, my honored lord, 'tis true. And we did think it writ down in our duty to let you know of it.
- HAMLET
- Indeed, sirs, but this troubles me. Hold you the watch tonight?
- ALL
- We do, my lord.
- HAMLET
- I would I had been there.
- HORATIO
- It would have much amazed you.
- HAMLET
- I will watch tonight. Perchance 'twill walk again.
- HORATIO
- I warrant it will.
- HAMLET
- If it assume my noble father's person, I'll speak to it. Let it be tenable in your silence still; and whatsomever else shall hap tonight, give it an understanding but no tongue. Upon the platform, 'twixt eleven and twelve, I'll visit you.
- ALL
- Our duty to your Honor.

- *All exit but Hamlet.*
  - HAMLET
  - All is not well. Would the night were come!

- *He exits.*

- **Act 1, Scene 3**

- *In Polonius' home, Laertes says good-bye to his sister, Ophelia.*
  - LAERTES
  - Farewell, sister, and let me hear from you.
  - OPHELIA
  - Do you doubt that?
  - LAERTES
  - For Hamlet, hold it as a temporary flirtation, a violet in the youth of nature, not lasting the pleasure of a minute, no more.
  - OPHELIA
  - No more but so?
  - LAERTES
  - Think it no more.

- **Laertes to Ophelia**

- **Note my dear sister that nature's crescent**
- **Does not grow alone in muscle strength sent**
- **In youth; the mind and soul grow wide withal.**
- **Perhaps he loves you now, but his will is**
- **Not his own, but of the whole state, so fall**
- **With care. He may say he loves you, but his**
- **Words go no further than the main voice of**

- Denmark, so weigh loss of honor above
- The moment; a cautious maid's prodigal
- Enough if she unmask to the moon. Lie
- Not to thyself, knowing canker can gall
- Buds of spring and fresh blossoms know not why.
- Be wary, then; best safety lies in fear
- Knowing youth itself rebels when love's near.
- OPHELIA
- I shall the effect of this good lesson keep as watchman to my heart. But, good my brother, do not, as some ungracious pastors do, show me the steep and thorny way to heaven, whiles himself the primrose path of dalliance treads and heeds not his own advice.
- LAERTES
- O, fear me not.

- *Polonius enters.*
  - LAERTES
  - I stay too long. But here my father comes.
  - POLONIUS
  - Yet here, Laertes? Aboard. The wind sits in the shoulder of your sail, and you are stayed for. My blessing with thee.

  - **Polonius to Laertes**

  - Hold tight these percepts. Give thy thoughts no tongue,
  - Nor act too swiftly. Grapple friends when young,
  - My son. Tie them to thy soul with hoops of
  - Steel; then draw in new-hatched, unfledged comrades
  - With care. Beware of letting a course shove
  - Lead to a fight, but if there, let the lads
  - Know you're in. Give every man they ear, but
  - Few thy voice. Reserve judgment, but take what
  - Others say. Neither a borrower nor
  - Lender be. Borrowing, the devil's due;
  - Loans oft lose themselves and can make friends sore.
  - This above all
  - to thine own self be true.
  - And it must follow as the night the day
  - Thou canst not then be false in any way.
  - POLONIUS
  - The time invests you. Go, your servants tend.
  - LAERTES
  - Farewell, Ophelia, and remember well what I have said to you.
  - OPHELIA
  - 'Tis in my memory locked, and you yourself shall keep the key to it.

- *Laertes exits.*
  - POLONIUS
  - What is 't, Ophelia, he hath said to you?
  - OPHELIA
  - So please you, something touching the Lord Hamlet.

- POLONIUS
- 'Tis told me he hath very oft of late given private time to you, and you yourself have of your audience been most free and bounteous. What is between you? Give me up the truth.
- OPHELIA
- He hath, my lord, of late made many tenders of his affection to me.
- POLONIUS
- Affection! You speak like a green girl naive in such perilous circumstance.
- OPHELIA
- I do not know, my lord, what I should think.
- POLONIUS
- Tender yourself more dearly, or you'll tender me a fool.
- OPHELIA
- My lord, he hath importuned me with love in honorable fashion.
- POLONIUS
- Ay, "fashion" you may call it.
- OPHELIA
- And hath given countenance to his speech, my lord, with almost all the holy vows of heaven.

- **Polonius to Ophelia**

- **Ay, I know when the blood burns how lightly**
- **The soul lends the tongue vows. Do believe me**
- **Daughter, those blazes giving more light than**
- **Heat extinguish themselves as they are made,**
- **Not to be taken for fire. This is an**
- **Occurrence replayed, so as a fair maid,**
- **Be more meager. For Lord Hamlet, believe**
- **In him that he is young and free to leave**
- **With a larger tether than you. His vows**
- **Are not in true reports heard and in large**
- **Measure beyond what good judgment allows.**
- **This is for all: from this time forth I charge**
- **You not misuse any leisure minute**
- **To give words or talk with the Lord Hamlet.**
- OPHELIA
- I shall obey, my lord.

- *They exit.*

- **Act 1, Scene 4**

- *The scene is Elsinore*
  - HAMLET
  - The air bites shrewdly; it is very cold. What hour now?

- *A flourish of trumpets.*
  - HORATIO
  - What does this mean, my lord?
  - HAMLET

- The King stays awake tonight drinking. As he drains his draughts of Rhine wine down, the kettledrum and trumpet thus bray out the triumph of emptying the cup in one draft.
- HORATIO
- Is it a custom?
- HAMLET
- Ay, marry, is 't.

- **Hamlet to Horatio, No. 1**

- **This heavy-headed drinking goes a bit**
- **Too far, much defamed as we are for it.**
- **It takes from our great feats, Horatio,**
- **Fair Dane; loyal, good friend. It is a custom**
- **Better breached in honor than observed. So**
- **Oft it seems inherited, as if some**
- **Are guilty by birth, yet man can't choose his**
- **Origin or this trait that leads him. 'Tis**
- **Sad, for other virtues, be they pure as**
- **Grace, as infinite as any man may**
- **Have, he'll be publicly censured and has**
- **To live with it, because of it; the way**
- **Of misfortune's star. That dram of evil**
- **O'ergrows the noble to our own scandal.**

- *The Ghost enters.*
  - HORATIO
  - Look, my lord, it comes.
  - HAMLET
  - Be thy intents wicked or charitable, thou com'st in such a questionable shape that I will speak to thee. I'll call thee "Hamlet," "King," "Father," Royal Dane." O, answer me! Let me not burst in ignorance. What may this mean that we fools of nature so horridly to shake our disposition with thoughts beyond the reaches of our souls? What should we do?

- *The Ghost beckons.*
  - MARCELLUS
  - It waves you to a more removed ground. But do not go with it.
  - HORATIO
  - No, by no means.
  - HAMLET
  - It will not speak. Then I will follow it.
  - HORATIO
  - Do not, my lord.
  - HAMLET
  - Why, what should be the fear? I do not set my life at the cost of a pin. And for my soul, what can it do to that, being a thing immortal as itself?
  - HORATIO
  - What if it tempt you toward the flood, my lord? Or to the dreadful summit of the cliff and there assume some other horrible form which might deprive your sovereignty of reason and draw you into madness? Think of it.

- HAMLET
- It wave me still. Go on, I'll follow thee.

- *They hold back Hamlet.*
  - HAMLET
  - Hold off your hands. Unhand me, gentlemen. By heaven, I'll make a ghost of him that lets me!

- *Ghost and Hamlet exit.*
  - MARCELLUS
  - Let's follow. 'Tis not fit thus to obey him.
  - HORATIO
  - Have after. To what issue will this come?
  - MARCELLUS
  - Something is rotten in the state of Denmark. Let's follow him.

- *They exit.*

- **Act 1, Scene 5**

- *The Ghost and Hamlet enter.*
  - HAMLET
  - Whither wilt thou lead me? Speak. I'll go no further.
  - GHOST
  - Pay attention to me.
  - HAMLET
  - I will.
  - GHOST
  - Pity me not, but lend thy serious hearing to what I shall unfold.
  - HAMLET
  - Speak. I am bound to hear.
  - GHOST
  - So art thou to revenge, when thou shalt hear.
  - HAMLET
  - What?

- **Ghost to Hamlet**

- **I am thy father's spirit doomed to walk**
- **The night for a time, determined to stalk**
- **The truth. Listen, if thou didst ever thy**
- **Dear father love. Now, Hamlet, hear me. It**
- **Has been give out that, sleeping in my**
- **Orchard, a serpent stung me, but what bit**
- **Thy father's life now wears his crown, takes my**
- **Wife as his queen, and sent my soul to fly**
- **With my defects still on my head. If thou**
- **Hast a spirit in thee, keep it alive.**
- **However thou pursue this act, allow**
- **Not thy mind be stained nor thy soul contrive**
- **'Gainst thy mother. As each day comes to be,**
- **As the sun flares its fire, remember me.**

- *The Ghost exits.*
  - HAMLET
  - Remember thee? Yea, from the table of my memory I'll wipe away all trivial, fond records. And thy commandment all alone shall live within the book and volume of my brain. That one may smile and smile and be a villain. At least I am sure it may be so in Denmark.

- *Horatio and Marcellus enter.*
  - HORATIO
  - What news, my lord?
  - HAMLET
  - O, wonderful.
  - HORATIO
  - Good my lord, tell it.
  - HAMLET
  - No, you will reveal it.
  - HORATIO
  - Not I, my lord, by heaven.
  - MARCELLUS
  - Nor I, my lord.
  - HAMLET
  - There's never a villain dwelling in all Denmark but he's an arrant knave.
  - HORATIO
  - There needs no ghost, my lord, come from the grave to tell us this.
  - HAMLET
  - Why, right, you are in the right. Touching this vision here, it is an honest ghost. That let me tell you. And now, good friend, give me one poor request.
  - HORATIO
  - What is 't, my lord? We will.
  - HAMLET
  - Nay, but swear 't, upon my sword.
  - MARCELLUS
  - We have sworn, my lord, already.
  - GHOST CRIES UNDER THE STAGE
  - Swear.
  - HORATIO
  - Propose the oath, my lord.
  - HAMLET
  - Never to speak of this that you have seen. Swear by my sword.
  - GHOST BENEATH
  - Swear by his sword.
  - HORATIO
  - O day and night, but this is wondrous strange.
  - HAMLET
  - There are more things in heaven and earth, Horatio, than are dreamt of in your philosophy. Here, as before, never note that you know aught of me. This do swear, so grace and mercy at your most need help you.
  - GHOST BENEATH
  - Swear.
  - HAMLET
  - Rest, rest, perturbed spirit. Go, gentlemen, let us go in together, and still your fingers on your lips, I pray. The time is out of joint. O cursed spite that ever I was born to set it right! Nay, come, let's go together.

- *They exit.*

- **Act 2, Scene 1**

- *Polonius is on stage with his servant, Reynaldo, preparing to send him on a mission to Paris.*
  - POLONIUS
  - Give him this money and these notes, Reynaldo.
  - REYNALDO
  - I will, my lord.
  - POLONIUS
  - You shall do marvelous wisely, good Reynaldo, before you visit him, to make inquire of his behavior.
  - REYNALDO
  - My lord, I did intend it.
  - POLONIUS
  - Look you, sir, inquire me first what Danes are in Paris; and how, and who, what means, and where they keep what company, at what expense. Do you mark this, Reynaldo?
  - REYNALDO
  - Ay, very well, my lord.
  - POLONIUS
  - Sir, wanton, wild and usual slips are companions noted and most known to youth and liberty.
  - REYNALDO
  - As gaming, my lord.
  - POLONIUS
  - Ay, or drinking, fencing swearing, quarreling-----you may go so far.
  - REYNALDO
  - My lord, that would dishonor him.
  - POLONIUS
  - You must not put another scandal on him. That's not my meaning.
  - REYNALDO
  - But, my good lord!
  - POLONIUS
  - Marry, sir, here's my drift. Was he gaming or falling out at tennis----or so forth. You have me, have you not?
  - REYNALDO
  - My lord, I have.
  - POLONIUS
  - Farewell.

- *Reynaldo exits. Ophelia enters.*
  - POLONIUS
  - How now, Ophelia, what's the matter?
  - OPHELIA
  - O, my lord, I have been so affrighted!
  - POLONIUS
  - With what, i' th' name of God?
  - OPHELIA
  - My lord, as I was sewing in my closet, Lord Hamlet, with a look so piteous in purport, to speak of horrors, comes before me.

- POLONIUS
- Mad for thy love?
- OPHELIA
- My lord, I do not know, but truly I do fear it.
- POLONIUS
- What said he?
- OPHELIA
- He took me by the wrist and held me hard. Long stayed he so. He raised a sigh so piteous and profound as it did seem to shatter all his bulk and end his being. That done, he lets me go.
- POLONIUS
- Come, go with me. I will go seek the King. This is the very ecstasy of love, whose violent property fordoes itself and leads the will to desperate undertakings. What, have you given him any hard words of late?
- OPHELIA
- No, my good lord, but as you did command I did repel his letters.
- POLONIUS
- That hath made him mad. By heaven, it is as proper to our age to cast beyond ourselves in our opinions as it is common for the younger sort to lack discretion. Come, go we to the King.

- *They exit.*

- **Act 2, Scene 2**

- *Rosencrantz and Guildenstern, two longtime friends of Hamlet, enter with the King and Queen.*
  - KING
  - Welcome, dear Rosencrantz and Guildenstern. Something have you heard of Hamlet's transformation, so call it. I treat you both to draw him on to pleasures, and to gather so much as from occasion you may glean.
  - QUEEN
  - Good gentlemen, it will please you to show us so much goodwill for the supply and profit of our hope. Your visitation shall receive such thanks as fits a king's remembrance.
  - GUILDENSTERN
  - We both obey, and here give up ourselves in the full bent to lay our service freely at your feet, to be commanded.
  - QUEEN
  - Thanks, Guildenstern and gentle Rosencrantz. I beseech you instantly to visit my too much changed son.
  - GUILDENSTERN
  - Heavens make our presence and our practices pleasant and helpful to him!

- *Rosencrantz and Guildenstern exit. Polonius enters.*
  - POLONIUS
  - Th' ambassadors from Norway, my good lord, are joyfully returned.
  - KING
  - Thou still hast been the father of good news.
  - POLONIUS
  - I do think that I have found the very cause of Hamlet's lunacy.
  - KING

- O, speak of that! That do I long to hear.
- POLONIUS
- Give first admittance to th' ambassadors. My news shall be the fruit to that great feast.

- *Polonius exits.*
  - KING
  - He tells me, my dear Gertrude, he hath found the head and source of all your son's distemper.
  - QUEEN
  - I doubt it is no other but the main --- his father's death and our o'erhasty marriage.
  - KING
  - Well, we shall examine him.

- *Ambassadors Voltemand and Cornelius enter with Polonius.*
  - KING
  - Say, Voltemand, what from our brother Norway?
  - VOLTEMAND
  - Upon our first, he sent out to suppress his nephew's levies, which to him appeared to be a preparation 'gainst the Polack, but he truly found it was against your Highness. Whereat he sends out arrests on Fortinbras, which he, in brief, obeys, receives rebuke from Norway, and makes vow before his uncle never more to give th' assay of arms against your Majesty. Whereon old Norway, overcome with joy, then gives him three-score thousand crowns in annual fee to employ those soldiers against the Polack, that it might please you to give quiet pass through your dominions for this enterprise.

- *Voltemand gives the king a paper.*
  - KING
  - At our more considered time, we'll read, answer, and think upon this business. Meantime, go to your rest. Most welcome home.

- *Voltemand and Cornelius exit.*
  - POLONIUS
  - My liege, and madam, since brevity is the soul of wit, I will be brief. Your noble son is mad. "Mad" call I it, for, to define true madness, what is 't but to be nothing else but mad?
  - QUEEN
  - More matter with less art.
  - POLONIUS
  - Madam, I swear I use no art at all. I have a daughter who hath given me this.
  - POLONIUS READS
  - "To the celestial, and my soul's idol, the most beautiful Ophelia -----."
  - QUEEN
  - Came this from Hamlet to her?
  - POLONIUS
  - Good madam, stay awhile.
  - POLONIUS READS
  - "Doubt thou the stars are fire, doubt that the sun doth move, doubt truth to be a liar, but never doubt I love. O dear Ophelia, I love the best, O most best, believe it." Hamlet

- KING
- But how hath she received his love?
- POLONIUS
- What do you think of me?
- KING
- As of a man faithful and honorable.
- POLONIUS
- I would fain prove so. What might you think if I had looked upon this love with idle sight? Thus I did bespeak: "Lord Hamlet is a prince, out of thy star. This must not be." Then I prescripts gave her that she should lock herself from his resort, admit no messengers, receive no tokens; which done, she took the fruits of my advice, and he fell into a sadness, then into a fast, thence into a weakness, into the madness wherein now he raves and all we mourn for.
- KING TO THE QUEEN
- Do you think 'tis this?
- QUEEN
- It may be, very like.
- POLONIUS
- If circumstances lead me, I will find where truth is hid. You know sometimes he walks here in the lobby.
- QUEEN
- So he does indeed.
- POLONIUS
- At such a time I'll loose my daughter to him.
- POLONIUS TO THE KING
- Be you and I behind an arras then. Mark the encounter.
- KING
- We will try it.

- *Hamlet enters reading a book.*
  - POLONIUS
  - Away, I do beseech you both, away.

- *King and Queen exit.*
  - POLONIUS
  - How does my good Lord Hamlet?
  - HAMLET
  - Excellent well. You are a fishmonger.
  - POLONIUS
  - Not I, my lord.
  - HAMLET
  - Have you a daughter?
  - POLONIUS
  - I have, my lord.
  - HAMLET
  - Let her not walk i' th' sun.
  - POLONIUS ASIDE
  - Still harping on my daughter. Yet he knew me not at first; he said I was a fishmonger. He is far gone.
  - POLONIUS
  - What is the matter that you read, my lord.

- HAMLET
- Slanders, sir; for the satirical rogue says here that old men have gray beards, and that they have a plentiful lack of wit. For yourself, sir, I hold it you shall grow old as I am, if, like a crab, you could go backward.
- POLONIUS ASIDE
- Though this be madness, yet there is method in 't.
- POLONIUS
- I will take my leave of you.
- HAMLET
- You cannot, sir, take from me anything that I will more willingly part withal ---- except my life.
- POLONIUS
- Fare you well, my lord.
- HAMLET ASIDE
- These tedious old fools.

- *Polonius exits. Guildenstern and Rosencrantz enter.*
  - HAMLET
  - My excellent good friends! Good lads, how do you both? What news?
  - ROSENCRANTZ
  - None, my lord, but that the world's grown honest.
  - HAMLET
  - Then is doomsday near. What have you, my good friends, deserved at the hands of fortune that she sends you to prison hither?
  - GUILDENSTERN
  - Prison, my lord?
  - HAMLET
  - Denmark's a prison.
  - ROSENCRANTZ
  - We think not so, my lord.
  - HAMLET
  - Why, then, 'tis none to you, for there is nothing either good or bad but thinking makes it so. To me, it is a prison.
  - ROSENCRANTZ
  - Why, then, your ambition makes it one.
  - HAMLET
  - I could be bounded in a nutshell and count myself a king of infinite space, were it not that I have bad dreams.
  - GUILDENSTERN
  - Which dreams, indeed, are ambition, for the very substance of the ambitious is merely the shadow of a dream.
  - HAMLET
  - A dream itself is but a shadow.
  - ROSENCRANTZ
  - Truly.
  - HAMLET
  - Come, come, deal justly with me. Come, nay, speak.
  - GUILDENSTERN
  - What should we say, my lord?
  - HAMLET
  - Anything but to th' purpose. I know the good king and queen have sent for you.

- ROSENCRANTZ
- To what end, my lord.
- HAMLET
- That you must teach me. By the rights of our fellowship, be even and direct with me whether you were sent for or no.
- GUILDENSTERN
- My lord, we were sent for.

- **Hamlet to Guildenstern and Rosencrantz**

- **That your pledge to the king and queen need not**
- **Be disclosed, as to break their secret sought,**
- **I will tell you why. I have lost my mirth**
- **And forsaken exercise. Indeed, my**
- **Disposition's so bad that this good earth**
- **Seems a sterile rock and this air, the sky,**
- **This brave overhanging arch, fretted with**
- **The golden fire appeareth as a myth,**
- **As a pestilent set of vapors. What**
- **A piece of work is a man. Nobel must**
- **Be he in reason, form and action, but**
- **Yet to me, what's this quintessence of dust?**
- **Man delights me not, nor women I know,**
- **Though by your smiling you seem to say so.**
- ROSENCRANTZ
- My lord, there was no such stuff in my thoughts.
- HAMLET
- Why did you laugh, then, when I said "man delights me not?"
- ROSENCRANTZ
- To think, my lord, if you delight not in man, what Lenten entertainment the players shall receive from you. They are coming to offer you service.

- *The Players enter.*
  - GUILDENSTERN
  - There are the players.
  - HAMLET
  - Gentlemen, you are welcome to Elsinore. You are welcome. But my uncle-father and aunt-mother are deceived.
  - GUILDENSTERN
  - In what, my dear lord?
  - HAMLET
  - I am but mad north-north-west. When the wind is southerly, I know a hawk from a handsaw.

- *Polonius enters.*
  - POLONIUS
  - Well be with you, gentlemen.
  - HAMLET
  - Good my lord, will you see the players well bestowed? Do you hear, let them be well used, for they are the abstract and brief chronicles of the time.
  - POLONIUS

- My lord, I will use them according to their desert.
- HAMLET
- Use them after your own honor and dignity. Take them in.
- POLONIUS
- Come, sirs.
- HAMLET
- We'll hear a play tomorrow.
- HAMLET TO THE FIRST PLAYER
- Can you play "The Murder of Gonzago"?
- FIRST PLAYER
- Ay, my lord.
- HAMLET
- We'll ha 't tomorrow night.

- *First Player exits.*
  - HAMLET TO ROSENCRANTZ AND GUILDENSTERN
  - My good friends, I'll leave you till night. You are welcome to Elsinore.
  - ROSENCRANTZ
  - Good my lord.

- *Rosencrantz and Guildenstern exit.*
  - HAMLET
  - Now I am alone.

- **Hamlet to himself, No. 2**

- **O, what a rogue and peasant slave am I!**
- **How can this actor force his eyes to cry,**
- **His voice to break, his face to wan, when all**
- **A fiction be, for nothing? What would he**
- **Do had he my just motive and could call**
- **On the passion that is mine. Yet I be**
- **A pigeon-livered knave, like John-a-dreams**
- **And can say nothing. Do I lack the means**
- **To make oppression bitter? Hum, I've heard**
- **That guilty creatures sitting at a play**
- **Have proclaimed their malefactions when the word,**
- **Though it hath no tongue, speaks for itself. May**
- **The devil hath a role and the play ring**
- **Truth. I'll then catch the conscience of the king.**

- *He exits.*

- **Act 3, Scene 1**

- *The King, Queen, Polonius, Ophelia, Rosencrantz and Guildenstern enter.*
  - KING
  - Can you by no drift of conference get from him why he puts on this confusion?
  - ROSENCRANTZ
  - He does confess he feels himself distracted.
  - GUILDERSTERN

- With a crafty madness he keeps aloof.
- QUEEN
- Did you tempt him to any pastime?
- ROSENCRANTZ
- Madam, it so fell out that certain players we overtook on the way. They have already order this night to play before him.
- POLONIUS
- 'Tis most true, and he beseeched me to entreat your Majesties to hear and see the matter.
- KING
- Good gentlemen, give him a further edge and drive his purpose into these delights.

- *Rosencrantz and Guildenstern exit.*
  - KING
  - Sweet Gertrude, leave us, for we have closely sent for Hamlet hither, that he, as 'twere by accident, may here affront Ophelia, her father and myself.
  - QUEEN
  - I shall obey you. And for your part, Ophelia, I do wish that your good beauties be the happy cause of Hamlet's wildness.
  - OPHELIA
  - Madam, I wish it many.

- *Queen exits.*
  - POLONIUS
  - Ophelia, walk you here. I hear him coming. Let's withdraw, my lord.

- *They withdraw. Hamlet enters.*

- **Hamlet to himself, No. 3**

- **To be or not to be is the question.**
- **Is it nobler to bear the misfortune**
- **Of slings and arrows or by opposing**
- **A sea of troubles end them? To die, to**
- **Sleep and by a sleep to find the ending**
- **To the heartache and natural shocks you**
- **Are heir to is an ending to be sought.**
- **Yet to die with the chance to dream ought not**
- **Be sought, for not knowing in that sleep of**
- **Death what dreams may come must give us pause. There's**
- **The respect for life, for who'd suffer love,**
- **Accept oppressors, what the weakest bears,**
- **And the law's delays, when he might rather**
- **Relieve himself from life with a dagger.**

- **Hamlet to himself, No. 4**

- **Who would bear these burdens, to grunt and sweat**
- **Under a weary life if not to let**
- **The dread of what's after death, the unknown**

- **Far-off land from whose bourn no traveler**
- **Returns, make us rather bear these ills sown**
- **Than fly blindly alone to another**
- **That we know not of. Thus conscience doth make**
- **Us cowards all, afraid to die, to wake**
- **No more. Our natural resolution**
- **Becomes a look of sickness, cowering**
- **In a shadow of thought, as when action**
- **In great enterprises begins losing**
- **Its motion through fear, as when a river**
- **Deflected becomes mere stagnant water.**
- HAMLET
- Soft you now, the fair Ophelia.
- OPHELIA
- My lord, I have remembrances of yours that I have longed long to redeliver. I pray you now receive them.
- HAMLET
- No, not I. I never gave you aught.
- OPHELIA
- My honored lord, you know right well you did. Rich gifts wax poor when givers prove unkind.
- HAMLET
- Ha, ha, are you honest?
- OPHELIA
- My lord?
- HAMLET
- Are you fair?
- OPHELIA
- What means your lordship?
- HAMLET
- Ay, I did love you once.
- OPHELIA
- Indeed, my lord, you made me believe so.
- HAMLET
- You should not have believed me. I loved you not.
- OPHELIA
- I was the more deceived.
- HAMLET
- Get thee to a nunnery. Why wouldst thou be a breeder of sinners? I am myself indifferent honest, but yet I could accuse me of such things that it were better my mother had not borne me. What should such fellows as I do crawling between earth and heaven? We are arrant knaves all; believe none of us. Where's your father?
- OPHELIA
- At home, my lord.
- HAMLET
- Let the doors be shut upon him that he may play the fool nowhere but in 's own house. Farewell.
- OPHELIA
- O, help him, you sweet heavens!
- HAMLET
- If thou wilt needs marry, marry a fool, for wise men know well enough what monsters you make of them. Farewell.

- OPHELIA
- Heavenly powers, restore him!
- HAMLET
- I'll no more of it. It hath made me mad. I say we will have no more marriage. To a nunnery, go.

- *He exits.*
  - OPHELIA
  - O, what a noble mind is here o'erthrown! The courtier's, soldier's, scholar's, eye, tongue, sword, the rose of the fair state, the glass of fashion and the mold of form, th' observed of all observers, quite, quite down! O, woe is me t' have seen what I have seen, see what I see!
  - KING ADVANCING WITH POLONIUS
  - Love? There's something in his soul o'er which his melancholy sits on brood. I have in quick determination thus set it down; he shall with speed to England for the demand of our neglected tribute. Haply the seas, and countries different, shall expel this something-settled matter in his heart. What think you on 't?
  - POLONIUS
  - It shall do well. But yet do I believe the origin of his grief sprung from neglected love. My lord, after the play let his queen-mother all alone entreat him to show his grief. Let her be round with him; and I'll be placed, so please you, in the ear of all their conference.
  - KING
  - It shall be so. Madness in great ones must not unwatched go.

- *They exit.*

- **Act 3, Scene 2**

- *Hamlet enters offering instructions to three of the players.*
  - HAMLET
  - Speak the speech, I pray you, trippingly on the tongue, but if you mouth it, as many of our players do, I had as life the town-crier spoke my lines. Nor do not saw the air too much with your hand.
  - PLAYER
  - I warrant your Honor.
  - HAMLET
  - Be not too tame neither, but let your own discretion be your tutor. Suit the action to the word, the word to the action. For anything so o'erdone is from the purpose of playing, whose end was and is to hold, as 'twere, the mirror up to nature. O, there be players that I have seen play and have so strutted and bellowed that I have thought some of nature's journeymen had made men, and not made them well, they imitated humanity so abominably.
  - PLAYER
  - I hope we have reformed that indifferently with us, sir.
  - HAMLET
  - O, reform it altogether. Go make you ready.

- *Players exit. Horatio enters.*
  - HORATIO
  - Here, sweet lord, at your service.
  - HAMLET

- Horatio, thou art e'en as just a man as e'er my conversation coped withal.
- HORATIO
- O, my dear lord----

- **Hamlet to Horatio, No. 2**

- **Think not, Horatio, that I flatter,**
- **For what advancement hast thou to offer**
- **Me, having no revenue but thy good**
- **Spirits to feed and clothe thee? The absurd**
- **Pomp that flows from those with candied tongues should**
- **Be for gifts that may follow fawning heard.**
- **My mistress soul choose thee for herself as**
- **One who suffers not, having suffered, has**
- **Bourne Fortune's buffets and rewards, has been**
- **Blessed with the balanced judgment of the brave;**
- **Those who let not Fortune's fickleness win.**
- **Give me that man that is not passion's slave**
- **And I will wear him in the core of me,**
- **Ay, in my heart of heart as I do thee.**
- HAMLET
- There is a play tonight before the King. One scene of it comes near the circumstance which I have hold thee of my father's death. When thou seest that act afoot, observe my uncle. Give him heedful note, for I mine eyes will rivet to his face, and, after, we will both our judgments join in censure of his seeming.

- *A flourish sounds.*
  - HAMLET
  - They are coming to the play. I must be idle. Get you a place.

- *The King, Queen, Polonius, Ophelia, Rosencrantz, Guildenstern and others enter.*
  - HAMLET
  - Be the players ready?
  - ROSENCRANTZ
  - Ay, my lord.

- *Hamlet takes a place near Ophelia.*
  - POLONIUS TO THE KING
  - Oh, ho! Do you mark that?
  - HAMLET
  - Lady, shall I rest my head upon your lap?
  - OPHELIA
  - You are merry, my lord.
  - HAMLET
  - What should a man do but be merry? For look how cheerfully my mother looks, and my father died within 't two hours.
  - OPHELIA
  - Nay, 'tis twice two months, my lord.
  - HAMLET
  - So long? O heavens, die two months ago, and not forgotten yet? Then there's hope a great man's memory may outlive his life half a year.

- *Trumpets sound. A show without words follows. A King and Queen enter, very lovingly. He lies down upon a bank of flowers. She, seeing him asleep, leaves him. Along comes another man, takes off his crown, kisses it, pours poison in the sleeper's ears, and leaves him. The Queen returns, finds the King dead, makes passionate action. The poisoner comes in again, seems to console her. The dead body is carried away. The poisoner woos the Queen with gifts. She seems harsh awhile but in the end accepts his love. Players exit.*
  - OPHELIA
  - What means this, my lord?
  - HAMLET
  - It means mischief.

- *A Prologue enters.*
  - HAMLET
  - Is this a prologue?
  - OPHELIA
  - 'Tis brief, my lord.
  - HAMLET
  - As woman's love.

- *The Player King and Queen enter.*
  - PLAYER KING
  - Since love our hearts and our hands unite commutual in most sacred bands.
  - PLAYER QUEEN
  - Your are so sick of late, so far from cheer and from your former state, that I distrust you. Yet, though I distrust, my lord, it nothing must. Where love is great, the littlest doubts are fear; where little fears grow great, great love grows there.
  - PLAYER KING
  - Faith, I must leave thee, love, and shortly too. And thou shalt live in this fair world behind, honored, beloved.
  - PLAYER QUEEN
  - O, confound the rest! In second husband let me be accurst. None wed the second but who killed the first.
  - HAMLET
  - That's bitter.
  - PLAYER QUEEN
  - The instances that second marriage move are base respects of thrift, but none of love. A second time I kill my husband dead when second husband kisses me in bed.
  - PLAYER KING
  - I do believe you think what now you speak.

  - **Player King to Player Queen**

  - **Passion breeds promises too soon broken**
  - **When passion ends, like fruit falls unshaken**
  - **From a tree when mellow. We forget to**
  - **Pay ourselves what we said we owed ourselves.**
  - **Joy and grief can change quickly and they do;**
  - **Where passionate vows lead, no one foretells.**
  - **This world's not forever; so 'tis not strange**

- **That even love should with our fortunes change.**
- **The question's left for us to prove whether**
- **Love leads to fate or through fate comes love. Our**
- **Will and fates wonder knowing not what lure**
- **Awaits. Our thought ours, though their ends may sour.**
- **You say thou wilt no second husband wed,**
- **But thy thoughts die when thy first love is dead.**
- PLAYER QUEEN
- Nor earth to me give good, nor heaven light, sport and repose lock from me day and night, to desperation turn my trust and hope, an anchor's cheer in prison be my scope. Both her and hence pursue me lasting strife, if, once a widow, ever I be wife.
- PLAYER KING
- Sweet, leave me here awhile. My spirits grow dull, and fain I would beguile the tedious day with sleep.

- *He sleeps.*
  - PLAYER QUEEN
  - Sleep rock thy brain, and never come mischance between us twain.

- *Player Queen exits.*
  - HAMLET
  - Madam, how like you this play?
  - QUEEN
  - The lady doth protest too much, methinks.
  - HAMLET
  - O, but she'll keep her word.
  - KING
  - Have you heard the plot? Is there no offense in 't? What do they call the play?
  - HAMLET
  - "The Mousetrap." 'Tis a knavish piece of work, but what of that? Your Majesty and we that have free souls, it touches us not. Let the galled jade wince.

- *Lucianus enters.*
  - HAMLET
  - This is one Lucianus, nephew to the king.
  - LUCIANUS
  - Thoughts black, hands apt, drugs fit, and time agreeing, else no creature seeing, thou mixture rank.

- *Lucianus pours the poison in the Player King's ear.*
  - HAMLET
  - He poisons him i' th' garden for his estate. His name's Gonzago. The story is written in very choice Italian. You shall see soon how the murderer gets the love of Gonzago's wife.

- *Claudius rises.*
  - HAMLET
  - What, frighted with false fire?
  - QUEEN
  - How fares my lord?
  - KING

- Give me some light. Away!

- *All but Hamlet and Horatio exit.*
  - HAMLET
  - O good Horatio, I'll take the ghost's word for a thousand pound. Didst perceive?
  - HORATIO
  - Very well, my lord.
  - HAMLET
  - Upon the talk of the poisoning?
  - HORATIO
  - I did very well note him.

- *Rosencrantz and Guildenstern enter.*
  - GUILDENSTERN
  - The King, sir, is in his retirement marvelous distempered.
  - HAMLET
  - With drink, sir?
  - GUILDENSTERN
  - No, my lord, with choler.
  - HAMLET
  - Your wisdom should show itself more richer to signify this to the doctor.
  - GUILDENSTERN
  - The Queen your mother hath sent me to you.
  - HAMLET
  - My mother, you say.
  - ROSENCRANTZ
  - Then thus she says: your behavior hath struck her into amazement and admiration.
  - HAMLET
  - O wonderful son that can so 'stonish a mother!
  - ROSENCRANTZ
  - She desires to speak with you in her private chamber ere you go to bed.
  - HAMLET
  - We shall obey. Have you any further trade with us?
  - ROSENCRANTZ
  - Good my lord, what is your cause of distemper?
  - HAMLET
  - Sir, I lack advancement.
  - ROSENCRANTZ
  - How can that be, when you have the voice of the King himself for your succession in Denmark?
  - HAMLET
  - "While the grass grows, the horse starves."

- *Polonius enters.*
  - POLONIUS
  - My lord, the Queen would speak with you, and presently.
  - HAMLET
  - I will come to my mother by and by.
  - POLONIUS
  - I will say so.

- *All exit but Hamlet.*
  - HAMLET
  - Soft, now to my mother. Let me be cruel, not unnatural. I will speak daggers to her, but use none.

- *He exits.*

- **Act 3, Scene 3**

- *The King enters with Rosencrantz and Guildenstern, preparing to give them instructions.*
  - KING
  - I like him not, nor stands it safe with us to let his madness range. I your commission will forthwith dispatch, and he to England shall along with you.
  - GUILDENSTERN

- *We will ourselves provide.*
  - KING
  - Arm you, I pray you, to this speedy voyage, for we will fetters put about tis fear, which now goes too free-footed.

- *Rosencrantz and Guildenstern exit. Polonius enters.*
  - POLONIUS
  - My lord, he's going to his mother's chambers. Behind the arras I'll convey myself to hear the process.
  - KING
  - Thanks, dear my lord.

- *Polonius exits.*
  - KING
  - O, my offense is rank, it smells to heaven; it hath the primal eldest curse upon 't, a brother's murder. Pray can I not, though inclination be as sharp as will.

  - **Claudius to himself**

  - **My stronger guilt defeats my strong intent**
  - **To pray, and, like a motionless man bent**
  - **On two options, I know not where to start,**
  - **Neglecting both. To what end serves mercy**
  - **But to face the offense? What is the part**
  - **Of prayer but to be not tempted and be**
  - **Forgiven? What form of prayer would serve me**
  - **Best? "Forgive my foul murder?" That can't be**
  - **Since I am still possessed of those effects**
  - **For which I did the murder, my fair queen**
  - **And crown. I lose all if the state detects**
  - **The crime. Yet above the crime will be seen**
  - **For the truth it is? What is there to vent?**
  - **What can one do when one cannot repent?**
  - KING
  - Bow, stubborn knees, and heart with strings of steel be soft as sinews of the newborn babe. All may be well.

- *He kneels. Hamlet enters.*
  - HAMLET
  - Now he is a–praying, and now I'll do 't.

- *He draws his sword.*
  - HAMLET
  - And so he goes to heaven, and so am I revenged. A villain kills my father, and for that, I, his sole son, do this same villain send to heaven. Why, this is hire and salary, not revenge. No. Up sword.

- *He sheathes his sword.*
  - HAMLET
  - When he is drunk asleep, or in his rage, then trip him, that his heels may kick at heaven, and that his soul may be as damned and black as hell, whereto it goes.

- *Hamlet exits.*
  - KING RISING
  - My words fly up, my thoughts remain below; words without thoughts never to heaven go.

- *He exits.*

- **Act 3, Scene 4**

- *The Queen enters with Polonius, who plans to hide behind the drapes.*
  - POLONIUS
  - He will come straight. I'll silence me even here. Pray you, be round with him.
  - QUEEN
  - I'll warrant you. Fear me not. Withdraw.

- *Polonius hides behind the arras. Hamlet enters.*
  - QUEEN
  - Hamlet, thou hast thy father much offended.
  - HAMLET
  - Mother, you have my father much offended.
  - QUEEN
  - Come, come, you answer with an idle tongue. Have you forgot me?
  - HAMLET
  - No. You are the Queen, your husband's brother's wife. You are my mother.

- *Come and sit you down; you shall not budge.*
  - QUEEN
  - What wilt thou do? Thou wilt not murder me?
  - POLONIUS FROM BEHIND THE ARRAS
  - What ho! Help!
  - HAMLET
  - How now, a rat? Dead for a ducat, dead.

- *He kills Polonius, thrusting a rapier through the arras.*
  - POLONIUS FROM BEHIND THE ARRAS
  - O, I am slain!
  - QUEEN

- O me, what hast thou done?
- HAMLET
- Nay, I know not. Is it the King?

- *Hamlet pulls Polonius' body from behind the arras.*
  - HAMLET
  - Thou wretched, rash, intruding fool, farewell. I took thee for the better.
  - HAMLET TO THE QUEEN
  - Leave wringing of your hands. Peace, sit you down, and let me wring your heart.
  - QUEEN
  - What have I done, that thou dar'st wag thy tongue in noise so rude against me?
  - HAMLET
  - Such an act that blurs the grace and blush of modesty, calls virtue hypocrite, takes off the rose from the fair forehead of an innocent love and sets a blister there, makes marriage vows as false as dicers' oaths.
  - QUEEN
  - Ay, me.
  - HAMLET
  - Look here upon this picture and on this, the counterfeit presentment of two brothers. This was your husband. Look you now what follows. Here is your husband, like a mildewed ear blasting his wholesome brother.

- **Hamlet to his Mother**

- **Have you eyes? This cannot be called love, for**
- **At your age the thrill in the blood is more**
- **Tame. Your senses must be paralyzed or**
- **Your mind enslaved; what judgment would have stepped**
- **To this? Madness would not err like this nor**
- **Should bliss be so bonding for you to've leapt**
- **To this fantasy; not reserving some**
- **Quantity of choice. What devil has come**
- **To trick you at blindman's bluff? If this love,**
- **Love is mad. If thou in matron's bones lacks**
- **Reason and will, how can the virtue of**
- **A flaming maid not melt as heated wax?**
- **Shaming youth for ardor is not your turn**
- **When frost itself as actively doth burn.**
- QUEEN
- O Hamlet, speak no more! These words like daggers enter in my ears. No more, sweet Hamlet

- *The Ghost enters.*
  - HAMLET
  - What would your gracious figure?
  - QUEEN
  - Alas, he's mad.
  - HAMLET
  - Do you not come your tardy son to chide, that, lapsed in time and passion, lets go by th' important acting of your dread command?

- GHOST
- Do not forget. But look, amazement on thy mother sits. O, step between her and her fighting soul. Speak to her, Hamlet.
- HAMLET
- How is it with you, lady?
- QUEEN
- Alas, how is 't with you, that you do bend your eye on vacancy and with th' incorporal air do hold discourse? O gentle son, upon the heat and flame of thy distemper sprinkle cool patience! Whereon do you look?
- HAMLET
- On him, on him! Look you how pale he glares.
- QUEEN
- To whom do you speak this?
- HAMLET
- Do you see nothing there?
- QUEEN
- Nothing at all; yet all that is I see.
- HAMLET
- Nor did you nothing hear?
- QUEEN
- No, nothing but ourselves.
- HAMLET
- Why, look you there, look how it steals away! My father, in his habit as he lived!

- *The Ghost exits.*
  - QUEEN
  - This is the very coinage of your brain.
  - HAMLET
  - It is not madness that I have uttered. Mother, for love of grace, lay not that flattering unction to your soul that not your trespass but my madness speaks. Confess yourself to heaven, repent what's past, avoid what is to come. Forgive me this my virtue, for virtue itself of vice must pardon beg.
  - QUEEN
  - O Hamlet, thou hast cleft my heart in twain!
  - HAMLET
  - O, throw away the worser part of it and live the purer with the other half! Good night. For this same lord (pointing to Polonius) I do repent. So, again, good night. I must be cruel only to be kind.
  - QUEEN
  - What shall I do?
  - HAMLET
  - Ravel all this matter out that I essentially am not in madness, but mad in craft.
  - QUEEN
  - Be thou assured, if words be made of breath and breath of life, I have no life to breathe what thou hast said to me.
  - HAMLET
  - I must to England, you know that.
  - QUEEN
  - Alack, I had forgot! 'Tis so concluded on.
  - HAMLET
  - My two schoolfellows, whom I will trust as I will adders fanged, they bear the mandate; they must sweep my way and marshal me to knavery. Let it

work. This man shall set me packing (pointing to Polonius). I'll lug the guts into the neighbor room. Come, sir, to draw toward an end with you. Good night, mother.

- *They exit, Hamlet tugging in Polonius.*

- **Act 4, Scene 1**

- *The King, Queen, Rosencrantz and Guildenstern are on stage.*
  - KING
  - Where is your son?
  - QUEEN
  - Bestow this place onus a little while.

- *Rosencrantz and Guildenstern exit.*
  - KING
  - How does Hamlet?
  - QUEEN
  - Mad as the sea and wind when both contend which is the mightier. In his lawless fit, behind the arras hearing something stir, whips out his rapier, cries "A rat, a rat," and in this brainish apprehension kills the unseen good old man.
  - KING
  - O heavy deed! His liberty is full of threats to all. Alas, how shall this bloody deed be answered? It will be laid to us. Where is he gone?
  - QUEEN
  - To draw apart the body he hath killed. He weeps for what is done.
  - KING
  - The sun no sooner shall the mountains touch but we will ship him hence; and this vile deed we must with all your majesty and skill both countenance and excuse. Ho, Guildenstern!

- *Rosencrantz and Guildenstern enter.*
  - KING
  - Friends both, Hamlet in madness hath Polonius slain, and from his mother's chambers hath he dragged him. Go seek him out, speak fair, and bring the body into the chapel.

- *Rosencrantz and Guildenstern exit.*
  - KING
  - Come, Gertrude, we'll call up our wisest friends and let them know both what we mean to do and what's untimely done. O, come away! My soul is full of discord and dismay.

- *They exit.*

- **Act 4, Scene 2**

- *Hamlet is on stage.*
  - HAMLET
  - Safely stowed.

- *Rosencrantz and Guildenstern enter.*
  - ROSENCRANTZ

- What have you done, my lord, with the dead body? Tell us where 'tis, that we may take it thence and bear it to the chapel.
- HAMLET
- Do not believe it.
- ROSENCRANTZ
- Believe what?
- HAMLET
- That I can keep your counsel and not mine own. Besides, to be demanded of a sponge, what replication should be made by the son of a king?
- ROSENCRANTZ
- Take you me for a sponge, my lord?
- HAMLET
- Ay, sir, that soaks up the King's favorable looks, his rewards, his authorities. When he needs what you have gleaned, it is but squeezing you, and, sponge, you shall be dry again.
- ROSENCRANTZ
- I understand you not, my lord.
- HAMLET
- I am glad of it. A knavish speech is not understood in a foolish ear.
- ROSENCRANTZ
- My lord, you must tell us where the body is and go with us to the King.
- HAMLET
- The body is with the King, but the King is not with the body. The King is a thing----
- GUILDENSTERN
- A "thing," my lord.
- HAMLET
- Of nothing.

- *They exit.*

- **Act 4, Scene 3**

- *The King is on stage.*
  - KING
  - I have sent to seek him and to find the body. How dangerous is it that this man goes loose! But he is loved of the distracted multitude, who like not in their judgment, but their eyes. This sudden sending him away must seem deliberate pause.

- *Rosencrantz enters.*
  - ROSENCRANTZ
  - Where the dead body is bestowed, my lord, we cannot get from him.
  - KING
  - But where is he?
  - ROSENCRANTZ
  - Without, my lord.
  - KING
  - Bring him before us.

- *They enter with Hamlet.*
  - KING
  - Now, Hamlet, where's Polonius?
  - HAMLET
  - At supper.

- KING
- At supper where?

- **Hamlet to Claudius**

- **It's not where he eats, but where he's eaten.**
- **A group of crafty worms are e'en 'im.**
- **Your worm is the emperor of eaters.**
- **We fatten all creatures to fatten us,**
- **And the fattening of ourselves defers**
- **To the maggots and worms. The worms don't fuss**
- **Over a fat king and skinny beggar,**
- **Considering them both fine meals; rather**
- **Like two different dishes at one table.**
- **A man may fish with the worm that was led**
- **To a king and eat the fish 'twas able**
- **To feed on that worm, which shows a king fed**
- **May progress through a beggar. You shall all**
- **Nose him as you go up into the hall.**
- KING TO ATTENDANTS
- Go, seek him there.
- HAMLET
- He will stay till you come.

- *Attendants exit.*
  - KING
  - Hamlet, this deed, for thine especial safety must we send thee hence. Therefore prepare thyself. The bark is ready, and the wind at help.
  - HAMLET
  - For England?
  - KING
  - Ay, Hamlet.
  - HAMLET
  - Good. But come, for England. Farewell, dear mother.

- *He exits.*
  - KING
  - Follow him at foot; tempt him with speed aboard. Delay it not.

- *All but the King exit.*
  - KING
  - The present death of Hamlet. Do it, England.

- *He exits.*

- **Act 4, Scene 4**

- *Fortinbras with his army march over the stage.*
  - FORTINBRAS
  - Go, Captain, from me greet the Danish king. Tell him that by his license Fortinbras craves the conveyance of a promised march over his kingdom.
  - CAPTAIN
  - I will do 't, my lord.

- *All but the Captain exit. Hamlet, Rosencrantz and Guildenstern enter.*
  - HAMLET
  - Good sir, whose powers are these?
  - CAPTAIN
  - They are of Norway, sir.
  - HAMLET
  - How purposed, sir.
  - CAPTAIN
  - Against some part of Poland.
  - HAMLET
  - Who commands them, sir?
  - CAPTAIN
  - The nephew to old Norway, Fortinbras.
  - HAMLET
  - Goes it against the main of Poland, sir, or for some frontier?
  - CAPTAIN
  - We go to gain a little patch of ground that hath in it no profit but the name. To pay five ducats, five, I would not farm it.
  - HAMLET
  - Why, then, the Polack never will defend it.
  - CAPTAIN
  - Yes, it is already garrisoned.
  - HAMLET
  - Two thousand souls and twenty thousand ducats will not debate the question of this straw. This is th' abscess of much wealth and peace, that inward breaks and shows no cause on the outside why the man dies.
  - CAPTAIN
  - God be wi' you, sir.

- *He exits.*
  - ROSENCRANTZ
  - Will 't please you to go, my lord?

- *All exit but Hamlet.*
  - HAMLET
  - How all occasions do inform against me and spur my dull revenge.

- **Hamlet to himself, No. 5**

- **Is man no more than a beast if his chief**
- **Good is to sleep and feed during his brief**
- **Stay? Since God gave us the power of thought,**
- **Surely he didn't intend we grow stale**
- **From unuse. Why do I say "This I ought**
- **Do" and yet not do it? Norway doth rail**
- **And this tender prince doth risk all for his**
- **Country, even for an eggshell. It is**
- **To find quarrel in a straw when honor's**
- **At stake; otherwise fight only if the**
- **Argument is great. This trick of fame bores**
- **Me, knowing they to die for fantasy.**
- **O, for the rest of my pale life on earth**

- **I'll hold bloody thoughts or be nothing worth.**

- *He exits.*

- **Act 4, Scene 5**

- *Horatio, the Queen and a Gentleman enter.*
  - QUEEN
  - I will not speak with her. What would she have?
  - GENTLEMAN
  - She speaks much of her father. Her speech is nothing, yet the unshaped use of it doth move the hearers to conclusions.
  - HORATIO
  - 'Twere good she were spoken with, for she may strew dangerous conjectures in ill-breeding minds.
  - QUEEN
  - Let her come in.

- *Gentleman exits. Ophelia enters distracted.*
  - OPHELIA SINGS
  - "How should I your true love know from another one?"
  - QUEEN
  - Alas, sweet lady, what imports this song?
  - OPHELIA SINGS
  - "He is dead and gone, lady, he is dead and gone."

- *King enters.*
  - KING
  - How do you, pretty lady?
  - OPHELIA
  - They say the owl was a baker's daughter. Lord, we know what we are but know not what we may be.
  - KING
  - She is thinking about her father.
  - OPHELIA SINGS
  - "Tomorrow is Saint Valentine's day, all in the morning betime, and I a maid at your window, to be your Valentine."
  - KING
  - Pretty Ophelia.
  - OPHELIA SINGS
  - "You promised me to wed."
  - KING
  - How long hath she been thus?
  - OPHELIA
  - I hope all will be well. We must be patient, but I cannot choose but weep to think they would lay him i' th' cold ground. My brother shall know of it. Good night, ladies, good night.

- *She exits.*
  - KING
  - Follow her close; give her good watch, I pray you.

- *Horatio exits.*

- **Claudius to Gertrude**

- **O, Gertrude, this is the poison of deep**
- **Grief; it's from her father's death. Sorrows keep**
- **Coming; her father's slain and your son's gone,**
- **The author of his removal. People**
- **Are talking and the whispering goes on;**
- **These sudden events are taking their toll.**
- **By not having properly interred him**
- **And with Ophelia split by this ill whim,**
- **We're but the picture of mere beasts. And her**
- **Brother has in secret come from France, feeds**
- **On these rumors, hearing each gossiper**
- **Draw it to me. I know not where this leads.**
- **O, dear Gertrude, these are frightening days**
- **Murd'ring me piece by piece in many ways.**
- **A Messenger enters.**
- MESSENGER
- Save yourself, my lord. The ocean eats not the flats with more impiteous haste than young Laertes o'erbears your officers. The rabble call him "lord." They cry "Choose we, Laertes shall be king!"
- QUEEN
- You are following the wrong trail, you false Danish dogs!

- *Laertes enters with others.*
  - LAERTES
  - Where is this king? O thou vile king, give me my father!
  - QUEEN
  - Calmly, good Laertes.
  - KING
  - What is the cause, Laertes? There's such divinity doth hedge a king that treason can but peep to what it would, acts little of his will. Tell me, Laertes, why thou art thus incensed.
  - LAERTES
  - Where is my father?
  - KING
  - Dead.
  - QUEEN
  - But not by him.
  - LAERTES
  - How came he dead? I'll not be juggled with. To this point I stand; let come what comes, only I'll be revenged most thoroughly for my father.
  - KING
  - Good Laertes, if you desire to know the certainty of your dear father, is 't writ in your revenge that you will draw both friend and foe, winner and loser?
  - LAERTES
  - None but his enemies.
  - KING
  - Will you know them, then?
  - LAERTES
  - To his good friends thus wide I'll open my arms.
  - KING

- Why, now you speak like a good child and a true gentleman. That I am guiltless of your father's death and am most sensibly in grief for it.

- *Ophelia enters.*
  - LAERTES
  - O heat, dry up my brains! Dear maid, kind sister, sweet Ophelia! O heavens, is 't possible a young maid's wits should be as mortal as an old man's life?
  - OPHELIA SINGS
  - "They bore him barefaced on the bier, and in his grave rained many a tear."
  - LAERTES
  - This nonsense speaks more eloquently than does serious speech.
  - OPHELIA
  - There's rosemary, that's for remembrance. Pray you, love, remember. And there is pansies, that's for thoughts.
  - LAERTES
  - A document in madness.
  - OPHELIA
  - There's a daisy. I would give you some violets, but they withered all when my father died. They say he made a good end.
  - LAERTES
  - Thought and afflictions, passion, hell itself she turns to favor and to prettiness.
  - OPHELIA SINGS
  - "And will he not come again? No, no, he is dead. His beard was as white as snow. He is gone, God 'a mercy on his soul."
  - OPHELIA
  - And of all Christians' souls, God be wi' you.

- *She exits.*
  - LAERTES
  - Do you see this?
  - KING
  - Laertes, make choice of whom your wisest friends you will, and they shall hear and judge 'twixt you and me. If they find us touched, we will our kingdom give, our crown, our life, and all that we call ours. But if not, be you content to lend your patience to us.
  - LAERTES
  - Let this be so. His means of death, his obscure funeral cry to be heard, as 'twere from heaven to earth that I must call 't in question.
  - KING
  - So you shall, and where th' offense is, let the great ax fall.

- *They exit.*

- **Act 4, Scene 6**

- *Horatio and a Gentleman are on stage.*
  - HORATIO
  - What are they that would speak with me?
  - GENTLEMAN
  - Seafaring men, sir.
  - HORATIO
  - Let them come in.

- *Gentleman exits. Sailors enter.*
  - SAILOR
  - There's a letter for you, sir. It came from th' ambassador that was bound for England, if your name be Horatio, as I am let to know it is.

- *He hands Horatio a letter.*
  - HORATIO READS THE LETTER
  - "Horatio, when thou shalt have overlooked this, give these fellows some means to the King. They have letters for him. Ere we were two days old at sea, a pirate of very warlike appointment gave us chase. In the grapple I boarded them. I alone became their prisoner. They have dealt with me like thieves of mercy, but they knew what they did: I am to do a good turn for them. Let the King have the letters I have sent, and repair thou to me with as much speed as thou wouldst fly death. I have words to speak in thine ear will make thee dumb. These good fellows will bring thee where I am. Rosencrantz and Guildenstern hold their course for England; of them I have much to tell thee. Hamlet."
  - HORATIO
  - Come, direct me to him from whom you brought them.

- *They exit.*

- **Act 4, Scene 7**

- *The King and Laertes are on stage.*
  - KING
  - You must put me in your heart for friend, since you have heard that he which hath your noble father slain pursued my life.
  - LAERTES
  - It well appears. But tell me why you proceeded not gainst these feats.
  - KING
  - O, for two special reasons. The Queen his mother lives almost by his looks, and for myself she is so closely joined to my life and soul that I could not but by her. The other motive is the great love the common people bear him.
  - LAERTES
  - And so have I a noble father lost and a sister driven into desp'rate terms. But my revenge will come.
  - KING
  - Break not your sleeps for that. You must not think that we are made of stuff so flat and dull that we can let our beard be shook with danger and think it pastime.

- *A Messenger enters.*
  - MESSENGER
  - Letters, my lord, for Hamlet. These to your Majesty, this to the Queen.
  - KING
  - From Hamlet? Who brought them?
  - MESSENGER
  - Sailors, my lord, they say.

- *Messenger exits.*
  - KING READS
  - "High and mighty, tomorrow shall I beg leave to see your kingly eyes, when I shall recount the occasion of my sudden return. Hamlet"

- KING
- In the postscript here, he says "alone." Can you advise me?
- LAERTES
- I am lost in it, my lord. But let him come. I shall tell him to his teeth "Thus didst thou."
- KING
- If it be so, Laertes, will you be ruled by me?
- LAERTES
- Ay, my lord, so you will not o'errule me to a peace.
- KING
- I will work him to an exploit under the which he shall not choose but fall; and for his death no wind of blame shall breathe.
- LAERTES
- My lord, I will be ruled, the rather if you could devise it so that I might be the agent.
- KING
- It falls right. You have been talked of a quality wherein they say you shine.
- LAERTES
- What part is that, my lord?
- KING
- Here was a gentleman of Normandy. I have seen him myself. He made confession of you and gave you such a masterly report for your rapier most especial, that he cried out 'twould be a sight indeed if one could match you. This report of his did Hamlet so envenom with his envy that he could nothing do but wish and beg your sudden coming-o'er. Laertes, was your father dear to you? Or are you like the painting of a sorrow, a face without a heart?
- LAERTES
- Why ask you this?

- **Claudius to Laertes, No. 1**

- **Laertes, know that I think you did then**
- **Love your father, but there is a time when**
- **Love begins, and, with proof from my past, I**
- **Know that time qualifies the spark and fire**
- **Of it. In the very flames of love lie**
- **Snuff that will abate it. Goodness doth tire**
- **In its own too-much. We should right-away**
- **Do what we would for "would" can find delay,**
- **And delay feeds on itself finding ways**
- **To abate and postpone action, changing**
- **Woulds to inactions. Then what should be stays**
- **Undone. To the quick, Hamlet's back. Using**
- **More than words, what processes should be done**
- **To show yourself indeed your father's son?**
- LAERTES
- To cut his throat i' th' church.

- **Claudius to Laertes, No. 2**

- **No safe place should protect a murderer.**

- Good Laertes, stay within your chamber.
- Hamlet shall know you have returned. We'll praise
- The fame attached to thy French-learned fencing
- Skills, and with Hamlet's guilelessness, he'll raise
- Unaware a foil. By then anointing
- Your sword with that rare poison that can bring
- Death to one scratched withal, you serve the king.
- But if this should fail, make your motions more
- Violent that he soon becomes hot and dry,
- Calling for drink. I'll have a chalice for
- The prince, whereon but sipping, if he by
- Chance escapes your venom stuck, will give us
- The second chance to achieve our purpose.
- LAERTES
- I will do it. And for that purpose I'll anoint my sword. I'll touch my point with this poison, that, if I scratch him slightly, it may be death.

- *The Queen enters.*
  - QUEEN
  - One woe doth tread upon another's heel, so fast they follow. Your sister's drowned, Laertes.
  - LAERTES
  - Drowned? O, where?
  - QUEEN
  - There is a willow grows across the brook. There on the pendant boughs an envious sliver broke, when down she fell in the weeping brook. But long it could not be till that her garments, heavy with their drink, pulled the poor wretch to muddy death.
  - LAERTES
  - Alas, then she is drowned.
  - QUEEN
  - Drowned, drowned.
  - LAERTES
  - Too much of water hast thou, poor Ophelia, and therefore I forbid my tears. But yet nature her custom holds; let shame say what it will.

- *He exits.*
  - KING
  - Let's follow, Gertrude. How much I had to do to calm his rage! Now fear I this will give it start again. Therefore, let's follow.

- *They exit.*

- **Act 5, Scene 1**

- *Gravediggers are on stage in a graveyard.*

  - Gravedigger to another gravedigger

  - The coroner ruled that she doth deserve
  - A Christian burial though she did serve
  - Out her own salvation, so it seems. Say

- **She drowned herself in her own defense; it**
- **Cannot be else. If one takes life that way**
- **Wittingly, it argues the act doth fit.**
- **But if the water comes to her, not sought**
- **By her, she drowns not herself; then she's not**
- **Guilty of her own cruel death that shortened**
- **Her own favored life. The truth is if she**
- **Weren't a gentlewoman, she'd not received**
- **A Christian burial. 'Tis a pity**
- **That great folk don't have more approval to**
- **Drown themselves than their fellow Christians do.**
- **The Gravedigger sings. Hamlet and Horatio enter.**
- HAMLET
- Has this fellow no feeling of his business? He sings in grave-making.
- HORATIO
- Custom hath made it in him a property of easiness.
- HAMLET
- 'Tis e'en so.

- *The Gravedigger sings. He digs up a skull.*
  - HAMLET
  - That skull had a tongue in it and could sing once. This might be of a courtier, which could say "Good morrow, sweet lord! How dost thou, sweet lord?" Might it not?
  - HORATIO
  - Ay, my lord.

- *The Gravedigger digs up more skulls.*
  - HAMLET
  - There's another. Why may not that be the skull of a lawyer? Where be his hair-splitting definitions now, his cases, and his tricks. Why does he suffer this mad knave now to knock him bout the head with a dirty shovel and will not tell him of his action of battery? Whose grave's this, sirrah?
  - GRAVEDIGGER
  - Mine, sir.
  - HAMLET
  - I think it be thine indeed, for thou liest in 't.
  - GRAVEDIGGER
  - You lie out on 't, sir, and therefore 'tis not yours. For my part, I do not lie in 't, yet it is mine.
  - HAMLET
  - What man dost thou dig it for?
  - GRAVEDIGGER
  - For no man, sir.
  - HAMLET
  - What woman then?
  - GRAVEDIGGER
  - For none, neither.
  - HAMLET
  - Who is to be buried in it?
  - GRAVEDIGGER
  - One that was a woman, sir, but, rest her soul, she's dead.

- HAMLET
- How precise the knave is! How long hast thou been grave maker?
- GRAVEDIGGER
- Of all the days i' th' year, I came to 't that day that our last King Hamlet overcame Fortinbras.
- HAMLET
- How long is that since?
- GRAVEDIGGER
- Cannot you tell that? Every fool can tell that. It was that very day that young Hamlet was born --- he that is mad, and sent into England.
- HAMLET
- Ay, marry, why was he sent into England?
- GRAVEDIGGER
- Why, because he was mad. He shall recover his wits there. Or if he do not, 'tis no great matter there.
- HAMLET
- Why?
- GRAVEDIGGER
- There the men are as mad as he.
- HAMLET
- How long will a man lie i' th' earth ere he rot?
- GRAVEDIGGER
- Faith, if he be not rotten before he die he will last you some eight year or nine year. A tanner will last you nine year. Here's a skull now hath lien you i' th' earth three-and-twenty years.
- HAMLET
- Whose was it?
- GRAVEDIGGER
- This same skull, sir, was, sir, Yorick's skull, the King's jester.
- HAMLET
- This?
- GRAVEDIGGER
- E'en that.

- *Hamlet takes the skull.*
  - HAMLET
  - Alas, poor Yorick! I knew him, Horatio --- a fellow of infinite jest, of most excellent fancy. Where be your gibes now? Your songs? Your flashes of merriment that were wont to set the table on a roar?

- *Hamlet puts the skull down. The King, Queen, Laertes and others bearing the corpse of Ophelia enter.*
  - HAMLET
  - Here comes the King, the Queen, the courtiers. Who is this they follow? This doth betoken the corpse they follow did with desp'rate hand fordo its own life. 'Twas of some estate.

- *They step aside.*
  - LAERTES
  - What ceremony else?
  - HAMLET
  - That is Laertes, a very noble youth.

- DOCTOR
- Her death was suspicious, and, but that great command o'ersways the order, she should in ground unsanctified been lodged till the last trumpet.
- LAERTES
- Must there no more be done?
- DOCTOR
- No more be done.
- LAERTES
- Lay her i' th' earth, and from her fair and unpolluted flesh may violets spring!
- HAMLET TO HORATIO
- What, the fair Ophelia?
- QUEEN
- Sweets to the sweet, farewell!

- *She scatters flowers.*
  - QUEEN
  - I hoped thou shouldst have been my Hamlet's wife.
  - LAERTES
  - Hold off the earth awhile till I have caught her once more in mine arms.

- *He leaps in the grave. Hamlet advances.*
  - HAMLET
  - What is he whose grief bears such an emphasis? This is I, Hamlet the Dane.

- *Laertes comes out of the grave.*
  - LAERTES
  - The devil take thy soul!

- *They grapple.*
  - HAMLET
  - I prithee take thy fingers from my throat. Hold off thy hand.
  - QUEEN
  - Hamlet, Hamlet!
  - ALL
  - Gentlemen!

- *Hamlet and Laertes are separated.*
  - HAMLET
  - Why, I will fight with him upon this theme until my eyelids will no longer wag!
  - QUEEN
  - O my son, what theme?

- **Hamlet to Laertes, No. 1**

- **I loved Ophelia. Some forty thousand**
- **Brothers' love could not make up my sum, and**
- **What wilt thou do for her, Laertes? Show**
- **Me what thou'lt do. Wilt thou weep, wilt thou fight,**
- **Wilt thou drink vinegar or eat a crow?**
- **I'll do it. Dost thou come within my sight**

- To whine or to outface me with leaping
- In her grave? Let all earth come cascading
- On us, millions of acres, enough to
- Bury us to the earth's burning zone. When
- Thou'lt mouth, I will rant as thou. Why do you
- Use me like this? But then so what. Even
- Hercules could try to do what he may,
- Yet cats will mew and dogs will have their day.

- *Hamlet exits.*
  - KING
  - I pray thee, good Horatio, wait upon him.

- *Horatio exits.*
  - KING TO LAERTES
  - Strengthen your patience in our last night's speech.
  - KING TO QUEEN
  - Good Gertrude, set some watch over your son.

- *They exit.*

- **Act 5, Scene 2**

- *Hamlet and Horatio are on stage.*
  - HAMLET
  - You do remember all the circumstance?
  - HORATIO
  - Remember it, my lord!
  - HAMLET
  - Sir, in my heart there was a kind of fighting that would not let me sleep.

- **Hamlet to Horatio, No. 3**

- Since impulsive acts sometimes serve us, we
- Should learn, dear friend, there's a divinity
- That shapes our ends. With my gown wrapped about
- Me, I groped to find them and fingered their
- Packet. As I withdrew I did find out
- An exact command that was writ with care
- To have my head struck off. I sat me down,
- Devised a new command and with a frown
- Took my father's seal and, sensing the row,
- Folded, sealed and placed it safely before
- The next day's sea fight; and what followed thou
- Knowest already. 'Tis dangerous for
- Baser nature's to get involved when it's
- Between the points of mighty opposites.
- HAMLET
- Without debatement further, more or less, he should those bearers put to sudden death.
- HORATIO

- So Guildenstern and Rosencrantz go to 't.
- HAMLET
- They are not near my conscience. Their defeat does by drawing themselves into the affair.

- *Osric, a courtier, enters.*
  - OSRIC
  - Your lordship is right welcome back to Denmark.
  - HAMLET
  - I humbly thank you, sir.
  - OSRIC
  - If your lordship were at leisure, I should impart a thing to you from his Majesty.
  - HAMLET
  - I will receive it, sir, with all diligence of spirit.
  - OSRIC
  - My lord, his Majesty bade me signify to you that he has laid a great wager on your head. Sir, this is the matter----
  - HAMLET
  - I beseech you, remember.
  - OSRIC
  - Sir, here is newly come to court Laertes --- believe me, an absolute gentle-man, of very soft society and great showing. I take him to be a soul of great article.
  - HAMLET
  - What imports the naming of this gentleman?
  - OSRIC
  - Of Laertes?
  - HAMLET
  - Of him, sir.
  - OSRIC
  - You are not ignorant of what excellence Laertes is -----
  - HAMLET
  - I dare not confess that, lest I should compare with him in excellence. But to know a man well were to know himself.
  - OSRIC
  - I mean, sir, for his weapon.
  - HAMLET
  - What's his weapon?
  - OSRIC
  - Rapier and dagger.
  - HAMLET
  - That's two of his weapons.
  - OSRIC
  - The King, sir, hath wagered with him six Barbary horses, against which he has impawned, as I take it, six French rapiers and daggers.
  - HAMLET
  - But on. Six Barbary horses against six French swords. That's the French bet against the Danish. Why is this all "impawned," as you call it?
  - OSRIC

- The King, sir, hath laid, sir, that in a dozen passes between yourself and him, he shall not exceed you three hits. He hath laid on twelve for nine, and it would come to immediate trial if your lordship would vouchsafe the answer.
- HAMLET
- Sir, I will walk here in the hall. Let the foils be brought, the gentleman willing, and the King hold his purpose. I will win for him, as I can. If not, I will gain nothing but my shame and the odd hits.
- OSRIC
- I commend my duty to your lordship.

- *Osric exits.*
  - HAMLET
  - He does well to commend it himself.

- *A Lord enters.*
  - LORD
  - My lord, his Majesty sends to know if your pleasure hold to play with Laertes, or that you will take longer time.
  - HAMLET
  - I am constant to my purposes. If his fitness speaks, mine is ready now or whensoever.
  - LORD
  - The King and Queen and all are coming down.

- *Lord exits.*
  - HORATIO
  - You will lose, my lord.
  - HAMLET
  - I do not think so. Since he went into France, I have been in continual practice.
  - HORATIO
  - Nay, good my lord.
  - HAMLET
  - It is such a kind of misgiving as would perhaps trouble a woman.
  - HORATIO
  - If your mind dislikes anything, obey it. I will forestall their coming hither and say you are not fit.
  - HAMLET
  - There is a special providence in the fall of a sparrow. If it be not now, yet it will come. The readiness is all.

- *A table is prepared with foils, daggers and wine. The King, Queen, Osric and Laertes enter.*

- **Hamlet to Laertes, No. 2**

- **As all in this presence know, I have done**
- **You wrong, Laertes. Accept my pardon.**
- **But, as you must have heard, I've been punished**
- **With a sore distraction. 'Tis no one's guess**
- **That what I did roughly awakened**

- **Your honor resulted from my madness.**
- **If madness takes Hamlet away, and when**
- **He's not himself he wrongs Laertes, then**
- **Hamlet does it not. His madness is host;**
- **His madness is poor Hamlet's enemy.**
- **Hamlet is a faction wronged. In your most**
- **Kind thoughts, from this evil please do free me**
- **As if I had shot my arrow over**
- **The house and by mistake hurt my brother.**
- LAERTES
- I am satisfied in nature. But in my terms of honor I stand aloof. I do receive your offered love like love and will not wrong it.
- HAMLET
- I embrace it freely. Give us the foils.
- LAERTES
- Come, one for me.
- HAMLET
- I'll be your foil, Laertes; in mine ignorance your skill shall stand out in brilliant contrast,
- LAERTES
- You mock me, sir.
- HAMLET
- No, by this hand.
- KING
- Give them the foils, young Osric. Cousin Hamlet, you know the wager?
- HAMLET
- Very well, my lord. Your Grace has laid the odds o' th' weaker side.
- KING
- I do not fear it; I have seen you both. But, since he is better, we have therefore odds.

- *They prepare to play.*
  - KING
  - Set me the stoups of wine upon that table. Give me the cups. Now the King drinks to Hamlet. Come, begin. And you, the judges, bear a wary eye.

- *They play.*
  - OSRIC
  - A hit, a very palpable hit.
  - KING
  - Stay, give me drink. Hamlet, this pearl is thine. Here's to thy health.

- *He drinks and then drops the pearl in the cup.*
  - HAMLET
  - Another hit. What say you?
  - LAERTES
  - A touch, a touch. I do confess 't.
  - KING
  - Our son shall win.
  - QUEEN
  - He's fat and scant of breath. Here, Hamlet, take my napkin; rub thy brows.

- *She lifts the cup.*
  - KING
  - Gertrude, do not drink.
  - QUEEN
  - I will, my lord; I pray you pardon me.

- *She drinks.*
  - KING ASIDE
  - It is the poisoned cup. It is too late.
  - HAMLET
  - I dare not drink yet, madam --- by and by. Come, for the third, Laertes. You do but dally. I pray you pass with your best violence.
  - LAERTES
  - Say you so? Come on.

- *They play.*
  - LAERTES
  - Have at you now!

- *Laertes wounds Hamlet. Then in scuffling they change rapiers. Hamlet wounds Laertes.*
  - KING
  - Part them.
  - HAMLET
  - Nay, come again.

- *The Queen falls.*
  - OSRIC
  - Look to the Queen there, ho! How is 't, Laertes?
  - LAERTES
  - Why as a woodcock caught in my own trap, Osric.

- *He falls.*
  - LAERTES
  - I am justly killed with mine own treachery.
  - HAMLET
  - How does the Queen?
  - KING
  - She swoons to see them bleed.
  - QUEEN
  - No, no, the drink, the drink! O, my dear Hamlet! I am poisoned.

- *She dies.*
  - HAMLET
  - O villainy! Ho! Let the door be locked.

- *Osric exits.*
  - LAERTES
  - It is here, Hamlet. Hamlet, thou art slain. No med'cine in the world can do thee good. In thee there is not half an hour's life. The treacherous instrument is in thy hand. The foul practice hath turned itself on me. Lo, here I lie, never to rise again. Thy mother's poisoned. I can no more. The King, the King's to blame.

- HAMLET
- The point envenomed too! Then, venom, to thy work.

- *He hurts the King.*
  - HAMLET
  - Drink off this potion.

- *He forces the King to drink the poison.*
  - HAMLET
  - Follow my mother.

- *King dies.*
  - LAERTES
  - He is justly served. It is a poison tempered by himself. Exchange forgiveness with me, noble Hamlet, mine and my father's death come not upon thee, nor thine on me.

- *He dies.*
  - HAMLET
  - Heaven make thee free of it. I follow thee. I am dead, Horatio. Wretched queen, adieu. Horatio, I am dead. Thou livest, report me and my cause aright to the unsatisfied.
  - HORATIO
  - Never believe it. I am more an antique Roman than a Dane.

- *He picks up the cup.*
  - HAMLET
  - Give me the cup. Let go! Be heaven, I'll ha 't. If thou didst ever hold me in thy heart draw thy breath in pain to tell my story.

- *Osric enters.*
  - OSRIC
  - Young Fortinbras, with conquest come from Poland, to th' ambassadors of England give this warlike volley.
  - HAMLET
  - O, I die, Horatio! The potent poison quite triumphs over my spirit. I cannot live to hear the news from England. But I do prophesy th' election lights on Fortinbras; he has my dying voice. So tell him. The rest is silence.

- *He dies.*
  - HORATIO
  - Now cracks a noble heart. Good night, sweet prince, and flights of angels sing thee to thy rest.

- *Fortinbras with the English Ambassadors enter.*
  - FORTINBRAS
  - Where is this sight?
  - HORATIO
  - If aught of woe or wonder, cease your search.
  - FORTINBRAS
  - This quarry cries of havoc.
  - AMBASSADOR

- The sight is dismal, and our affairs from England come too late. The ears are senseless that should give us hearing to tell him that Rosencrantz and Guildenstern are dead.
- HORATIO
- You from the Polack wars, and you from England, are here arrived. So shall you hear of carnal, bloody acts of accidental judgments, of deaths put on by cunning cause, purposes mistook fall'n on th' inventors' heads. All this can I truly deliver.
- FORTINBRAS
- Let us haste to hear it. For me, I have some rights of memory in this kingdom, which now to claim my vantage doth invite me.
- HORATIO
- Of that I shall have also cause to speak, and from his mouth whose voice will draw on more. But let this same be presently performed even while men's minds are wild, lest more mischance on plots and errors happen.
- FORTINBRAS
- Let four captains bear Hamlet like a soldier to the stage, for he was likely to have proved most royal. Take up the bodies. Such a sight as this becomes the field but here shows much amiss.

- *They exit.*

"The Masque of the Red Death," Edgar Allan Poe 1842

Edgar Allan Poe (1809–1849), an American Romantic author and critic, wrote tales of mystery and horror, and his stories are among the most popular among readers today. Although his stories are set in the nineteenth century, the events and emotions are *universal* (that is, applicable to all people in all times and relevant to our lives today).

The Masque of the Red Death

By Edgar Allan Poe

THE "Red Death" had long devastated the country. No pestilence had ever been so fatal, or so hideous. Blood was its Avatar and its seal—the redness and the horror of blood. There were sharp pains, and sudden dizziness, and then profuse bleeding at the pores, with dissolution. The scarlet stains upon the body and especially upon the face of the victim, were the pest ban which shut him out from the aid and from the sympathy of his fellow-men. And the whole seizure, progress and termination of the disease, were the incidents of half an hour.

But the Prince Prospero was happy and dauntless and sagacious. When his dominions were half depopulated, he summoned to his presence a thousand hale and light-hearted friends from among the knights and dames of his court, and with these retired to the deep seclusion of one of his castellated abbeys. This was an extensive and magnificent structure, the creation of the prince's own eccentric yet august taste. A strong and lofty wall girdled it in.

This wall had gates of iron. The courtiers, having entered, brought furnaces and massy hammers and welded the bolts. They resolved to leave means neither of ingress or egress to the sudden impulses of despair or of frenzy from within. The abbey was amply provisioned. With such precautions the courtiers might bid defiance to contagion. The external world could take care of itself. In the meantime it was folly to grieve, or to think. The prince had provided all the appliances of pleasure. There were buffoons, there were improvisatori, there were ballet-dancers, there were musicians, there was Beauty, there was wine. All these and security were within. Without was the "Red Death."

It was toward the close of the fifth or sixth month of his seclusion, and while the pestilence raged most furiously abroad, that the Prince Prospero entertained his thousand friends at a masked ball of the most unusual magnificence.

It was a voluptuous scene, that masquerade. But first let me tell of the rooms in which it was held. There were seven—an imperial suite. In many palaces, however, such suites form a long and straight vista, while the folding doors slide back nearly to the walls on either hand, so that the view of the whole extent is scarcely impeded. Here the case was very different; as might have been expected from the duke's love of the bizarre. The apartments were so irregularly disposed that the vision embraced but little more than one at a time. There was a sharp turn at every twenty or thirty yards, and at each turn a novel effect. To the right and left, in the middle of each wall, a tall and narrow Gothic window looked out upon a closed corridor which pursued the windings of the suite. These windows were of stained glass whose color varied in accordance with the prevailing hue of the decorations of the chamber into which it opened. That at the eastern extremity was hung, for example, in blue—and vividly blue were its windows. The second chamber was purple in its ornaments and tapestries, and here the panes were purple. The third was green throughout, and so were the casements. The fourth was furnished and lighted with orange—the fifth with white—the sixth with violet. The seventh apartment was closely shrouded in black velvet tapestries that hung all over the ceiling and down the walls, falling in heavy folds upon a carpet of the same material and hue. But in this chamber only, the color of the windows failed to correspond with the decorations. The panes here were scarlet—a deep blood color. Now in no one of the seven apartments was there any lamp or candelabrum, amid the profusion of golden ornaments that lay scattered to and fro or depended from the roof. There was no light of any kind emanating from lamp or candle within the suite of chambers. But in the corridors that followed the suite, there stood, opposite to each window, a heavy tripod, bearing a brazier of fire that protected its rays through the tinted glass and so glaringly illumined the room. And thus were produced a multitude of gaudy and fantastic appearances. But in the western or black chamber the effect of the fire-light that streamed upon the dark hangings through the blood-tinted panes, was ghastly in the extreme, and produced so wild a look upon the countenances of those who entered, that there were few of the company bold enough to set foot within its precincts at all.

It was in this apartment, also, that there stood against the western wall, a gigantic clock of ebony. Its pendulum swung to and fro with a dull, heavy, monotonous clang; and when the minute-hand made the circuit of the face, and the hour was to be stricken, there came from the brazen lungs of the clock a sound which was clear and loud and deep and exceedingly musical, but of so peculiar a note and emphasis that, at each lapse of an hour, the musicians of the orchestra were constrained to pause, momentarily, in their performance, to hearken to the sound; and thus the waltzers perforce ceased their evolutions; and there was a brief disconcert of the whole gay company; and, while the chimes of the clock yet rang, it was observed that the giddiest grew pale, and the more aged and sedate passed their hands over their brows as if in confused reverie or meditation. But when the echoes had fully ceased, a light laughter at once pervaded the assembly; the musicians looked at each other and smiled as if at their own nervousness and folly, and made whispering vows, each to the other, that the next chiming of the clock should produce in them no similar emotion; and then, after the lapse of sixty minutes, (which embrace three thousand and six hundred seconds of the Time that flies,) there came yet another chiming of the clock, and then were the same disconcert and tremulousness and meditation as before.

But, in spite of these things, it was a gay and magnificent revel. The tastes of the duke were peculiar. He had a fine eye for colors and effects. He disregarded the decora of mere fashion. His plans were bold and fiery, and his conceptions glowed with barbaric lustre. There are some who would have thought him mad. His followers felt that he was not. It was necessary to hear and see and touch him to be sure that he was not.

He had directed, in great part, the moveable embellishments of the seven chambers, upon occasion of this great fete; and it was his own guiding taste which had given character to the masqueraders. Be sure they were grotesque. There were much glare and glitter and piquancy and phantasm—much of what has been since seen in "Hernani." There were arabesque figures with unsuited limbs and appointments. There were delirious fancies such as the madman fashions. There was much of the beautiful, much of the wanton, much of the bizarre, something of the terrible, and not a little of that which might have excited disgust. To and fro in the seven chambers there stalked, in fact, a multitude of dreams. And these—the dreams—writhed in and about, taking hue from the rooms, and causing the wild music of the orchestra to seem as the echo of their steps. And, anon, there strikes the ebony clock which stands in the hall of the velvet. And then, for a moment, all is still, and all is silent save the voice of the clock. The dreams are stiff-frozen as they stand. But the echoes of the chime die away—they have endured but an instant—and a light, half-subdued laughter floats after them as they depart. And now again the music swells, and the dreams live, and writhe to and fro more merrily than ever, taking hue from the many-tinted windows through which stream the rays from the tripods. But to the chamber which lies most westwardly of the seven, there are now none of the maskers who venture; for the night is waning away; and there flows a ruddier light through the blood-colored panes; and the blackness of the sable drapery appals; and to him whose foot falls upon the sable carpet, there comes from the near clock of ebony a muffled peal more solemnly emphatic than any which reaches their ears who indulge in the more remote gaieties of the other apartments.

But these other apartments were densely crowded, and in them beat feverishly the heart of life. And the revel went whirlingly on, until at length there commenced the sounding of midnight upon the clock. And then the music ceased, as I have told; and the evolutions of the waltzers were quieted; and there was an uneasy cessation of all things as before. But now there were twelve strokes to be sounded by the bell of the clock; and thus it happened, perhaps, that more of thought crept, with more of time, into the meditations of the thoughtful among those who revelled. And thus, too, it happened, perhaps, that before the last echoes of the last chime had utterly sunk into silence, there were many individuals in the crowd who had found leisure to become aware of the presence of a masked figure which had arrested the attention of no single individual before. And the rumor of this new presence having spread itself whisperingly around, there arose at length from the whole company a buzz, or murmur, expressive of disapprobation and surprise—then, finally, of terror, of horror, and of disgust.

In an assembly of phantasms such as I have painted, it may well be supposed that no ordinary appearance could have excited such sensation. In truth the masquerade license of the night was nearly unlimited; but the figure in question had out-Heroded Herod, and gone beyond the bounds of even the prince's indefinite decorum. There are chords in the hearts of the most reckless which cannot be touched without emotion. Even with the utterly lost, to whom life and death are equally jests, there are matters of which no jest can be made. The whole company, indeed, seemed now deeply to feel that in the costume and bearing of the stranger neither wit nor propriety existed. The figure was tall and gaunt, and shrouded from head to foot in the habiliments of the grave. The mask which concealed the visage was made so nearly to resemble the countenance of a stiffened corpse that the closest scrutiny must have had difficulty in detecting the cheat. And yet all this might have been endured, if not approved, by the mad revellers around. But the mummer had gone so far as to assume the type of the Red Death. His vesture was dabbled in blood—and his broad brow, with all the features of the face, was besprinkled with the scarlet horror.

When the eyes of Prince Prospero fell upon this spectral image (which with a slow and solemn movement, as if more fully to sustain its role, stalked to and fro among the waltzers) he was seen to be convulsed, in the first moment with a strong shudder either of terror or distaste; but, in the next, his brow reddened with rage.

"Who dares?" he demanded hoarsely of the courtiers who stood near him—"who dares insult us with this blasphemous mockery? Seize him and unmask him—that we may know whom we have to hang at sunrise, from the battlements!"

It was in the eastern or blue chamber in which stood the Prince Prospero as he uttered these words. They rang throughout the seven rooms loudly and clearly—for the prince was a bold and robust man, and the music had become hushed at the waving of his hand.

It was in the blue room where stood the prince, with a group of pale courtiers by his side. At first, as he spoke, there was a slight rushing movement of this group in the direction of the intruder, who at the moment was also near at hand, and now, with deliberate and stately step, made closer approach to the speaker. But from a certain nameless awe with which the mad assumptions of the mummer had inspired the whole party, there were found none who put forth hand to seize him; so that, unimpeded, he passed within a yard of the prince's person; and, while the vast assembly, as if with one impulse, shrank from the centres of the rooms to the walls, he made his way uninterrupt-edly, but with the same solemn and measured step which had distinguished him from the first, through the blue chamber to the purple—through the purple to the green—through the green to the orange—through this again to the white—and even thence to the violet, ere a decided movement had been made to arrest him. It was then, however, that the Prince Prospero, madden-ing with rage and the shame of his own momentary cowardice, rushed hur-riedly through the six chambers, while none followed him on account of a deadly terror that had seized upon all. He bore aloft a drawn dagger, and had approached, in rapid impetuosity, to within three or four feet of the retreating figure, when the latter, having attained the extremity of the velvet apartment, turned suddenly and confronted his pursuer. There was a sharp cry—and the dagger dropped gleaming upon the sable carpet, upon which, instantly after-wards, fell prostrate in death the Prince Prospero. Then, summoning the wild courage of despair, a throng of the revellers at once threw themselves into the black apartment, and, seizing the mummer, whose tall figure stood erect and motionless within the shadow of the ebony clock, gasped in unutterable hor-ror at finding the grave-cerements and corpse-like mask which they handled with so violent a rudeness, untenanted by any tangible form.

And now was acknowledged the presence of the Red Death. He had come like a thief in the night. And one by one dropped the revellers in the blood-bedewed halls of their revel, and died each in the despairing posture of his fall. And the life of the ebony clock went out with that of the last of the gay. And the flames of the tripods expired. And Darkness and Decay and the Red Death held illimitable dominion over all.

"The Mark on the Wall," Virginia Woolf 1921

Virginia Woolf (1882–1941) was one of the leading **modernists** (those who thought the traditional forms of art, literature, religion, social organization, and activities of daily life were inappropriate for the new industrialized world) as well as one of the early feminist writers, and her novels, essays, and short stories gained critical and popular success. She was an important figure in the Bloomsbury Group, an intellec-tual group of writers and artists in England. One of her most well-known works is *A Room of One's Own* (1929) in which she asserts, "A woman must have money and a room of her own if she is to write fiction." "The Mark on the Wall" is an example of **stream of consciousness**, a type of first person narration, which attempts to trace a character's thinking, often associative and realistic.

The Mark on the Wall
By Virginia Woolf

PERHAPS it was the middle of January in the present that I first looked up and saw the mark on the wall. In order to fix a date it is necessary to remem-ber what one saw. So now I think of the fire; the steady film of yellow light upon the page of my book; the three chrysanthemums in the round glass bowl on the mantelpiece. Yes, it must have been the winter time, and we had just finished our tea, for I remember that I was smoking a cigarette when

I looked up and saw the mark on the wall for the first time. I looked up through the smoke of my cigarette and my eye lodged for a moment upon the burning coals, and that old fancy of the crimson flag flapping from the castle tower came into my mind, and I thought of the cavalcade of red knights riding up the side of the black rock. Rather to my relief the sight of the mark interrupted the fancy, for it is an old fancy, an automatic fancy, made as a child perhaps. The mark was a small round mark, black upon the white wall, about six or seven inches above the mantelpiece. *1*

How readily our thoughts swarm upon a new object, lifting it a little way, as ants carry a blade of straw so feverishly, and then leave it.... If that mark was made by a nail, it can't have been for a picture, it must have been for a miniature—the miniature of a lady with white powdered curls, powder-dusted cheeks, and lips like red carnations. A fraud of course, for the people who had this house before us would have chosen pictures in that way—an old picture for an old room. That is the sort of people they were—very interesting people, and I think of them so often, in such queer places, because one will never see them again, never know what happened next. They wanted to leave this house because they wanted to change their style of furniture, so he said, and he was in process of saying that in his opinion art should have ideas behind it when we were torn asunder, as one is torn from the old lady about to pour out tea and the young man about to hit the tennis ball in the back garden of the suburban villa as one rushes past in the train. *2*

But as for that mark, I'm not sure about it; I don't believe it was made by a nail after all; it's too big, too round, for that. I might get up, but if I got up and looked at it, ten to one I shouldn't be able to say for certain; because once a thing's done, no one ever knows how it happened. Oh! dear me, the mystery of life; The inaccuracy of thought! The ignorance of humanity! To show how very little control of our possessions we have—what an accidental affair this living is after all our civilization—let me just count over a few of the things lost in one lifetime, beginning, for that seems always the most mysterious of losses—what cat would gnaw, what rat would nibble—three pale blue canisters of book-binding tools? Then there were the bird cages, the iron hoops, the steel skates, the Queen Anne coal-scuttle, the bagatelle board, the hand organ—all gone, and jewels, too. Opals and emeralds, they lie about the roots of turnips. What a scraping paring affair it is to be sure! The wonder is that I've any clothes on my back, that I sit surrounded by solid furniture at this moment. Why, if one wants to compare life to anything, one must liken it to being blown through the Tube at fifty miles an hour—landing at the other end without a single hairpin in one's hair! Shot out at the feet of God entirely naked! Tumbling head over heels in the asphodel meadows like brown paper parcels pitched down a shoot in the post office! With one's hair flying back like the tail of a race-horse. Yes, that seems to express the rapidity of life, the perpetual waste and repair; all so casual, all so haphazard.... *3*

But after life. The slow pulling down of thick green stalks so that the cup of the flower, as it turns over, deluges one with purple and red light. Why, after all, should one not be born there as one is born here, helpless, speechless, unable to focus one's eyesight, groping at the roots of the grass, at the toes of the Giants? As for saying which are trees, and which are men and women, or whether there are such things, that one won't be in a condition to do for fifty years or so. There will be nothing but spaces of light and dark, intersected by thick stalks, and rather higher up perhaps, rose-shaped blots of an indistinct colour—dim pinks and blues—which will, as time goes on, become more definite, become—I don't know what.... *4*

And yet that mark on the wall is not a hole at all. It may even be caused by some round black substance, such as a small rose leaf, left over from the summer, and I, not being a very vigilant housekeeper—look at the dust on the mantelpiece, for example, the dust which, so they say, buried Troy three times over, only fragments of pots utterly refusing annihilation, as one can believe. *5*

The tree outside the window taps very gently on the pane.... I want to think quietly, calmly, spaciously, never to be interrupted, never to have to rise from my chair, to slip easily from one thing to another, without any sense of hostility, or obstacle. I want to sink deeper and deeper, away from the surface, with its hard separate facts. To steady myself, let me catch hold of the first idea that passes.... Shakespeare.... Well, he will do as well as another. A man who sat himself solidly in an arm-chair, and looked into the fire, so— A shower of ideas fell perpetually from some very high Heaven down through his mind. He leant his forehead on his hand, and people, looking in through the open door,—for this scene is supposed to take place on a summer's evening—But how dull this is, this historical fiction! It doesn't interest me at all. I wish I could hit upon a pleasant track of thought, a track indirectly reflecting credit upon myself, for those are the pleasantest thoughts, and very frequent even in the minds of modest mouse-coloured people, who believe genuinely that they dislike to hear their own praises. They are not thoughts directly praising oneself; that is the beauty of them; they are thoughts like this: *6*

"And then I came into the room. They were discussing botany. I said how I'd seen a flower growing on a dust heap on the site of an old house in Kingsway. The seed, I said, must have been sown in the reign of Charles the First. What flowers grew in the reign of Charles the First?" I asked—(but, I don't remember the answer). Tall flowers with purple tassels to them perhaps. And so it goes on. All the time I'm dressing up the figure of myself in my own mind, lovingly, stealthily, not openly adoring it, for if I did that, I should catch myself out, and stretch my hand at once for a book in self-protection. Indeed, it is curious how instinctively one protects the image of oneself from idolatry or any other handling that could make it ridiculous, or too unlike the original to be believed in any longer. Or is it not so very curious after all? It is a matter of great importance. Suppose the looking glass smashes, the image disappears, and the romantic figure with the green of forest depths all about it is there no longer, but only that shell of a person which is seen by other people— what an airless, shallow, bald, prominent world it becomes! A world not to be lived in. As we face each other in omnibuses and underground railways we are looking into the mirror that accounts for the vagueness, the gleam of glassiness, in our eyes. And the novelists in future will realize more and more the importance of these reflections, for of course there is not one reflection but an almost infinite number; those are the depths they will explore, those the phantoms they will pursue, leaving the description of reality more and more out of their stories, taking a knowledge of it for granted, as the Greeks did and Shakespeare perhaps—but these generalizations are very worthless. The military sound of the word is enough. It recalls leading articles, cabinet ministers—a whole class of things indeed which as a child one thought the thing itself, the standard thing, the real thing, from which one could not depart save at the risk of nameless damnation. Generalizations bring back somehow Sunday in London, Sunday afternoon walks, Sunday luncheons, and also ways of speaking of the dead, clothes, and habits—like the habit of sitting all together in one room until a certain hour, although nobody liked it. There was a rule for everything. The rule for tablecloths at that particular period was that they should be made of tapestry with little yellow compartments marked upon them, such as you may see in photographs of the carpets in the corridors of the royal palaces. Tablecloths of a different kind were not real tablecloths. How shocking, and yet how wonderful it was to discover that these real things, Sunday luncheons, Sunday walks, country houses, and tablecloths were not entirely real, were indeed half phantoms, and the damnation which visited the disbeliever in them was only a sense of illegitimate freedom. What now takes the place of those things I wonder, those real standard things? Men perhaps, should you be a woman; the masculine point of view which governs our lives, which sets the standard, which establishes Whitaker's Table of Precedency, which has become, I suppose, since the war half a phantom to many men and women, which soon—one may hope, will be laughed into the dustbin where the phantoms go, the mahogany sideboards and the Landseer prints, Gods and Devils, Hell and so forth, leaving us all with an intoxicating sense of illegitimate freedom—if freedom exists.... *7*

In certain lights that mark on the wall seems actually to project from the wall. Nor is it entirely circular. I cannot be sure, but it seems to cast a perceptible shadow, suggesting that if I ran my finger down that strip of the wall it would, at a certain point, mount and descend a small tumulus, a smooth tumulus like those barrows on the South Downs which are, they say, either tombs or camps. Of the two I should prefer them to be tombs, desiring melancholy like most English people, and finding it natural at the end of a walk to think of the bones stretched beneath the turf.... There must be some book about it. Some antiquary must have dug up those bones and given them a name.... What sort of a man is an antiquary, I wonder? Retired Colonels for the most part, I daresay, leading parties of aged labourers to the top here, examining clods of earth and stone, and getting into correspondence with the neighbouring clergy, which, being opened at breakfast time, gives them a feeling of importance, and the comparison of arrow-heads necessitates cross-country journeys to the county towns, an agreeable necessity both to them and to their elderly wives, who wish to make plum jam or to clean out the study, and have every reason for keeping that great question of the camp or the tomb in perpetual suspension, while the Colonel himself feels agreeably philosophic in accumulating evidence on both sides of the question. It is true that he does finally incline to believe in the camp; and, being opposed, indites a pamphlet which he is about to read at the quarterly meeting of the local society when a stroke lays him low, and his last conscious thoughts are not of wife or child, but of the camp and that arrowhead there, which is now in the case at the local museum, together with the foot of a Chinese murderess, a handful of Elizabethan nails, a great many Tudor clay pipes, a piece of Roman pottery, and the wine-glass that Nelson drank out of—proving I really don't know what. *8*

No, no, nothing is proved, nothing is known. And if I were to get up at this very moment and ascertain that the mark on the wall is really—what shall we say?—the head of a gigantic old nail, driven in two hundred years ago, which has now, owing to the patient attrition of many generations of house-maids, revealed its head above the coat of paint, and is taking its first view of modern life in the sight of a white-walled fire-lit room, what should I gain?— Knowledge? Matter for further speculation? I can think sitting still as well as standing up. And what is knowledge? What are our learned men save the descendants of witches and hermits who crouched in caves and in woods brewing herbs, interrogating shrew-mice and writing down the language of the stars? And the less we honour them as our superstitions dwindle and our respect for beauty and health of mind increases.... Yes, one could imagine a very pleasant world. A quiet, spacious world, with the flowers so red and blue in the open fields. A world without professors or specialists or house-keepers with the profiles of policemen, a world which one could slice with one's thought as a fish slices the water with his fin, grazing the stems of the water-lilies, hanging suspended over nests of white sea eggs.... How peaceful it is drown here, rooted in the centre of the world and gazing up through the grey waters, with their sudden gleams of light, and their reflections—if it were not for Whitaker's Almanack—if it were not for the Table of Precedency! *9*

I must jump up and see for myself what that mark on the wall really is—a nail, a rose-leaf, a crack in the wood? *10*

Here is nature once more at her old game of self-preservation. This train of thought, she perceives, is threatening mere waste of energy, even some collision with reality, for who will ever be able to lift a finger against Whitaker's Table of Precedency? The Archbishop of Canterbury is followed by the Lord High Chancellor; the Lord High Chancellor is followed by the Archbishop of York. Everybody follows somebody, such is the philosophy of Whitaker; and the great thing is to know who follows whom. Whitaker knows, and let that, so Nature counsels, comfort you, instead of enraging you; and if you can't be comforted, if you must shatter this hour of peace, think of the mark on the wall. *11*

I understand Nature's game—her prompting to take action as a way of ending any thought that threatens to excite or to pain. Hence, I suppose, comes our slight contempt for men of action—men, we assume, who don't think. Still, there's no harm in putting a full stop to one's disagreeable thoughts by looking at a mark on the wall. *12*

Indeed, now that I have fixed my eyes upon it, I feel that I have grasped a plank in the sea; I feel a satisfying sense of reality which at once turns the two Archbishops and the Lord High Chancellor to the shadows of shades. Here is something definite, something real. Thus, waking from a midnight dream of horror, one hastily turns on the light and lies quiescent, worshipping the chest of drawers, worshipping solidity, worshipping reality, worshipping the impersonal world which is a proof of some existence other than ours. That is what one wants to be sure of.... Wood is a pleasant thing to think about. It comes from a tree; and trees grow, and we don't know how they grow. For years and years they grow, without paying any attention to us, in meadows, in forests, and by the side of rivers—all things one likes to think about. The cows swish their tails beneath them on hot afternoons; they paint rivers so green that when a moorhen dives one expects to see its feathers all green when it comes up again. I like to think of the fish balanced against the stream like flags blown out; and of water-beetles slowly raiding domes of mud upon the bed of the river. I like to think of the tree itself:—first the close dry sensation of being wood; then the grinding of the storm; then the slow, delicious ooze of sap. I like to think of it, too, on winter's nights standing in the empty field with all leaves close-furled, nothing tender exposed to the iron bullets of the moon, a naked mast upon an earth that goes tumbling, tumbling, all night long. The song of birds must sound very loud and strange in June; and how cold the feet of insects must feel upon it, as they make laborious progresses up the creases of the bark, or sun themselves upon the thin green awning of the leaves, and look straight in front of them with diamond-cut red eyes.... One by one the fibres snap beneath the immense cold pressure of the earth, then the last storm comes and, falling, the highest branches drive deep into the ground again. Even so, life isn't done with; there are a million patient, watchful lives still for a tree, all over the world, in bedrooms, in ships, on the pavement, lining rooms, where men and women sit after tea, smoking cigarettes. It is full of peaceful thoughts, happy thoughts, this tree. I should like to take each one separately—but something is getting in the way.... Where was I? What has it all been about? A tree? A river? The Downs? Whitaker's Almanack? The fields of asphodel? I can't remember a thing. Everything's moving, falling, slipping, vanishing.... There is a vast upheaval of matter. Someone is standing over me and saying— *13*

"I'm going out to buy a newspaper." *14*

"Yes?" *15*

"Though it's no good buying newspapers.... Nothing ever happens. Curse this war; God damn this war!... All the same, I don't see why we should have a snail on our wall." *16*

Ah, the mark on the wall! It was a snail.

You may go to any of the following web sites in order to further introduce yourself to English literature:

Robert Frost at this link http://www.poetryfoundation.org/poem/173536

Edgar Allan Poe at this link http://poestories.com/poetry.php

Virginia Woolf at this link http://www.litera.co.uk/virginia_woolf_love_poem/

Jane Austen at this link excerpt from Pride and Prejudice http://www.pemberley .com/etext/PandP/chapter8.htm

John Milton at this link http://www.poemhunter.com/poem/paradise-lost-book-01/

African American Literature

"We wear the Mask," Paul Laurence Dunbar 1895

Paul Laurence Dunbar (1872–1906) was one of the first African-American poets to gain national and international receognition. His parents were freed slaves from Kentucky and in his writings Dunbar often drew upon their stories of plantation life. In this poem, he describes the psychological situation of African Americans after the Civil War, however, the *symbolic* wearing of masks is *universal*.

We Wear the Mask

By Paul Laurence Dunbar

We wear the mask that grains and lies,

It hides our cheeks and shades of our eyes,--

This debt we pay to human guile;

With torn and bleeding hearts we smile,

And mouth with myriad subtleties.   5

Why should the world be over-wise,

In counting all our tears and sighs?

Nay, let them only see us, while

    We wear the mask.

We smile, but, O great Christ, our cries   10

To thee from tortured souls arise.

We sing, but oh the clay is vile

Beneath our feet, and long the mile;

But let the world dream otherwise,

    We wear the mask!   15

"Those winter Sundays," Robert Hayden 1962

Robert Hayden (1913-1980) is an American poet, essayist, and educator, From 1976 to 1978, he served as US Poet Laureate, the first African American to hold this office. In 2012, the US Postal Service issued a stamp to recognize the accomplishments, especially as a poet. In this poem, the speaker is an adult remembering his childhood.

Videos of this poem being read are available on YouTube, and the first web site in the list below contains the poem.

You may go to any of the following web sites in order to further introduce yourself to African American literature:

Robert Hayden at this link http:www.poets.org/poetsorg/poem/those-winter-sundays

Alice Walker excerpt from The Color Purple at this link http://www.luminarium.com/contemporary/purplexcerpt.htm

William Blake at this link http://www.brainyquote.com/quotes/authors/w/william_blake.html

Tupac Shakur at this link http://allpoetry.com/poem/8574647-I-Cry-by-Tupac-Shakur

Langston Hughes at this link http://www.tnellen.com/cybereng/matoson.html

Maya Angelou at this link http://www.poetryfoundation.org/poem/178948

Phillis Wheatley at this link http://www.poemhunter.com/phillis-wheatley/

Hampton Helped Me!

Michael Stewart Wortham

Photo courtesy of Hampton University

Michael Stewart Wortham, affectionately known as "Rev. Mike," is a native of Fairfield, Alabama, and currently resides in Atlanta, Georgia.

Rev. Mike graduated cum laude in 2007 from Hampton University with a BS degree in Finance and in 2010 from the Candler School of Theology at Emory University with a Master of Divinity degree with a concentration in Race and Religion and certificates from the Black Church Studies and Baptist Studies programs.

Rev. Mike received his license to preach in August 2007 from the Sixth Avenue Baptist Church in Birmingham, Alabama. He was ordained in October 2011 at the Historic Ebenezer Baptist Church in Atlanta, Georgia, and currently serves there as the Assistant Pastor for Youth, College, and Young Adult Ministries.

Hampton Helped Me!

Brian Davis

Photo courtesy of Hampton University

As a Digital Advertising Account Executive at Microsoft, **Brian Davis** develops, executes, and manages the online advertising campaigns of top brands such as Wrigley, Burger King, DeVry, and US Cellular. In a media industry that commingles creativity and data, Brian leverages the principles learned at Scripps to influence thoughts and behaviorsofthe online audience through advertising.

Brian is a 2007 graduate of the Scripps Howard School of Iournalism and Communications at Hampton University, where he was a member of the Student Leadership Program, a National Coca-Cola Scholar, and a recipient of the President's Cup. He was also the Basileus of the Gamma Epsilon Chapter of Omega Psi Phi at Hampton University and the 2007 International Scholar ofthe Year for the fraternity.

CHAPTER 10

Hampton's Collections and Connections with African American Art

"Just don't give up what you're trying to do. Where there is love and inspiration, I don't think you can go wrong."

—Ella Fitzgerald

Upon completion of this chapter, you will be able to:

- **Review and discuss** 200 years of African American art and history on the campus
- **Discuss** the growth and development of the Hampton University Museum
- **Explain** Hampton's art collections and connections to world culture
- **Identify and summarize** the contribution of Hampton's photographers who produce an extraordinary visual record of the life of the University

Hampton's Collections and Connections with African American Art

Welcome from the Hampton University Museum

Welcome to Hampton University and an experience with the culture of not only this historic campus but the historic museum that now belongs to you. As old as the school itself, the museum was founded in 1868 when the founder, Samuel Chapman Armstrong, son of missionaries and educators, asked his mother who lived in Hawaii, "to send natural articles, such as coral and lava, from the Pacific." "I would prefer that you send what you have to send not in money, but in rare specimens of all kinds." The collections for the museum or Curiosity Room as they were called quickly grew.

The material that is provided for you to learn about the museum is the most comprehensive overview of the museum's collection to date. *The International Review of African American Art* is the only journal in the United States that writes about African American art and artists. Founded by Hampton alumnus, Dr. Samella Sanders Lewis, the journal has been housed at Hampton University since the early 1990s. This special issue, published in 2005 was written by museum staff that may not work at the university any longer . So, if you have questions you will have to visit the museum and ask for the current staff. Any of us will be happy to assist you. You will find this overview beneficial as you visit the museum not only for a class but for your edification and enjoyment. Again, this museum belongs to you.

You will notice that there are old photographs and documents included in some of the articles you are about to read. The originals of these materials may be found in the Hampton University Archives which was established in 1972. It is renowned for documentation of the institution's beginnings in the Reconstruction era, the history of the university, and the role of African Americans and Native peoples in the history of American education.

We also have a membership program for students, *The Biggers' Circle*. The Hampton University Museum's *Biggers' Circle* is dedicated to promoting and enhancing the student's experience with the museum through student initiated programming, volunteerism, and community outreach. **WE ARE LOOKING FOR MEMBERS!!** The organization is named in honor of Dr. John Thomas Biggers, painter, sculptor, printmaker, muralist, educator and author. John Biggers came to Hampton Institute in 1941 where he was inspired to pursue a career in art. Dr. John Biggers is among the best known and most renowned American artists. Dr. Biggers was Hampton University's Artist-in-Residence for the 1990-91 academic year when he painted *Tree House* and *House of the Turtle*, the two large and impressive murals in the William R. and Norma B. Harvey Library. Dr. Biggers died January 2001. Also, do not forget to visit Clark Hall where you will see our first mural, *The Contribution of the Negro to Democracy in America*, painted in 1943 by Charles White, one of John Biggers mentors.

Photo courtesy of Hampton University

By the way, I am Vanessa Thaxton-Ward, Ph. D., Curator of Collections at the Hampton University Museum. I returned to my Home-By-the Sea in 1991 and have worked in several capacities at the museum from Director of Membership to Curator of History. I have a Bachelor of Arts in English from Virginia Wesleyan, a Master of Arts in Museum Studies from Hampton University; a Doctor of Philosophy in American Studies from the College of William and Mary. Please stop by the museum to visit with me and the outstanding staff of the Hampton University Museum and Archives.

The following pages are from *The International Review of African American Art: Hampton's Collections and Connections*, Volume 20 Number 1. Copyright © Hampton University. Reprinted by permission.

A CAMPUS FULL OF ART AND HISTORY

For years art lovers and scholars have inquired about a catalogue of our extensive holdings — collections that, in a number of ways, are second to none. While we have published occasional monographs and small catalogues on aspects of the collections, we have not yet published a comprehensive catalogue.

This special issue of the *IRAAA*, then, is the seed of such a catalogue. It is published with the intent to bring increased visibility to the collections and to pave the way for a book based on them. Because the collections are an excellent resource for the study of African American topics in many disciplines — history, fine art, music, material culture etc. — the book-format catalogue project will support scholars coming to campus to research topics in specific areas and the publication of essays based on this research with numerous illustrations including full-page, color plates of artworks.

Hampton University — a campus full of art and history — offers a unique cultural experience for visitors. The Museum is open to the public, free of charge, Monday through Friday, 8 am to 5 pm; Saturdays, noon to 4 pm. Significant works of art are also located around the campus along with a number of historic landmarks.

Next door to the museum, for example, is the architectural landmark, Virginia Cleveland Hall, "sung up" by Hampton Institute students at fund-raising concerts around the country and completed in 1874. Designed by Richard M. Hunt, the first American to study at the Ecole des Beaux Arts and a leading New York architect, the large Victorian building replete with turrets and lofty towers was intended to serve as a grand symbol, not just good student housing. Hampton Institute founder Samuel Armstrong dedicated the building to the psychological elevation of this first generation of free black young people; it symbolized his belief in their abilities.

Across from Virginia Cleveland is Mansion House, an 1828, river-front, plantation manor that today serves as the home of the university president. Also nearby are: the public reception area of the president's office where works by Henry O. Tanner, Grafton Tyler Brown (another 19th-century African American artist),

Lois Mailou Jones and Claude Clark are hung; Memorial Chapel (1886); the second Academy Hall completed in 1881, after the first building burnt down; and Clarke Hall which houses the Charles White mural, *The Contribution of the Negro to Democracy in America* (1943).

Two notable features of the Hampton University Harvey Library are the 20-foot high John Biggers murals in the atrium — a dazzling meditation on metaphysics, Hampton history and environmental ecology — and the George F. Peabody Collection of rare books, monographs and vertical file materials on the fourth floor.

Containing more than 30,000 items by and about African Americans, the George Foster Peabody Collection is one of the oldest and one of the best repositories of its kind. In 1905 Peabody, a Hampton Institute trustee, obtained 1,400 books and pamphlets relating to African American history and culture from bibliophile Tucker A. Malone and lent them to Hampton's library. In 1908 this loan was converted to a gift. Six years later, the library of Phil Broome Brooks, an African American physician in Washington D.C., was purchased for the collection; over 200 of the titles in Broome's library were by black authors. In subsequent years, other collections, such as that of Wendell P. Dabney, a black publisher, were added.

Scholars from around the country and abroad travel to do research in the Hampton University Archives — a repository of more than 50,000 photographs of people and events associated with the history of the university; volumes of the *Southern Workman*, a journal on African American achievement published between 1872 and 1939; files on artists Henry O. Tanner, Charles White, and John T. Biggers; the papers of pioneering African American explorer William Sheppard, composer R. Nathaniel Dett, Booker T. Washington and other figures prominent in the history of Hampton and the larger society.

Currently, the Hampton University Museum is organizing a major, new collection — the Samella Lewis Archive of African American Art. Over five decades, artist and art historian Samella Lewis collected a voluminous amount of materials on African American art — catalogues, clippings, pamphlets, photos, slides, correspondence, manuscripts, transcripts of personal interviews with master artists such as Romare Bearden, audio tapes and assorted ephemera. She also saved now-historically significant items stemming from her own broad experience in art, including her personal correspondence with Elizabeth Catlett. She has given Hampton these materials and this unparalleled collection on African American art will be made available to the public.

The beautiful, waterfront campus of Hampton University is located at the juncture of the Hampton River and the Chesapeake Bay on the Virginia peninsula, an area filled with many more historic sites.

An early photo of the women's dormitory, Virginia Hall (1874), a symbol of lofty aspiration for freedom's first generation. Cleveland Hall, built with funds contributed by former pupils, was connected to the back of Virginia Hall in 1901, and the building became known as Virginia-Cleveland Hall.

HAMPTON'S COLLECTIONS AND CONNECTIONS

A UNITY OF ART AND LIFE

The history of Hampton University Museum's art collections is extensively intertwined with the history of African American achievement in art. Today the HU Museum's distinctions include being the oldest African American museum and holding one of the world's largest collections of fine art by African Americans. With the acquisition of two paintings by Henry O. Tanner in 1894, Hampton Institute (as it was called then) was the first institution to establish a collection of African American art.

The people behind the story of the art collections at Hampton University ranged from northern philanthropists like Hampton trustee Robert C. Ogden, a partner in the Wannamaker department store, and real estate magnate William E. Harmon, to students such as John Biggers and Samella Sanders (Lewis) both of whom rose from humble origins in the South. What they had in common was the belief that visual art does matter — that making and viewing art can make a vital difference in people's lives.

In 1866, Ogden's parlor in New York had been the site of a meeting on the founding of the school that became Hampton Normal and Agricultural Institute in 1868. During his 45-year service as a trustee and board director, Ogden raised over $2,000,000 for the school. The trustee's gifts to

the school also included the nucleus of the school's African American art collection — several paintings by Henry O. Tanner, one of the highly-acclaimed artists of his time in both the United States and France.

Henry O. Tanner had taken an active interest in the black subject during the years 1889–1890 and 1893–94, and during the second period, produced the large painting, *The Banjo Lesson* (1893), which became his best-known work. Leaving behind a land of limited opportunities for African American artists, Tanner sailed to Europe in 1891, and returned periodically to the States.

Although they were both from Philadelphia, Ogden and Tanner met in Paris, France. The prosperous businessman soon became a benefactor and friend to the artist and in May 1894, Tanner accompanied Ogden to the commencement ceremony at Hampton Institute. Tanner's *The Bagpipe Lesson* (1893) was displayed at the commencement and, on this occasion, Ogden donated Tanner's *The Lion's Head* (1892) to the Institute. The fall of the same year Ogden made a gift of Tanner's *The Banjo Lesson* to Hampton Institute.

According to Ogden's biographer Philip W. Wilson, "what Ogden hoped for him [Tanner] was that his brush would illuminate the life of his own race, so revealing its

Henry Ossawa Tanner (1859-1937)
The Bagpipe Lesson
1893
oil on canvas
45" x 68 3/4"
COLLECTION HAMPTON UNIVERSITY MUSEUM

Opposite page:
Rotunda, Hampton University Museum,
with view of 1997 John Biggers exhibit
Photos: Alexander Kravets

Henry Ossawa Tanner

inner dignity and heroism." Hampton's monthly publication *Southern Workman* reported in November 1894 that there "will be great pleasure and profit to our students in having before them this fine achievement of a Negro artist."

In 1895, at Ogden's urging, Tanner entered three paintings, including *The Bagpipe Lesson*, into the Cotton States and International Exposition in Atlanta — the fair where Booker T. Washington made his famous, separate but equal speech. Although exhibited in the fair's special Negro Building, *The Bagpipe Lesson* won a medal. Ogden set the value of *The Bagpipe Lesson* at "something over $1,000" in a letter to Booker T. Washington. In 1905, Ogden purchased *The Bagpipe Lesson* and donated it to Hampton Institute.

Hampton continued to acquire works by Henry O. Tanner and today has 16 works by the artist — 14 paintings and two etchings. Other African American artists active in the 19th century and represented in Hampton's collection are Robert Scott Duncanson (1821–1872), Edward Mitchell Bannister (1828–1901) and Charles Ethan Porter (1847?–1923). The oldest work in the collection is an 1805 painting by Joshua Johnson (1765–1830), the nation's first-known, professional artist of African ancestry.

Following in Tanner's footsteps was William Edouard Scott, a graduate of the Art Institute of Chicago, who studied in Paris between 1910 and 1913; his teachers included Tanner who became his main mentor. In 1912, he became the second African American artist to exhibit in the Paris Salon, Tanner, having been the first. Scott's *Weighing Dye Logs*, in Hampton's collection, was inspired by the artist's year-long stay in Haiti in 1931.

Another figure in the intertwined story of Hampton's collections and connections is William E. Harmon, a successful New York City realtor who used his wealth to form a foundation in 1924. In the mid-1920s, Harmon visited the studio of an accomplished African American artist and asked what the artist charged for a portrait. Stating a low

price, the artist explained, "because I am a Negro I cannot command a price commensurate with the amount of training I have had, the time consumed or perhaps the actual ability which I have shown in my production." After the visit with the artist, in 1926, William Harmon started a program to give awards to black people in eight fields including fine art. The art program soon expanded to include exhibitions and other activities and became the Harmon Foundation's primary component.

During the 41 years of its operation, the Harmon Foundation's art program was linked in various ways with Hampton Institute via persons such as Hampton Institute trustee George Foster Peabody. In 1931, James Lesesne Wells, a Howard University art professor, won the Harmon gold award for his painting, *Flight into Egypt*. Peabody purchased the painting for $400 and donated it to Hampton Institute. After the award, Wells was invited to have one-man shows at the Delphic Studios and Brooklyn Museum in New York. (In 1931, the trustee's generosity also led to the formation at Hampton Institute of one of the finest collections of books and manuscripts on Negro subjects in the country — the George Foster Peabody Collection.)

In 1938, Robert Russa Moton, an 1890 Hampton graduate and president emeritus of Tuskegee Institute, offered a eulogy at George Foster Peabody's funeral that was transcribed and printed in Hampton's *Southern Workman's* journal. Peabody was "interested in Negro art and did much to help individuals who showed talent in painting, music, drawing, etc.," Moton recalled. Both Peabody and James Wells were from Georgia which may have been a factor in the philanthropist's interest in this particular artist.

Joshua Johnson (ca. 1765– ca. 1830)
A Portrait of an Unidentified Young Lady
1805
oil on canvas
22" x 18"
HAMPTON UNIVERSITY MUSEUM; MUSEUM ACQUISITION FUND

In 1933, in memory of her father, Robert C. Ogden, Mrs. Alexander Purves of Hampton, VA, donated $150 for the top prize in the Harmon art competition. The Robert C. Ogden Prize for "outstanding artistry in combination of material" was awarded to Sargent Johnson for *Pearl*, a porcelain figure with bronze, blue-green glaze of a seated baby (his daughter).

In sharp contrast to the more than $1,000 value set for the single Tanner painting in the 1890s is the $100 loan that Jacob Lawrence got four decades later after offering a complete series of his paintings as collateral to the lender, the Harmon Foundation. During this period, 1937–1941, Jacob Lawrence was finding his niche as an artist as he depicted a sweeping history of black people through the lives of Toussaint L'Ouverture, Harriet Tubman and Frederick Douglass, John Brown and the *Migration of the Negro* series.

In 1939, Jacob Lawrence gave the 32 Frederick Douglass panels to the Harmon Foundation as collateral for the loan of about $100. Harmon support for Lawrence continued and, in 1967, the Foundation donated the 32 Douglass panels and 31 Harriet Tubman panels to the Hampton Institute Museum.

When Jacob Lawrence was growing up in Harlem, historical figures such as Douglass and Tubman were popular folk heroes. "People would speak on these things on the street," Lawrence explained in 1984 to art historian Ellen Harkins Wheat. "I was encouraged by the community to do [narrative] works of this kind; they were interested in them." The Hampton University Museum is publisher of Wheat's book, *Jacob Lawrence: The Frederick Douglass and Harriet Tubman Series of 1938–40* (in association with University of Washington Press, 1991).

Jacob Lawrence's expressionistic painting was not the only experimental work being done by African American artists associated with the Harmon Foundation. In the late 1930s, foreshadowing the abstract expressionist movement, Beauford Delaney began creating non-objective paintings such as the later one shown in Hampton's collection. Moving to New York in 1929, Delaney frequented Charles Alston's "306" group as well as the artistic community center in Greenwich Village, and exhibited in the 1933 and 1935 Harmon shows.

The Harmon Foundation was also interested in the art of sub-Saharan Africa where, according to assistant director Evelyn Brown, "design and function went hand-in-hand." In 1961, the Foundation began collecting the work of contemporary African artists and, in 1962, its trail-blazing show of this art traveled to Hampton Institute.

In November 1962, when Hampton's driver and truck returned the exhibit to the Foundation at 140 Nassau Street, the artist Palmer Hayden helped to bring the African pieces back up to the 6th-floor office. Hayden also checked the condition of the returned pieces. By this time, Hayden was working as an assistant at the Harmon Foundation. Several years earlier Hayden assisted Mary Beattie Brady with the rescue of the William H. Johnson works in a storage unit. The works were going to be dumped as trash because of unpaid storage company bills. William H. Johnson was suffering syphilis-related dementia and confined to an institution.

As she and her long-time assistant Evelyn S. Brown neared retirement, Mary Beattie Brady regarded Hampton as the primary institution to carry on the Foundation's mission to — not only collect work by black artists — but to increase the visibility of this art nationwide through "cultural service projects." In 1963 Hampton Institute art instructor Lorraine Bolton went to New York to confer with Brady on how the two institutions could work together to promote the art.

In her report about the visit, Bolton was optimistic about mounting the numerous local and national "cultural service projects" that she and Brady discussed. For a while, Hampton's bookstore sold African artifacts supplied

SOUTHERN WORKMAN COVERS ART

From its beginning in 1872 to 1939 when it folded, Hampton Institute's *Southern Workman* journal was a seminal chronicle of African American achievement.

The *Workman's* reportage on visual arts in the 1920s and 1930s is particularly noteworthy. During this period the journal documented a pronounced rise in African American visual arts production and commented on the African aspects of the artists' heritage.

A record of now-obscure African American artists such as Louise Latimer is also found in the pages of the *Workman*. In the teens and 1920s, when American women's careers generally were cut short by marriage and only a very few young African American women were working in the visual arts, Louise Latimer, an African American painter and illustrator, was designing covers for the *Crisis* magazine, working deftly in the "treacherous" medium of watercolor, and exhibiting around the East Coast. She also skillfully colored motion pictures and managed art exhibits at the New York Public Library and elsewhere. The December 1924 *Southern Workman's* profile of the artist also notes the influence of her father, Lewis H. Latimer, a mechanical illustrator and patent draftsman.

The journal's criticism of the 1931 Harmon exhibition reflected Alain Locke's central thesis — that African American artists should draw ideas from their own ethnic backgrounds. Repeatedly praising evidence of a coalescing "racial" school of art in the Harmon show, *Southern Workman* reviewer Rose Henderson noted that the show "revealed a gratifying advance in those qualities and themes which are inherently Negro." Richmond Barthe's sculptures, she said, presented "Negro character with revealing insight and a touch of primitive vigor and richness"; indeed, she exulted, two of these works "have still more of the racial opulence and candor." At this time, when southern black colleges strove to instill in their students the values of the larger Euro-American culture, Henderson's critique shows that an African American identity also was being cultivated at Hampton.

NEGRO ARTISTS IN THE FIFTH
HARMON EXHIBITION
BY ROSE HENDERSON

The *Southern Workman* covers the Harmon exhibitions. Shown on this page from the April 1933 issue is Sargent Johnson's *Pearl*, recipient of the Robert C. Ogden Prize. Also in the article are photos of artwork by Palmer Hayden, James Porter and William Artis.

Robert Scott Duncanson (1817-1872 [suicide])
Landscape with Hawk
1848-49
oil on canvas
15" x 12"
COLLECTION HAMPTON UNIVERSITY MUSEUM

Edward Mitchell Bannister
(1828-1901)
Landscape: Figures and Cattle
1890
oil on canvas
24" x 36"
MUSEUM ACQUISITION FUND

Henry Ossawa Tanner (1859–1937)
Landscape in Moonlight
1913, oil on canvas board, 10 $\frac{1}{8}$" x 13 $\frac{7}{8}$"
COLLECTION HAMPTON UNIVERSITY MUSEUM; MUSEUM ACQUISITION FUND

Henry Ossawa Tanner
Lion's Head
1892
oil on linen
31 $\frac{1}{2}$" x 27 $\frac{1}{2}$"
COLLECTION HAMPTON UNIVERSITY MUSEUM; GIFT OF ROBERT OGDEN

Charles Ethan Porter
Untitled (Still Life)
Ca. 1905
oil on cavas
COLLECTION HAMPTON UNIVERSITY MUSEUM;
GIFT OF ROBERT S. HARRISON AND THOMAS D. HARRISON

Robert S. Pious (1908–1983)
Portrait of Singer
1932
pen and chalk on paper
COLLECTION HAMPTON UNIVERSITY MUSEUM;
GIFT OF THE HARMON FOUNDTATION

by the Foundation. But Bolton and the College Museum director soon realized that major projects such as traveling exhibitions would require an enormous amount of time, energy and supplies. And the Foundation, in the final stage of its operation, only had funds to support its own office operations. Bolton's rapport with Brady, never-the-less, did help pave the way for the donation of major works of art to come.

In 1966, when Hampton museum director and art instructor Evert Johnson visited the Harmon Foundation to make arrangements for a William H. Johnson exhibit, he and Brady went over several hundred works by William H. Johnson and selected 50 representing a good cross-section of the work. In a June 22, 1966 memo, Johnson told Hampton Institute President Jerome Holland, "if we handle this exhibit in a manner of the art works and one that pleases Miss Brady she will probably let us keep the paintings in our collection...."

Evert Johnson explained that Hampton was central to Harmon's deaccession planning. While most of the Harmon papers would go to the National Archives and some of the William H. Johnson's paintings would go to the Smithsonian, Hampton stood to gain significantly from the liquidation of Harmon's holdings:

> The idea of Hampton Institute being the artistic leader among predominantly Negro colleges is very dear to Miss Brady. She lectured me at great length concerning the sociological benefits of art, the bringing of "culture" to the Negro, and the role she hoped Hampton Institute would take in all this....She has a strong desire to feel that the Harmon Foundation has been instrumental in helping Hampton Institute take a leading position in "bringing culture" and a sense of artistic fullness to this campus and community, and to the whole Negro community in the United States

In October 1968, Hampton's museum received the Harmon Foundation's final William H. Johnson donation bringing the total number of Johnson works donated by Harmon to Hampton to 58. This was the second of two major Harmon gifts to the Institute that year.

In early Spring 1967, Palmer Hayden packed 42 cartons containing original art work, art reproductions, photographs, and photographic equipment that was shipped to Hampton by truck on April 7. Original art in the shipment included works by Malvin Gray Johnson, Archibald Motley, Jr., Claude Clark, Albert Alexander Smith, Ellis Willis, James Lesesne Wells, Hale Woodruff, Allan Rohan Crite, Richmond Barthe, Palmer Hayden, John Wesley Hardrick, Wilmer Jennings, Sargent Johnson, William Edouard Scott, William Artis, Hilda W. Brown, Teodoro Ramos-Blanco, Aaron Douglas, and several lesser known African American artists who had exhibited at the competitions. The Foundation also donated works by a number of modern African artists including Ben Enwonwu, Skunder Boghossian, Bruce Onobrakpeya and Ibrahim el Salahi.

Through the negotiations of the new College Museum director Richard A. Long, the Harmon Foundation had also donated the Jacob Lawrence panels to Hampton Institute in 1967. On May 18, 1967 Long wrote to Brady:

> When I saw Jacob Lawrence Tuesday, after having seen you, he confirmed my impression that he would be delighted to have his early works here at Hampton. If they are included in the Harmon gift a special exhibition featuring them would be arranged for the school year 1968–69.

Richmond Barthé (1901–1989)
Black Madonna
1961
bronze
COLLECTION HAMPTON UNIVERSITY MUSEUM;
GIFT OF SAMELLA LEWIS

The next day, May 19, Richard Long reported to President Holland that he had elicited from Brady "a willingness to consider giving Hampton one of her most valuable holdings — the Jacob Lawrence group of historical sketches. In support of this, I have received Mr. Lawrence's assurance that he would be most pleased if the sketches came to the College Museum."

In addition to the major gifts of art from Harmon to Hampton, Brady oversaw the donation of art books and now-rare print materials such as catalogues for the 1939 *Contemporary Negro Art* (Baltimore Museum of Art) and the 1945 *Negro Artist Comes of Age* (Albany Institute) exhibitions as well as early Harmon Foundation exhibition catalogues. Among the items in the April 1967 shipment was a rare visual record: glass slides, taken between 1927 and 1934, of African American artists and their works, some of which are not part of the published record.

The College Museum's 1968 William H. Johnson exhibit (March 3–April 14) was the culminating event of Hampton's association with the Harmon Foundation which had closed in 1967. Organized by Richard A. Long, the exhibition was the first major retrospective of Johnson's work. Unfortunately the 67-year-old artist was oblivious of this career milestone.

Over the years, the key liaison between Hampton Institute and the Harmon Foundation had been Marie V. Wood, executive assistant to President Holland. In April 1969, Wood received a long, hand-written letter from Mary Beattie Brady. Most poignant in the intimate letter detailing her failing health was Brady's remark that she had collapsed in November 1967, the day after she had closed the door to the Foundation for the final time. Having worked at the Foundation since November 1923, it had been her life's work. And, in the end, her hopes for its legacy rested with Hampton.

A CENTURY-LONG TRADITION

That visual art was a centerpiece of Hampton's 1968 centennial celebration was true to the institute's tradition. In August 1868, Samuel Chapman Armstrong, the founder of Hampton Normal and Agricultural Institute, took the initial steps to establish a museum collection. Although the earliest objects came from Oceanic, African and American Indian cultures, interest in ethnicity and a concern for African American culture and its roots have characterized the school from its founding. The museum collection was carefully selected and documented to support and enhance a curriculum combining industrial education and a solid academic program. Over the decades, these collections served as resources that helped to develop a strong self-image and pride in heritage.

The school's philosophical concept of the unity of life and art was advanced in the 1940s by Viktor Lowenfeld, a professor at Hampton and mentor to three great African

John Wesley Hardwick (1891-1968)
Portrait of a Woman
1932
oil on board
HAMPTON UNIVERSITY MUSEUM;
GIFT OF THE HARMON FOUNDATION

Augusta Savage (1900-1962)
Lift Every Voice and Sing
1939
cast iron
10 $^7/_8$" x 9 $^1/_4$"
COUNTEE CULLEN ART COLLECTION,
HAMPTON UNIVERSITY MUSEUM; MUSEUM ACQUISITION FUND

James Lesesne Wells (1902-1993)
The Flight into Egypt
1930
oil on board
16" x 20"
COLLECTION HAMPTON UNIVERSITY MUSEUM; GIFT OF GEORGE FOSTER PEABODY

Aaron Douglas (1899-1979)
Power Plant in Harlem
1939
oil on canvas
20" x 22"
COLLECTION HAMPTON UNIVERSITY MUSEUM; GIFT OF THE HARMON FOUNDATION

Lois Maïlou Jones (1917-1998)
Montmartre (Street Scene)
1938
oil on canvas
21 1/4" x 16"
COLLECTION HAMPTON UNIVERSITY MUSEUM; MUSEUM ACQUISITION FUND

Ellis Wilson (1899-1977)
Caribbean Vendor, Bird Vendor
1953
oil on canvas
39" x 24"
COLLECTION HAMPTON UNIVERSITY MUSEUM

Malvin Gray Johnson (1886-1934)
The Old Mill
1934
oil on canvas
COLLECTION HAMPTON UNIVERSITY MUSEUM; GIFT OF THE HARMON FOUNDATION

Archibald Motley, Jr. (1891-1981)
Black Belt
1934
oil on canvas
31 3/4" x 39 3/8"
COLLECTION HAMPTON UNIVERSITY MUSEUM; GIFT OF THE HARMON FOUNDATION

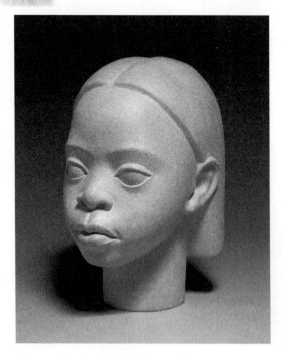

William Artis (1914-1977)
Head of a Girl
n.d.
terra-cotta
13 1/2" x 5 1/2" x 7 1/2"
COLLECTION HAMPTON UNIVERSITY MUSEUM; GIFT OF THE HARMON FOUNDATION

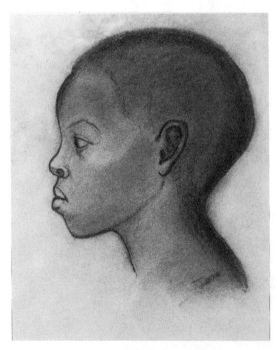

Sargent Johnson (1887-1967)
Head of A Boy
n.d.
pastel on paper
COLLECTION HAMPTON UNIVERSITY MUSEUM; GIFT OF THE HARMON FOUNDATION

American artist-educators: John Biggers, Joseph Gilliard and Samella Lewis. (see article beginning on p. 38)

Combining a background in psychology and art education, Lowenfeld, an Austrian of Jewish heritage who fled the Nazi persecution, discouraged his students from imitating the canon of Western art that excluded them. In doing so, he believed, they inhibited themselves and perpetuated their own feelings of inferiority. Lowenfeld urged his students to paint from the heart and to express the pain and adversity of black people's condition. He also used African sculpture as a teaching resource.

Late in 1942, Lowenfeld worked on a Hampton student art show that culminated in an exhibit in the Museum of Modern Art in New York City. Lowenfeld was a member of a college art teachers' association and he made arrangements with other members who were representatives of various East Coast colleges for the exhibit to first be shown on their campuses.

Among the works of the Hampton students in the *Young Negro Art* exhibit at MoMA October 6 through November 28, 1943 were Joseph Mack's *Pieta* and Alfred James Martin's *Jazz*. John Biggers had the greatest number of works, which included his murals, *The Dying Soldier* and *The Rural Preacher*. Also on view was Junius Redwood's *Night Scene* which was purchased by MoMA.

Especially significant in the interwined story of Hampton and African American art history are Lowenfeld's students John Biggers, Joseph Gilliard and Samella Lewis.

Joseph Gilliard came to Hampton in 1935 to study building construction and technology. Through Lowenfeld's effort, he was one of the recipients of the first art fellowships at Hampton. Upon graduation from Hampton in 1941, Gilliard was recruited by Lowenfeld to teach a program in ceramics. Gilliard's ceramics studio at Hampton was marked by invention. He built the first kiln himself, and, using natural elements such as fish scales, oyster and crab shells, seaweed and plant ash, invented new techniques to produce visual textures in glazes. He earned his master's degree at Hampton and spent time in the chemistry and physics labs, experimenting with his craft. In 1988, the museum presented a retrospective exhibition of Gilliard's work that demonstrated his long-standing interest in creating new glazes, textures and colors. *Rock Pile* (1975) was acquired by the museum after the retrospective ended.

During his more than 40 years at Hampton, Gilliard created striking ceramics and mentored hundreds of students such as David MacDonald, Winnie Owens-Hart, Benjamin Wigwall and Samella Lewis as well as John Biggers and others who teach at, or retired from, the art departments of schools, colleges and universities around the country. On November 22, 2004, as this issue was being prepared, Joseph Gilliard passed on.

John Biggers enrolled at Hampton in 1941 with a penchant for art but intending to major in plumbing. He enrolled in one Lowenfeld's evening art classes as an elective during his first semester. "At last I had found a way to deal with the life-long yearning to speak in line, form and color of the aspirations of the black man I had become," Biggers later recalled. "Man, I'm telling you, that Lowenfeld turned me on! In my second year, I became an art major."

Another major influence in Biggers' development was his close observation of Charles White's creation of a mural at Hampton. In 1942, the 24-year-old Charles White had been awarded a one-year, $2,000 fellowship to paint a mural at a southern school. White had selected the medium of mural painting because, he said, "My main concern is to get my work before ordinary people.... A work of art was meant to belong to people.... Art should take its place as one of the necessitates (*sic*) of life, like food, clothing and shelter."

On January 4, 1943, Charles White and his wife Elizabeth Catlett arrived on the Hampton Institute campus. The school agreed to provide $200 in painting supplies and room and board while the work was in progress. The school was reluctant, however, to provide the same for Catlett, and initially billed the couple $50 per month for her room and board. The situation was ultimately resolved when Catlett began teaching sculpture classes without pay and Hampton decided to compensate her at the rate of $50 a month.

Nearly six months went into the creation of the mural which was titled *The Contribution of the Negro to Democracy in America*. According to Biggers, White spent the first three of these months in a small room off the balcony in the auditorium planning and sketching. White gave the initial pencil sketch to Biggers and it is now on loan to Hampton. Biggers helped prepare the egg tempera pigments used in the mural and often swept the floor just to be near the master muralist. White used Biggers as a model and the student's hands, arms and even his likeness as the runaway slave are in the finished mural. (See p. 46 for Alona Horn's article on an aspect of this mural.)

Elizabeth Catlett had taught at Dillard University where one of her students was Samella Sanders (later Lewis). Catlett convinced Sanders to transfer to Hampton in March 1943. "Coming to Hampton saved my life," recalled Samella Sanders Lewis many years later. Lewis described her New Orleans hometown as a city where people were "extremely active" and the black population was "very aggressive":

> *Every Friday night we had what we called "Bump Night." That's the time you bumped your enemies off the sidewalk to relieve your aggressions. So we were very independent kinds of people.... When I came here (to Hampton), I didn't like teachers and I didn't like anybody to tell me what to do and I didn't like administrators most of all.*

Lowenfeld and Catlett, independent spirits themselves, were exceptions to Lewis' general dislike of teachers and she graduated from Hampton Institute in 1945. Recounting her college experience in 1993, Samella Lewis said that when she entered graduate school at Ohio State University (OSU), she felt that she was "moving back in time" because much of what she was taught in the master's program she had learned at Hampton. The museum's holdings include two important student works by Samella Sanders (Lewis), *Waterboy* and *Sharecropper Family*, both executed in 1944. These paintings reveal the artist's attempt to juxtapose pure colors (one next to the other) to create intense feeling.

In 1951, Samella Lewis earned the Ph.D. in art history at OSU, becoming the first African American to earn the degree. Over five decades, her extraordinary career included many other "firsts" as she distinguished herself as an author, educator, curator, artist and publisher, founding this journal in 1976. *Royal Sacrifice* (1976) the painting Lewis selected to be on the cover of the first edition (1978) of her pioneering text, *Art: African American*, was acquired by Hampton.

By the time of his death on January 25, 2001, John Biggers was a towering figure in American art. He founded and headed the art department at Texas Southern University, earned a Ph.D. in education in 1954, and in 1957, was one of the first African American artists to travel to Ghana. A prolific artist, he produced a complex yet distinctive body of work linking concepts and motifs from African and African American material cultures and spirituality, environmental ecology and sacred geometry.

LASTING CONNECTIONS

There is a thread that stretches from Aaron Douglas, the preeminent visual artist of the Harlem Renaissance up to the present Hampton University President William R. Harvey. Harvey began collecting art in 1969 when he was an administrator at Fisk University. Although he had retired a few years earlier as chair of the Fisk art department, Aaron Douglas, continued to frequent the campus, attracting other artists of note and mentoring David Driskell, his successor. Driskell had taught Harvey as an undergraduate at Talladega College and encouraged the young administrator to begin collecting.

Not only did Harvey continue collecting after he left Fisk, acquiring a diverse personal collection of 19th- and 20th-century masterworks, he has overseen the expansion of the Hampton University Museum's collections since he assumed the leadership of the school in 1978. In a continuing pursuit of excellence at the university, he has provided acquisition monies, funded an artist-in-residence program, commissioned major works of public art for the campus and acquired donations of art from private collectors to the museum. Over 500 significant works have been added to the collection of African American art since 1978.

Harvey's vision of creating "an environment on the Hampton University campus where the arts can flourish" was manifested in a monumental outdoor sculpture honoring the school's most well-known graduate, Booker T. Washington. In 1983, Louisville sculptor Ed Hamilton was commissioned to create the realistic work. A photograph taken of Washington at the 1898 Cotton States and International Exposition in Atlanta served as inspiration for the 9-foot 4-inch, 2000-pound bronze sculpture. Hamilton read Washington's speeches and autobiography to get into the "mystique of the man." Historical accuracy was insured as the artist reviewed photographs and sketches of the coat Washington wore during the Atlanta speech. The Booker T. Washington Memorial Garden and sculpture, dedicated on May 13, 1984, is a lasting tribute to the achievements of African Americans in education.

William R. Harvey's dream for the collection was shared and implemented by Jeanne Zeidler, HU Museum director from 1981 to 2001. The goal of the acquisition plan implemented under her leadership was to enhance the depth and breadth of the collection with an eye to developing permanent exhibition galleries that would provide museum visitors with an opportunity to view a comprehensive chronology of African American art.

In 1986 the museum made its first major purchase of an outstanding collection of African American art with the acquisition of the Countee Cullen art collection. The 29 paintings and sculptures assembled by the poet and his wife are rare and valuable for the quality of the individual pieces and for the historical significance of the collection.

William Edouard Scott (1884–1964)
Weighing Dye Logs, Cap-Haitian
Ca. 1931
oil on canvas
COLLECTION HAMPTON UNIVERSITY MUSEUM;
GIFT OF THE HARMON FOUNDATION

Twenty-eight of the works of art in the collection are by six major twentieth-century American artists: Palmer Hayden, Hale Woodruff, Jacob Lawrence, Augusta Savage, William Artis, and Charles Sebree. The majority of the collection was built by Countee Cullen over a period of nearly two decades, until his untimely death in 1946. Most of the artists represented in the Cullen collection were personal and long-time friends of Countee's and Ida's. Several are themselves also strongly identified with the Harlem Renaissance Movement

The earliest works in the collection were acquired by Countee before he and Ida married, while he was living in Europe. In 1928, when the poet received a Guggenheim Fellowship and went to France, he joined what Ida Cullen described as "a community of black artists that had gone to Paris to study." Palmer Hayden, Hale Woodruff and Augusta Savage were among these artists and Cullen purchased works from each of them.

From Hale Woodruff, Countee purchased three watercolor paintings which thereafter were always displayed in the Cullen home. *Paris Landscape*, dated 1927, is the earliest and is personally inscribed to Countee by the artist. The Chartres paintings, both dated 1928, were particular favorites. In 1928, Countee also acquired an oil painting, *Parisian Landscape*, from Palmer Hayden. The bookends which the poet commissioned Augusta Savage to create that same year depict a man standing at a latrine, a common sight in Paris.

Sixteen of the works are original book illustrations for Cullen's book, *The Lost Zoo* (1940). In 1939, the poet commissioned Charles Sebree to illustrate the animals of the world which no longer exist because they could not get on Noah's ark. Sebree maintained possession of these original illustrations for many years until Ida Cullen purchased them as part of her on-going efforts to keep Cullen's writings before the public and to get them back in print. Two additional works by Sebree are included in the collection — two portraits of women that were gifts from Sebree to Countee and Ida Cullen on the occasion of their marriage in 1940.

In 1944, two years before Countee Cullen's death, the couple purchased Jacob Lawrence's 1943 gouache on paper, *The Peddlers*, also known as *Peddlers Reduce Their Prices in the Evening to Get Rid of Their Perishables*, and *Fruit and Vegetable Peddlers*. One of more than 20 gouache on paper works created between 1942–43 focusing on the theme of Harlem and originally exhibited with caption-like titles, this work was included in the recent retrospective exhibition *Over the Line: The Art and Life of Jacob Lawrence*.

After Countee's death, Ida Cullen added several pieces to the collection. From the Harmon Foundation, she purchased the sculpture, *Eddie*. From a dentist in Harlem, she purchased William Artis' *Lift Every Voice and Sing*, Augusta Savage's maquette for the sculpture installed at the 1939 New York World's Fair. This small cast iron sculpture is the

Below:
Hampton's recently acquired *Along the Eure at Chartres* (top) is very similar to the two Chartres watercolors that the museum acquired in 1986 as part of the Countee Cullen Collection.

Hale Woodruff (1900-1980)
Along the Eure at Chartres
1928
oil on canvas
25 3/4" x 21 1/2"
(EX-COLLECTION MARY BEATTIE BRADY)
COLLECTION HAMPTON UNIVERSITY MUSEUM; GIFT OF ED ROECH

Hale Woodruff (1900-1980)
Chartres
1928
watercolor
18 1/2" x 21 3/8"
COUNTEE CULLEN ART COLLECTION,
HAMPTON UNIVERSITY MUSEUM; MUSEUM ACQUISITION FUND

Palmer Hayden (1890–1973)
Carousel and Balloons
ca. 1950
watercolor
23 1/2" x 26 3/4"
COUNTEE CULLEN ART COLLECTION
HAMPTON UNIVERSITY MUSEUM; MUSEUM ACQUISITION FUND

Jacob Lawrence (1917–2000)
The Peddlers
1943
gouache on paper
23 1/2" x 26 3/4"
COUNTEE CULLEN ART COLLECTION
HAMPTON UNIVERSITY MUSEUM; MUSEUM ACQUISITION FUND

Andre Stener Dufo
Portrait of Countee Cullen
1935
watercolor
23 1/2" x 18 1/4"
COUNTEE CULLEN ART COLLECTION
HAMPTON UNIVERSITY MUSEUM; MUSEUM ACQUISITION FUND

Beauford Delaney (1901–1979)
Untitled
1968
oil on canvas
COLLECTION HAMPTON UNIVERSITY MUSEUM; MUSEUM ACQUISITION FUND

Herman "Kofi" Bailey (1931–1981)
Our Image
Ca. 1961
mixed media
COLLECTION HAMPTON UNIVERSITY MUSEUM; MUSEUM ACQUISITION FUND

only known maquette in a museum collection of the original plaster sculpture that was destroyed after the fair. In the mid-1970s, Ida Cullen added Jacob Lawrence's serigraph, *The Builders*, to the collection. And in 1976, or early 1977, she bought the painting, *Carousel and Balloons*, from Palmer Hayden's widow, Miriam.

Ida Cullen's decision in 1985 to sell the collection stemmed from her attachment to the works and her awareness of their importance. At 86 years of age, she wanted to place the collection where it would remain together as a lasting tribute to Countee and his work; where the collection would serve to keep his work alive and remembered; and where the pieces would be protected, cared for and would be available and known to people for generations to come. At Hampton, Ida Cullen found such a home for her collection.

Another collecting goal during the Harvey administration has been the acquisition of representative works by the major African American artists of the 19th century. The first work to be entitled was a religious painting by Henry O. Tanner, *In The Holy Land* (ca. 1890). In 1991, two Tanner etchings, *The Wreck* and *Street-Scene Tangiers* (1913) were purchased to show the range of his work. In 1989, a major commitment was made which resulted in the purchase of paintings created in the 19th century by Joshua Johnson, Robert Scott Duncanson, and Edward Mitchell Bannister. Landscapes by Charles Ethan Porter and Grafton Tyler Brown and two lithographs by New Orleans-based printmaker and photographer Jules Lyon acquired over the next two decades have also added to the museum's nineteenth-century holdings.

HAMPTON TRADITION IN ART

Uniquely important for the development of Hampton University Museum's fine art collection over the past two decades has been the major effort to collect works of art by distinguished artists trained at or associated with Hampton University. This effort has been supported by a number of exhibitions organized around the theme of documenting the visual arts at Hampton University. These exhibitions include: *Joseph Gilliard: Hampton Artist, Teacher, and Inventor* (1988); *The Homecoming: Charles Young* (1989); *Five Decades: John Biggers and the Hampton Art Tradition* (1990); *The Art of Samella Sanders Lewis* (1990); *Objects Ceremonial and Mundane: Works by David MacDonald* (1991); *Memory and Oblivion: Legacies of Enslavement in the Americas* (2003); and *Painting History: The Murals of Charles White and John Biggers* (2003). From these exhibitions, the museum has acquired works by Charles White, Joseph Gilliard, Junius Redwood, Persis Jennings, John Bean, Michael Portilla, Annabelle Baker, Benjamin Wigfall, Charles Young, David MacDonald, Gerry Lang, Lloyd Toone, Kwabana Ampofo-Anti, Marianetta Porter, Greg Henry, and others.

Through a combination of gifts and purchases, the Hampton University Museum has built up significant holdings of works representing all decades of the careers of three important figures connected to the visual arts at Hampton: John T. Biggers, Elizabeth Catlett, and Samella Sanders Lewis.

In 1989 Hampton acquired more than 80 drawings, paintings, prints and sculpture created by John Biggers. The collection features more than 20 works the artist created as a student at Hampton and includes the 1942 oil painting, *Crossing the Bridge*, the first painting he did under the guidance of Viktor Lowenfeld. This collection — which includes *Fishing Village* (1962), one of the drawings from Biggers' book, *Ananse: The Web of Life in Africa* — formed the nucleus of works for the 1995 retrospective exhibition *The Art of John Biggers: View from the Upper Room* organized by the Museum of Fine Arts, Houston and Hampton University Museum and mounted in 1997 at Hampton's newly renovated Huntington Building.

John Biggers' most monumental presence on Hampton's campus is 20-feet high — the two murals, *Tree House* and *House of the Turtle*, inspired by the history of the university that were installed in the main library in 1992. The Biggers connection also has led to the museum exhibiting and collecting the fine art photography of Earlie Hudnall Jr. who studied with Biggers at Texas Southern University.

In 1992, Hampton University Museum organized the first comprehensive exhibition of Elizabeth Catlett's works on paper — 75 works created over five decades — and published an exhibition catalogue with essays by Samella Lewis and Richard Powell. (The exhibition has also traveled nationally.) The museum acquired the entire body of work in *Elizabeth Catlett: Works on Paper, 1944–1992* through a gift and purchase agreement.

In response to the museum's support of her artistic achievement, Catlett has made the museum the archive for her works on paper and Hampton has added more than 50 pieces to this outstanding repository of Catlett works.

Elizabeth Catlett's artistic development as a sculptor after her teaching stint at Hampton, is reflected in the three sculptures in the museum's collection. *Pensive* (1946), was created the same year the artist went to Mexico. A gift from the estate of the artist's sister Cera Leacock in 2004, the three-quarter-length bronze figure reveals the strength of the working woman. This work complements the museum's other Catlett sculptures — orange onyx and black marble torsos — both powerful abstracted studies of the female form that date to the 1970s.

A group of more than 20 works of art acquired from two exhibitions: *The Art of Samella Sanders Lewis* (1990) and *Samella Lewis: A Retrospective* (1997) show the depth and versatility of this major art figure and Hampton alumnae.

The collection has also grown through a magnanimous gesture made by Lewis. In 1997, when the museum was preparing to move into a large (34,300 sq. ft.) building with

HAMPTON UNIVERSITY MUSEUM CHRONOLOGY

1868	*General Samuel Chapman Armstrong establishes museum collection.*
1870s	*First African pieces acquired.*
1878	*First American Indian pieces acquired.*
1894	*First works acquired for African American fine art collection.*
1967	*Museum receives major gifts from the Harmon Foundation.*
1984	*Hampton Institute becomes Hampton University. The College Museum becomes the Hampton University Museum.*
1997	*With the completion of a $5 million renovation of the former Huntington Library and the addition of a new wing to the building, the Museum moves into a large, state-of-the-art facility which now houses about 10,000 objects.*

Joseph Gilliard (1914–2004; Hampton Institute Class of 1941)
The Rock Pile
Ca. 1960
terra cotta
25" x 11 ½"
COLLECTION HAMPTON UNIVERSITY MUSEUM; MUSEUM ACQUISITION FUND

William H. Johnson (1901–1970)
Three Great Freedom Fighters
oil on fiberboard
35 1/2" x 27 3/8"
COLLECTION HAMPTON UNIVERSITY MUSEUM

Albert Alexander Smith
Dancing Time
1930
oil on canvas
20" x 24"
COLLECTION HAMPTON UNIVERSITY MUSEUM; GIFT OF THE HARMON FOUNDATION

Claude Clark (1915–2001)
Combat
COLLECTION HAMPTON UNIVERSITY MUSEUM

John Biggers
Old Coffee Drinker
1945
oil on canvas
51 3/8" x 35 3/8"
COLLECTION HAMPTON UNIVERSITY MUSEUM; GIFT OF THE ARTIST

John Biggers, seated, with *Mother and Child* painting on easel, 1944. Art instructor Viktor Lowenfeld (second from left) encouraged the students to express their frustration with poverty and other conditions of oppression in the South. (Standing far right are Frank Steward and Ada Ferguson Vann.)
PHOTO: HAMPTON UNIVERSITY ARCHIVES

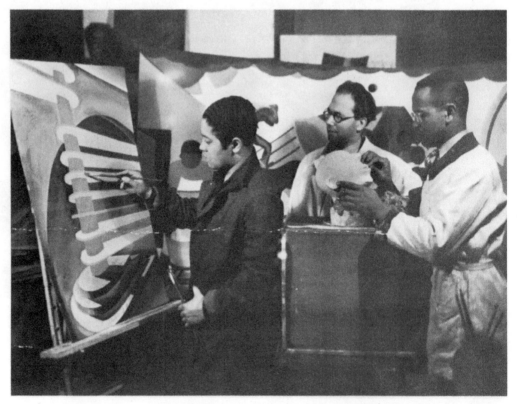

Viktor Lowenfeld (center) looking over the work of two of the first Hampton students to receive art fellowships, Michael Portilla (left) and Joseph Gilliard (right), 1941.

John Biggers
Four Sisters
1986
oil and acrylic on canvas
36" x 48"
COLLECTION HAMPTON UNIVERSITY MUSEUM

Persis Jennings (Hampton Institute Class of 1944)
Family
1984
wood
COLLECTION HAMPTON UNIVERSITY MUSEUM; MUSEUM ACQUISITION FUND

12,000 square feet of gallery space, and needed works by contemporary master artists to fill out the contemporary gallery, Lewis drew from her personal collection to provide works by Benny Andrews, Herman "Kofi" Bailey, Margo Humphrey, Sam Gilliam, Floyd Coleman, Joe Overstreet, Al Loving, and William Alexander among others. In 1999, Samella Lewis also made possible the acquisition of 21 sculptures by Richmond Barthé, which brings the number of Barthé sculptures in the collection to 23 as two sculptures were part of the 1967 Harmon Foundation gift.

NURTURING THE TRADITION

Hampton-affiliated artists and donors are just one aspect of the museum's collection. It also has grown through the university's institutional priority to nurture the development of an African American art tradition. This commitment is reflected in the both the exhibition by the Hampton University Museum, and its subsequent acquisition of works by a variety of contemporary artists. These include:

Richard Mayhew's *September* (1985), a gift of the artist, from the exhibition, *"West by Southwest": Drawings and Paintings by Richard Mayhew.*

Six prints by master printer Ron Adams collected since his 1989 artist in residency at the University.

Moe Brooker's *The Music of Space We Carry Deep Inside* (1990) from the 1992 exhibition "Recherche."

AfriCOBRA member James Phillips' *The Soul and Spirit of John Biggers* (1995) from the 1995 *"The Awesome Image"* exhibition.

Sonya Clark's four mixed media hats from her 1995 show.

William E. Pajaud's suite of three mixed media paintings Fifth Ward Series from the 1999 exhibition *"William E. Pajaud: Journeys of the Heart."*

James Brantley's *Quartet* (1996) from the 1998 exhibition *Faithful Voices.*

Award winning entries in the museum's inaugural juried exhibition *New Power Generation* in 2003: Teri Richardson's *Visiting the House that Angelline Built* (1999) and M. Scott Johnson's *The Judgment of Peter Norton* (2002).

Other HU Museum acquisitions occur though gifts such as the Norman Lewis painting, *Getting It Together* (1975), donated by the Hampton chapter of Jack and Jills of

America, and those listed in the "Recent Acquisitions" section of this article.

Equally important as acquiring works for the collection has been a concerted effort on the part of Hampton University to preserve the work of African American artists for future generations. Conservation of works of art has been an on-going priority during the Harvey administration and more than 100 works of art by artists of African descent have undergone conservation since 1978. A major conservation project to restore all of the Henry O. Tanner paintings in the collection was undertaken in 1988. Painter and conservator Felrath Hines, who was chief conservator for the Hirshhorn Museum and Sculpture Garden in Washington D.C., was selected to treat the Tanner masterpieces.

Out of this relationship, the museum acquired a major painting by Hines, who was a founding member of the Spiral Group. The short-lived group consisted of more than a dozen African American artists who joined together in 1962 in New York City to explore their common cultural connections. *From Dark to Light* (1965), acquired from Hines in 1993, was part of the 1964 path-breaking Spiral exhibition in New York City. All works in the Spiral exhibit were executed only in black and white to reflect the group's concern about racial equality and the affirmation of black identity.

Beginning in 1998, the museum mission expanded to include the exhibition and acquisition of works by self-taught African American artists. Anderson Johnson was the subject of the museum's first exhibition of this genre: *The Creative Spirit: The Work of Anderson Johnson*. Johnson converted the first floor of his two-story home in the East End section of Newport News, Virginia, into the Faith Mission and decorated the exterior and interior of the mission with 2,000

Mose Tolliver (1915-)
Untitled (Birds)
1994-6
paint on board

COLLECTION HAMPTON UNIVERSITY MUSEUM; GIFT OF BARON AND ELLIN GORDON

or so paintings — portraits, bible passages, visionary images of angelic faces, historical figures and contemporaries from his neighborhood. When the Faith Mission was destroyed in 1995, the murals decorating its interior walls were saved by the city of Newport News through the efforts of local art supporters, including Hampton University Museum.

The collection of self-trained artists currently numbers 80 works by 47 contemporary artists including, in addition to Anderson Johnson, Mose Tolliver, Bessie Harvey, Purvis Young, Mary T. Smith, and Thornton Dial, Sr. The majority of these works have come through the generosity of Williamsburg collectors Ellin and Baron Gordon. In 2004 the Wisconsin-based Kohler Foundation, Inc. donated five mixed media sculptures to the museum from the Dr. Charles Smith Collection.

The intertwining of the histories of the Harmon Foundation and Hampton University intersect at the start of the new millennium with the presentation to the museum of eight pochoir, or hand-painted screenprints, by William H. Johnson. The donor, Ed Roesch of nearby Williamsburg, Virginia, received the artwork as a gift from his great-aunt Mary Beattie Brady more than 30 years ago.

In 2001 Roesch donated an important oil painting by Hale Woodruff that he acquired from Brady. *Along the Eure at Chartres* (1928) was one of four oil paintings Woodruff sent to New York from France for inclusion in the 1929 Harmon Foundation's "Fine Arts Exhibit by Negroes" show. Brady acquired the painting sometime after the exhibition.

Its scene of medieval houses along the Eure River bank in the Beauce Valley is very similar to the two 1928 watercolors, entitled *Chartres*, which Countee Cullen acquired from the artist when they were studying in France. Together these works provide an opportunity to understand how Woodruff treated the same subject in different media and to explore his interest in reflections on water.

In 2002, Roesch donated another Harmon-related work acquired by Brady — a tempera painting by Congolese artist Rene Bokoko. The artist's work was included in the Harmon Foundation's 1962 contemporary African art exhibition that came to Hampton Institute and in the 1967 Harmon Foundation gift.

As a result of Jeanne Zeidler's direction, Hampton University Museum's collection of African American art contains the largest existing collections of works in any museum by the artists John Biggers, Elizabeth Catlett, Jacob Lawrence, Samella Lewis, Richmond Barthe, Gwen Knight and Earlie Hudnall, Jr. Among her other accomplishments was overseeing the five million dollar renovation of the Huntington Library building into a state-of-the-art museum facility for a collection of African American, African and American Indian pieces that today numbers more 9,000 pieces — the museum's home since 1997. Her extraordinary stewardship of the collection complemented William R. Harvey's unlimited aspiration. Together they worked to move the museum to national attention and admiration.

Feldrath Hines
From Dark to Light
1965
oil on linen
COLLECTION HAMPTON UNIVERSITY MUSEUM; MUSEUM ACQUISITION FUND

Henry Ossawa Tanner (1859-1937)
The Banjo Lesson
1893
oil on canvas
49" x 35 ½"
COLLECTION HAMPTON UNIVERSITY MUSEUM;GIFT OF ROBERT ODGEN

William Pajaud
Palm Sunday
mixed media
1989
COLLECTION HAMPTON UNIVERSITY MUSEUM; GIFT OF THE ARTIST

RECENT ACQUISITIONS

Hampton University acquired its ninth painting by Henry O. Tanner in May 2001 when Hampton President William R. Harvey purchased at auction the exquisite *Landscape in Moonlight*. The painting, which was originally owned by a former director of the Worcester Museum of Art, is signed, dated and inscribed: "To Raymond Henniker-Heaton with respect by H.O. Tanner, March 1st 1913."

Important acquisitions continued during the tenure of director Ramona Austin (2001–2004) with works by Charles Alston, Gwen Knight, Robert Reid, Philemona Williamson and Alan Rohan Crite coming in to the collection. Charles Alston's *Untitled (portrait of a woman)*, the second work by the artist in the collection, was donated by Atlanta law professor Lemoine D. Pierce in the name of her aunt, a Hampton Institute graduate, who taught her how to read.

In 2003, at the same time as the Romare Bearden retrospective was traveling the country, President Harvey undertook the acquisition of a major work by Romare Bearden for Hampton. The collage-on-panel, *Carolina Blue* (1969), was acquired from the Bearden Foundation.

The largest and most impressive group of acquisitions in the new century has come from the estate of Hampton alumnae Beryl O'Kelly Brooks, class of 1951.

These acquisitions will be discussed by William R. Harvey in an illustrated article in a forthcoming issue of the *International Review of African American Art*. Harvey was instrumental in these outstanding collections coming to the Hampton University Museum.

An unanticipated but most welcomed gift, a sculpture entitled *Pensive* by Elizabeth Catlett, arrived at the museum in December 2004. Catlett initially created the figure of a strong working woman, arms folded and deep in thought, in plaster in 1946. She gave the piece to her sister Cera Leacock, who moved with it many times during her husband's career in the military. In an effort to preserve the work, the artist had it cast in bronze in 1978. The work was in several exhibitions including *Significant Others: Artist*

Charles Alston (1907–1977)
Untitled (portrait of a woman)
Ca. 1960
oil on canvas
24" x 18"
COLLECTION HAMPTON UNIVERSITY MUSEUM; GIFT OF DR. LEMOINE D. PIERCE ("IN LOVING MEMORY OF MY GRANDPARENTS ALICE AND ROBERTA AND LUTHER DOGGET WHITE, PARENTS OF NANNIE ELDEAN WHITE, HAMPTON INSTITUTE CLASS OF 1938.")

William H. Johnson (1901-1970)
Training For War
Ca. 1941-42
pochoir
COLLECTION OF THE HAMPTON UNIVERSITY MUSEUM; GIFT OF ED ROESCH

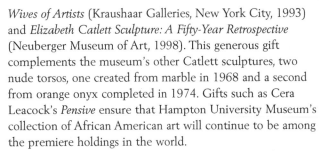

Charles Young (1930-)
Red Enclosure
acrylic
50" x 36"
COLLECTION HAMPTON UNIVERSITY MUSEUM

Wives of Artists (Kraushaar Galleries, New York City, 1993) and *Elizabeth Catlett Sculpture: A Fifty-Year Retrospective* (Neuberger Museum of Art, 1998). This generous gift complements the museum's other Catlett sculptures, two nude torsos, one created from marble in 1968 and a second from orange onyx completed in 1974. Gifts such as Cera Leacock's *Pensive* ensure that Hampton University Museum's collection of African American art will continue to be among the premiere holdings in the world.

In January 2005, Mary Lou Hultgren, curator of collections at the Hampton University Museum since 1984, was appointed director of the museum. Having worked closely with Zeidler and William Harvey in developing the collection, Hultgren says she plans to build on this remarkable experience by continuing to cement long-lasting relationships with artists and forging new links with artists. "Under Dr. Harvey's visionary leadership," she adds, "Hampton University will continue to strive for excellence as a leader in collecting, exhibiting and preserving the rich legacy of African American art through exhibitions and publications, and critically needed educational outreach resources that can be shared with students and teachers throughout the country."

This article was compiled by former and present staff members of the Hampton University Museum.

Nannette Acker-Clark (1948-)
Retreat at Blue Mountain
1991
mixed media
COLLECTION HAMPTON UNIVERSITY MUSEUM; MUSEUM ACQUISITION FUND

Moe Brooker (1940-)
The Music of the Space We Carry Deep Inside
1990
mixed media
COLLECTION HAMPTON UNIVERSITY MUSEUM; MUSEUM ACQUISTION FUND

Mask, Mukenga
raffia, hide, trade cloth, beads, wood, cowrie shells,
parrot feathers, animal hair, brass
H. 28 1/2"
MUSEUM ACQUISITION FUND

Collector William H. Sheppard explained: *The long top (of the mask) represents an elephant's trunk, i.e., strength. The palm (fringe) also signifies strength. Therefore the mass of it (is) around the neck. Leopard (skin on the front of the mask) also means strength. Shamba Bolongongo (an early Kuba ruler) is said to have founded a secret association whose members served as a kind of police force. One of three high officials of this society wore a beaded mask made of leopard skin and native palm fiber cloth at the ceremonies held for the initiation of new members into the society.*

THE AFRICAN ART COLLECTIONS
TO BE A GREAT SOUL'S INSPIRATION

by Mary Lou Hultgren

"O Hampton, a thought sent from heaven above,
To be a great soul's inspiration..."

(Lyrics from the Hampton University alma mater by Sarah Collins Fernandis, 1882)

Among Hampton University's 'great soul's inspirations' has been the museum's African collections. Consisting of exceptional pieces from traditional and contemporary sub-Saharan cultures, the African collections have been a source of special knowledge and pride for several generations of students. In 1929, for example, Dwight Sumner, a student from Sierra Leone, hailed the museum's recent acquisition of artifacts from a Gikuyu chief in Kenya. Writing in the student. newspaper, *The Script*, Sumner explained that viewers should appreciate the artistic merit of the collection and thus strive for a deeper understanding of its meaning. "It... gives an insight into the ethos of a people," he wrote. "A nation expresses its philosophy in art as much as it does in music or language." Two years later, Dwight Sumner deepened his experience of cultural philosophy as one of four students in Hampton's African Quartet.

The mission of the museum, founded in 1868, the same year as the school, did not specifically include collecting the art of Africa. However, from the beginning the museum collection included non-Western cultures. General Samuel Chapman Armstrong, the school's founder, planned the museum's collection to be "very instructive." Originally called the "Curiosity Room," a term used in the 19th century to refer to a tradition of collecting and displaying diverse anthropological, zoological, mineral, and botanical specimens primarily from non-western countries, the museum collection was developed to support the education of Hampton students. The son of missionary parents working in Hawaii, Armstrong solicited the help of his mother in obtaining the first objects, asking her to

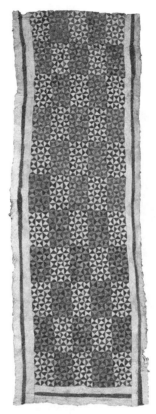

Barkcloth Overskirt
barkcloth
L. 24 1/2"

Sheppard explained: *Used as floor coverings, blanket or dress and for burial purposes (spread over dead body which rests in reclining position). These mats are considered a very valuable possession costing time and labor in the making.*

send "specimens of coral, lava and curiosities of all kinds found in the Pacific."

Museum records indicate that a neck ornament and headdress collected by former student Akrel E. White, Class of 1876, on Sherbro Island in Sierra Leone is the earliest African acquisition remaining after a fire in 1879 destroyed much of the early collection. A "country cloth" was acquired in 1880. In 1893, a folklore and ethnology department with an expressed interest in the "traditions of ancestry in Africa" was established by the school. Rooted in this context, the museum's African collection was selected and documented to enhance the education of African Americans and to encourage cross-cultural understanding.

The museum collection reflected Armstrong's educational philosophy of "teaching by the most practical method." Armstrong's initial goal in establishing the school was "to train selected Negro youth who should go out and teach and lead their people...." To accomplish this, he developed a program of study that sought to train "the head, the hand, and the heart." Instruction in world geography, cultures, and history was solidified through close examination of museum objects while students learned the dignity of labor by practical, hands-on training in the school's many workshops, and on the school's farms. The museum collection, which quickly encompassed diverse cultural materials from around the world, was carefully acquired to support the curriculum. As a direct resource for students, the museum had an indirect impact upon education throughout the South, for by 1880, Hampton graduates were teaching over ten thousand African American pupils throughout the region.

William H. Sheppard after his induction into the Royal Geographic Society, 1893.
PHOTO: COLLECTION ARTHUR R. WARE

Initially, the major links between Hampton students and Africa were maintained through contacts with African Americans who had direct contact with the continent. These included White, a Hampton graduate and an American Missionary Association missionary in Sierra Leone, and campus speakers such as the Americo-Liberian Edward Wilnot Blyden. In a September 1, 1890 letter posted from Stanley Pool, Congo Free State, West Central Africa, Hampton alumni William Henry Sheppard told General Armstrong that he was acquiring objects for the collection. The first African American missionary to be sent to the Congo Free State by the Southern Presbyterian Mission Board, Sheppard closed with the promise, "I have many spears, knives, idols, etc., saving them for the curiosity room at Hampton."

William H. Sheppard was born in Waynesboro, Virginia in 1865, the son of a barber and a bath maid who worked at the hot springs. Sheppard attended Hampton from 1881 through 1882, at which time he transferred to Stillman College in Tuscaloosa, Alabama. There he earned a theology degree and was ordained as a minister in the Southern Presbyterian Church. Sheppard's collection is the first systematic collection of African art assembled by an African American. The collection is unique in its intention to enhance the education of African Americans through the development of a respect for African peoples. In addition, this important resource is the earliest collection of Kuba objects in the West.

Much of the exceptionally rich art of the Kuba peoples is related to royal court art. Sheppard's collection is also notable in that it has special association with Kuba royalty. In 1892, William Sheppard became the first Westerner to visit the Kuba royal capital, Nsheng, and meet the paramount ruler Kot aMbweeky II. Although forewarned that the ruler had threatened death to any foreigner who should enter his dominion and to any of his people who would assist a foreigner, Sheppard set off into the heart of the kingdom. His facility in the Kuba language, learned through his close association with various local peoples while traveling in the Kasai region, aided Sheppard as he encountered Kuba traders during his journey from village to village. When Sheppard finally arrived at the capital unaccompanied by a guide and speaking the native language, the puzzled Kuba concluded that the missionary was in fact no foreigner but a makuba, the reincarnation of a member of the royal family. "You are Bo-pe Makabe who reigned before my father and who died," the King's son To-en-zaida informed Sheppard. "His spirit went to a foreign land; your mother gave birth to it, and you are that spirit."

In spite of Sheppard's attempt to repudiate this claim, the Kuba accepted Sheppard as one of them, and he was accorded a unique relationship with the king, the royal family, and the Kuba people. In a ceremony held at the capital's royal court, Sheppard was officially greeted by Kot aMbweeky II who "pulled from his belt a knife, and saying that it had been handed down in the red halls of the Lukengas through seven generations, presented it to me." This knife, which represents the "ties of blood" between Sheppard and the Kuba, is now in the collection of Hampton University Museum.

"I had seen nothing like it in Africa," Sheppard wrote of his visit to the royal court. During the four months Sheppard spent as the guest of the King, he had the opportunity to observe many aspects of Kuba society for the royal capital was the economic, political, religious, and artistic center of the realm. As the distinguished historian Jan Vansina has noted: "No introduction to the visual arts of Africa omits the Kuba, for theirs is no doubt one of the greatest artistic traditions on the continent."

Even before the school acquired Sheppard's collection, Kuba art objects that he collected were essential tools for the promotion of positive attitudes about Africa at Hampton. After being elected into the prestigious Royal Geographical Society in London in June of 1893, Sheppard returned for a

Harp
Mangetu peoples
wood, hide, fiber, bead inlay
L. 14"
COLLECTED BY RAOUL BLONDIAU, CA. 1900
BLONDIAU-THEATRE ARTS COLLECTION, HAMPTON UNIVERSITY MUSEUM

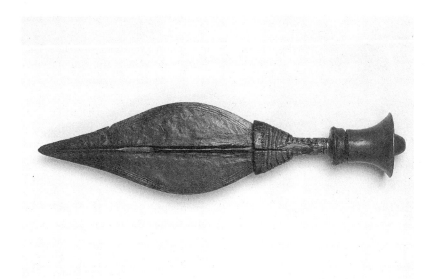

Knife
Ca. 17th century
iron, copper, wood, brass, L. 14.5 "
WILLIAM H. SHEPPARD COLLECTION, HAMPTON UNIVERSITY MUSEUM

This knife was gift to Sheppard four days after he arrived in the Kuba capital. The collector noted "as he
(the Lukenga or paramount ruler) pleasantly greeted me he pulled from his belt a knife and,
saying it had been handed down in the red halls of the Lukengas through several
generations, presented it to me."

Box used by women to hold sewing utensils.
wood
L. 13 ¹/₂"

Hampton student Peter Mbiyu Koinange dressed in the
objects a Kikuyu chief would wear for an ordinary ceremony,
ca. 1929.
HAMPTON UNIVERSITY ARCHIVES

year to the United States and eventually to Hampton where he addressed the student body on November 14, 1893. During this lecture he showed Kuba objects he had acquired, giving his American audiences concrete examples of the Kuba culture. The knife presented to him by Kot aMbweeky II at their initial meeting the year before at the royal court was one of the objects that Sheppard brought with him. In his efforts to foster cross-cultural understanding and pride in heritage, Sheppard employed the same type of object lessons that Hampton museum curators would utilize repeatedly over the years.

In 1911, Hampton Institute purchased Sheppard's impressive collection of more than a hundred objects for the sum of five hundred dollars. The July 1911 issue of the *Southern Workman*, the school's widely distributed magazine, announced the purchase noting that the 150 objects included "many rare and interesting articles with a decided artistic as well as ethnic value." The article concluded that the "many varieties of fibre cloth, beautiful in design and texture, with mats and baskets of artistic form and pattern, give one a new idea of the ancestors of the American Negro and are of special interest to their descendants." That same year the museum curator, Cora Mae Folsom, described the teaching benefits provided by Sheppard's collection in her annual report when she wrote: "To the Negroes it is a great aid to respect of race to find their ancestors capable of the taste and skill exhibited by these articles that have come from the hand of African men and women. Things African prove to be the favorite theme. The boys and the girls find great interest in this really fine exhibit...I open the cases and let them [the students] handle most of the objects while explaining them." Her 1917 report noted that "the African... collections should and do have a large mission in stimulating race pride."

Throughout her years as curator (1903–1922) Cora Mae Folsom lobbied for larger exhibition and storage spaces, using as a model Boston's art museum. By 1918 the museum had

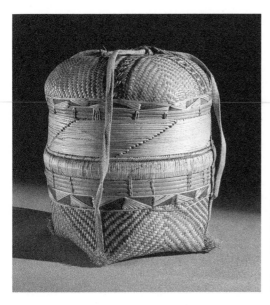

Basket
Songye peoples
cane, raffia
H. 12 1/2"
WILLIAM H. SHEPPARD COLLECTION,
HAMPTON UNIVERSITY MUSEUM

Made by women to carry personal belongings when traveling...Carried on the head.

5,400 square feet of exhibition space in Marshall Hall, the administration building, and a collection representing many world cultures.

During the first three decades of the 20th century, the African collection expanded with gifts coming through students from West, South and East Africa. Additional objects continued to be acquired in an ad hoc manner from staff, trustees, school supporters, missionaries and travelers to the continent.

Hampton's African collection was recognized as having important implications beyond the campus. It was a community resource and, as a 1920 curator's report noted, Hampton was also the only museum in the South open to African Americans. As knowledge of Hampton's collection spread, in part through articles published in the *Southern Workman*, the African pieces, appreciated both as material culture and art, were reported by Folsom to be "inspiring —helpful ...not only at Hampton, but to students of African ethnology in other places, and to artists in search of the new designs and suggestions."

During this period, New York City served as an important site where visual artists looked to African art for inspiration. On February 7, 1927, a major exhibition of African art that would impact Hampton's African holdings opened at the New Art Circle Gallery on West 57th Street. Alain L. Locke, often called the "Father of the Harlem Renaissance," authored the foreword for the exhibition catalogue, the Blondiau-Theatre Arts Collection of Primitive African Art, expressing his hope that the exposure to and appreciation of African art would lead Americans of African descent "to recapture this heritage of creative originality and to carry it to distinctive new achievement in the plastic arts."

This exhibition, which was only the third such exhibition of its kind in New York City, was drawn from a collection of nearly 1,000 Central African art objects assembled over a twenty-five year period by Belgian diplomat Raoul Blondiau. Locke arranged for Edith Isaacs, publisher of the *Theatre Arts* magazine, to purchase the collection and bring it to America to preserve the artistic heritage of Africa and to inspire African American artists. At the conclusion of the exhibition, Hampton trustee George Foster Peabody arranged for Hampton to acquire some 50 pieces that would complement the Sheppard collection. The collection included examples of regalia and personal adornment, household objects and musical instruments.

At Hampton, where a fine art department was not established until 1941, many of these new works of art proved to be of special interest and inspiration to students in the music department. The acquisition of the African musical instruments reflected the school's long-standing goals of encouraging the performance of traditional music by African American students.

In the school's annual reports, Hampton documented the classroom use of the museum collection. A domestic science class is shown studying Kuba textiles from the Sheppard Collection, ca. 1920.

A unique collection of nearly fifty Kikuyu objects from Kenya, assembled by Senior Chief Koinange-wa-Mbiyu to represent his culture, arrived at the museum in 1929. The year before, his eldest son, Peter Mbiyu Koinange, the first Kenyan to attend Hampton, visited the museum and "suddenly said to the curator, 'You have nothing from my tribe. I don't like that. I shall tell my father when I write to him.'" Described by the museum's second curator, social studies instructor Sara Lane, as "valuable articles such as only a chief would be able to obtain," the collection is a rare example of objects selected by a cultural insider to represent his culture to a Western audience. The gifts, which include ceremonial headdresses, personal adornment objects, weapons and household items, provide an interesting view of cultural representation. Koinange, a 1929 graduate of Hampton, provided documentation on the pieces for the museum records as to the meaning of the objects and how and when they were worn and used.

The music and dance of the Zulu peoples served as the inspiration for another unique group of "hands on" objects procured by cultural insiders for the museum to further cross-cultural understanding. The collection was assembled by Reuben T. Caluza, Class of 1936, a Zulu student from Edendale, Natal, South Africa. Caluza, a music major and an accomplished composer and arranger of Zulu songs, organized a performing arts group at Hampton called "The African Quartet." The quartet included Caluza and three West African students to whom Caluza taught Zulu songs and dances. Dressed in Zulu dance regalia, the quartet performed extensively on campus and throughout the South with the goal of conveying an understanding of African music to American audiences. Prior to his return to South Africa, Caluza donated to the museum more than 40 pieces of the quartet's performance costumes that included beaded necklaces, belts, head and wrist bands, headdresses, courting shields, skirts, capes and outfits said to be worn by "carriers of

burden" or "rickshaw boys" in Durban, South Africa. These art objects, coupled with a traditional Zulu bride's costume that was purchased from Caluza in 1933 by curator Sara Lane, constitute the largest lot of the museum's Zulu collection.

The 1939 arrival on campus of Viktor Lowenfeld, a Jewish refugee scholar from Vienna, Austria, served as a catalyst for a period of intense interest in the African collection among Hampton students. An art educator and artist, Lowenfeld had studied at the Austrian Museum for Art and Industry and understood the influence African art had on European modernism. He also brought with him a background in working with African art gained while serving as director of an African art and pottery museum in Vienna. In addition to his teaching duties in the art department that he established, Lowenfeld served as the curator of the museum in 1942 and again in 1946, his last year on the faculty. His appointment as part-time curator began a 30-year practice where the position of museum curator was assigned to a member of the art faculty.

Former Lowenfeld student and renowned artist John Biggers, reflecting on his introduction to the African art collection in 1941, stated that students came to Hampton with a "stereotyped concept" of African art. It "was something not to be embraced [because] it represented savagery and barbarism." Biggers, who went on to become a pioneer in translating the rich heritage of African art, African culture, and African civilization into American art, recalled:

> In our culture, when black represents something that's terrible and bad and the devil, and he [Lowenfeld] picked up these beautiful, these very — I wanted to say almost glistening black things — and starts telling us the profound meaning of it, the great meaning of African art, its humanistic tradition and how old all this must have been, here was a new experience entirely for me....I realized that I had a

Hampton's African Quartet, 1931. Left to right: George Taylor (Sierra Leone), Dwight Sumner (Sierra Leone), Reuben Caluza (South Africa), John Cooper (Liberia). The Zulu dance costumes, acquired by Reuben Caluza for the the quartet, were donatedto the museum when Caluza graduated from Hampton in 1936.
HAMPTON UNIVERSITY ARCHIVES

Gallery view: *Primitive Art of Africa, North America and Oceania from the* (Hampton) *College Museum* exhibit, Union Carbide Building in New York City, November 6-22, 1967

heritage, and inheritance that I was entirely unaware of before coming here.

During the administration of Hampton Institute President Jerome H. Holland in the 1960s, a renewed attention was drawn to the African art collection. During the 1960s the museum hosted several special exhibitions focusing on the African art collection and mounted an ambitious exhibition in New York City celebrating the school's one hundred year anniversary.

The 1962 exhibition *Art from Africa — Of Our Time* was one of several exhibitions organized by the Harmon Foundation and brought to campus by museum director Friedrich Gronstedt. The exhibition not only exposed students to contemporary examples of African art, but it also served as a catalyst for new acquisitions. Five years later the museum acquired a portion of the Harmon Foundation Collection of Contemporary African Art. With the sponsorship of Nigerian artist Ben Enwonwu's 1950 visit to the United States, the Foundation had become an advocate for contemporary African art. The Foundation continued promoting contemporary African art into the mid-1960s, publishing the pathbreaking book *Africa's Contemporary Art and Artists* in 1966.

By 1967, the Harmon Foundation began dispersing its art collections and gave a significant portion to Hampton. Included in the gift were more than 200 paintings, prints and sculpture by more than 40 African artists. Hampton's collection includes Nigerian artists Ben Enwonwu (1921–1994), Akinola Lasekan (1916–1972), Jacob Afolabi (b.1940), Lamidi Fakeye (b.1928) and Bruce Onobrakepya (b.1932); South African artists Peter Clarke (b. 1929) and Gerard Sekoto (1913–1993); Sudanese artist Ibrahim

El Salahi (b.1930); Ghanaian artist Vincent Akwete Kofi (1923-1974); Tanzanian artist Sam J. Ntiro (1923–1993); Ethiopian artist Alexander Skunder Boghossian (1937–2003); and Congolese artist Pili-Pili Molongoy (b.1914).

During the 1960s, one Hampton student was particularly motivated by her contact with the school's African collection. On Sundays Rosalyn Walker's family had gone to the State Museum in Baton Rouge, Louisiana, and since then she had always wanted to work in a museum. Enrolling at Hampton in the Fall of 1962, Walker was aware that the school had a museum and was soon working there. The museum director "needed help and I volunteered for the job," she recalls. "The African objects were fascinating and I was meeting Africans for the first time — students from Sierra Leone and Nigeria." During Walker's junior or senior year, Peace Corps volunteers were being trained on Hampton's campus and noted historian of African art Roy Sieber came to lecture the volunteers about African art and aesthetics. While Sieber was on campus he did an appraisal of the African collection and Walker "shadowed" him. She would go on to study with Sieber at the University of Iowa and earn her Ph.D. in African art history. Rosalyn Walker currently holds a distinguished position at the Dallas Museum of Art: senior curator for the arts of Africa, the Pacific and the Americas and Margaret McDermott Curator of African Art.

Hampton's Centennial Celebration (1967–1968) brought widespread attention to the African collection through the efforts of museum director and interdisciplinary scholar Richard A. Long.

In 1944, when Richard A. Long was a 17-year-old student at Howard University he met Alain Locke, the great philosopher who urged African American artists to look to the sophisticated design aesthetics of African art as inspiration for their own. One of the last times, Long saw Locke was in 1953 at an African art exhibit organized by James V. Herring at Howard. "I arrived at the door at Founders Library (where the gallery was) at the same moment with Locke and we viewed the exhibit together," Long recently recalled.

Because of his early, expert exposure to African art, Richard Long naturally gravitated towards the Kuba objects in Hampton Institute's museum when he accepted a faculty appointment here in 1966. With a Ph.D. in linguistics from the University of Poitiers, France, he had come to Hampton to teach and head the French department. But soon he was also director of the College Museum which contained magnificent examples of late-19th- and early-20th-century Kuba art from the Congo.

As Long learned about William H. Shepard, the first African American explorer to southern Africa, who had collected the Kuba items, an idea took hold. "There had not been a lot of scholarly investigation of African art," Long explained. "There were a few specialists, but not in the College Art Association. I wanted to make them aware of the Sheppard collection and initiate group activity around African art." Long had met Jan Vansina, one of the foremost scholars of African history in Belgium. "He had heard about Shepard but didn't know where his collection was."

Over the next two years, the public recognition of Hampton's African art collection mushroomed. With the help of anthropologist Margaret Mead, Long organized the Primitive Art of Africa, North America and Oceania from the College Museum at the Union Carbide Building in New York City, November 6–22, 1967. A Hampton Institute trustee Margaret Mead "threw herself into the planning of the exhibition and attended the opening," Long recalled.

The African art collection drew international attention the following year when the school hosted a five-day "Symposium on Traditional African Art," also organized by Richard A. Long. This Centennial Celebration conference, held from May 6–10, 1968 on the college's historic campus, introduced leading scholars in the field to Hampton's collection and "to the pioneering role of Black Americans in bringing Africa to the consciousness of the West," Long would later write in *Art Forum*. The symposium sessions were rounded out by special exhibitions of the Sheppard Collection, the Bloudiau Theatre-Arts Collection and a complementary exhibition of 37 of the photographs of Kuba art and life taken in 1947 by Eliot Elisofon, who also attended the conference.

Attracting African art specialists from around the country and abroad, the symposium included presentations by William Fagg of the British Museum and two others from Europe; and from American universities: Jan Vansina, Eugene Grigsby, Robert F. Thompson, S.I. Hayakawa, and Douglas Fraser, among others. Hampton's landmark symposium ultimately evolved into the International Triennial Symposium on African Art, with the second meeting held at Harvard's Peabody Museum. Seeded by Sheppard's example,

Long's original idea grew into a stream that contributed to the development of African studies at American universities around the nation; a stream indeed flowing back to 1873 when Hampton Institute initiated an African studies program, one of the earliest in the nation.

By 1970, with the school's multicultural collections of African, African American, American Indian, Asian, and Pacific art were housed together under one roof in the recently renovated, historic landmark Academy Building, the first full-time museum director, Julia Vodicka, began the task of professionalizing the museum. The 1971 loan of four objects from the Sheppard Collection to The Museum of Modern Art's groundbreaking exhibition African Textiles and Decorative Arts, curated by Roy Sieber, marked the first time works from the collection were included in a major national traveling exhibition.

Between 1970 and 1980, more than 600 African pieces, mainly gifts, were added to the collection. The donors included supporters of African American education like Franklin H. Williams, the president of the Phelps-Stokes Foundation and former ambassador to Ghana, and collectors of African art such as Donna and Lee Bronson and Jay T. Last. The most heralded donations came from the seven members of the musical group the Commodores. Presented in honor of Hampton's new president, William R. Harvey, who had assisted the group during their student-years at Tuskegee Institute where Harvey was an administrator, the gift expanded the museum's holdings from West African cultures. Notable among the gifts is a highly decorated hunter's shirt from Sierra Leone/Liberia donated by trumpeter William King.

The expansion of the collection allowed for more extensive exhibitions and assisted the museum in its continued mission as a resource for students and the wider community. On the role that the museum played in her life, painter and North Carolina State University art chair Chandra Cox, class of 1976, said: "I came here as a student at Hampton and had to study African sculpture and that was the seed of my interest in traditional African art, which is a thriving theme in my work today. The museum very much is exemplified in the Ghanaian proverb, 'Until the lion has his own historians, the tale will always glorify the hunter.'"

Under the leadership of Jeanne Zeidler (museum director, 1980–2001), concerted effort was directed toward making the museum's multicultural collections accessible to wider and more diverse audiences. To accomplish this, considerable support was focused on new exhibitions, developing publications, selectively enlarging the collections and expanding the museum's facilities. In 1983, the first interpretative exhibition of the African collection, *Thy Rooftrees Outspread: African Roots and Limbs*, was installed in the museum. This permanent exhibition utilized images, maps and documents from Hampton's archives to interpret more than 100 objects in a historical and cultural context that included information on how the collections were

Skunder Boghossian
Ghosts of the Atlantic Ocean
1964
mixed mediums (including opaque watercolor, acrylic, and ink on paper board)
40 $\frac{1}{4}$" x 27 $\frac{5}{8}$"
COLLECTION HAMPTON UNIVERSITY MUSEUM; GIFT OF THE HARMON FOUNDATION

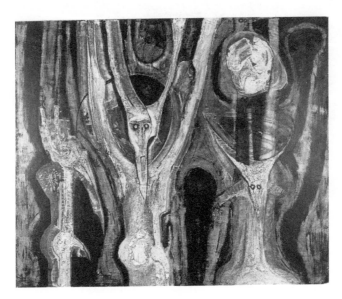

Ibrahim el Salahi
Victory of Truth
n.d.
39 $\frac{1}{4}$" x 48"
mixed mediums on masonite board
COLLECTION HAMPTON UNIVERSITY MUSEUM; GIFT OF THE HARMON FOUNDATION

Akinola Lasekan
Pots for Market, Okitipupa
1960
tempera and mixed mediums on canvas
16" x 20"
COLLECTION HAMPTON UNIVERSITY MUSEUM; GIFT OF THE HARMON FOUNDATION

used in early classes to support the school's philosophy of education.

The unique history of Hampton's collection was paramount in the selection of 67 African objects to be included in the groundbreaking traveling exhibition *Art/artifact* curated by Susan Vogel in 1988. The decision to participate in the exhibition, organized by the Center for African Art, was based on the fact that *Art/artifact* was a multifaceted vehicle for showcasing Hampton University Museum's historic collection. Not only did one theme of the exhibit feature the recreation from a photograph of Hampton's museum at the turn of the century but the much discussed exhibition and accompanying catalog brought the history of Hampton's African collection to national and international audiences.

The Hampton museum's first publication on the African collection, *A Taste for the Beautiful: Zairian Art from the Hampton University Museum*, was published in 1993. Conceived as an overview of the historic Kuba collection, the book was aimed at non-specialists as well as specialists seeking to learn about African art, African American history and the history of museum collections.

Installed in 1998 in the new Hampton University Museum building (a renovation of the school's 1903 Beaux Arts style–former library), the current African exhibition features more than 240 works.

The African collection was carefully expanded with the aim of building on and updating core groupings already in the museum's holding under Zeidler's 21-year tenure. A group of objects from Kenyan cultures was acquired to complement the historic Koinange Collection. Special emphasis was also placed on adding objects from the Kuba peoples that would "complete" the Sheppard Collection. More than 150 additional Kuba works of art, including textiles, masks, household objects, decorative arts, prestige regalia and objects of personal adornment have been acquired since 1987. Many of these objects have links to the current Kuba ruler His Majesty Nyimi Kwete Mbuek III and his immediate predecessor Bope Mabiinc. Continuing Hampton's tradition of engaging Africans in the development and interpretation of the collection, Ngoloshang Mbeky, (Hampton University, Class of 1993, MBA), the youngest brother of the current paramount ruler, assisted in documenting the objects and provided information on the changing role of the contemporary Kuba leader. In addition, Ngoloshang facilitated the visit of his brother, Kwete Mbuek III, to the museum in 2000 to view the more than 130 Kuba art objects in the permanent African exhibition, *The Art of Africa: Power, Beauty and Community*. This type of collection building is unique among African art collections.

Efforts to make the African collection accessible to a broader audience have continued into the new millennium. One hundred African pieces, including twenty-five works by contemporary Nigerian artists from the Harmon Foundation collection, were entered into the database of the Museum Loan Network in 2000. The following year international attention was brought to Hampton's Harmon Foundation collection of contemporary African art through two groundbreaking, critically acclaimed exhibitions: *The Short Century: Independence and Liberation Movements in Africa 1945–1994* curated by Okwui Enwenzor for Munich's Museum Villa Stuck and *Century City: Art and Culture in the Twentieth Century Metropolis* mounted at the Tate Modern in London and curated by Okwui Enwezor and Olu Oguibe. Paintings by Ibrahim El Salahi, Skunder Boghossian, and Ben Enwonwu were loaned to these exhibitions.

Hampton's African art collection, which currently numbers more than 3,600 objects, continues to support the museum's time-honored mission of enhancing the education of African Americans and encouraging cross-cultural understanding. As the 21st century unfolds, the firm foundation of Hampton's African art collection remains deeply rooted in the mission of the museum and the university for, as noted artist and alumni John Biggers has stated, "It is the richness of the past that gives us a meaning for the future."

Mary Lou Hultgren is director of the Hampton University Museum.

NOTES

Information for this article was mostly drawn from the archives of Hampton University, Hampton University Museum records and the Hampton Institute publication, The *Southern Workman*.

Other references include:

Biggers, John. Interview by Jeanne Zeidler, Hampton, Virginia, 19 November 1991, Video recording, Hampton University Museum.

Brown, Evelyn S. *Africa's Contemporary Art and Artists: A Review of Creative Activities in Painting, Sculpture, Ceramics and Crafts of More than 300 Artists Working in the Modern Industrialized Society of Some of the Countries of Sub-Saharan Africa*. New York: Harmon Foundation, Inc, 1966.

Cox, Chandra. Interview by Sherri Fisher Staples, Hampton, Virginia, 4 May, 2003. Video recording, Hampton University Museum.

Engs, Robert Francis. *Educating the Disfranchised and Disinherited: Samuel Chapman Armstrong and Hampton Institute, 1839-1893*. Knoxville: The University of Tennessee Press, 1999.

Hultgren, Mary Lou and Jeanne Zeidler. "A Taste for the Beautiful," in *A Taste for the Beautiful: Zairian Art from the Hampton University Museum*. Hampton: Hampton University Museum, 1993.

Southern Workman 40, no. 6 (1911): 448.

Vansina, Jan. *The Children of Woot: A History of the Kuba Peoples*. Madison: University of Wisconsin Press, 1978.

Wardlaw, Alvia J. "Metamorphosis: The Life and Art of John Biggers," in *The Art of John Biggers: View from the Upper Room*. New York: Harry B. Abrams, 1995.

SURPRISE ENCOUNTER AT HU MUSEUM

by Kagbare Onobrakpeya

I came to Hampton University to attend graduate school on a very cold day in January. Even though I had seen pictures of the school on the web and in my application package, nothing had prepared me for such a breath-taking experience. Hampton University offered me a scenic home by the sea and all the resources I would need to grow to become a successful part of any society. Getting a Hampton MBA was "value added." My first interesting observation was that my dorm was not a dorm at all. It was a lovely little white cottage that I shared with Saori, a Japanese graduate student.

I have always been drawn to water so I often would walk to the bay to admire the view of boats and sunsets, but what captivated me the most was the Hampton University Museum. My cottage was located right across from the museum. *Hmmm... what are the chances?*, I thought. I had lived with art all my life and I just loved it. I visited the museum when I had a break between classes or at weekends by myself or with my friends.

I met Jean Zeidler who was the museum director at the time and struck a friendship with collections curator Mary Lou Hultgren. I thought it would be wonderful to work around art and enjoy the art at the same time. When I ran into Mary Lou again, I asked her if the museum had part-time, graduate assistant positions. She said there were no openings but if something came up she'd let me know. Even though I was disappointed, I was hopeful. In fact, I was very hopeful, and after a brief wait, she told me something had opened up — a part-time position documenting the modern African art pieces in the storage area for the Museum Loan Network.

I was so excited because it was an opportunity to see the great contemporary African artists in the museum's permanent collection that are not on display. The collection includes Nigerian artists like Lamidi Fakeye, Ben Enwonwu, Uche Okeke, Yusuf Grillo *et al.*, several of whom I had met growing up as the daughter of an artist. Yes, in the collection were pieces of art by my dad! My father is Bruce Onobrakpeya, one of Nigeria's foremost painters and printmakers.*

As I documented each piece, I began to understand the depth of imagery and meaning in each abstract piece. Being in the presence of the masterpieces made me very nostalgic; the familiarity in the names, styles and techniques helped me understand that this wasn't just chance because nothing just happens. I'd been given the opportunity to dialogue with those great African artists who had worked so hard to give meaning to what we stood for as a continent. I thought about this over and over again, and my promise to the artists was never to let them down. I innately knew that this wasn't just another coincidence, but an auspicious occasion. I was there to interpret and represent them. It was so strong, this feeling, yet so very spiritual. And the great thing was that I knew it.

———————————————————

Kagbare Onobrakpeya is program director at the Southstar Community Development Corporation in Atlanta, Georgia.

*Acclaimed on three continents and Listed in the *International Who's Who of Art and Antiques*, Bruce Onobrakpeya draws from both traditional and contemporary styles of art and combines them, often using experimental printmaking techniques of his own invention. His work is in the collections of the Smithsonian Institution, Fisk and Hampton Universities and other museums in the United States, Canada, Nigeria, the Netherlands and the Vatican in Rome. — ed.

Kagbare Onobrakpeya with her father, Bruce Onobrakpeya
PHOTO: KAGBARE ONOBRAKPEYA

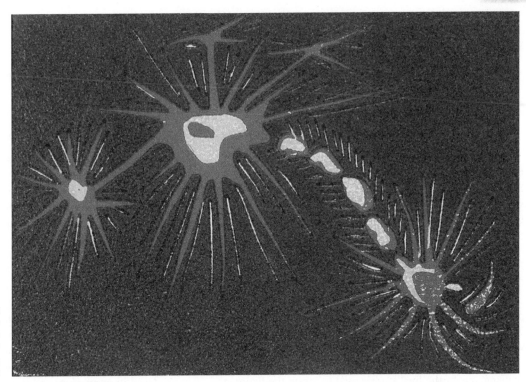

Bruce Onobrakpeya
Negritude
1960
12 1/8" x 13 1/4"
lithograph
COLLECTION HAMPTON UNIVERSITY MUSEUM

Ben Enwonwu
Tete-a-tete
1950
oil on canvas
24 1/8" x 13 1/4"
COLLECTION HAMPTON UNIVERSITY MUSEUM

STUDY OF A CHARLES WHITE STUDY

by Alona C. Wilson

In the Spring of 2004, Charles M. Young, a private art dealer, acquired a Charles W. White drawing through the Swann Auction Galleries of New York. The drawing was shown to me last Spring during Young's visit to the Smith College Museum of Art. Although the title was not recorded on the charcoal and graphite drawing, Swann Galleries identified it as *Study of a Man Singing*. It was signed and dated 1943 by Charles White with his characteristic style of lettering.

To clarify the record, I've identified the drawing as *Study of Huddie William Ledbetter (Leadbelly)*, for the 1943 mural *The Contribution of the Negro to Democracy in America*, at Hampton University, then Hampton Institute. Because of the style and figure placement, it is most likely a "finished" drawing, one of the final studies used to create the figure at the lower right corner of the mural. Throughout the history of art, the drawing medium forms a critical intersection between an idea and the manifestation. It is considered the most intellectual medium in the visual arts and a discipline to be mastered by the artist for successful development. The Ledbetter study is a detailed drawing of the face and head of the popular blues singer and guitarist of the 1930s.

White was an excellent draftsman. While a student at the School of the Art Institute of Chicago in 1937-38, he completed at least five drawing courses, two in figure drawing. Improving with each course, he earned a grade of "A" in his final course. The study is created with charcoal and graphite on cream- colored Whatman paper, specifically Whatman Drawing Board. Whatman papers are considered the finest drawing papers because of the smooth tightly woven surface. Because the mural is tempera, a slow, methodical painting process in which changes are not easily made, White would have prepared many drawings prior to the execution of the mural. The paper texture provided White with a surface that would emulate the smooth surface of a tempera mural, an egg-based paint applied to plaster.

Because the mural is located on a wall behind a shallow stage in a small auditorium with a semi-circular balcony, White had to consider the placement of the figure. The drawing is animated with Ledbetter's head turned upward, mouth open, and eyes fixed above. In the mural, Ledbetter's position draws the viewer back into the composition. White changed the position of the figure from one looking outward to one looking inward and he defined the figure as Ledbetter.

He placed the image of Ledbetter below that of Paul Robeson and within the figure grouping that includes Marian Anderson — both politically outspoken performers. More

than just a performer himself, Ledbetter infused his lyrics with biting social and political commentary on topics such as the Scottsboro Boys case. His "Bourgeois Blues," recorded in 1938, was motivated by the discrimination and condescension he encountered from both blacks and whites when he visited Washington, D.C. to record for the Library of Congress. The selection of these particular performers and their grouping was probably a deliberate decision by White. It demonstrates the many contradictions of democracy and the importance of the lessons of history.

Alive at the time of the painting of the mural, Ledbetter is portrayed in photographs and prints of the period, frequently playing a six-string guitar with his mouth open in song. Photographs or prints of Ledbetter were often reproduced in promotions and it is probable that White referred to these printed images to create the detailed drawing, making modifications to create an archetypal yet realistic figure.

White placed a halo directly behind Ledbetter's head, visible in the drawing with repetitive lines and in the mural with the use of lighter tones. With broad cross-hatches, a technique that translates effectively to tempera paintings,

Charles White
Study of Huddie William Ledbetter (Leadbelly)
for the 1943 mural *The Contribution of the Negro to Democracy in America*
graphite and charcoal on Whatman Drawing Board
26 13/16" x 19 1/4"; signed and dated at lower right: Charles White 1943
PHOTO: R. J. PHIL, EAST HAMPTON, CONNECTICUT

White extracts lines to create a soft shadow on the forehead of a thinking man. The drawing is rendered in outline form with broad, dark charcoal lines. The outline method can be seen in White's easel paintings of the same period. Sinuous lines of graphite form the cheek bones to build a solid facial structure that is defined in the mural with bold colors.

White worked from live models, mostly students at Hampton, in the development of many of the mural figures. John Biggers, the renowned artist and then Hampton art student, was the model for the figure of the slave in the upper right corner.

In 1942, Charles White, with the award of a Julius Rosenwald Fellowship, received funding for research, site selection and the execution of a historical mural. He spent a year preparing for the mural by studying tempera techniques with Harry Sternberg, an experienced artist and teacher at the Art Student League in New York City and hours of library research to determine the subject of the mural. He selected Hampton Institute, one of the oldest African American colleges, to be the installation site, and the subject, Negro achievement.

The artist had earned a considerable reputation prior to his arrival at Hampton, having received several awards for his drawings and paintings, mural commissions, and notable exhibitions in Chicago and Washington, D.C. A political activist, voicing his views for equality and justice, White found a community at Hampton that supported his politics as well as his process of creation. The young artists who assisted White were studying under Viktor Lowenfeld who used approaches that were considered radical at the time. (For more about this era, see the "Hampton Tradition" section of the "Unity of Art and Life" article in this issue.)

This drawing, *Study for Huddie William Ledbetter*, was formerly in the collection of Leo Katz, chairman of the art department at Hampton Institute, 1946–47. He replaced Viktor Lowenfeld who left for a position at Pennsylvania State University. At the time of this writing, it is unknown if Leo Katz and Charles White would have crossed paths or how the drawing came into Katz's possession. It survives in excellent condition, demonstrating that it was well cared for in the intervening years and also that the paper and drawing materials were of high quality.

Alona Horn is curatorial assistant, Smith College Museum of Art, and a doctoral student in art history at Boston University.

Charles White
The Contribution of the Negro to Democracy in America
1943
egg tempura (fresco secco)
11' 9" x 17' 3"
CLARKE HALL, HAMPTON UNIVERSITY

Anonymous Hampton Camera Club Photographer
Untitled (man and woman repairing cabin)
Ca. 1900
gelatin silver print
4 $\frac{5}{8}$" x 6 $\frac{11}{16}$"
HAMPTON UNIVERSITY ARCHIVES

FROM POEM TO PHOTOGRAPH
HAMPTON STAFF ILLUSTRATES DUNBAR'S BOOKS

by Nancy B. McGee

By the time of the poet's death, the romantic story of Paul Laurence Dunbar had been established by myth and legend, by controversy and criticism, by fact and fiction, that together made him a hero among African Americans. In the decade before his death the literary career of Dunbar had progressed rapidly, with recognition and praise coming from the great of the land. For thousands of Dunbar admirers, the "dark youth, singing in the dawn of a new freedom," had become the symbol of the artistic and intellectual potential of black folk. The poet's blossoming achievements, interrupted before the peak by his untimely death, evoked excesses of praise, recollections, and critical evaluations. In the short span of one decade — from the publication of *Lyrics of Lowly Life* (1896) to *Joggin' Erlong* (1906) — Paul Dunbar looked into the smiling face of fame and also suffered inexpressibly the pains of his frail body intermingled with the weakness, sorrows, and depression of the human spirit.

Three years after *Lyrics of Lowly Life*, Dunbar published his first illustrated collection of poems, *Poems of Cabin and Field* (1899). By this time, he had become a national figure and was busily writing and making appearances reciting his poems. A job at the Library of Congress, for which a friend recommended him, gave him an opportunity to settle in Washington, D.C., where his circle of associates were many of the Negro leaders of the day. He had previously gained the friendship of Kelly Miller, Mary Church Terrell, and other well-known personalities of his race living in Washington. Among his contemporaries in the arts, he associated continuously with the Johnson brothers, J. Rosamond and James Weldon. Will Marion Cook, Bert Williams, Ford Dabney, Harry Burleigh, Sr., and other musical artists who gathered at the Marshall Hotel in New York also became his friends.

Dunbar was also making his poems known through readings at black colleges, such as Howard University, Tuskegee Institute, and Hampton Institute. Several letters written by Principal Hollis B. Frissell of Hampton Institute and addressed to Paul Laurence Dunbar at the Congressional Library, Washington, D.C., confirm the opinion that a cordial relationship between the Hampton administration and the young author was developing as early as 1898. On December 24, 1897 Principal Frissell wrote to the poet:

Our Armstrong Association in New York has engaged the Astor Gallery for a meeting on the 13th of February, Monday afternoon. We shall be glad to pay you fifty dollars for your services on that afternoon.

As far as I know the hour of the meeting has not been arranged, but presume that it will be three o' clock as last year.

I should like very much to have you come to Hampton whenever you can, but as I do not feel that we can pay you the amount for a reading that you usually obtain, as I do not like to ask you to come without it, I feel we shall be deprived of the pleasure of seeing you. Miss Bacon has, I think, already written you asking for some contribution for "The Southern Workman."

Kindly let me know as soon as convenient in regard to the New York meeting as we shall have to make some other arrangement if you can not come.

Apparently the invitation was accepted, for it appears that the letters of Frissell and Dunbar crossed in the mail. On December 29, 1897, the principal replied:

Your kind letter on the 23rd is at hand and we shall expect you for the further afternoon of February 13th. I think that the story was altogether satisfactory, though perhaps Miss Bacon would rather it had been reference to colored rather than white people, but that is not of very great importance.

I hope you will realize that you will always be a welcome guest whenever it may suit your convenience to come to us.

The reference to "the story" is very likely to Dunbar's "A Southern Silhouette," a short story that appeared in the *Southern Workman* in January 1899.

Further explanation of the plans for the Armstrong meeting in New York appear in Frissell's letter of January 10, 1898:

I am glad to know from your card of the 8th that you are likely to be at the meeting in New York on the afternoon of February 11th. I have not myself yet heard the details of the meeting, but the plan was to have an author's reading at which Mr. John Kendrick Bangs is to preside, and then Hopkinson Smith and Mrs. Ruth McEnery Stuart and others whose names I do not know, have promised to take part.

The meeting will be under the general care of Armstrong Association of New York, of which Dr. William Shieffelin is president. The first thought in regard to it was to have it a reading for colored authors entirely, but after consideration it seemed to me wiser to make it more general. I hope very much that you will be able to be present for my thought was that it would be well to give some prominence to what has been done in literature by members of the colored race.

Please remember that we should at any time be pleased to see you here at Hampton, and you may always be sure of a very cordial welcome. I shall be glad to have the School meet you and know you, for we are very proud of what you have accomplished.

I called to see you on Saturday of last week, but was not able to get at you.

It is evident that the arrangement for this meeting involved several well-known personalities and that the Hampton Institute principal was unable to be present. Yet he had personally arranged for the fee to be paid to the poet to avoid inconvenience, according to his letter of February 6, 1898, referring to the $50 to be paid to Dunbar in New York, and requesting that the poet occupy "considerable time" in the reading of poems, and "possibly" some of the prose writings.

The *Southern Workman* described the meeting at the Waldorf as an occasion planned " for the benefit of Hampton Institute" and promised that Dunbar would read "some of his Lyrics of Lowly Life." As an added attraction, the article announced that "the Hampton Quartette will sing plantation melodies and an Indian boy from Hampton will give an account of the Indian Medicine Man." Other southern authors of note were expected to appear, including the popular writer Mrs. Ruth McEnery Stuart, who would read selections from her own short stories. In a later letter to the poet, Principal Frissell, exhibiting his usual active interest in literacy and artistic life of Hampton Institute, requested Dunbar to become a regular contributor to the *Southern Workman*, along with numerous other rising young literary artists and outstanding community leaders.

The humor and pathos of the Dunbar poems and short stories embellished the color and luster of the *Southern Workman*; most of his works from 1899 to 1906 were reviewed and many of them were published in the journal. Six of the seven illustrated volumes of Dunbar poems, moreover, owe their illustration and decorations to the interest, imagination and artistic talents of approximately 20 members of the faculty and staff of Hampton Institute.

CAMERA CLUB FORMS AT HAMPTON

The minutes of Kiquotan Kamera Klub dated October 21, 1893, read:

"A party of Hampton teachers met in Room 21, Science Building on the evening of October 21, 1893, for the purpose of organizing a Camera Club. Mr. Brown called the meeting to order and presided until Mr.

Turner was elected President. Mr. Brown and Miss Davis were appointed a committee to suggest a name for the club at the next meeting, and Mr. Turner, Mr. Briggs and Mrs. Armstrong, a committee to formulate a constitution or statement of the clubs aim and regulation." (Kiquotan is an Indian name for an area near the Hampton campus.)

With this meeting the camera began its artistic life, which continued until November 22, 1926.

The amateur photographers had made advances in the techniques of picture taking and developing prints, acquired and decorated a room in the science building and made considerable progress in studying and selecting provocative subjects for their pictures. There is little doubt that teachers at Hampton had read Keat's poems illustrated by Will H. Low, published in 1885 and 1886, as well as the edition of Rossetti's *Blessed Damozed*, illustrated by Kenyon Cox, 1886. They might even have seen Dunbar's "A Coquettel Conquered" from *Lyrics of Lowly Life* (1896) reprinted in the *Century* with a sketch illustration by Peter Newell, the first published illustration for a Dunbar poem.

During the period of incubation between examining illustrated editions and actually producing their own, the members of the Kiquotan Kamera Klub produced three albums of blue prints which, according to Eleanor Gillman, assistant to the director of the Hampton Archives, depicted scenes "of the campus and boats on Hampton Creek and the neighboring Hampton Roads." Among the club's other activities was the annual 12-page calendar depicting historical scenes on campus and exhibitions of photographs to which the public was invited. Critiques in the local press pointed out the progress made by the members who won prizes and honors for their choice of subject as well as for their photographic skills.

At the October 20, 1897 and January 28, 1898 camera club meetings, Paul Laurence Dunbar's poem, "The Deserted Plantation," was suggested for illustrating, and members were requested to bring in negatives at the next meeting. On January 29, negatives and prints for illustrating the poem were examined, others were to be brought in at the next meeting, and the poem was read. For the regular club meeting in May 1898, the minutes offer the following information:

The subject for the illustrations for "The Deserted Plantation" was discussed and the committee reported that only five or six of the illustrations were lacking. It was suggested that if the illustrations are satisfactory Mr. Turner submit the collection of the club to Dodd and Mead, in N. Y....

It was voted that a meeting be held as late as the presence of the members allowed, and that a copy of the lines still requiring illustration be given to each member of the club by the Librarian. It was decided that the subject for work should be the frontispiece for "The Deserted Plantation" to be handed in accompanied by a negative to some other line. The price was left to be determined at the next meeting….

Fourteen negatives were handed in at this meeting. The prize was awarded to Mrs. Armstrong for her picture of Dan.

With this exchange of ideas at the club meeting the story of the Kiquotan Kamera Klub and its study of Dunbar's poetry began. Evidently, the procedure of the club had become fairly clear:

1. Each member was expected to produce a minimum number of photographs.
2. Each member was responsible for interpretive illustration of designated poems of lines from poems or other literary works.
3. Samples of the clubs work at the April 15, 1898 Exhibition indicate that the members sought to penetrate "every field of amateur work…. through out-door photography, both landscape and marine dominated."

A letter from the publisher, Dodd, Mead & Company, read at a special club meeting on January 21, 1899, proposed that the club expand its commitment beyond illustration of the one poem, "The Deserted Plantation," to a set of illustrations for a small volume of selected poems, later entitled *Poems of Cabin and Field*. In February 1899 the club met again in Griggs Hall and learned that the firm now offered $150 instead of $100. There were to be 50 pictures to be ready by the middle of June. Selections from photographs already submitted for "The Deserted Plantation" had been made by the publisher, and those not used would be returned to the club for possible use in the illustration of other poems. The club studied the poems and voted to undertake the work, asking the same committee which collected illustrations for "The Deserted Plantation" to serve for the larger assignment.

The rather involved process of reading and studying poems, conceiving and planning appropriate illustrations, and persuading reluctant subjects to participate in the project was a time-consuming endeavor. Persons who posed for the photographs would need to be contacted, the purpose of the photographer precisely explained, and a time set for the picture-taking exercise. Patience, diplomacy, and a high degree of dedication must have abounded among club members to achieve the results desired by author, publisher, photographer, and screening committee.

Written in what critics recognize as the plantation tradition, exemplified by Joel Chandler Harris and Thomas Nelson Page, *Poems of Cabin and Field* reflects general attitudes expressed in the following statement from the *Southern Workman* of June 1899:

The Camera Club is pushing to completion

its work of illustrating Mr. Dunbar's poems for the publishers, Messrs. Dodd, Mead & Co. of New York. There are eight of these poems, most of which have already appeared elsewhere…with about fifty illustrations from negatives which the club is making for this purpose.

This club has been in existence among the teachers here for several years, and has made a more or less valuable collection of pictures of the school and its surroundings, including many studies of Negro cabins.

But the study of the old-time life of coloured people which is involved in these illustrations is by far the most interesting if not valuable work which it has undertaken.

The poems themselves are wonderfully true in their descriptions of a life which is rapidly passing away.

After the members read and studied the poems selected for illustration, they finally decided that each member of the club should undertake what he or she pleased and efforts for special pictures should be made later. The eight poems chosen for the first venture were (from the table of contents of the 1899 *Poems of Cabin and Field*): "The Deserted Plantation," "Hunting Song," "Little Brown Baby," "Chrismus is a-Comin'," "Signs of the Times," "Time to Tinker 'Round," "Lullaby," and "Banjo Song."

Although the old way of life was fading from the Hampton community at the turn of the century, the illustrations for Dunbar's lifelike plantation images came from actual scenes of nature, the cabins, and roads, the old farms and fences bearing clearly the ravages of time. The poems presented provocative scenes that stimulated the members of the camera club to search the Hampton community for the most appropriate illustration of the lifelike poetic images. Almost every stanza of the eight poems

Hampton Camera Club illustration for Dunbar's *Lil' Gal*. Photographer: Leigh Minor.

was illustrated by the camera. These illustrations from real scenes around the Hampton Institute community are both imaginative interpretations of nature and realistic renditions of the man-made enviroment.

The poem most industriously illustrated by club members, according to their records, "Chris'mus is a-Comin'," must have given author and publisher some concern. The usual competitive work on this poem is suggested by the Kiquotan Kamera Klub minutes of January 21, 1899, where it is recorded that for the Dunbar book the club wished to add "Chris'mus is a-Comin'," a poem published in the December issue of the *Bookman*. It appears that this addition was necessary in view of the feeling that several other poems which the publisher seems to have suggested were deemed too difficult to illustrate.

It is also evident that Dunbar reviewed the pictures which the club offered as illustration of his words, because handwritten notes in the dummy read: "Mr. Dunbar says no to the first picture" (referring to one which appears in full page following the title of the poem). The full-page picture of a landscape snow scene must have seemed to Dunbar less specifically a Christmas picture, for the print that he recommended more definitely reflects the Christmas holiday. The scene is inside the "Big House" where the mistress is decorating with holly wreaths and pine branches. The lady is standing on a stool at the window, while an old "uncle" holds more holly for her. On the floor in front of the spacious fireplace a little white boy plays, completing a typical plantation tableau.

On rainy days there is "Time to Tinker 'Roun'," mending harness for the mule and catching up on chores. The dramatic voice of the poem very clearly characterizes the speaker:

> Den you men's de mule's of ha'ness,
>
> An' you men's de broken chair.
>
> Hummin' all de time you's wo'kin'
>
> Some of common kind o'air.

Notes in the dummy for this poem suggest that familiar persons in the Hampton community posed for the pictures. The published pictures differ from those submitted to the committee for the dummy. The unpublished picture shows an older man mending harness in the doorway of a barn; a portion of a wagon wheel is visible at the door amidst trash or scraps of harness littering the floor. The picture published is less striking, portraying a younger man near the doorway of a workroom; a scene that easily could have originated in the Harness Shop on the Hampton campus, in view of the penciled note "Captain Moton made substitute." Offering many pictorial options, the poem perhaps stimulated the imaginations of Robert Russa Moton and his colleagues, eliciting so many illustrations that the camera club committee judged several nominations worthy of inclusion. (Moton

would go on to succeed Booker T. Washington as principal of Tuskegee Institute.)

CANDLE-LIGHTIN' TIME

In the first meeting of the club for the school year 1899-1900, the club asked its executive committee to "continue correspondence with Dodd and Mead, publishers," although the attention of the club was focused on such matters as the very real probability of building a small clubhouse on the campus. It is obvious that the Kiquotan Kamera Klub had a full schedule of activities in the fall of 1900 with discussions about the clubhouse occupying the center stage, and the individual photographic contributions to such contests as that sponsored by the *Ladies Home Journal* occasionally coming to the forefront. The committee which had been appointed to plan the year's photography projects recommended that the club undertake:

1. *To make illustrations for Dunbar's poem "Fishin'" before December 1st.*
2. *To help carry out Dr. Frissell's wish to obtain the teacher's pictures by making amateur portraits.*
3. *To make booklets of photographs of Southern Negro types for sale.*

On November 9, when the club met at the "Nutshell" to consider more carefully its possibilities as a clubhouse, it also voted to submit pictures for Dunbar's poem "Fishin' " at the next meeting, November 23. The records show that four

Hampton Camera Club illustration for "Dinah Kneading Dough," the opening poem in *Candle-Lightin' Time*

negatives for "Fishin'" were submitted, but the club took no action on these prints. In the meantime, working to arrange a substitute building as a clubhouse and also endeavoring to fulfill commitments for negatives, the club found itself frustrated and its plans thwarted when the faculty changed its mind in regard to allowing the club to use the "Nutshell." However, one bright ray filtered through the clouds of confusion and dissatisfaction by way of "a proposition from Dodd, Mead & Co., who wished to know if the Camera Club would undertake to illustrate a book of Dunbar's poems similar to his 'Cabin and Field' and containing about the same number of pictures."

With this offer under discussion, the club appears to have found the stimulation it needed, and "at a special meeting on February 11, 1901, the club voted unanimously to undertake the illustration of the new book for Dodd, Mead & Co. on condition that [the club] receive $200.00 for the entire work and that [they] have until July 1st to finish it."

In planning to illustrate the new Dunbar book, the club was better organized than previously; they had learned from the experience of illustrating *Poems of Cabin and Field*. At the March club meeting, the group made specific assignments of committees to provide illustrations of each of the poems which the club had selected, thereby fixing responsibility for the work. In general three persons were assigned to a poem and deadlines were established. Apparently this plan was productive because most readers agreed that the second illustrated collection of poems was superior to

the earlier collection. Concurring with this opinion, the *Southern Workman* in its section on "Hampton Incidents" concluded "that the photographic work in this instance is an improvement over that in the previous book" and quoted the *Dial* in commending the book:

> *Mr. Paul Laurence Dunbar has already won wide recognition as a poet, using the dialect of his race. A selection of nine of these poems, bearing the name, "Candle-Lightin' Time" which is beautifully illustrated with photography by the Hampton Institute Camera Club, and with marginal decorations by Miss Margaret Armstrong will be likely to win him fresh popularity. The book also reveals the great possibilities of artistic photography for purposes of illustration. No studied "composition by the engraver or etcher could surpass some of these glimpses of picturesque nature, or the poses of the human figures."*

Books of this type frequently become cherished gifts, and *Candle-Lightin' Time* came off the press at a most appropriate time for Christmas shopping.

The poems were bound in a handsome little book and the illustrations of the opening poem, "Dinah Kneading Dough," struck many readers as pleasantly as they affected the reviewer of the book in the *Dial*, who said that "the three interiors and one landscape…are enough to establish the artistic value of the book, and those following are equally good."

The frontispiece is the photograph of an African American woman, holding a candle in her right hand while shielding the candle with her left hand. According to the plan of the camera club, from four to six pictures were selected to illustrate each poem. Usually key words or lines of especially strong visual imagery gave the photographer his clue, since the poems are all relatively short.

Candle-Lightin' Time was a collection of nine poems that had appeared in periodicals such as the *Saturday Evening Post*, ("Lullaby") and the *Southern Workman* ("Fishin'").

In content, style and illustration, the first poem in the volume is different from those in *Poems of Cabin and Field* as well as the remaining poems in *Candle-Lightin' Time*. This poem focuses on a beautiful black girl, pert, lively, bright-eyed, seen at first in full-page portrait standing in front of an open fireplace, one hand placed saucily on her hip, the other on the mantel as though she is on the verge of a flippant remark. This must be "Dinah," whose young admirer praises her beauty, which seems enhanced by such domestic chores as kneading dough. More significant is its standard English usage; the only poem in the illustrated editions not written in dialect. It focuses on the favorite Dunbar themes, love and nature, with the latter yielding to love:

> I have seen full many a sight
> Born of day or drawn by night:
> Sunlight on a silver stream,

Hampton Camera Club illustration for *Candle-Lightin' Time*

Golden lillies all a-dream,
Lofty mountains, bold and proud

Veiled beneath the lacelike cloud;
But no lovely sight I know
Equals Dinah kneading dough.

The photographs clearly portray the charming Dinah as she works, "Brown arms buried elbow-deep / Their domestic rhythm keep," thus embellishing the duties of simple, real life with the allurements of her personality.

The other love poem in this illustrated collection, "A Spring Wooing," fulfills the promise of the title by intermingling a poet's keen sensitivity to the myriad signs of awakening nature with the incipient feelings of love:

Come on walkin' wid me, Lucy; `tain't no time
    to mope erroun'
W'en de sunshine's shoutin' glory in de sky,
An' de little Johnny-Jump-Ups jes' a-springin'
    f'om de groun',
Den a-lookin' roun' to ax each othah w'y.

Obviously, club members located ample scenes for pictures of spring in Hampton, Virginia. There the luxuriant foliage half hiding the cabins and farmhouses, brought vivid color — the pink and white dogwood, the yellow forsythia, the red, pink, white, and purple azaleas served as picturesque background for the strolling couples.

In contrast to these poems in which the lovers speak their feeling respectively for the young ladies Dinah and Lucy, the other poem in this collection dealing with young love is pragmatic and humorous. The voice of the poem is that of the prospective "father of the bride," who finally recalls his own youth when he "cou'ted Sally Jane," and ceases grumbling about propping up "The Old Front Gate."

The photograph illustrating the last verse of the poem brings together the daughter, her young man and her parents on the steps at the door of a very rustic cabin, perhaps to relieve the old front gate that will "keep on saggin' low" until all "de gals is ma'ied off."

The very favorable review of *Candle-Lightin' Time* in the December issue of the *Southern Workman* suggested the interest aroused in these poems of simple homelife among black people and pointed out the similarities to *Poems of Cabin and Field*: "All the contents are new [that is, never previously anthologized]. 'A Spring Wooing' and 'Song of Summer' take the place of the Christmas and Thanksgiving lyrics; there is 'Fishin' instead of 'Huntin' and 'The Little Brown Baby' has a 'Lullaby' all to herself…The tragedies brought by war to both races on the old plantation touch our hearts anew in 'When dey 'Listed Colored Soldiers'." Dramatic contrasts of blacks with whites, between soldiers in blue and soldiers in gray, highlight the emotions of the black girl whose low-key account suggests the pain and suffering of the war-ravaged plantation people, the blacks as well as the whites:

Bofe my mastahs went in gray suits, an' I loved de
    Yankee blue,
But I t'ought dat I could sorrer for de losin' of'em
    too;
But I couldn't, for I did n't know de ha'f o' what I
    saw,
Twell dey'listed colo'ed sojers an' my 'Lias went to
    wah.

In two other poems Dunbar creates vivid scenes from homely, everyday affairs on the plantation. These scenes evoked from members of the camera club an unusual number of choices for illustration.

"At Candle-Lightin' Time," the title poem of the collection, stresses a theme Dunbar repeated many times in his interpretation of the plantation tradition. This theme emerges in his conception of the unifying elements in the black family — the love of the father for his children, the time he spends with them after his workday and his storytelling.

When Malindy Sings cover

WHEN MALINDY SINGS

On January 5, 1902, the Kiquotan Kamera Klub held a special meeting, with 17 members present, during which "the work committee reported the offer of Dodd, Mead & Co. to have the club illustrate a new book of Mr. Dunbar's poems." Discussion of the proposal brought suggestions that "the competition be divided between the members doing the work and the club." Following the usual procedure of reading and discussing the poems in the meetings, each member was asked to hand to the secretary a list of those poems he considered suitable for illustration. Throughout January 1902 the club was busy negotiating with Dodd, Mead &

Frontispiece and title page for *When Malindy Sings*

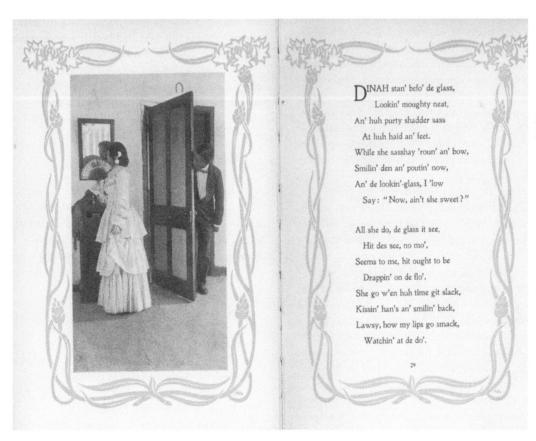

DINAH stan' befo' de glass,
    Lookin' moughty neat,
An' huh purty shadder sass
    At huh haid an' feet.
While she sasshay 'roun' an' bow,
Smilin' den an' poutin' now,
An' de lookin'-glass, I 'low
    Say: "Now, ain't she sweet?"

All she do, de glass it see,
    Hit des see, no mo',
Seems to me, hit ought to be
    Drappin' on de flo'.
She go w'en huh time git slack,
Kissin' han's an' smilin' back,
Lawsy, how my lips go smack,
    Watchin' at de do'.

29

Hampton Camera Club illustration for *When Malindy Sings*

Hampton Camera Club illustration for *When Malindy Sings*

Company. They agreed on the publisher's offer and requested that the club be allowed to set up a plan for arrangement of the poems in the book. When "Mr. Miner suggested that the club ask for permission to make a dummy of the book as we prepare to illustrate it," members began to establish more specific regulations for illus-trating the new collection.

Learning from experience with the two previously illustrated volumes, the club no doubt realized the problems that could arise in the preparation of a larger group of illustrations. A committee was appointed to have charge of the general arrangement of the book and to submit to the club a plan for each poem. It was voted that final decision on pictures be made by the whole club at the regular weekly meetings after pictures had been submitted, numbered and placed on exhibition for more than one evening. Selection of pictures was made by ballot. Each member of the club would submit an itemized bill when the period for making pictures had passed. By February 1903, it appears that Leigh Miner had conferred directly with the publishers, explaining plans of the camera club on such details as the title and the possible introduction of color.

It was not until October 12, 1903, that the club completed its illustrations for the Dunbar book that would be called *When Malindy Sings*. At that time 80 pictures had been accepted by the publishers. According to the club minutes, "Mrs. Brown reported her interview with Mr. Dodd concerning the book, during which its merits were generally discussed and all the pictures criticized favorably. In comparison with previous books, Mr. Dodd expressed his opinion that this last is the best." Apparently the dummy was in the possession of the publishers because Mrs. Brown reported that she had "asked for the sample book we loaned them. Mr. Dodd asked if he could keep it until their book was definitely planned. The request was granted."

The number of poems requiring illustration in *When Malindy Sings* was greater than twice the combined number of the two volumes previously illustrated. In this collection are some of the best-loved Dunbar poems, including the title poem of the volume. The review in the December 1903 *Southern Workman* was indeed favorable:

As an illustration of Mr. Dunbar's insight into human nature and especially that found under the brown skin of his people, this latest volume of verses is eminently satisfactory. They are rollicking, pathetic,, amusing, sad, sentimental, clever, weird, and altogether charming. The volume is uniform with *Candle-Lightin' Time* and *Poems of Cabin and Field*, being illustrated, as they were, by the Hampton Institute Camera Club. The decorations in this volume are by Margaret Armstrong and consist of slightly conventionalized flowers and vines outlined in light blue. The illustrations are perhaps even better than those in the two previous books, being less literal and showing more artistic power as well as better workmanship. Some of the illustrations are deserving of special mention. Those in "Two Little Boots" show the greatest power and feeling.

As usual in a volume of Dunbar verses, there are several poems in *When Malindy Sings* whose major theme is love and courtship in the African American community. These poems portray a different level of rural beauty in the middle-class setting, not now a broken-do' "front gate" or crude cabin. The lines of "The Lookin' Glass" demand that the camera focus on a beautiful young lady, one fit to rival Alice Moore, whose charms captured the heart of young Paul Dunbar. In the poem the flirtatious beau entertains guests and smiles enchantingly into the mirror which the lover envies: "while she sasshey' roun' an' bow, / Smilin' de an' poutin' now." In contrast to this sophisticated beauty who tantalizes the young man, Mandy Lou, the heroine of "A Plantation Portrait," is equally attractive in a wooded setting. Her personal charms are delicate and modest, suggesting serenity of spirit complementing the beauty of face and form:

> Eyes ez big an' roun' an' bright
>   Ez de light
> Whut de moon gives in de prime
>   Harvest time.

The popular title poem, "When Malindy Sings," is illustrated by four pictures, one of which shows a young white girl sitting at the piano looking up at a well-dressed black man standing near by and talking to her, seeming to say

> G'way an' quit dat noise, Miss Lucy-
>   Put dat music book away;
> What's de use to keep on tryin'?
>   Ef you practise twell you're gray,
> You cain't sta't no notes a-flyin'
>   Lak de ones dat rants and rings
> F'om de kitchen to de big woods
>   When Malindy sings
> But fu' real melojous music,
>   Dat jes' strikes yo' heat and clings,
> Jes' you Stan' an' listen wif me
>   When Malindy sings.

Hampton Camera Club page decoration and illustration for *Lil' Gal*

The three illustrated collections, *Poems of Cabin and Field*, *Candle-Lightin' Time*, and *When Malindy Sings*, were well received by the reading public, according to the reviews and notices in popular periodicals and newspapers. Of *Candle-Lightin' Time*, a reviewer in the December 5, 1901 *New York Observer* said "this book is a striking proof of what the black man can do in poetry and art, Margaret Armstrong's decorations being the only white work in the volume." Obviously, the reviewer was unaware that the Hampton Institute staff and the Kiquotan Kamera Klub included black and white members.

THE FINAL VOLUMES

The next three illustrated volumes continued the conventional style of illustrated poems popularized by *Poems of Cabin and Field*. These later volumes appeared in successive years: *Li'l Gal*, in 1904, with 22 poems; *Howdy, Honey, Howdy!*, 1905, with 21 poems; *Joggin' Erlong*, 1906, with 20 poems. Dodd, Mead & Company continued as publisher, but the illustrations were provided by one member of the camera club, Leigh Richmond Miner. Decorations for all but the last volume remained in the hands of Margaret Armstrong. John Rae created the decorations for *Joggin' Erlong*.

This last illustrated edition was published in October following the death of Dunbar in February 1906 and from all evidence was prepared for publication with the poet's cooperation and advice. Leigh Miner, its illustrator, had worked with the earlier photographic illustrations arranged by the club and was actively involved in the work on *When Malindy Sings*. The camera club minutes record that at the regular meeting on October 21, 1907, the nominating committee presented a slate of officers headed by the name of Miner for president. After a unanimous vote, however,

Miner found it necessary to offer his resignation, which was accepted with regret.

Leigh Richmond Miner, who came to Hampton Institute in 1898 as an art teacher, was, like Dunbar, "a builder of beauty," according to the *Norfolk Journal and Guide* in its tribute upon his death in June 1935. Similar to the famous poet whose writings he so well illustrated, Miner is described as "a quiet efficient worker, who not only wrote poetry but transmitted it into lovely arrangements of walks, bowers, and stately trees." Because of his tastes, temperament, and professional competence as both a poet and visual artist, Miner best understood the sensitive insights and clearly etched images that Dunbar projected. Admirably suited for this demanding task, Miner used the camera creatively to translate into pictures Dunbar's poetic world of work and play and to convey the emotions experienced by black people in the South.

Undertaking an assignment that had originally taxed the productivity of 20 to 25 club members, Miner would carry to completion the activity that had brought to the club and the school significant national notice. These last illustrated volumes were being circulated while Dunbar was in failing health, and at a time when his suffering had elicited the concern and sympathy of hundreds of his readers.

Dunbar, as well as his admirers, realized that his poetic genius would soon cease. Each poem dictated, "Joggin' Erlong," for example, was in a sense distilled from his life's blood, and therefore more precious. Artist-photographer Leigh Miner must have spent many thoughtful hours in illustrating these last Dunbar poems. Dunbar spoke not only to the artistic temperament such as that possessed by Leigh Miner but also to semiliterate black people who, particularly at this time in their racial history, yearned for one who could voice their joys and sorrows, their hopes and longings. The first African American professional poet — "a poet of his people" — Dunbar said to them:

> Be proud, my Race, in mind and soul;
> Thy name is writ on Glory's scroll
>   In characters of fire.
> High 'mid the clouds of Fame's bright sky
> Thy banner's blazoned folds now fly,
>   And truth shall lift them higher.

This article is a modified version of an essay by Nancy McGhee that was published in *Stony the Road: Chapters in the History of Hampton Institute* (University Press of Virginia, 1977). The copy was abridged to fit in this issue.

Nancy McGhee (1908–1995) was Avalon Professor of the Humanities at Hampton Institute (now University).

Leigh Richmond Miner
Portia in Drawing Room (at Hampton Institute)
1907
cyanotype
COLLECTION OF HAMPTON UNIVERSITY ARCHIVES

HAMPTON'S PHOTOGRAPHIC COLLECTIONS
AN EXTRAORDINARY VISUAL RECORD

by Vanessa Thaxton-Ward

Hampton University, from its beginnings, has a rich tradition in photography. Founder Samuel Chapman Armstrong understood the importance of using the new technology as a promotional medium to raise funds and to recruit new students for the "institution that was to be second to none." Today the Hampton University Archives houses over 50,000 photographs and glass negatives. Over 1,000 of these images were produced by Hampton's first camera club, a group organized in 1893 to cultivate and promote photography among interested amateurs, and active for 26 years. (For more on the camera club, see article beginning on page 49.)

Among Hampton's photographers, three have made outstanding contributions in documenting the life of the institution: Leigh Richmond Miner, Frances Benjamin Johnston and Reuben V. Burrell.

LEIGH RICHMOND MINER

The school employed its own talent in Leigh Richmond Miner who joined the faculty in 1898 as a teacher of drawing and served in that position until 1904. Archival documents indicate that Miner left Hampton in 1904 to operate a photography studio in New York. Invited back to Hampton in 1907, Minor retired from the institute in 1933, died in 1935, and is buried in the campus cemetery.

Leigh Miner was not only deeply involved in photography but was proficient as a visual artist, a landscape artist, interior designer and poet. Today, one can see remnants of Miner's landscape artistry on Hampton's campus. His photographs of campus life and the surrounding community were reproduced in the catalog of the traveling exhibition, *To Conserve a Legacy*, organized by the Addison Gallery of American Art and The Studio Museum in Harlem, 1999-2001.

Also known for his work on St. Helena Island, located off the coast of South Carolina, Miner documented a life that was fast disappearing on the secluded Sea Islands. During this period, Hampton teachers made a practice of visiting their former students. When Minor visited his students who were teaching at St. Helena's Penn School, he was fascinated by the people and the beauty of the island. Photographs taken by Miner during that visit include shots of an elderly man, a sea grass basket-maker, who had learned the craft from an African-born relative, and was passing it on to young boys.

Minor visited St. Helena again in 1923 and photographed Penn School students and Island residents. Many years later, glass negative plates of Minor's photographs from that visit were found in an attic on the campus of Penn Center and published in Edith M. Dabbs' *Face of An Island: Leigh Richmond Miner's Photographs of Saint Helena Island* (Grossman, 1971).

FRANCES BENJAMIN JOHNSTON

Frances Benjamin Johnston (1864-1952) was given her first camera by family friend George Eastman. Opening a studio in Washington, D.C. in 1890, she was the first woman press photographer and became known for photographing dignitaries such as Presidents Harrison, Cleveland, Roosevelt and Taft.

After hearing of Johnston's success in photographing a project for the Washington, D.C. public schools, Johnston was commissioned by Hampton's second principal, Hollis B. Frissell, to document through "picture stories and monograms" the story of the Institute for the Negro Educational Exhibit at the Paris Exposition of 1900. She produced 150 photographs for *The Hampton Albums*; prints of all of these images are preserved in the Hampton University Archives.

During the World War II years, prints of Johnston's Hampton photographs were discovered in an old, scuffed album in Washington, D.C., and in 1966, were published in book form as *The Hampton Album* by the Museum of Modern Art. Crisp, beautiful and simply shot, Johnston's platinum prints reveal the dignity of her subjects, and are a link between the photographs of Leigh Richmond Miner and the visual record of a man who came after.

REUBEN V. BURRELL

Known to generations of students and staff, Reuben V. Burrell has photographed the campus for more than 60 years. He became interested in photography in high school and was one of the first members of the new camera club that sprang up among students at Hampton Institute during the early 1940s.

Completing his course requirements in auto mechanics in 1940, Burrell was sent by Hampton to Hemphill Diesel School in New York to learn diesel mechanics. He returned to Hampton and taught, as a civilian, in a naval progam on campus until he, himself, was drafted into the navy. In the service, he learned aviation metalsmithing, an "all white" trade he was not allowed to practice when he was stationed

Frances Benjamin Johnston
*Physics at Hampton:
estimating the combined
draught of horses*
1899-1900
platinum print
7 1/2" x 9 3/8"
COLLECTION OF THE
HAMPTON UNIVERSITY ARCHIVES

in Norfolk, Virginia. Instead, he worked as a stevedore. Upon his discharge, Burrell resumed his studies at Hampton Institute, earning a B.S. in industrial arts in 1947. After earning the M. A. in industrial arts education from New York University in 1949, Burrell was hired in the part-time position of photographer at Hampton Institute and, as a self-employed photographer, took photographs in schools and communities in Hampton and Newport News. He became Hampton's full-time photographer in the 1960s under President Jerome Holland's administration.

Referring to himself as a "self-taught" photographer, Burrell experimented, read and practiced, becoming a master known for the sensitivity of his lens and the quality of his prints. Beyond their formal documentation, and like the works of Miner and Johnston, Burrell's images have an artistic dimension. His special skills also go into restoring old, fragile photographs from the university's archives. Explaining the process, he says:

> *I need to be Houdini to figure out the best way to bring the old prints back ... many of the early prints made by the first camera club members were glass plates that were covered with a light sensitive silver emulsion. The emulsion at that time was orthochromatic, in other*

Reuben V. Burrell
Hampton trade school student, Billy B. Smith, ca. 1940
black and white print
COLLECTION OF THE HAMPTON UNIVERSITY MUSEUM

Reuben V. Burrell
Marian Anderson on a visit to campus
1956
black and white print
COLLECTION OF THE HAMPTON UNIVERSITY MUSEUM

Reuben V. Burrell
Hampton's Terpsichoreans
Ca. 1950s
black and white print
COLLECTION OF THE HAMPTON UNIVERSITY MUSEUM

words 'blind' to red. Film used today is panchromatic or sensitive to all colors. The older prints are in various states of deterioration, some are faded; some have stains; some are on the blue print paper (cyanotype), this, in addition to being very brittle makes for a very sensitive job and the images must be handled with a lot of tender love.

With a steady hand and wealth of experience, Burrell converts the aged images to black and white prints, bringing them back to their original beauty and continuing the legacy of his predecessors Leigh Richmond Miner and Frances Benjamin Johnston.

Reuben V. Burrell turned 86 in February 2005. Still working full time as campus photographer, he remains remarkably agile as he stoops, bends and climbs to get the good shot.

———————————

Vanessa Thaxton-Ward is curator of history and director of membership and community programs at Hampton University Museum.

Reuben V. Burrell
Hampton University waterfront at dusk
1980, color print
COLLECTION OF THE HAMPTON UNIVERSITY ARCHIVES

Reuben Burrell at the 2004 Hampton University Commencement.
PHOTO: JACQUELINE BONTEMPS

CALL FOR PAPERS
EAST-WEST MEET IN ART & AFRICAN AMERICAN LIVES

Because the art of seeing inevitably leads to insight into the nature of perception and the physical reality, many visual artists have explored questions of consciousness along the way. However, an influence that is little-examined in the lives and work of African American artists are the consciousness-centered practices and philosophies of the East such as Buddhism and the Vedanta.

Such influenced African American artists range from Aaron Douglas who was interested in the metaphysical teachings of George Gurdjieff to contemporary artists such as Barbara Chase-Riboud (*Tantra* series), James Watkins (A Raku ceramicist who travels extensively in Asia), and Adrian Piper (who writes and lectures about various forms of yoga and practices it). Some of these artists (like M. Scott Johnson and Al Smith) find parallels and confluence in the philosophies of Africa and the East. Some, like Aaron Douglas, use their understanding of consciousness to better serve an interest in expressing African American themes. Others may seek transcendence from racial and cultural identities.

The *International Review of African American Art* is planning an issue on this east-west topic in our visual culture and invites suggestions and abstracts for essays. Contact *IRAAA* editor: juliette.harris@hamptonu.edu.

Consulting editor for this special issue is writer/philosopher/visual artist Charles Johnson, Ph.D., who writes about relations between the history of African American suffering and loss, creativity and dharma practice. Johnson's books include *Turning The Wheel: Essays on Buddhism and Writing* (2003) and *Middle Passage* (1990, a National Book Award winner), and he is a contributor to the anthology, *The Best Buddhist Writing of 2004* (2004). He holds the S. Wilson and Grace M. Pollock Professorship for Excellence in English at the University of Washington in Seattle.

SEE THE ARTISTS, REVISIT THE OPENINGS

A number of the artists in Hampton's modern and contemporary collections have visited the Museum for exhibit openings and other events. See the artists, donors, friends, students, staff and gallery shots, as we revisit our gala openings and other special events. The photographic record is on the journal's website at:

www.hamptonu.edu/museum/publication.htm

Jacob Lawrence with student at 1991 Hampton University Museum members' event.

J.L. Thornton Fine Arts and Antiques

Indianapolis, Indiana
46208
(317) 501-3773

Southern Living
John Wesley Hardwick
(1891–1968)
Oil on Board, 28" x 36"

WILLIAM R. & NORMA B HARVEY LIBRARY

The William P. & Norma B. Harvey Library at Hampton University and
(right) the library lobby with the John Biggers' murals
House of the Turtle (back cover image) and *Tree House.*

Back cover image:
John Biggers (1924-2001)
House of the Turtle
1991–92
acrylic on canvas
20' x 10'
THE WILLIAM R. & NORMA B. HARVEY LIBRARY HAMPTON UNIVERSITY

House of the Turtle, the right panel of the Biggers' murals,
depicts buildings and themes of Hampton University history.

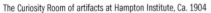

The Curiosity Room of artifacts at Hampton Institute, Ca. 1904

View of 1998 installation, African Gallery, Hampton University Museum

Hampton Helped Me!

Dr. Shaundau (Shaun) Woodly

Photo courtesy of Hampton University

A 2004 graduate of Hampton University, **Shaun Woodly** obtained his bachelor of arts in music education and his masters in teaching in 2005. While at Hampton, Shaun was an active member of the university bands program and the Gamma Iota Chapter of Alpha Phi Alpha Fraternity, Inc. After graduation, he took his love for music and education to serve as a director of bands in the Norfolk Public Schools system. In this role, he demonstrated excellence in music education with measurable evidence of student performance gains along with numerous honors that included blue ribbon recognition from the state of Virginia, teacher of the year, a district inspiration award, and several commendations of distinction for outstanding teaching in music education.

Additionally, Shaun served as a department chair, where he coached teachers and designed faculty professional development for effective instructional techniques to achieve school and district goals. Shaun's collaborative style of leadership harnesses the power of others and promotes a sense of teamwork and community, all to provide a first class education that prepares students to become effective, contributing members of society. While at Norfolk, he completed his doctoral studies in education from Capella University in 2014.

Outside of his career, Shaun is active in his local community, humbly serving as a new teacher mentor, director of the Hampton University alumni band, and founder (and former director) of the Sixth Mount Zion Baptist Temple orchestra. In his spare time, Shaun enjoys developing his craft as a percussionist and musician, traveling, reading, and spending time with friends and family. He currently resides in Atlanta, GA with his fiancé and fellow Hamptonian Jetaun Adkins, and their son Brayden, where they make a conscious effort to take advantage of all life has to offer while letting their lives do the singing!

Part 3
EXCEL

© Kendall Hunt Publishing Company

"Don't just dream about success,
work for it
and make it reality"

KAREN MIKHAI

"Nothing ever comes to one, that is worth having, except as a result of hard work."

—Booker T. Washington

CHAPTER 11

Beyond the Classroom

"Happiness is a state of activity."

– Aristotle

Upon completion of this chapter, you will be able to:

- **Review** extracurricular activities on campus
- **List** the divine 9 African American Fraternities and Sororities
- **Select** available sports and athletics of interest
- **Identify** successful Hampton graduates in sports, TV, music, theater and other fields

Hampton Helped Me!

Ruth Carter

Photo © JaxonPhotoGroup

Ruth E. Carter's unparalleled ability to develop an authentic story through costume and character has made her one of the most sought after and renowned costume designers today. She has garnered two Academy Award (Oscar) nominations for "Best Costume Design," for Spike Lee's MALCOM X (1993) and Steven Spielberg's AMISTAD (1998) as well as an Emmy nomination in 2016 for the reboot of ROOTS.

She has worked in the industry for over three decades and has been credited with over forty films and counting. It includes working with Spike Lee on over ten films beginning with SCHOOL DAZE and including DO THE RIGHT THING, MALCOLM X and OLD BOY.

Known for her research and diligence to the craft, specifically for her outstanding work for period ensemble films like the highly praised Lee Daniels' THE BUTLER and Ava Duvernay's, SELMA, she proudly presents: BLACK PANTHER, her recent work directed by Ryan Cooglar, which premiered in February 2018, and MARSHALL, directed by Reginald Hudlin, which premiered in October 2017. Last Fall, Carter completed work on YELLOWSTONE, an upcoming television series starring Kevin Costner and directed by Taylor Sheridan. She is currently working on Season 2 of YELLOWSTONE as well as the Netflix film, DOLEMITE IS MY NAME, starring Eddie Murphy.

Firsts/Additional Info

1. Ruth E. Carter is the first African-American to be nominated for an Academy Award in Costume Design.
2. Ruth E. Carter has been a member of the Academy for over 25 years.
3. Ruth E. Carter holds the most African-American historic films and series than any other Costume Designer in the film and television industry.
4. Ruth E. Carter created a curriculum for herself in Costume Design while attending and then graduating from Hampton University, a private historically black university, in Virginia.
5. Ruth E. Carter has designed 14 of Spike Lee's Films holding an Academy (Oscar) Nomination for Malcolm X.
6. Ruth E. Carter holds another Oscar Nomination for Amistad directed by Steven Spielberg.
7. Ruth E. Carter holds an Emmy Nomination for Roots.
8   Ruth E. Carter designed Marvel's Black Panther. If nominated for Oscar she will be in line to be the first woman ever to win for a super hero film and the first African American woman to ever win for BEST COSTUME DESIGN.

Beyond the Classroom

HBCU Extracurricular Life

Making Connections on Campus

Going to college is a major milestone in your life. You will find yourself in the center of culture and new ideas. The college environment will provide the opportunity for you to grow and blossom socially. You will meet new people, many with whom you share much in common. At the same time, you will also meet and interact with people from different cultural backgrounds. One common misperception about HBCUs is that all students are alike. Nothing could be farther from the truth. The reality is that HBCU students represent a diverse group. While most are black, they nonetheless hail from different parts of the country, indeed the world, social strata, religious backgrounds, and ethnic groups. The HBCU experience will mold you into a well-rounded individual, a true citizen of the world.

The best way to be a part of and feel engaged in the school community is to get involved in extracurricular activities. While attending college will involve a few years of your life, the rewards and benefits will last a lifetime. So take advantage of as many things as possible, both academic and extracurricular. Doing so will make you more likely to succeed academically and leave you feeling fulfilled and self-assured.

What Types of Extracurricular Activities Are There on Campus?

HBCU campuses are home to numerous clubs and special activities. There are Greek organizations (fraternities and sororities), student government, religious groups, newspapers, political groups, radio or TV stations, recreation centers and activities, choir, band, special interest groups, special events (homecoming, step-shows, spring dance), film festivals, intercollegiate sports, intramural sports, concerts, symposiums, and lectures. This chapter will identify the major extracurricular activities at HBCUs. It also explains the history of these organizations and their purpose vis-à-vis the larger college experience.

Student Government Association

The Student Government Association (SGA) is a major extracurricular organization on HBCU campuses. SGA provides a leadership opportunity that places students at the center of the college experience. It formulates policy governing the activities and welfare of students on campus and represents the overall interests of students. SGA also facilitates the representation of the student viewpoint on administrative and faculty committees. Participation in SGA provides students practical experience and develops leadership skills necessary for success in the larger

From *A Customized Version of Thriving in College and Beyond* by Carolyn W. Mbajekwe. Copyright © 2012 by Kendall Hunt Publishing Company. Reprinted by permission.

world. Many prominent African American business and civic leaders held SGA leadership positions as undergraduates.

Choir

Music is an integral aspect of the HBCU extracurricular experience. This phenomenon is reflective of the larger significance of music in black culture. With regards to the HBCU experience, the musical tradition gave rise to the existence of choirs and marching bands as key extracurricular activities.

The origin of the HBCU choir tradition dates back to the 1870s and the rise of the Fisk University Jubilee Singers. In 1871, a struggling Fisk University sent a chorus of students on an international tour to raise money for the college. The "Jubilee Singers" toured the northern United States, Europe, and the British Isles, where they introduced "Negro spirituals" to the world. On one acclaimed visit to Europe, they sang for the royal families of Holland, Germany, and Great Britain. Monies collected from the tours not only paid the school's debt, but were also used to purchase the site of the present campus.

Today, HBCU choirs embrace a wide variety of music genres, including new age, gospel, and classical music. The HBCU Choir offers students the opportunity to be part of a musical tradition.

Marching Band

The HBCU musical tradition is further enhanced by marching bands. The marching band performance is the must-see event during halftime at HBCU football games. Here spectators see drum majors and musicians march and dance to the latest R&B and Hip Hop tunes. The soulful music is accompanied by on-field designs and dance performances that leave many audiences in awe. Several HBCUs, including South Carolina State University (Marching 101), Florida Agricultural and Mechanical University (Marching 100), Grambling State University (Tiger Band), Southern University (Human Jukebox), and North Carolina A&T State University (Blue and Gold Marching Machine), have received national recognition for their outstanding marching bands.

The "Divine Nine": Black Fraternities and Sororities

Black Greek letter organizations (fraternities and sororities) are a key aspect of the HBCU experience. There are presently nine historically black fraternities and sororities. As a group, they constitute the National Pan-Hellenic Council, and collectively, are referred to as the "Divine Nine."

The "Divine Nine" members include Alpha Phi Alpha Fraternity, Alpha Kappa Alpha Sorority, Kappa Alpha Psi Fraternity, Omega Psi Phi Fraternity, Delta Sigma Theta Sorority, Phi Beta Sigma Fraternity, Zeta Phi Beta Sorority, Sigma Gamma Rho Sorority, and Iota Phi Theta Fraternity.

Why Do Black Greek Letter Organizations Exist?

Black fraternities and sororities have a rich history. Most black Greek letter organizations were founded between 1906 and 1920. The first black Greek organization, Alpha Phi Alpha Fraternity, was founded in 1906 on the campus of Cornell

Snapshot

The Divine Nine

African American Fraternities and Sororities

Alpha Phi Alpha Fraternity (ΑΦΑ)

Alpha Kappa Alpha Sorority (AKA)

Kappa Alpha Psi Fraternity (AKΨ)

Omega Psi Phi Fraternity (ΩΨΦ)

Delta Sigma Theta Sorority (ΔΣΘ)

Phi Beta Sigma Fraternity (ΦΒΣ)

Zeta Phi Beta Sorority (ZΦB)

Sigma Gamma Rho Sorority (ΣΓΡ)

Iota Phi Theta Fraternity (IΦΘ)

University. Two years later, in 1908, Alpha Kappa Alpha Sorority was founded on the campus of Howard University. This was a time period many historians call the "nadir," or low point, of race relations in America. Blacks were separated from the larger society by mandate of "Jim Crow" segregation laws, deprived of the right to vote, denied equal opportunity in education, economically exploited under the southern sharecropping system, and lived under the constant threat of racial violence. Black Greek letter organizations—like most black institutions founded in this time period, including the NAACP and the National Urban League—were established to provide a counterbalance to this hostile environment. Their primary mission was to "uplift" or improve the conditions of African Americans. The black Greek letter organizations developed leaders, promoted brotherhood and sisterhood and encouraged academic excellence, while providing service and advocacy for the black community. Overall, the young college students who founded these organizations towered as leaders in the black community, providing models of excellence and service that other blacks could aspire to emulate.

Membership Benefits: Why Should I Join a Fraternity or Sorority?

Participation in a black Greek letter organization is extremely beneficial to students. First, these organizations provide a supportive environment for their members during college. Secondly, since a college education is a prerequisite for membership, participation grants students entrée into vast social and business networks. Many of black America's "movers and shakers" belong to Greek letter organizations. Participation in such networks could be extremely useful beyond college. Finally, membership in a fraternity or sorority allows students to render service to the community. Most black Greek letter organizations continue the tradition of service by sponsoring a number of initiatives to improve conditions in the community as well as expand opportunities for young people. These include college scholarships, voter registration drives, health clinics, and tutoring clubs. If you are a socially conscious person, membership in a fraternity or sorority will allow you to be connected to a cohort of like-minded people.

Black Greek Letter Organizations—Profiles

Alpha Phi Alpha Fraternity, Incorporated (AΦA)
Founded: December 4, 1906 at Cornell University
Official Colors: Black and Gold
Official Symbol: Sphinx
Notable Members:
- Norman Manley: Jamaican Prime Minister
- Dr. Martin L. King, Jr.: Nobel Prize winner
- Thurgood Marshall: Supreme Court justice
- Andrew Young: United Nations ambassador
- Maynard Jackson: Atlanta mayor
- Jesse Owens: Olympian

Alpha Kappa Alpha Sorority, Incorporated (AKA)
Founded: January 15, 1908 at Howard University
Official Colors: Salmon Pink and Apple Green
Official Symbol: Ivy Leaf
Notable Members:
- Marian Anderson: opera singer
- Dr. Maya Angelou: writer

- Dr. Mae Jemison: astronaut, physician
- Coretta Scott King: civil rights activist
- Jada Pinkett-Smith: actress
- Star Jones: talk show host ("The View"), attorney

Kappa Alpha Psi Fraternity, Incorporated (KAΨ)
Founded: January 15, 1911 at Indiana University, Bloomington, Indiana
Official Colors: Crimson and Cream
Official Symbol: Kappa Diamond
Notable Members:
- Adrian Fenty: former mayor of Washington, DC
- Tavis Smiley: talk show host, political commentator
- Montell Jordan: R&B musician
- Dr. Calvin O. Butts: President of The State University of New York at Old Westbury
- Dr. Michael K. Fauntroy: Professor of Public Policy at George Mason University; author of the book, *Republicans and the Black Vote*
- John Singleton: movie director

Omega Psi Phi Fraternity, Incorporated (ΩΨΦ)
Founded: November 17, 1911 at Howard University
Colors: Purple and Gold
Official Flower: African Violet
Notable Members:
- Jesse Jackson: President & CEO of Rainbow Coalition
- L. Douglas Wilder: former governor of Virginia
- Shaquille O'Neal: NBA player (Phoenix Suns)
- Tom Joyner: radio show host
- Michael Jordan: NBA player (Chicago Bulls)
- Earl Graves: publisher of *Black Enterprise Magazine*
- Dr. Walter E. Massey: President of Morehouse College

Delta Sigma Theta Sorority, Incorporated (ΔΣΘ)
Founded: January 13, 1913 at Howard University
Official Colors: Crimson and Cream
Official Flower: African Violet
Notable Members:
- Brigadier General Hazel Johnson Brown, Ph.D.: first African American woman general in the U.S. Army
- Alexa Canady: pediatric neurosurgeon
- Darlene Clark Hine: noted historian
- Shirley Jackson, Ph.D.: President of Rensselaer Polytechnic Institute
- Carol Moseley Braun: first black woman elected to U.S. Senate
- Marian Wright Edelman: founder of Children's Defense Fund

Phi Beta Sigma Fraternity, Incorporated (ΦBΣ)
Founded: January 9, 1914 at Howard University
Official Colors: Royal Blue and Pure White
Official Symbol: Dove
Notable Members:
- Preston Edwards: founder of *Collegiate Magazine*
- Blair Underwood: actor
- John Lewis: U.S. Congressman and civil rights activist

- Jerry Rice: NFL player (San Francisco 49ers)
- Les Brown: motivational speaker
- Dr. Willie Adams, Jr.: mayor of Albany, Georgia
- Herman J. Russell: owner of largest black-owned general contractor firm in the U.S.

Zeta Phi Beta Sorority, Incorporated (ZΦB)
Founded: January 16, 1920 at Howard University
Official Colors: Royal Blue and Pure White
Official Symbol: Dove
Notable Members:
- Yvonne Miller: Virginia State Senator, District 5
- Julia Carson: U.S. House of Representatives, Indiana
- Sheryl Underwood: comedian
- Dionne Warwick: singer
- Dr. Tommie Morton: author
- Cynthia Willard-Lewis: New Orleans City Councilwoman

Sigma Gamma Rho Sorority, Incorporated (ΣΓΡ)
Founded: November 12, 1922 in Indianapolis, Indiana
Official Colors: Royal Blue and Gold
Official Flower: Yellow Tea Rose
Notable Members:
- Corrine Brown: U.S. Representative, Florida
- MC Lyte: Hip Hop recording artist
- Cynthia Horner: magazine editor, *Right On!*
- Jetta Jones: comedian
- Dr. Lorraine Hale: Executive Director of Hale House, Inc
- Cynthia Broussard: financial advisor and author of *Sister CEO*

Iota Phi Theta Fraternity, Incorporated (ΙΦΘ)
Founded: September 19, 1963 at Morgan State University
**   in Baltimore, Maryland**
Official Colors: Charcoal Brown and Gilded Gold
Official Symbol: The Centaur
Notable Members:
- Raymond Grady: President and CEO of Evanston Hospital
- Zemira Jones: Vice President of Operations of Radio One
- Elvin Hayes: NBA Hall of Fame
- Dr. J. Keith Motley: Chancellor, University of Massachusetts, Boston
- Chidi Iwuoma: NFL player (Tennessee Titans)
- Dr. Steven Ray: Professor of Theology, Louisville Seminary

Athletics

In addition to numerous social and civic opportunities, the HBCU extracurricular experience also affords students the opportunity to participate in intercollegiate athletic competition. Participation in sports can have a positive impact on a student's life. It teaches the value of teamwork and helps build character. It inspires self-confidence and a feeling of achievement. It teaches students how to deal with adversity, and ultimately, the value of perseverance.

Most HBCUs compete in one of four historically black athletic conferences. These include the Southwestern Athletic Conference (SWAC), the Mid-Eastern Athletic Conference (MEAC), the Central Intercollegiate Athletic Association (CIAA), and the Southern Intercollegiate Athletic Conference (SIAC). These various conferences sponsor a wide range of sports competition, including basketball, football, baseball, bowling, cheerleading, dance, golf, soccer, softball, tennis, track and field, and volleyball.

Historically Black Athletic Conferences: Member Institutions

Southwestern Athletic Conference: Alabama A&M University, Alabama State University, Alcorn State University, University of Arkansas at Pine Bluff, Grambling State University, Jackson State University, Mississippi Valley State University, Prairie View A&M State University, Southern University, Texas Southern University

Mid-Eastern Athletic Conference: Bethune-Cookman University, Coppin State University, Delaware State University, Florida A&M University, Hampton University, Howard University, University of Maryland Eastern Shore, Morgan State University, Norfolk State University, North Carolina A&T State University, South Carolina State University

Central Intercollegiate Athletic Association: Bowie State University, Elizabeth City State University, Lincoln University, St. Paul's College, Virginia State University, Virginia Union University, Fayetteville State University, Johnson C. Smith University, Livingstone College, Saint Augustine's College, Shaw University

Southern Intercollegiate Athletic Conference: Albany State University, Benedict College, Clark Atlanta University, Fort Valley State University, Kentucky State University, Lane College, LeMoyne Owen College, Miles College, Morehouse College, Paine College, Stillman College, Tuskegee University

HBCU Graduates in the NFL and NBA: The historically black athletic conferences have produced many students who've gone on to successful careers in professional sports. Some current and retired National Football League (NFL) and National Basketball Association (NBA) players who played at HBCUs include:

- Ben Wallace (Cleveland Cavaliers/Virginia Union University)
- Michael Strahan (New York Giants/Southern University)
- Steve McNair (Baltimore Ravens/Alcorn State University)
- Jerry Rice (San Francisco 49ers/Mississippi Valley State University)
- Tyrone Poole (Carolina Panthers/Fort Valley State University)
- Shannon Sharpe (Denver Broncos/Savannah State University)
- Walter Payton (Chicago Bears/Jackson State University)
- Doug Williams (Washington Redskins/Grambling State University)
- Robert Porcher (Detroit Lions/South Carolina State University)
- Fred Lester (New York Jets/Alabama A&M University)
- Roosevelt Blackmon (Green Bay Packers/Morris Brown)
- Avery Johnson (San Antonio Spurs/Southern University)

11.1 Identifying Extracurricular Activities on Your Campus

List five extracurricular activities for students on your campus.

1. _____

2. _____

3. _____

4. _____

5. _____

Hampton Helped Me!

Anita Blanton

Photo courtesy of Hampton University

Anita Blanton is an award-winning journalist, who joined the WAVY-TVIO/WVBT FOX43 family from KOCO-TV in Oklahoma City, Oklahoma, where she served as a morning anchor for 4 years.

She began her journalism career as a reporter at KTXS-TV in Abilene, Texas, before heading to Central Texas to work at KWTX-TV in Waco and WRlC-TV in Richmond, Virginia.

Anita is a proud alumna of Hampton University in Hampton, Virginia (a former Miss Hampton University). Go Pirates! She earned a Bachelor of Arts degree in Broadcast Journalism and Political Science from the Scripps Howard School of Journalism and Communications.

Anita has won numerous awards from the Society of Professional Journalists and the Associated Press for her work as an anchor and reporter. She has also received several community service awards, including a citation signed by the Governor of Oklahoma for her dedication to giving back. She has volunteered, served as a spokesperson, and sat on boards for several organizations as well as helping to create mentoring groups for pre-teens and teens. And Anita is a fitness enthusiast with a deep love for music, having been selected to sing the National Anthem for the Oklahoma City Thunder NBA team for 2 years.

Anita is a member of the National Association of Black Journalists and Delta Sigma Theta Sorority, Inc.

Learning the Language of Higher Education

A Dictionary of College Vocabulary

Academic Affairs the unit or division of the college that deals primarily with the college curriculum, course instruction, and campus services that support academic success (e.g., library and learning center).

Academic Calendar the scheduling system used by a college or university to divide the academic year into shorter terms (e.g., semesters, trimesters, or quarters).

Academic Credits (Units) what students are credited with after completing courses that are counted toward completion of their college degree; course credit is typically counted in terms of how many hours the class meets each week (e.g., a course that meets for three hours per week counts for three credits).

Academic Standing where a student stands academically (cumulative grade point average) at a given point in their college experience (e.g., after a term or a year).

Academic Transcript a list of all courses a student has enrolled in, the grades received in those courses, and the student's grade point average.

Advanced Placement (AP) Tests tests designed to measure college-level work that are taken while a student is in high school; if the student scores high enough, then college credit is awarded in the subject area tested or the student is granted advanced placement in a college course.

American Psychological Association (APA) Style a particular style of citing references in a research report or term paper that is endorsed by the APA and is most commonly used in fields that comprise the behavioral sciences (e.g., psychology and sociology) and natural sciences (e.g., biology and chemistry).

Analysis (Analytical Thinking) a form of higher-level thinking that involves breaking down information, identifying its key parts or underlying elements, and detecting what is most important or relevant.

Associate (A.A. or A.S.) Degree a two-year college degree that represents completion of general education requirements and prepares students for transfer to a four-year college or university.

Bachelor's (Baccalaureate) Degree a degree awarded by four-year colleges and universities, which represents the completion of general education requirements plus completion of an academic specialization in a particular major.

Breadth Requirements the required general education courses that span a range of subject areas.

From *Thriving in College and Beyond: Research-Based Strategies for Academic Success and Personal Development* by Cuseo et al. Copyright © 2013 by Kendall Hunt Publishing Company. Reprinted by permission.

Certificate a credential received by students at a community college or technical college who have completed a one- or two-year vocational or occupational training program, which allows them entry into a specific occupation or career.

College Catalog (a.k.a. College Bulletin) an official publication of a college or university that identifies its mission, curriculum, and academic policies and procedures, as well as the names and educational backgrounds of the faculty members.

Combined Bachelor-Graduate Degree Program a program offered by some universities that allows students to apply for simultaneous admission to both undergraduate and graduate school in a particular field and to receive both a bachelor's degree and a graduate degree in that field after completing the combined program (e.g., a bachelor's and master's degree in physical therapy).

Counseling Services the personal counseling provided by professionals on campus that is designed to promote self-awareness and self-development in emotional and social aspects of life.

Cross-Registration a collaborative program offered by two colleges or universities that allows students who are enrolled at one institution to register for and take courses at another institution.

Dean a college or university administrator who is responsible for running a particular unit of the college.

Distance Learning enrolling in and completing courses online rather than in person.

Doctoral Degree an advanced degree obtained after completion of the bachelor's (baccalaureate) degree, which typically requires five to six years of full-time study in graduate school, including completion of a thesis or doctoral dissertation.

Double Major attaining a bachelor's degree in two majors by meeting the course requirements of both academic fields.

Drop-Add the process of changing an academic schedule by dropping courses or adding courses to a preexisting schedule; at most colleges and universities, adding and dropping courses can be done during the first week of the academic term.

Fine Arts a division of the liberal arts curriculum that focuses largely on artistic performance and appreciation of artistic expression by pursuing such questions as "What is beautiful?" and "How do humans express and appreciate aesthetic (sensory) experiences, imagination, creativity, style, grace, and elegance?"

Full-Time Student a student who typically enrolls in and completes at least 24 units per academic year.

General Education Curriculum a collection of courses designed to provide a broad rather than narrow education and develop skills needed for success in any major or career.

Graduate Record Examination (GRE) a standardized test for admission to graduate schools, which is used in a manner similar to the way that the SAT and ACT tests are used for admission to undergraduate colleges and universities.

Graduate Student a student who has completed a four-year (bachelor's) degree and is enrolled in graduate school to obtain an advanced degree (e.g., master's degree or Ph.D.).

Health Services on-campus services provided to help students who are experiencing physical illnesses or injuries and to educate students on matters relating to health and wellness.

Higher Education formal education beyond high school.

Honors Program a special program of courses and other learning experiences designed for college students who have demonstrated exceptionally high levels of academic achievement.

Humanities a division of the liberal arts curriculum that focuses on the human experience, human culture, and questions that arise in a human's life, such as "Why are we here?" "What is the meaning or purpose of our existence?" "How should we live?" "What is the good life?" and "Is there life after death?"

Impacted Major an academic major in which there are more students wishing to enter the program than there are spaces available in the program; thus, students must formally apply and qualify for admission to the major by going through a competitive screening process.

Interterm (a.k.a. January Interim or Maymester) a short academic term, typically running three to four weeks, during which students enroll in only one course that is studied intensively.

Learning Habits the usual approaches, methods, or techniques a student uses while attempting to learn.

Living-Learning Environment an on-campus student residence that is designed and organized in such a way that students' learning experiences are integrated into their living environment (e.g., study groups, tutoring, and student development workshops).

Lower-Division Courses courses taken by college students during their freshman and sophomore years.

Master's Degree a degree obtained after completion of the bachelor's (baccalaureate) degree, which typically requires two to three years of full-time study in graduate school.

Matriculation the process of initially enrolling in or registering for college. (The term is derived from the term *matricula*, a list or register of people belonging to a society or community.)

Multicultural Center a place on campus that is designed for interaction among and between members of diverse cultural groups.

Natural Sciences a division of the liberal arts curriculum that focuses on observing the physical world and explaining natural phenomena, asking such questions as "What causes physical events in the natural world?" and "How can we predict and control physical events and improve the quality of interaction between humans and the natural environment?"

Nonresident Status the status of out-of-state students who typically pay higher tuition than in-state students because they are not residents of the state in which their college is located.

Orientation an educational program designed to help students make a smooth transition to college that is delivered to students before their first academic term.

Part-Time Student a student who typically enrolls in and completes less than 24 units per academic year.

Pass-Fail (Credit-No Credit) Grading a grading option offered in some courses whereby students do not receive a letter grade (A–F) but only a grade of pass (credit) or fail (no credit).

Phi Beta Kappa a national honor society that recognizes outstanding academic achievement of students at 4-year colleges and universities.

Phi Theta Kappa a national honor society that recognizes outstanding academic achievement of students at two-year colleges.

Placement Tests tests administered to new students upon entry to a college or university designed to assess their basic academic skills (e.g., reading, writing, and mathematics) to place them in courses that are neither too advanced nor too elementary for their particular level of skill development.

Postsecondary Education formal education beyond secondary (high school) education.

Preprofessional Coursework undergraduate courses that are required or strongly recommended for gaining entry into professional school (e.g., medical school or law school).

Proficiency Tests tests given to college students before graduation that are designed to assess whether they can perform certain academic skills (e.g., writing) at a level advanced enough to qualify them for college graduation.

Quarter System a system for scheduling courses in which the academic year is divided into four quarters (fall, winter, spring, and summer terms), each of which lasts approximately 10 or 11 weeks.

Registrar's Office the campus office that maintains college transcripts and other official records associated with student coursework and academic performance.

Resident Assistant a undergraduate student (sophomore, junior, or senior) whose role is to enforce rules in student residences and help new students adjust successfully to residence hall life.

Resident Director a student development professional who is in charge of residential (dormitory) life and the person to whom resident assistants report.

Resident Status the status of in-state students who typically pay lower tuition than out-of-state students because they are residents of the state in which their college is located.

Residential Students students who live on campus or in a housing unit owned and operated by the college.

Semester System a system for scheduling courses in which the academic year is divided into two terms (fall and spring) that are approximately 15 or 16 weeks long.

Self-Regulation adjusting learning strategies in a way that best meets the specific demands of the subject being learned.

Social and Behavioral Sciences a division of the liberal arts curriculum that focuses on the observation of human behavior, individually and in groups, asking such questions as "What causes humans to behave the way they do?" and "How can we predict, control, or improve human behavior and interpersonal interaction?"

Student Activities cocurricular experiences offered outside the classroom that are designed to promote student learning and student involvement in campus life.

Student-Designed (Interdisciplinary) Major an academic program offered at some colleges and universities in which a student works with a college representative or committee to develop a major that is not officially offered by the institution.

Student Development Services (Student Affairs) the division of the college that provides student support on issues relating to social and emotional adjustment, involvement in campus life outside the classroom, and leadership development.

Student Handbook an official publication of a college or university that identifies student roles and responsibilities, violations of college rules and policies, and opportunities for student involvement in cocurricular programs, such as student clubs, campus organizations, and student leadership positions.

Summer Session courses offered during the summer between spring and fall terms that typically run for four to six weeks.

Transfer Program a two-year college program that provides general education and premajor coursework to prepare students for successful transfer to a four-year college or university.

Trimester System a system for scheduling courses in which the academic year is divided into three terms (fall, winter, and spring) that are approximately 12 or 13 weeks long.

Undeclared students who have not committed to a college major.

Undergraduate a student who is enrolled in a two- or four-year college.

University an educational institution that offers not only undergraduate degrees but graduate degrees as well.

Upper-Division Courses courses taken by college students during their junior and senior years.

Vocational-Technical Programs community college programs of study that train students for a particular occupation or trade and immediate employment after completing a two-year associate degree (e.g., Associate of Applied Science) or a one-year certificate program.

Volunteerism volunteering personal time to help others.

Withdrawal dropping a class after the drop-add deadline, which results in a student receiving a W for the course and no academic credit.

Writing Center a campus support service where students can receive assistance at any stage of the writing process, whether it be collecting and organizing ideas, composing a first draft, or proofreading a final draft.

Appendix

Hampton University Chronology of Events

1863
The Emancipation Oak is the site of the first reading of the Emancipation Proclamation to former slaves within the City of Hampton. It was under this oak tree that Mrs. Mary Peake, daughter of a "free colored woman and an Englishman" conducted some of the first lessons for newly freed African American men and women.

1863
When the need of the freed people became too extensive, General B. F. Butler, chief in command at Fortress Monroe, used government funds and erected a large wooden building known as "The Butler School."

1865
The "Butler" school-house was turned over by the government in 1865 to the American Missionary Association, that supplied it with teachers until it became the property of the trustees of Hampton Institute upon whose grounds it stood.

1866
The overcrowding at The Butler School was eventually relieved by the erection of another school at "slabtown" (an impromptu suburb of Hampton), and by the building of the "Lincoln School" in 1866 by General Samuel Armstrong.

1867, October 1
A 160 acre Wood Farm was purchased for $9,000 by General Samuel Chapman Armstrong as site of Hampton Normal and Agricultural Institute. The Southern Colonial style Mansion House on the property was built before 1867 at a cost of $3,766.

1868, April 1
Hampton Normal and Agricultural Institute was founded by General Samuel Chapman Armstrong with two teachers and fifteen students. General Armstrong solicited first objects to establish a museum collection.

1868, September 21
Commonwealth of Virginia grants charter to Hampton Institute.

1869, November 12
Cornerstone laid for Academic Hall, the first permanent classroom building.

1870, June 4
Hampton Normal and Agricultural Institute was incorporated.

1870
Original Academy Building was erected.

1871
First class graduated with five women and 14 men.

1872, March 19
First issue of Southern Workman was published. Virginia Governor approved awarding of one-third of the state's Morrill Act land grant funds to Hampton.

1874
The book Hampton and Its Students, published in 1874, was written by two Hampton Institute teachers: Mrs. M. F. Armstrong and Helen W. Ludlow. The book was sold to raise funds as the Hampton Singers travelled throughout the North.

1874, June 11
Virginia Hall was dedicated. It was partly sung up by the Hampton Singers at a cost of $98,000. It was built by students and outside labor.

1875, June 9
First official seal of the Institute was accepted by Board of Trustees.

1875, June 18
Booker T. Washington graduated.

1877, August 20
First meeting of the National Hampton Alumni Association was held in Saratoga Springs, N.Y.

1878, April 13
First American Indian students arrived.

1878, April 14
First Alumni Reunion was held.

1878, September 12
Ground was broken for Wigwam, the dormitory for male American Indian students. It was planned by the staff and built by Hampton Institute students. Construction cost was $14,700.

1879, November 9
First Academic Hall was destroyed by fire.

1880
"Shellbanks," a stock and grain farm, was purchased to provide an agricultural laboratory for students and to supply the school.

1881, May 19
Academy Building, was constructed on the foundations of the Academic Hall, was dedicated.

1882
Winona Lodge, a residence for Native American females was constructed. This building was demolished in the 1950's and replaced by Twitchell and Davidson Halls.

1882, April 15
Stone Manor was completed. Marshall Hall (The Administration Building) was completed to house the library and offices of the principal and treasurer.

1886
Memorial Church was built at the original cost of $65,000 is an Italian Romanesque structure. The original and current yellow pine pews were built by Hampton Trade School students.

1891
Faculty member Alice Bacon began the Hampton Training School for Nurses on the campus.

1893, May 11
General Samuel Chapman Armstrong died. Hollis Burke Frissell was appointed second principal.

1894, November
Hampton acquired Henry O. Tanner's painting, "The Banjo Lesson."

1896, November 6
Armstrong-Slater Memorial Trade School was dedicated.

1898, September
Business Department, the forerunner of the School of Business, was established.

1901
Cleveland Hall, an addition to Virginia Hall, was completed at a cost of $51,973.

1903
Collis P. Huntington Memorial Library was dedicated. This facility would house the library until 1992.

1904
Academic course year was lengthened from three years to four years of study.

1906, July 26
Land was acquired from Hampton Institute by National Home for Disabled Volunteer Soldiers (Current site of the VA Hospital).

1909, November 20
U.S. President William Howard Taft visited Hampton as a recently elected trustee of the school.

1912
Federal appropriations for American Indian students at Hampton are withdrawn.

1913
Clarke Hall was dedicated.

1914
First Annual Ministers' Conference was held.

1916
Hampton Normal and Agricultural Institute was approved as a four-year secondary school by the Department of Public Instruction for the Commonwealth of Virginia.

1918, April 1
James E. Gregg was appointed as third principal. Robert C. Ogden Hall completed. R. Nathaniel Dett established the Musical Arts Society.

1918
Marshall Hall was enlarged. The addition named Palmer Hall. The building became the Marshall-Palmer Hall. It is the current "Administration Building."

1922
First bachelor's degree was awarded in agricultural education.

1923
Coleman Dupont Hall was completed to house natural sciences, biology, mathematics, chemistry and physics.

1928, May 12
First issue of the student newspaper, The Hampton Script, was published.

1928, October 6
Armstrong Field was dedicated. The original stadium cost was $12,900.

1930, January 30
George P. Phenix was appointed as fourth principal.

1930, April 21
Dr. Nathaniel Dett and choir sang before President Herbert Hoover at the White House.

1930, July 1
The name Hampton Normal and Agricultural Institute was changed to Hampton Institute and the title of "principal" was changed to "president."

1931
School of Nursing was established, offering diplomas after a three-year program.

1931, January 3
Arthur Howe became the fifth president.

1931, June 3
First class of the School of Music graduated.

1931
Kelsey Hall, a dormitory for girls, was erected.

1932, April 21
Hampton Institute was accredited by Southern Association of Colleges and Secondary Schools as a "Class B" school.

1932, May 21
First master's degree was awarded. George P. Phenix School, which served as the City of Hampton's Senior High School for African Americans until the 1960s, was completed on the campus.

1933, January 24
Hampton Institute was accredited by Southern Association of Colleges and Secondary Schools as a "Class A" school.

1933, May
In a vote conducted by The Hampton Script, students select "Pirates" as the name of the school mascot.

1938, May
Hampton Institute commissioned its first class of Army officers.

1940, October
First Annual Fall Convocation was held.

1940, November 25
Malcolm MacLean was inaugurated as the sixth president.

1941, March 1
Land (on the northern side of what is now I-64 East) that was acquired by the Virginia Department of Transportation (VDOT) at an unknown date, was conveyed to the City of Hampton.

1942, July 8
U.S. Naval Training School, the first offered at a black college, activated and continued until August 1945. In addition to other sites on campus, students coming from other black schools were housed in the attic of Stone building. They carved their names with dates on the beams.

1943
Baccalaureate nursing program began under the Hampton Institute Division of Nurse Education, with first class of three women graduating in 1946.

1943, June 25
Charles White mural, "The Contribution of the Negro to Democracy in America," was dedicated in Clarke Hall.

1943, October 29
Scrolls were presented to 39 charter members of the Quarter Century Club during convocation.

1944
Division of Trades and Industries closed.

1944, February 12
Ralph P. Bridgman appointed seventh president.

1944, October
Graduate courses in education and guidance techniques began.

1949, April
Alonzo G. Moron became the eighth president and first African-American president of Hampton Institute.

1950
Entrance Gate, designed by William Moses and built by Trade School students was completed.

1950, February 2
John Biggers' bronze Armstrong was unveiled.

1953
Aerial maps of 1953 show one low bridge only between downtown Hampton and East Queen Street leading to the main entrance to the campus.

1956
Auditorium of Clarke Hall named in honor of John H. Wainwright (Class of 1888) was dedicated.

1957, February 15
Land where I-64 East now runs past the campus was acquired for Right of Way (ROW) by the Virginia Department of Transportation (VDOT). This includes land behind the Hampton National Cemetery in Phoebus and almost to Mallory Street.

1957, December 5
Hampton Institute was admitted to the Southern Association of Colleges and Secondary Schools.

1960, July 1
Jerome H. Holland became the ninth president.

1960, December 28
Land on the northern side of I-64 East along Woodlawn Road that was acquired by VDOT was conveyed to Zion Baptist Church.

1962, October 8
Land acquired by VDOT behind the Hampton National Cemetery and almost to Mallory Street for ROW to build I-64 East was conveyed to Frederick Helmer.

1968, September 26
Martin Luther King Hall, the Social Sciences Building, was dedicated. The Natural Sciences Building was also completed and would later be dedicated Thomas W.

Turner Hall on January 29, 1978. Dr. Thomas Wyatt Turner, the first black to earn a doctorate degree in botany, served on the Hampton Institute faculty from 1924 to 1945.

1969, February 6
Dedication was held for William A. Freeman Hall, the Nursing Building.

1969
The National Register nominated 201 acre Hampton campus as Historic Landmark District acres. It was approved by the Keeper of the National Register, citing the historical importance of Virginia Hall, Academy Building, Mansion House, Memorial Chapel, Wigwam and Emancipation Oak.

1970, August 1
Roy D. Hudson became the tenth president.

1972, May 28
Ceremonial Mace was presented to Hampton Institute at Commencement.

1973, January 2
W.E.B. DuBois Hall was dedicated.

1976, July 28
Corrine S. Pelligrin, Registrar of the Virginia Historic Landmarks Commission, sent a letter to Dr. William J. Murtagh, Keeper of the National Register, National Register of Historic Places, indicating that "at its April 20, 1976 meeting of the Virginia Historic Landmarks Commission, the boundaries of the Hampton Institute were reduced to 15 acres" requesting that the same be reflected in the Hampton Institute nomination to the National Register to Historic Places.

1977, April 22
Carl M. Hill became the eleventh president.

1977, June
William J. Murtagh, Keeper of the National Register, sent a letter to Mr. Tucker Hill, Executive Director, Virginia Historic Landmarks Commission, in which he emphasized the need "to be certain that the historic integrity of Hampton Institute has been identified and preserved..."

1978, January
In a letter from William J. Murtagh, Keeper of the National Register, to Mr. Tucker Hill, Executive Director, Virginia Historic Landmarks Commission, Dr. Murtagh states, "After careful consideration we cannot concur with your request for a revision of the boundaries of Hampton Institute."

1978, January 29
Early Childhood Education Laboratory School, named in honor of Dr. Eva C. Mitchell was dedicated.

1978, February 17
Mr. Tucker Hill, Executive Director, Virginia Historic Landmarks Commission, sent a letter to Mr. Robert L. Hundley, Environmental Quality Division, Virginia Department of Highways and Transportation. This letter states as follows:

> Dear Bob:
> Here is the letter which we received in response to our request for a change in the Boundaries of the Hampton Institute register listing. I hope that you realize the lengths to which we have gone to convince the National Register people but apparently to no avail.

1978, March 11
Dedication service was held of Jerome H. Holland Physical Education Center.

1978, May 20
Ethel C. Buckman Hall, the Business School, was dedicated.

1978, July 1
Dr. William R. Harvey became the twelfth president.

1978
Modulars I residence hall was completed.

1979, March
First Annual Conference on the Black Family was held. Three modular units were constructed for students' housing. Degree program in marine science was initiated.

1980
First Elderhostel Program was held at HU.

1980
Armstrong Press Box was completed.

1981, March 12
There was a Rededication of the Charles White mural in Clarke Hall, "The Contribution of the Negro to Democracy in America."

1981, June 4
Charles H. Flax Monument was unveiled during Hampton Institute's 67th Ministers' Conference. Navy ROTC program began at HU. Master's programs in business administration, chemistry, museum studies, nursing and physics were approved. Bachelor's programs in building construction technology and criminal justice were approved.

1981
Marine Science Lab was completed.

1982, February
Men's basketball team captured its first CIAA title.

1982, February 27
Dedication of Marine Science Center was held.

1982
Modulars II-A and II-B were completed.

1982, November 2
Hattie McGrew Towers was dedicated. Hampton

Institute Business Assistance Center was established. College of Continuing Education expanded program to include distance learning in Guantanamo Bay Naval Base in Cuba.

1984, May 12
Booker T. Washington Sculpture and Memorial Garden was dedicated.

1984, July
Board of Trustees adopted the name Hampton University and reorganized the University to include Hampton

Institute as the undergraduate college; the Graduate College; and the College of Continuing Education.

1985, September
Airway science program began. Bachelor's degree program in fire administration was established. Teaching Learning Technology Center established.

1985
Central Warehouse building was completed.

1986
Initial plans were made for the establishment of the Honors College and the Queen Street Honors Hall opened. Nursing Center was also established.

1986
Armstrong CC Generator House, Computer Center Generator House, Electrical Switch House, and the Marine Storage Building were completed.

1987
Center for Teaching Excellence was instituted.

1987
Olin Engineering Building and Science and Technology Building completed.

1988
Women's basketball team won NCAA Division II championship. First annual Hampton University Read-In was held.

1988
Grounds Facility Building was completed.

1988, September 18
Dedication of Olin Engineering Building was held.

1988, October 27
Groundbreaking held for Hampton Harbor Inc. project, a 250 unit apartments and shopping village.

1989
American Indian Education Opportunities Program was initiated.

1989, May
Tennis team won CIAA and NCAA Division II championships.

1989, June 8
Groundbreaking for 8,000-seat Convocation Center held during the 75th Annual Ministers' Conference.

1990
Dr. Oscar Prater was named president of Fort Valley State University. Dr. Prater was the first administrator or vice-president to be named president or chief executive officer at another institution using Dr. Harvey's Model for Administrative Success. Dr. Prater was later named President of Talladega College in 2005.

1990
Renovation of Whipple Barn was completed to become Administrative Services Center. School of Arts and Letters merged with School of Education to become the School of Liberal Arts and Education.

1990, January 28
L. Douglas Wilder Hall, a men's dormitory, was dedicated and named for the Governor of Virginia, the nation's first elected black governor.

1990, September
Hampton Harbor apartment complex was completed and accepted first residents. Campus-wide renovations included Armstrong-Slater Hall, Dupont Hall, Virginia-Cleveland Hall, and James Hall.

1991, May
U.S. President George Bush served as Commencement speaker.

1991
Armstrong Stadium was renovated. Neilson-Screen Tennis Stadium was completed. Armstrong Press Box expanded.

1992, January
William R. and Norma B. Harvey Library was dedicated.

1992, June
Job Education and Training Corps Program begun. Hampton University acquired The International Review of African American Art.

1993
First Ph.D. program (in physics) was offered.

1993
Hampton University celebrated its 125th Anniversary.

1993
Code of Conduct was approved and instituted for faculty, staff, and students.

1993, September
Convocation Center was dedicated. Center for Entrepreneurial Studies was established.

1993, November
Football team completed first undefeated season 11-0 and won CIAA championship.

1994
Dr. Harold Wade was named president of Atlanta Metropolitan College. Dr. Wade was the second administrator or vice-president to be named president or chief executive officer at another institution.

1994
School of Engineering and Technology was established. Sailing team, the first at a historically black college or university, was established.

1995
Hampton University was named to the Honor Roll for Character Building Colleges by the John Templeton Foundation.

1995, April
Miss Hampton University Pageant inaugurated as franchise of Miss America Pageant.

1995, May
South African Peace Train made a three-day stop at Hampton University to celebrate the African nation's first anniversary of democracy.

1995, June
Hampton University joined Mid-Eastern Athletic Conference and moved to Division I (Division I-AA in football).

1995, August
Hampton University/Hughes Aero science Center was inaugurated.

1995, September
Hampton University Environmental Justice Information Center opened in downtown Hampton. Women's tennis team was established. Endowment surpassed $100 million.

1996
Hampton University was named to the Honor Roll for Character Building Colleges by the John Templeton Foundation.

1996, March 16
Academic Technology Mall opened.

1996
University embarked on $12 million campus renovation project including Virginia-Cleveland Hall, Kennedy Hall, Kelsey Hall and Huntington Building.

1996, September
First students enrolled in the University' second doctoral/professional program - pharmacy.

1997
Dr. Carlton Brown was named president of Savannah State University. Dr. Brown was the third administrator or vice-president to be named president or chief executive officer at another institution. Later he was also named President of Clark Atlanta University in 2009.

1997
Hampton University was named to the Honor Roll for Character Building Colleges by the John Templeton Foundation.

1997, January
Concert Choir performed at the second inauguration ceremony for President William Jefferson Clinton.

1997, February
First annual W.E.B. DuBois Invitational Honors Conference was held for high achieving high school students.

1997, April
University Museum celebrated its grand opening in the Huntington Building after moving from the Academy Building.

1997, September
Women's golf team was established.

1998
Hampton University receives its Southern Association of Colleges and Schools reaffirmation of accreditation.

1998
Dr. Elnora Daniel was named president of Chicago State University. Dr. Daniel was the fourth administrator or vice-president to be named president or chief executive officer at another institution.

1998
Hampton University was named to the Honor Roll for Character Building Colleges by the John Templeton Foundation.

1998, March
First African-American Jewish Community Relations Symposium was held, featuring Julian Bond.

1998, May
Nation's first African-American Poetry Archive was established. First doctoral degrees and associates degrees were awarded at Commencement.

1998, October
Public phase of record-setting $200 million fundraising Campaign for Hampton was launched including special guests the Rev. Jessie Jackson, poet Maya Angelou, and Count Basie Orchestra, actress Diahann Carroll, and singer Peabo Bryson.

1999, January
Hampton University Business Incubator opened in downtown Phoebus. Students enrolled in third doctoral/professional degree program– physical therapy.

1999
Dr. Warren Buck was named chancellor of the University of Washington-Bothell. Dr. Buck was the fifth administrator or vice-president to be named president or chief executive officer at another institution.

1999
Hampton University was named to the Honor Roll for Character Building Colleges by the John Templeton foundation. Dr. William R. Harvey was named to Templeton's Presidential Leadership Honor Roll. Only fifty presidents in the country were given this prestigious honor.

1999, March
School of Nursing established registered nurse to bachelor's degree curriculum.

1999, May
Hampton University's first African-American received doctoral degree (in physics).

1999, June
First web-based course offered through the University, a finance course in the College of Continuing Education. Women's bowling team was established. Students enrolled into fourth doctoral/professional degree program-the Ph.D. in nursing.

1999, August
Hampton University received its unconditional National Collegiate Athletic Association (NCAA) Division I Athletic Certification.

1999, October 30
Williams Student Union was razed and University broke ground on new student center.

1999, December 18
Football team won the Heritage Bowl, playing in a nationally televised game.

2000, January
Dr. Dianne Boardley Suber was named president of St. Augustine's College. Dr. Suber, the first female president of Saint Augustine's College was the sixth administrator or vice-president to be named president or chief executive officer at another institution.

2000, February
Women's basketball team won MEAC tournament, earned berth to the NCAA Division I tournament for the first time in school history.

2000, March 21
Hampton University opened Data Conversion and Management Laboratory. Hampton University was named one of the nation's 100 Most Wired Universities according to Yahoo! Website.

2000, April
Hampton purchased Strawberry Banks Motel and resort property.

2000, May
Dr. Calvin Lowe was named president of Bowie State University. Dr. Lowe was the seventh administrator or vice-president to be named president or chief executive officer at another institution.

2000, September 22
University broke ground on Scripps Howard Center, the new home for the Department of Mass Media Arts – School of Journalism and Communications.

2000, October 14
University broke ground on White Hall and Holmes Hall, new residence halls, for women and men, respectively.

2000, October 26
Board of Trustees announced $200 Million fundraising Campaign exceeded goal by $16 million; Campaign increased to $250 million.

2000, November
Mr. Leon Scott was named president of the Consolidated Bank and Trust Company. Mr. Scott was the eighth administrator or vice-president to be named president or chief executive officer at another institution.

2001, January
Dr. Rodney D. Smith was named president of Ramapo College of New Jersey. Dr. Smith was the ninth administrator or vice-president to be named president or chief executive officer at another institution. Dr. Smith was later named president of the College of The Bahamas in 2004.

2001

The No. 15 seeded Pirates basketball team stunned the nation with its upset over No. 2 Iowa State in its first ever trip to the NCAA Division I Tournament.

2001

Dr. and Mrs. William R. Harvey donate $1 million for student scholarships; specifically, for students wanting to become teachers.

2001

First annual William R. Harvey Executive Leadership Summit was held.

2002

Dr. Dennis Thomas named commissioner of the Mid-Eastern Athletic Association Conference (MEAC). Dr. Thomas was the tenth administrator or vice-president to be named president or chief executive officer at another institution.

2002

School of Pharmacy was granted full accreditation from the American Council on Pharmaceutical Education.

2002

Dr. Phyllis Henderson was awarded the first HBCU Ph.D. in Nursing at Hampton University.

2002

Holmes and White residence halls opened.

2003

Rev. Dr. Leah Gaskin Fitchue was named president of Payne Theological Seminary. She is the first woman to serve as President of Payne Theological Seminary. Dr. Fitchue was the eleventh person from Hampton to be named president or chief executive officer at another institution.

2003

Dr. Michael Battle was named president of Interdenominational Theological Seminary. Dr. Battle was the twelfth former administrator or vice-president to be named president or chief executive officer at another institution.

2004

General Wallace Arnold was named president of Cheyney University. General Wallace was the thirteenth administrator or vice-president to be named president or chief executive officer at another institution.

2005

Hampton University initiated efforts to create a world-class Proton Beam Therapy Center.

2005

Dr. Joann W. Haysbert named president of Langston University. Dr. Haysbert, the first female president of Langston University was the fourteenth administrator or vice-president to be named president or chief executive officer at another institution.

2006

NASA, Hampton University launched the Cloud-Aerosol Lidor and Infrared Pathfinder Satellite Observation (CALIPSO) satellite from Vandenberg Air Force Base in California.

2006

Intel Corporation and Center for Digital Education named Hampton University one of America's Top 50 colleges for wireless internet capability (No. 39).

2006

Dr. William R. Harvey established the Presidential Fellows Program.

2007

The University became the first Historically Black College and University to have total mission responsibility for a NASA satellite mission.

2007

Groundbreaking was held for the new Frank Fountain Interdisciplinary Research Center (Research I).

2007

U. S. Senator Barack Obama addressed attendees of the 93rd Annual Hampton University Ministers' Conference and the 73rd Annual Choir Directors' and Organists Guild.

2007
The University made history when it had a Division 1-AA record of five players invited to the NFL Combine in Indianapolis.

2008
Construction was completed on the 98,000 square-foot, world's largest free-standing proton therapy facility, using 85 million pounds of concrete and 70 tons of steel.

2008
The Commission on Colleges of the Southern Association of Colleges and Schools (SACS) reaffirmed accreditation for Hampton University through 2018.

2008
President-elect Barack Obama and Vice President-elect Joe Biden Inaugural Committee officially extended an offer to Hampton University Marching Force to participate in the 56th Inaugural Parade on January 20, 2009.

2009
Schools of Nursing, Architecture and Pharmacy receive accreditation.

2009
On March 31, 2009 Dr. William R. Harvey raised the Singapore flag at the Circle of Nations in observance of the first 12 students from Singapore enrolled at Hampton University.

2009
The Rev. Deborah L. Haggins was named University Chaplain and Pastor of the Hampton University Memorial Church. She is the first female to be named in this position.

2009
Dr. William R. Harvey was appointed to the National Collegiate Athletic Association (NCAA) Division I Board of Directors.

2009
Dr. William R. Harvey was appointed by U.S. President Barack Obama as Chair of the White House Initiative on Historically Black Colleges and Universities (HBCUs).

2009
U. S. Senator Mark Warner sponsored the Virginia Summit on Energy Opportunities at Hampton University on July 9th with over 500 entrepreneurs and activists in attendance.

2009
Dr. John Silvanus Wilson, Jr., Executive Director of the White House Initiative on HBCU's delivered the HU Convocation address.

2009
The inaugural Hampton University Athletics Hall of Fame welcomed its first members when 15 legendary names were inducted in November 2009.

2010
President Barack Obama, the first African-American, 7th sitting president and 10th U. S. president to speak at Hampton University, delivered the Commencement address. He was presented with a seedling from the Emancipation Oak, which was planted on the South Lawn of the White House.

2010
U. S. Secretary of Education Arne Duncan spoke at the 2010 Ministers' Conference.

2010
Hampton University received $8 million to build a new Biomedical Research Center for research activities such as cardiovascular disease, diabetes, adolescent health, HIV/AIDS, bio-molecular cancer imaging, medical chemistry and Alzheimer's. This building is referred to as Research II.

2010
Hampton U Online was launched, offering online programs to distance education students in 23 program areas, including certificates, associates, bachelor's, master's, and doctoral degrees.

2010

Hampton University's President Dr. William R. Harvey was awarded PepsiCo's Harvey C. Russell Inclusion Award. The award is part of PepsiCo's prestigious Chairman's Award, the highest honor the company bestows.

2010

Hampton University was named a top research institution by Washington Monthly College Guide; and listed No. 32 in the Top 50 Master's Universities category out of more than 500 such institutions surveyed.

2010

Hampton University celebrated the opening of the world's largest proton therapy institute. HUPTI will ultimately treat approximately 2,000 patients per year with prostrate, breast, brain, lung, ocular, and pediatric cancers. HUPTI's 200-ton cyclotron originates and spins the protons at 60 percent of the speed of light, sending the resulting beam down a beam line to the treatment room.

2011

The Multi-use facility, replacing the former Alumni House, dedicated on Founder's Day 2011. The 35,798 square-foot facility houses Offices of Alumni Affairs, University Relations and the Career Center on the first floor. The second and third floors are a woman's residence hall. This is the first building at Hampton University to use a geothermal heating and cooling system. Geothermal grids are installed beneath Armstrong Lawn across from the Multi-purpose Building.

2011

The Virginia Chamber of Commerce honored Hampton University with the presentation of the Virginia Torchbearer Award in recognition as a leading economic development organization.

2011

Dr. and Mrs. William R. Harvey donated a second $1 million to Hampton University to be utilized as incentives to increase faculty salaries.

2011

Dr. William R. Harvey was named the Daily Press Citizen of the Year for 2010.

2011

Hampton University became a National Center of Academic Excellence in Information Assurance Education (CAE/IAE), a designation from the National Security Agency and the Department of Homeland Security.

2011, October

First Annual Gala of Hope held to raise funds for cancer patients who cannot afford treatment.

2011, October 25

Dr. William R. Harvey accepted a request from the Mayor of the City of Hampton, to head a city-wide representative committee to spearhead the redevelopment of Downtown Hampton.

2011, October 27

Hampton University purchased Hampton City's tallest office building. The 13-story Harbour Centre building was partly donated to HU by Armada Hoffler, a Virginia Beach real estate company. The rest was paid in an undisclosed amount of cash.

2012

Dr. William R. Harvey was appointed to the National Geographic Society Board of Trustees.

2012

Hampton University senior, Kendyl Crawley-Crawford was selected as a 2012 Marshall Scholar.

2012

The Hampton University Honors College was named the Dr. Freddye T. Davy Honors College.

2012

Former Hampton University track and field standout, Francena McCorory, became Olympic gold medalist in Team USA Relay. Alumna Kellie Wells won the bronze medal in the 100m hurdles.

2012

The new state-of-the-art waterfront student dining facility opened. It is on the site of the old Queen Street residence hall and sage Court houses.

2012

The Softball Stadium was completed.

2013

Former Miss Hampton University, Desiree Williams, was named Miss Virginia 2013.

2013

Dr. Deborah White was named president of North Carolina Central University. Dr. White was the fifteenth former administrator or vice-president to be named president or chief executive officer at another institution.

2013

Hampton University endowment exceeded $260 million.

2013

A five-time MEAC Lady Volleyball Player of the Week, Vendula Strakova led the nation and the conference in points and kills. On Sept. 3, Strakova became the first Hampton player named Div. I Player of the Week by the American Volleyball Coaches Association (AVCA).

2013

Lady Pirates Volleyball Team won first ever MEAC Championship. The team played #7 Stanford University in the NCAA Division I Tournament.

Photo courtesy of Hampton University

Title IX Policy

Table of Contents

I.   Notice of Non-Discrimination

Hampton University ("University") adheres to the principle of equal education and employment opportunity and does not discriminate against anyone in education or employment on the basis of age, sex, pregnancy, sexual orientation, gender identity, race, color, creed, religion, disability, genetic information, national origin, military or veteran status or for engaging in protected activity. This policy extends to all students and employees and applicants for admission and/or employment. Further, it extends to all programs and activities supported by the University; including the Undergraduate College, College of Continuing Education, College of Virginia Beach, the Graduate College, University sponsored study abroad and University sponsored internships.

The following persons have been designated to handle inquiries regarding the University's policies prohibiting discrimination based on sex in accordance with Title IX of the Education Amendments of 1972 ("Title IX"):

Title IX Coordinator
for Hampton University:

Kelly Harvey-Viney, J.D.
Wigwam Building – Rm 205
Hampton University
Hampton, VA 23668
757-727-5426
kelly.harvey@hamptonu.edu

Title IX Specialist
for Hampton University:

Terri Haskins
Wigwam Building – Rm 205
Hampton University
Hampton, VA 23668
757-727-5426
terri.haskins@hamptonu.edu

Title IX Investigator
for Hampton University:

Rebecca Ennis
Wigwam Building – Rm 205
Hampton University
Hampton, VA 23668
757-727-5426
rebecca.ennis@hamptonu.edu

In addition, information concerning Title IX can be obtained from:

Office for Civil Rights
U.S. Department of Education
400 Maryland Avenue, SW
Washington, D.C. 20202-1475
Telephone: 202-453-6020
FAX: 202-453-6021   TDD: 800-877-8339
Email: OCR.DC@ed.gov

For other inquiries concerning the University's policy on nondiscrimination or to make a complaint of discrimination, please contact:

STUDENTS
Woodson Hopewell
Dean of Judicial Affairs & Housing
2nd Floor Student Center
Hampton, VA 23668
757-757-5303
Email: woodson.hopewell@hamptonu.edu

EMPLOYEES INCLUDING FACULTY
Rikki R. Thomas
Director of Human Resources
53 Marshall Avenue
Hampton, VA 23668
757-727-5250
Email: rikki.thomas@hamptonu.edu

II.   Discrimination Complaint Procedures

Hampton University has adopted an internal grievance procedure providing for prompt and equitable resolution of complaints alleging discrimination and/or harassment in violation of its policies of non-discrimination, adopted in accordance with the various state and federal civil rights acts governing employees and students in education and employment including, but not limited to, Titles VI and VII of the Civil

Rights Acts, Title IX of the Education Amendments Act ("Title IX"), Section 504 of the Rehabilitation Act, the Americans with Disabilities Act and the Age Discrimination in Employment Act.

A. Complaints Alleging Sex Discrimination and/or Harassment in Violation of Title IX

Complaints by Students and Employees including Faculty alleging sex discrimination and/or harassment in violation of Title IX should be directed to one of the following University officials:

Title IX Coordinator	**Title IX Specialist**	**Title IX Investigator**
Kelly Harvey-Viney, J.D.	Terri Haskins	Rebecca Ennis
Wigwam Building – Rm 205	Wigwam Building – Rm 205	Wigwam Building – Rm 205
Hampton University	Hampton University	Hampton University
Hampton, VA 23668	Hampton, VA 23668	Hampton, VA 23668
(757) 727-5426	(757) 727-5426	(757) 727-5426
kelly.harvey@hamptonu.edu	terri.haskins@hamptonu.edu	rebecca.ennis@hamptonu.edu

See Section III, Policy and Procedures on Sexual Discrimination and Misconduct (Title IX).

B. Complaints Alleging Discrimination and/or Harassment NOT Involving Title IX

i. Employees Including Faculty

Complaints by Employees including Faculty alleging discrimination and/or harassment in violation of Hampton University's policies on non-discrimination not involving Title IX should be directed to:

Rikki R. Thomas
Director of Human Resources
53 Marshall Avenue
Hampton, VA 23668
757-727-5250
Email: rikki.thomas@hamptonu.edu

For details concerning these complaint procedures, please see either: Education Support Staff Handbook or Faculty Handbook.

ii. Students

Complaints by Students alleging discrimination and/or harassment in violation of Hampton University's policy on Non-Discrimination involving claims other than those arising under Title IX should be directed to:

Woodson Hopewell
Dean of Judicial Affairs & Housing
2nd Floor Student Center
Hampton, VA 23668
Telephone: 757-727-5303
Email: woodson.hopewell@hamptonu.edu

iii.   Student Complaint Procedures Not Involving Title Ix

a.   The student should make the complaint verbally or in writing to the Dean of Judicial Affairs & Housing. If, however, the complaint involves the Dean of Judicial Affairs & Housing, then the complaint should be directed to the Director of Human Resources and will be handled in accordance with the Faculty Handbook procedures, Section 1.3.1.

b.   In making a complaint, the student should provide sufficient information to identify the parties involved, any witnesses, the alleged discrimination and all facts that support the allegations of discrimination.

c.   The Dean of Judicial Affairs & Housing (hereinafter "Investigator") shall immediately begin an investigation of the complaint. The investigation will involve meeting with all parties and witnesses. The complainant and the person(s) against whom the allegation of discrimination have been made and their respective representatives, if any, will be provided an opportunity to submit information, written statements and documentation regarding the complaint allegations. To the extent appropriate, interim measures for the protection of the complaining party may be taken while the investigation is pending.

d.   Within 30 days of receipt of the complaint, unless the Investigator has notified the parties in writing that the facts require a longer investigation, the Investigator shall issue a written determination as to the complaint, including the investigative findings, and provide such written determination to the Reporting Party and the Responding Party. The Dean of Judicial Affairs and Housing will implement prompt remedial action to remedy any discrimination or harassment that he concludes has occurred.

e.   Either party may appeal the findings of an investigation by submitting a written document within seven (7) days of notification of the determination to the Vice President for Administrative Services, Hampton University, Hampton, VA 23668 who shall refer the appeal to a three (3) member Appeals Committee consisting of a representative from Student Affairs, a Faculty representative and the Assistant Provost. The appeal must specify with particularity the irregularities of the Investigator's determination. The Vice President for Administrative Services must inform the parties of the appeal decision within fourteen (14) days of the receipt of the appeal.

f.   Although Hampton University will make every effort to comply with these timelines, circumstances such as school breaks, may justify an extension of time. If such an extension is warranted, the parties will be advised in writing.

g.   Retaliation against any person who files a complaint of alleged discrimination or harassment, participates in an investigation, or opposes a discriminatory or harassing education practice or policy is prohibited under University policy and by state and federal law. An individual who believes he or she was subjected to retaliation can file a complaint about the alleged retaliation under these procedures. If it is determined that retaliation has occurred, sanctions may be imposed, including, but not limited to, suspension or termination.

III.   Policy and Procedures on Sexual Discrimination and Misconduct (Title Ix)

Title IX of the Education Amendments of 1972

No person in the United States shall, on the basis of sex, be excluded from participation in, be denied the benefits of, or be subjected to discrimination under any education program or activity receiving Federal financial assistance.

~ 20 U.S. Code § 1681

A. Statement of Policy

The Hampton University Policy on Sexual Discrimination and Misconduct is designed to ensure an environment that is safe and free from sexual discrimination, harassment or misconduct for the members of the Hampton University community.

Sexual harassment is a form of sexual discrimination and includes sexual misconduct and/or sexual violence. The University is committed to maintaining an environment that is free from sex-based violence and in which the freedom to make individual choices regarding sexual behavior is respected by all.

Sexual discrimination, harassment or misconduct is unacceptable and will be addressed in a prompt, equitable fashion in accordance with this policy and the applicable procedures. Additionally, the University prohibits Retaliation against anyone who exercises his or her rights in accordance with this policy.

B. To Whom this Policy Applies

i This policy applies to all Students who are registered to take classes at Hampton University; all University employees including full-time and adjunct faculty; full-time, part-time and temporary staff; and contractors, vendors, visitors, guests and third-parties.

ii This policy applies to conduct that takes place on the campus of the University, at University sponsored events (including academic, social and athletic events), University sponsored Study Abroad Programs, University sponsored internships and may apply off-campus and to actions online if the Title IX Coordinator determines the conduct falls within the scope of Title IX and policies pertaining thereto.

C. Purpose

This policy is designed to help the University prevent sexual discrimination, harassment and misconduct on its campus and in its programs, and further help the University to comply with the following statutes:

- Title IX of the Education Amendments of 1972, which prohibits discrimination on the basis of sex in education programs or activities,
- the Violence Against Women and Department of Justice Reauthorization Act of 2005,
- the Higher Education Act of 1965, and
- the Clery Act, each as amended.

D. Jurisdiction

The University has jurisdiction over Title IX complaints and investigations. The applicable police department will have jurisdiction over criminal complaints and investigations.

IV. Hampton University Title Ix Office

Title IX Coordinator	**Title IX Specialist**	**Title IX Investigator**
Kelly Harvey-Viney, J.D.	Terri Haskins	Rebecca Ennis
Wigwam Building – Rm 205	Wigwam Building – Rm 205	Wigwam Building – Rm 205
Hampton University	Hampton University	Hampton University
Hampton, VA 23668	Hampton, VA 23668	Hampton, VA 23668
(757) 727-5426	(757) 727-5426	(757) 727-5426
kelly.harvey@hamptonu.edu	terri.haskins@hamptonu.edu	rebecca.ennis@hamptonu.edu

A.   Responsibilities of the Title IX Coordinator:

- Oversees compliance with Title IX at Hampton University;
- Responds to and investigates all sexual discrimination, harassment and misconduct complaints, to include analysis of policy, determination of violation, and the filing of detailed reports;
- Informs students and employees on the options of filing a formal complaint through the Title IX Office and/or filing of a criminal or civil complaint;
- Implements interim safety measures. This may include, but is not limited to, alternative housing arrangements, academic adjustments, no contact orders and referral to campus and local resources;
- Meets with students, faculty and staff to provide training and education on Title IX and the policies, procedures and services at Hampton University;
- Evaluates requests for confidentiality;
- Works with the appropriate University departments, offices or divisions to accommodate persons seeking services and support under Title IX, including counseling and health center services, campus safety measures with the University Police Department, if necessary, and the Director of Testing Compliance and Disability Services for pregnancy related medical accommodations; and
- Coordinates with local agencies to meet the support needs of persons seeking redress under Title IX, to include Transitions Family Violence Services, the Center for Sexual Assault Survivors, appropriate area law enforcement agencies, and area hospitals.

B.   Responsibilities of the Title IX Specialist:

- Coordinates with the Title IX Coordinator on compliance and training on Title IX policies at Hampton University;
- Provides administrative support to the Title IX Coordinator on projects and initiatives involving Title IX at Hampton University and in the community;
- Educates University employees, students, faculty and staff on Title IX policies and procedures at Hampton University;
- Provides resources and publications to faculty, staff and students to help in educating the University community about Title IX; and
- Updates the Hampton University community on changes to the Title IX policies and regulations from the state and federal government.

C.   Responsibilities of the Title IX Investigator:

- Reports to the Title IX Coordinator and assists in resolving complaints of sexual misconduct, sexual harassment, sexual assault, gender-related violence including stalking, dating violence and domestic violence involving undergraduate and graduate students, faculty and staff at the University;
- Identifies University policies and/or Student Conduct Code provisions relevant to a complaint;
- Conducts a prompt, equitable and impartial administrative investigation into complaints;
- Provides information to students, employees and others regarding the Title IX Policy and other University policies related to discrimination, harassment and sexual conduct;
- Creates and facilitates training/presentations to students and other campus constituencies regarding the University's Title IX policies and processes; and
- Develops and maintain relationships with campus and community partners. Collaborate with on and off campus resources including law enforcement and victim services in resolving complaints and work with the Title IX Coordinator to ensure that the University's processes, responses, and policies are consistent with federal and state laws and regulations related to compliance.

V. Resources

The following Confidential and Non-Confidential Resources are available for victims of sexual discrimination, harassment, or violence.

A. Confidential Resources

A Confidential Resource has no requirement to report incidents of sexual discrimination, harassment or violence. Below is a listing of Confidential Resources with their contact information:

Hampton University Student Counseling Center	(757) 727-5617
Hampton University Student Health Center	(757) 727-5315
Hampton University Chaplain	(757) 727-5340
Riverside Regional Emergency/Trauma Center	(757) 594-2050
Sentara Careplex Emergency Room	(757) 736-2010
The Center for Sexual Assault Survivors	(757) 599-9844
Transitions Family Violence Services	(757) 722-2261

B. Non-Confidential Resources

A Non-confidential Resource has an obligation to report incidents. Below is a listing of Non-confidential Resources with their contact information:

Hampton University Police Department	(757) 727-5300
Title IX Coordinator	(757) 727-5426
Title IX Specialist	(757) 727-5426
Dean of Judicial Affairs and Housing	(757) 727-5303
Dean of Residence Life	(757) 727-5486

VI. Prohibited Conduct and Definitions

A. In accordance with Title IX, the University prohibits any conduct that constitutes sexual discrimination, sexual misconduct, sexual harassment or retaliation against anyone who exercises his or her rights and privileges under Title IX, including, filing a complaint of sexual harassment, misconduct, and/or discrimination, participating in an investigation or hearing or opposing a discriminatory employment or education practice prohibited by this policy, or Title IX.

B. **Definitions**

The following definitions further explain the conduct prohibited under this policy and are applicable regardless of gender, sexual orientation or gender identification:

1. **Sexual Discrimination** includes denying an individual the right to participate in a program solely based on their gender, denying an individual a job or promotion solely based on their gender, or granting or denying benefits based on sexual stereotypes. It further includes sexual misconduct and sexual harassment. Sex discrimination also includes discrimination on the basis of pregnancy, childbirth, miscarriage, termination of pregnancy, or recovery from any of these conditions.

2. **Sexual Harassment** as a form of sexual discrimination refers to unwelcomed and unsolicited conduct of a sexual nature, whether by members of the same sex or of the opposite sex. It includes unwelcome sexual advances, requests for sexual favors and other verbal, nonverbal or physical conduct of a sexual nature, and is specifically prohibited when:

   a. Submission to such conduct is made explicitly or implicitly a term or condition for an individual's work performance or academic performance;

   b. Submission to or rejection of such conduct by an individual is used as a basis for employment decisions, performance evaluation, or academic performance evaluation concerning a member of the University; or

c. Such conduct has the purpose or effect of unreasonably interfering with an individual's work or academic performance, or ability to participate in or benefit from the University's programs, or of creating an intimidating, hostile, or offensive work or educational environment.

3. **Sexual Misconduct** is a form of sexual harassment. It includes a broad range of behaviors such as inappropriate physical touching, sexual exploitation, stalking, non-consensual sexual contact, non-consensual intercourse, domestic violence, dating violence, sexual assault, rape and other forms of sexual violence.

4. **Retaliation** for the purposes of this policy occurs when an individual is subjected to adverse action, intimidation, threats, coercion or discrimination in order to interfere with any right or privilege secured by Title IX or this policy or because of an individual's participation or involvement in any fashion in exercising rights under Title IX or this policy, including but not limited to making a complaint or report, participating in an investigation, or testifying as a witness.

5. **Hostile Environment** exists as a form of sexual harassment under Title IX when sexually harassing conduct is sufficiently severe or pervasive to alter the conditions of employment or education and creates an abusive work or educational environment. A single or isolated incident of sexual harassment may create a hostile environment if the incident is sufficiently severe. An example of the latter is a single instance of rape.

6. **Sexual Assault** is a form of sexual misconduct. It encompasses sexual assault and battery, non-consensual sexual contact, non-consensual sexual intercourse and other violent sexual behavior. Sexual assault and battery includes, but is not limited to, forced sexual intercourse, rape or any intentional unpermitted or unwanted sexual contact by the accused, acquaintance or stranger, either directly or through the clothing, or with the victim's genitals, breasts, thighs, buttocks, or mouth, without the victim's consent. Sexual assault and battery also includes touching or fondling of the victim by the accused when the victim is forced to do so against his or her will.

7. **Sexual Exploitation** is taking sexual advantage of another person without effective consent and includes, by way of example but not limitation, causing the prostitution or other incapacitation of a person for a sexual purpose; electronically recording, photographing or otherwise transmitting intimate or sexual utterances, sounds or images of another person; voyeurism; exposing one's genitals or inducing another to do so or knowingly transmitting a sexually transmitted disease.

8. **Coercion** occurs when an unreasonable amount of pressure is used to engage in sexual activity, and/or the practice of persuading or forcing someone to do something by use of force or threats.

9. **Domestic Violence** occurs when a current or former spouse, intimate partner or other person with whom the victim has shared a close family or living relationship within the previous 12 months uses or threatens physical or sexual violence. Domestic violence also may take the form of a pattern of behavior that seeks to establish power and control through emotional abuse or by causing fear of physical or sexual violence.

10. **Dating Violence** occurs when a person with whom the victim has shared a close social relationship of a romantic or intimate nature uses or threatens physical or sexual violence.

11. **Stalking** is engaging in a course of behavior directed at a specific person that would cause a reasonable person to fear for his or her own safety or the safety of others or to suffer substantial emotional distress.

12. **Intimidation** involves inducing fear, especially to cause or force an individual to engage in a specific action.

13. **Consent** is a voluntary agreement to engage in sexual activity. Consent for sexual activity can only be obtained in situations where all people involved have equal power and full awareness in deciding what sexual activity will and will not happen during an encounter.
    - Consent cannot be gained by force, intimidation, threat, coercion, or by taking advantage of another's incapacitation.
    - The use of alcohol or drugs may affect a person's ability to consent to sexual contact.
    - Silence, previous consent, or absence of resistance does not imply consent.
    - Consent to engage in sexual activity with one person does not imply consent to engage in sexual activity with another.

- Consent is not final or irrevocable and can be withdrawn at any time.
- Members of the University community choosing to engage in any form of sexual activity – from touching or kissing to intercourse – must obtain consent from their partner(s) prior to engaging in such activity.

14. **Incapacitation** is the physical and/or mental inability to make informed, rational judgments. One who is incapacitated cannot provide effective consent. States of incapacitation include sleep, unconsciousness, intermittent consciousness, and blackouts. Incapacitation may result from the consumption of alcohol or the use of drugs.

VII. Policy and Procedure on Pregnancy and Pregnancy-Related Conditions

Title IX prohibits discrimination on the basis of sex in education and in programs and activities that receive federal funding. This prohibition includes discrimination on the basis of pregnancy, childbirth, miscarriage, termination of pregnancy, or recovery from any of these conditions.

Students have the right to continue participating in classes and extracurricular activities during pregnancy. Students may request adjustments based on general pregnancy needs. Requests for adjustments must be made in writing to the Title IX Office. Such requests will be handled on a case-by-case basis depending on the student's medical needs and academic requirements.

In addition, if a student is unable to attend classes or complete academic requirements due to a medical condition related to pregnancy or childbirth, the student can request a reasonable accommodation. Such a request must be made in writing to the Title IX Office. The Title IX Office may coordinate with the Director of Testing Compliance and Disability Services in considering and reviewing such requests for accommodations. Requests for accommodations based on a medical condition due to a pregnancy-related condition must be accompanied by medical documentation detailing: 1) the pregnancy-related disability; 2) how it limits the student's participation in courses, programs, services, jobs, or activities; and 3) specifics concerning the accommodation that is needed. The University will consider requests for reasonable accommodation on a case-by-case basis.

Title IX requires the University to excuse a student's absences due to pregnancy or related conditions, including recovery from childbirth, with medical approval. Students requiring a medical leave must make a request in writing to the Title IX Office. Such a request must be

accompanied by medical documentation supporting the need for the medical leave. The Title IX Office may coordinate with the Director of Testing Compliance and Disability Services in reviewing such requests for accommodations.

The University must allow a student to return to the same academic and extracurricular status as before a medical leave began, including providing the student to make up any missed work. The University may offer the student alternatives to making up missed work, such as retaking a semester, taking a leave of absence or allowing the student additional time in a program to continue at the same pace and finish at a later date. The Title IX Coordinator and the student's Academic Advisor or appropriate academic representative in the student's field of study will meet with the student to discuss options available to the student based on the student's current status and program requirements.

VIII. Reporting Sexual Discrimination, Misconduct and Retaliation

Under Title IX, it is the responsibility of the University to ensure that students are not denied the benefit of or limited in participating in any University education program or activity on the basis of sex. Hampton University has an obligation to respond to reports and notifications of sexual violence. When the University has jurisdiction and has received notice of sexual violence, by law, the University must take prompt and effective steps to end the sexual violence, prevent its recurrence, and remedy its effects.

The University is committed to fostering a safe environment for victims of sexual discrimination, sexual harassment, sexual violence and retaliation, and is committed to offering help and support. Victims are encouraged to report incidents of sexual discrimination, harassment, misconduct or retaliation.

A. Responsible Employee

   i.   A Responsible Employee is anyone at the University, including faculty, administration, the Hampton University Police Department, Title IX Coordinator, Title IX Specialist, Title IX Investigator, the Dean of Judicial Affairs and Housing, and the Dean of Residence Life, with authority or a duty to respond and/or report sexual discrimination, sexual harassment, sexual violence and retaliation to the Title IX Coordinator or appropriate personnel.

   ii.   The University requires Responsible Employees, who in the course of their employment obtain information that an act of sexual discrimination, harassment and/or misconduct or retaliation has occurred against a student attending the University on campus, in or on a non-campus building or property used or controlled by the University, or on any public property that is adjacent to or accessible from a campus building or University-controlled facility, to report promptly the incident to the University's Title IX Coordinator.

   iii. In addition, Hampton University also encourages anyone who is or knows someone who has been a victim of sexual violence and/or misconduct to report promptly the incident to the Hampton University Police Department (HUPD).

   iv. HUPD may be reached at (757) 727-5300 and is available to explain the procedures for pursuing a criminal investigation of the alleged sexual misconduct or violence. HUPD will investigate every incident reported to determine if a crime has been committed. Any criminal investigation will be separate and distinct from any investigation undertaken in accordance with Title IX. A criminal complaint and investigation may run simultaneously with a Title IX complaint and investigation. For immediate assistance call HUPD at (757) 727-5666 or 911.

   v.   Pursuant to the Clery Act, the University is required to disclose statistics of certain crimes, including sexual offenses, violations of drug, liquor, or weapons laws, and hate crimes that result in an arrest or disciplinary referral.

B. Amnesty for Complainant and Witnesses

The reporting of sexual discrimination, sexual harassment or sexual misconduct and retaliation by complainants and witnesses is encouraged by Hampton University. In support of a Reporting Party and witness who participate in the complaint process, Hampton University may offer amnesty from other student conduct policies at the University. This determination will be made by the Vice President for Administrative Services and other appropriate University Administrators.

IX. Confidentiality

A. Confidentiality and Privacy

   i.   The University will make every effort to protect the confidentiality and privacy of students who report, are third-party complainants, or are named in a report of sexual discrimination, harassment and/or misconduct. The University will also strictly enforce the prohibition on retaliation.

   ii.   Information reported will be shared only on a need-to-know basis. The University will also take steps to protect members of its community against further misconduct.

iii.   Confidentiality, privacy and retaliation protections exist in part to help encourage students who experience sexual discrimination and/or misconduct to come forward and to permit an investigation to proceed.

iv.   The University will not begin an internal administrative investigation or make a referral to law enforcement without the consent or knowledge of the reporting party; however, the University must consider its obligation to other students and the campus community.

v.   The Title IX Coordinator will decide whether an investigation or referral is required after evaluating the risk of the alleged offender harming other members of the campus community, and, the likelihood of the University being able to proceed without the active participation of the reporting party (if applicable), by considering:

    a.   The nature of the alleged misconduct, including whether it involved a weapon or use of physical force;

    b.   The existence of evidence of predatory behavior;

    c.   Any prior credible reports of misconduct by the alleged perpetrator; and

    d.   The existence of evidence other than the reporting party's testimony, such as physical evidence, recordings, documentary evidence, or written statements provided by the reporting party.

B.   If Confidentiality cannot exist

While the University is supportive of a student's request for confidentiality, if that request must be denied due to safety or other concerns as determined by the Title IX Coordinator, the University will inform the Reporting Party.

X.   Filing a Complaint of Sexual Discrimination and/Or Misconduct or Retaliation

To file a complaint of sexual discrimination, harassment and/or misconduct or retaliation, an individual should contact the Title IX Office.

A.   Process of Reporting a Complaint

i.   The following steps should be taken to file a complaint:

1.   Report the incident to the Title IX Coordinator.

2.   Once an incident is reported, the Title IX Coordinator will provide information concerning the University's policies and services for victims of sexual discrimination, harassment and/or misconduct, other applicable offenses under Title IX, (See Section VI, B 1-14), and its procedures for determining, investigating, and handling such complaints, including the procedures for proceeding with a formal complaint and investigation.

3.   The Title IX Coordinator will make an initial assessment to determine the specific violations under the University's Title IX Policy, assess the needs of the Reporting Party, and provide interim measures if necessary which may include when appropriate:

    a.   Academic accommodations,

    b.   Safety measures,

    c.   Issuance of No Contact Orders,

    d.   Modification of schedules,

    e.   Changes in housing or work locations,

    f.   Campus escort services,

    g.   Leaves of absence.

4.   Following the Title IX violations assessment, either an informal resolution or a formal investigation of the complaint will occur.

ii. Informal Resolution

The Title IX Coordinator may facilitate the informal resolution of a complaint between the parties, including mediation, provided the following conditions are met:

a. All parties voluntarily agree to participate in an informal resolution after full disclosure of the allegations and their options for a formal investigation, and

b. The Title IX Coordinator concludes that the particular Title IX complaint is appropriate for informal resolution If this conclusion is reached, the matter is referred to Judicial Affairs for resolution.

iii. Formal Investigation

A formal investigation will include the following:

a. An interview with the Reporting Party, the Responding Party and other possible witnesses.

b. Recordings –All interviews conducted by the Title IX Coordinator and a Reporting Party, Responding Party or witnesses will be recorded with appropriate consent according to the laws of the Commonwealth of Virginia. A Reporting Party will not be allowed to record any meeting pursuant to this process.

c. The Title IX Coordinator will also gather other related information or documents.

d. A Reporting Party or a Responding Party has **one week** following the initial interview to provide further evidence or documentation in support of his or her claims. This includes evidence such as pictures, videos, screen shots of text messages, letters, or other written materials, like Protective Orders or other court documents.

iv. Failure to Comply

When a Reporting Party, Responding Party or witness is contacted by the Title IX Coordinator or other appropriate University officials requesting an interview for the purposes of carrying out a Title IX investigation, students are expected to comply. Failure to comply, by not responding to inquiries to make an appointment with the Title IX Coordinator for an interview or scheduling an appointment, but failing to show up, will result in student sanctions pursuant to the Student Code of Conduct Policy on Personal Honesty and Integrity. (*See Sanctions*)

v. Investigation Timeline

The investigation will be conducted in accordance with the following timeline, unless the Title IX Coordinator determines that sufficient extenuating circumstances exist as to necessitate an extension of time:

a. The formal investigation shall be completed within thirty (30) calendar days of a report being filed.

b. The investigation and adjudication before the Sexual Discrimination and Misconduct Committee, including notification of the outcome, will be completed within sixty (60) calendar days of a report being filed,

c. If the Title IX Coordinator determines in his or her discretion that an extension of time is required, he or she will notify both the Reporting Party and the Responding Party in writing.

B. Complaints of Sexual Violence and the Sexual Assault Threat Assessment Team

Any complaint involving sexual violence will be forwarded to the Sexual Assault Threat Assessment Team, following an initial assessment by the Title IX Coordinator, for review and a determination of whether disclosure to local law enforcement is warranted.

Pursuant to the Code of Virginia § 23.1-806, the **Sexual Assault Threat Assessment Team** ("Team") shall:

i. Consist of three (3) members with representatives from the Title IX Office, Student Affairs, and the HUPD who will review all information relating to acts of sexual violence. The Threat Assessment team may obtain law enforcement records, criminal history records, health records, institutional conduct or personnel records and any other known facts or information on record and known to the university or law enforcement.

    ii.   Upon receipt of a complaint involving sexual violence, convene within 72 hours to review the information relating to the complaint of sexual violence and determine if the incident, circumstances or the parties involved are a threat to the health and/or safety of the campus at large.

    iii. If the Team determines there is no threat, the Title IX Coordinator continues the investigation into the incident and comports with the mandates and timeline as outlined in the University policy.

    iv. If the Team determines there IS a threat, the HUPD representative on the Team will disclose and route the information to the City of Hampton Police Division who is responsible for investigating the act of sexual violence.

    v.   When such disclosure is made to local law enforcement, the Title IX Coordinator shall notify the Reporting Party of the disclosure in writing.

C. Criminal Complaints

The Title IX investigation is independent of any criminal proceeding and can continue separately, yet concurrently with any criminal investigation.

D. Non-Student Involvement

Should an incident of sexual discrimination, harassment or misconduct involve a University student and a person or student that is not affiliated with the University, appropriate steps will be taken including, an investigation, reporting and coordination with, for example, the visiting school or law enforcement.

The Vice President for Administrative Services will communicate all findings to parties involved, including action and remedies for the victim and the University at large.

E. False Allegations

Reporting deliberately false or malicious allegations under this policy is a serious offense. If proven to be false, the party found guilty of making false allegations will be subject to appropriate University disciplinary action.

F. Conclusion of Formal Investigation

At the conclusion of the formal investigation, the Title IX Coordinator will refer the case and all investigation findings to the Sexual Discrimination and Misconduct Committee. The matter will then be handled in accordance with Hampton University's Sexual Discrimination and Misconduct hearing process as set forth below.

XI. Proceedings Before the Sexual Discrimination and Misconduct Committee

A. Hearing Determination

The Sexual Discrimination and Misconduct Committee is responsible for adjudicating complaints that allege violations of Title IX and Title IX regulations including retaliation claims.

If a complaint falls under Title IX, as determined by an investigation by the Title IX Coordinator, the formal report is then handed over to the Sexual Discrimination and Misconduct Committee for review as follows:

 i. Within thirty (30) days of receipt of the findings from the Title IX Coordinator's investigation, the Sexual Discrimination and Misconduct Committee ("Committee") will convene to review documentation, meet with all parties and conduct a hearing.

 ii. The standard of review will be based on the Preponderance of the Evidence, which means it is more likely than not that sexual discrimination, harassment, or misconduct occurred. The preponderance of the evidence does not require proof beyond a reasonable doubt.

 iii. Each party will be provided the opportunity to submit any and all information in support of their respective positions, including documentary evidence and witnesses.

 iv. Evidence regarding a Reporting Party's sexual history unrelated to the Responding Party will not be permitted.

 v. Each party will also be provided with the option of having only **two** advisors present, including a professor, parent, legal guardian, or lawyer during the hearing process. Advisors are allowed for support of the Reporting Party or the Responding Party but are not allowed to speak or provide testimony during the hearing.

B. Post Hearing Procedures

 i. Within ten (10) days of convening a hearing, the Committee will render its final determination based on the preponderance of the evidence presented to it and will forward its decision in writing to the appropriate administrator: the Vice President for Administrative Services for students; the Executive Vice President and Provost for a Faculty member; or the Vice President for Business Affairs and Treasurer for a Staff member. The appropriate administrator will then forward the final decision including any determination as to disciplinary action to the party under their respective jurisdictions.

 ii. This written decision shall be received by all parties within sixty (60) calendar days of a report being filed, unless the Title IX Coordinator in her discretion has granted an extension and informed all parties in writing of such extension.

 iii. **The decision of the Sexual Discrimination and Misconduct Committee is final.**

XII. Student Sanctions

A. Definition of Penalties:

The following definitions are established in order that penalties may be clearly understood:

 i. **Warning**: Notice, orally or in writing, that continuation or repetition of misconduct, within a period of time stated in the warning, may be cause for more severe disciplinary action.

 ii. **Disciplinary Probation**: Exclusion from participation in privileged or co-curricular institution activities as set forth in the notice for a period of time not exceeding one school year.

 iii. **Censure**: A written reprimand for violation of specified regulations, including the possibility of more severe disciplinary sanctions in the event of being found in violation of any university policy within a specified period of time.

 iv. **Interim (Immediate) Suspension**: Suspension pending a hearing upon the recommendation of the Sexual Assault Threat Assessment Team of imminent danger to person or property on the campus. In such cases, a hearing will be held as soon as practicable.

v. **Suspension (Indefinite/Contingent):** The exclusion of a student from the University for an unspecified or specified period of time.

vi. **Suspension, held in abeyance:** A disciplinary measure imposed for violation of University policy that warrants separation, but in which some merit is found to allow the student to continue academic work only, or while further investigation or review of other evidence is being done. Failure to follow prescribed restrictions during any period of abeyance or additional violations of university policies will result in the immediate imposition of separation from the university up to and including expulsion.

vii. **Expulsion:** Permanent separation from the University. The student is not permitted to enroll or matriculate at any time.

- NOTE: A student who is suspended or expelled from Hampton University is denied any privileges of the University during the period specified.
- Notification of such action will be in writing.
- The student will be given no longer than 24 hours to remain on campus without written permission from the Vice President for Administrative Services.
- This policy also applies to academic suspension or expulsion.

XIII. Transcript Notation

In accordance with Virginia Code §23.1-900, the Registrar shall include a prominent notation on the academic transcript of each student who has been suspended for, has been permanently dismissed for, or withdraws from the institution while under investigation for an offense involving sexual violence. Such notation shall be substantially in the following form: "[Suspended, Dismissed, or Withdrew while under investigation] for a violation of university's policy for sexual discrimination, harassment and/or misconduct."

A. Notification of Transcript Notation

Hampton University shall notify each student that any such suspension, permanent dismissal, or withdrawal will be documented on his or her academic transcript.

Transcript notation determinations are made by the Vice President for Administrative Services.

B. Removal of Transcript Notation

The University shall remove from a student's academic transcript any notation placed on the transcript if the student is subsequently found not to have committed the offense involving sexual violence under the University's Sexual Discrimination and Misconduct Policy, or has completed the term of the suspension and any conditions thereof.

Following verification of the above, the transcript notation will be removed following a determination by the University that the student is in good standing according to the University's standards and policies.

XIV. Education, Prevention And Awareness Programs

Hampton University is committed to the education, ongoing training, and awareness of its Sexual Discrimination and Misconduct Policy and prevention of the specified prohibited conduct on campus. Training, Awareness campaigns and related education programs are provided to new and returning students, new and returning faculty and staff, and other specific campus populations biannually and on an as needed basis by the Title IX Office.